REST
The Case For Sabbath

Bible Proof
No Theologian
Can Dispute
And Every
Believer
Should
Know

TIMOTHY SCHWAB
ANNA ZAMORANOS

Foreward By
BGen. Bienvenido Gerardo C. Casis, Jr., AFP (Ret.)

Copyright © 2021 by Timothy Schwab, Anna Zamoranos, The God Culture.

Library Of Congress Control Number: 1-10619255321
ISBN Number: 979-8-523-66875-3

To order additional copies of this book, contact:

The God Culture
thegodculture@gmail.com
Facebook: The God Culture - Original
www.OphirInstitute.com
www.TheGodCulture.com

Contents

THE Levite BIBLE
THE Levite BIBLE
LeviteBible.com

WHY REST?
the GOD culture
יהוה

Foreward

By BGen. Bienvenido Gerardo C. Casis, Jr., AFP (Ret.) *(Pictured left with wife, Rowie.)*

Greetings in The Most Precious Name of Our Creator YHWH and Our Messiah YAHUSHA from the Casis-Yema Family here in Cavalier's Home Subdivision, Marcos Highway, Metro Baguio!

It has been approximately three years since a Pastor friend from the USA asked me about my opinion regarding the Sabbath Day. I vividly remember that it was the start of my journey in the most important topic in Scripture next to The Name of The Creator! I did not immediately respond to his inquiry because I was apprehensive that it would embarrass me if I sent him wrong answers. What I did was search through my electronics gadget for the word Sabbath in the KJV Bible which I had downloaded. In order to be sure of a correct response, I read not only the verses containing the word Sabbath, but also read the whole chapters with those Sabbath verses, hoping to get their proper contexts as to what Sabbath meant. As I read further, the topic Sabbath had captured my interest more and more. Isaiah 58:13-14 really struck me very profoundly! I concluded then that Sabbath Day is the Right Worship Day (versus Sunday which had been taught to us). Then I sent my response to my Pastor friend. Hence, I am forever grateful to Dr. Alberto Nuñez, of Vallejo, California, USA, for (humanly) bringing my consciousness to the topic of Sabbath.

I have read my KJV forty two times over by then. My eldest sister Macris has done so 100+ times; my youngest brother Lloyd over 70 times. I cite them never to boast about our readings (Oh, we love the Scripture!), but to emphasize an important point: that despite our zeal in reading the Scripture, we were oblivious to the Sabbath since we had been in the Baptist Church for decades already! Obviously, the same predicament could be true for most, if not all, Sunday church-goers since the topic Sabbath was never given deeper study nor taught in-depth in the pulpits.

I shared my conviction to my beloved wife Rowie, and that same week we began to observe Sabbath immediately. From then on, Saturday became our worship and rest day! We also ceased attending Sunday church services; instead, we began to conduct our own Sabbath Services by reading the Scripture from Genesis 1 and 2, and other chapters containing the Sabbath verses. Such a simple start brought us to a deeper conviction on the Sabbath observance. We started learning more Truths about Sabbath. Observance of the Sabbath Day led us to practically overhaul our "faith and worship" life. It was a re-birth into the correct, right, true, deeper and Scriptural relationship with Our Creator YHWH! The very week we "implemented" the Sabbath observance in our life, we received tremendous and unprecedented blessings, spiritually and physically! We were convicted deeper that it was the right thing to do! Moreover, we have experienced the real profound peace in our spiritual life: it was incomparable to that which we lived by when we were still in the church system!

As I read more about Sabbath, I wished then, that The God Culture (TGC) would produce a series or even discuss the Sabbath so that I could confirm even more that what we were practicing was truly right! And, it came! The TGC Sabbath Series was indeed a great blessing, confirming our observance to be truly Scriptural! I thank YHWH for all their presentations (I never missed any; in fact, I recorded them all!) which really revolutionized my belief in YAHUAH. For fifty-nine years, I was blinded by the man-made Sunday worship! Many of the preachings and lessons taught in the churches and bible schools are "mindsets" which blind believers from the right contexts of the Scripture. Hence, many simply believe what is taught and preached, but do not search the Scripture again whether those things were true as did the Bereans in Acts 17:11. I am indeed blessed and chosen to have known still the True Holy Day of Our Creator, The Sabbath Day, a privilege which I received before I would sleep with my forefathers.

Learning more about Sabbath compels me to share it patiently and diligently to the rest of my family, relatives, friends, former church-mates, and to all people as far as is practicable. I suffer persecution. I am scorned and branded as cultic and a heretic. Some relatives, friends, and brethren have even chosen to dissociate from me. It is sad, but I know that YAHUAH is on my side. Sabbath (Genesis 2:1-3) is the very gateway to a truly holy relationship with Our Creator. Sabbath (Exodus 20:8-11), #4 in The Decalogue, led me to the Torah, to the Mo'edim or Appointed Times (Leviticus 23), and to the Dietary Law (Leviticus 11) which is very crucial in order to be holy. The RUACH HA'QODESH has taught me many more Truths because of Sabbath observance. It was a fulfilling journey in my spiritual life when I started all over again with the Sabbath! It is an experience beyond compare to any! I strongly believe that I am now on the right track, the old paths (Jeremiah 6:16): all because of Sabbath! Meanwhile, I continue to pray for loved ones.

The RUACH'S conviction brought new friends and brethren, like the Old Paths Torah Assembly (OPTA) led by Preachers MB Sioco (UAE) and Gary Ambrad (KSA), who are likewise seeking the truth about Sabbath! Upon the suggestion and sponsorship of Sis. Vivien Cruz and Sis. Carol Dollentas, former members also of a Baptist Church, we, as Sabbath Believers Congregation (SBC), have held Sabbath conferences for all who were interested to learn about Sabbath: YAHUAH provided so graciously that everything was free for all attendees! With the RUACH'S guidance, we were able to connect with The God Culture (TGC) Team led by Bro. Timothy and Sis. Anna, and with the Office of the Presidential Adviser on Religious Affairs (OPARA) led by Secretary Dr. Grepor "Butch" Belgica. They were the key speakers in the Sabbath 2nd Conference held on 30 January, 2021, at the Armed Forces of the Philippines Commissioned Officer's Country (AFPCOC), Camp General Emilio Aguinaldo, Quezon City. The succeeding conferences, however, are indefinitely suspended due to the current pandemic.

To all those I mentioned by names, as well as those who were not cited but have prayed for YAH'S providence, suffer me to profoundly express my heartfelt gratitude for your invaluable contribution to Sis. Rowie and me and to our sons, Bro. Ashton, Bro. Rex, and Bro. Stephen and to our beloved families, in our Sabbath faith! We are for ever grateful to YAHUAH for giving all of you to journey with us!

To all readers of this book about Sabbath, I enjoin you to seriously consider every point. It is never too late to reconsider a life in the Sabbath faith! Rejoice in your reading journey! Verily, you will be blessed like us! **YHWH BLESS US ALL! MABUHAY!**

The New Testament
SABBATH
STANDARD
WORK
STRESS
WORRIES
THE SABBATH STANDARD
THE SABBATH STANDARD
the GOD culture
יהוה
OPENING STATEMENT

Introduction

If you are a believer, you have probably heard from the pulpit that the Sabbath has passed away. Sure, we have heard that but is that what the Bible says? If you are a Pastor, you have likely taught the Sabbath is fulfilled which somehow you have learned a redefinition of the word fulfill and interpret it as meaning passed away. It never means such. Sure, that's what seminaries teach and we learned and used to teach the same but is that what the Bible says? Your Sunday service is not representative of the Sabbath and we'll show you. Meeting on Sunday should not actually be objectionable to anyone, however, as you can meet any day but you cannot redefine that as Sabbath nor is it in practice. We are to prove all things hold fast that which is good *(1 Thessalonians 5:21)*.

This book represents the Bible's Case for Sabbath – not ours and not any organization's as we are affiliated with none. This makes us an equal opportunity offender as even James says the Word offends those of us who are not perfect *(Jas. 3:2)* and all have sinned and fallen short *(Rom. 3:23)*. Thus, this book is not about condemnation but the restoring of the Word in interpretation will most certainly offend some and we are happy to do so. You will find this book wholly rooted and grounded in scripture not church doctrine that should agree but does not for many.

The God Culture is a group of independent researchers with extensive Bible backgrounds but this is not about titles, it is about what the Bible says verses the traditions of men. The Word is and must be the authority not initials after one's name that actually should require such person to provide even more proof because they are supposedly more learned.

Certainly, we will interpret and you must prove all things for yourself but these are pretty straight forward references and they are not just abundant, the Sabbath is a theme of the New Testament even after Messiah ascended to Heaven and even in Revelation for those remnant believers according to the words of Jesus*(Yahusha)*. We will explore this and in this introduction, we will prove from the New Testament this is fact. Are we really saying the New Testament is about the Sabbath?

The Book of Hebrews goes so far as to say we operate in unbelief if we do not keep the Sabbath yet this is completely overlooked by the "New Testament" church generally.

Hebrews 4:1-11 KJV

*Let us therefore fear, lest, a promise being left us of **entering into his rest**, any of you should seem to come short of it. For unto us **was the gospel preached**, as well as unto them: but the word preached did not profit them, not being mixed with faith in them that heard it. **For we which have believed do enter into rest**, as he said, As I have sworn in my wrath, if they shall enter into my rest: although the works were finished **from the foundation of the world**. For he spake in a certain place of the **seventh day** on this wise, And **God did rest the seventh day from all his works**. And in this place again, If they shall **enter into my rest**. Seeing therefore **it remaineth** that some must enter therein, and they to whom it was first preached **entered not in because of unbelief**: Again, he limiteth **a certain day**, saying in David, To day, after so long a time; as it is said, To day if ye will hear his voice, harden not your hearts. **For if Jesus had given them rest, then would he not afterward have spoken of another day**. There **remaineth therefore a rest to the people of God**. For he that is entered into **his rest**, he also hath **ceased from his own works, as God did from his**. Let us **labour therefore to enter into that rest**, lest **any man fall after the same example of unbelief**.*

Did the Book of Hebrews pass away? No, His Sabbath rest remains after Messiah's ascension. "It remaineth..." This is written in rebuke of the exact doctrine much of the modern church espouses as the first ekklesia was already dealing with such false doctrines. We did not write it so don't get angry with us. It is right there in the New Testament and yet New Testament believers are supposed to go against what Hebrews says?

This is a literal Sabbath sermon from the New Testament which specifically explains what Jesus*(Yahusha)* was actually saying in His Sabbath sermon on the Sabbath even in Matthew 11:28-12:1 which we will explain. The Bible interprets itself many times and when it does, no scholar can debate it. One will have a hard time observing this when they mislabel the Bible generally as allegory which truly allows them to change it or they just plain change what is very obvious in interpretation such as this passage. This is accomplished by a paradigm that mostly reads fragments out of context and that leads to much misunderstanding intended or not. We will expose this.

If Messiah would have spoken of another day for the Sabbath, this passage even tells you only He could have changed it and only He could have abolished it. He did not. However, after His ascension into Heaven, Hebrews explains if you are not keeping the Biblical Sabbath, you are an example of unbelief. Ouch! That struck us like a ton of bricks. He proclaims those not entering the Sabbath rest are of no faith. It even says Sabbath is part of the Gospel. Are you preaching that Biblical Gospel or another gospel that Paul and the apostles never preached? That got us too and we will prove it is applicable in this case.

His works put into action were finished from the Foundations of the World which this verse is also attesting the Sabbath originated at Creation and not the time of Moses just as Genesis does. This affirms Sabbath is a Creation concept on the 7th Day. How can the church not realize the hypocrisy in claiming something from Creation has passed? We still have the earth, Heaven, plants, animals, humans and everything represented in the other 6 days yet we are actually expected to believe that the 7th day's Creation somehow passed away. Imagine how the Creator feels about being misrepresented in such fashion. How could we demean His largest miracle of Creation by eliminating part of it knowing His Creation has not passed away?

The writer tells us again those did not enter into the Sabbath rest because of their unbelief. What day did Yahuah rest and what day does this refer to in the days of David? The 7th day Sabbath *(Genesis 2:2-3)*. Did Messiah speak of another day for Sabbath? Never. Not according to Hebrews or any other passage in context thus it remains the 7th day not the 1st EVER. This very passage links the antediluvian world with that of David and that of Messiah all the same regarding specifically the Sabbath. In fact, this section of Psalm being referenced begins in the KJV titled as "A Psalm or Song for the sabbath day" *(Psalm 92-97)*. "To day" is the Sabbath in this passage.

What day are we to cease from our own works as did Yahuah? The

7th Day Sabbath and this is the New Testament not Old yet there we have the Sabbath practice same as the Old. How does one labor in order to enter rest? The Sabbath rest requires preparation and a change in mindset as it is not like the other 6 days. Even this qualifier serves to affirm this is a Sabbath sermon which is confirmed a dozen times within this passage. Even the mention of Moses originates in this Sabbath Psalm in context as does much of Hebrews 4 as the writer is actually using the Old Testament to teach the Sabbath practice which still remained in his time. At least that is what he says. What scholar can overrule that? Why don't all pastors know and teach this? It's the Word. Test it.

However, there are works that can legally occur on the Sabbath and we will test this when we find Jesus*(Yahusha)* defines such also in the New Testament. He tells us "it is lawful to do good on the Sabbath" which is why He preached, healed and even allowed the disciples to eat as they were about ministry that day. He even compared it to David eating showbread from the Temple when hungry on the Sabbath which He, the only righteous Judge, deemed permissible then and now. He also notes the Temple Priests "work" on the Sabbath but it is permissible and lawful and always has been. Neither of these concepts are new in the New Testament. The problem is they are new to the Pharisees who defiled the Temple, exiled the Temple Priests, the sons of Zadok, and usurped the Priesthood illegally. They did not understand the Sabbath and they profaned it as well as the entire worship of Yahuah. They always have and this is no mystery as Messiah rebukes them throughout.

It is illiterate for any scholar to frame either of these occurrences as breaking the Sabbath. In order to believe their unsupported opinion, one then has to accept that Jesus*(Yahusha)* sinned which is against scripture and proves it wrong. We have an entire chapter on this. They would also have to accept the Pharisee Sabbath practice which was and is wrong and Jesus*(Yahusha)* rebuked it several times even telling us their interpretation of Torah *(the Talmud today)*, is against His Commandments *(Mark 7:9)* which includes the Sabbath. They are not reading and certainly not testing.

We will demonstrate the difference between the legalistic Pharisee Sabbath which Jesus*(Yahusha)* and Paul rebuked as opposed to the Bible Sabbath which they reinforced, taught and kept. In the end, this passage says twice, to abandon His Sabbath is unbelief. Are you a believer? Is

He your Lord? This is the New Testament after Messiah's ascension and something you have likely never heard in church especially not as part of the Gospel which Hebrews says it is. The whole of scripture agrees with the writer of Hebrews. If your church does not, ask why.

This passage then launches into the famous scripture that the Word is "quick, and powerful, and sharper than any two-edged sword" *(4:12)* which is a Sabbath context of spending an intense day weekly in His Word. This is so profound. He discusses the Word as having the power to divide the soul and spirit, joints and marrow and even a discerner of the thoughts and intents of the heart. Again, this is within a Sabbath context. For we are naked in His sight and nothing is hidden from Him. Again, though applicable any day, this is a Sabbath sermon specifically.

Hebrews proceeds with a section titled "Christ is our high priest" *(4:14)*. You mean the Lord of the Sabbath who leads Sabbath worship even teaching and performing miracles especially on the Sabbath as our example? Then, "Warning against spiritual immaturity" *(5:11)*. Are you getting this? If we are to mature, we are to learn and understand His ways not the church's or any denomination's, but His. As our High Priest, Messiah kept and taught the Sabbath. Are we mature enough to understand this importance and read in context rather than in fragments?

This continues as the next section is titled "Encouragement for the faithful" *(6:9)* and "Christ's eternal priesthood" *(7:1)* which both include the Sabbath. As you focus out on the big picture of this context, it is a continuation of the Sabbath sermon very appropriately full of encouragement. In 6:9, he discusses "things that accompany salvation." Sabbath is not salvation. Allow me to repeat as this is one of the idiotic opposition lines to the Sabbath, Sabbath is NOT salvation but it's practice is one of those things that accompany it. Just as baptism is an outward sign of your commitment, so is keeping His Sabbath. He reminds us the ways Abraham followed *(When did he sacrifice? Feasts and Sabbaths.)*, which included the Sabbath and even uses the term the "entered" referring to those who enter into His rest which he already defined as the Sabbath multiple times over ALL of time. Thus, he continues to invoke the Sabbath in relation as the foundation of this entire sermon. This is incredibly obvious yet you will not learn this in most seminaries today.

Continue in Hebrews and you will find the next section titled "The new covenant" *(8:1)* which includes the Sabbath. This author did not change it all of a sudden after affirming it. It would be illiterate to not notice the beginning of Chapter 8 "***Now of the things which we have spoken this is the sum***." This means the Sabbath as he is summing up the previous here which foundation was built on the Sabbath after Messiah's Ascension in the New Testament. Within, the writer tells us Jesus*(Yahusha)* is our "High Priest" in Heaven seated on the "right hand of the throne of the Majesty in the heavens." However, he is speaking on the Sabbath and the Biblical Feasts which he still keeps but more so, so does Heaven after Messiah's ascension. That is what Hebrews says as these sacrifices are an "example and shadow of heavenly things" *(8:5)*. Many wonder how Heaven operates and yet we have had such example patterned for us and we reject it claiming we are under a new covenant. Indeed, we are. However, Hebrews is incredibly clear that the Sabbath always was, remains and this is a section titled "The new covenant" which still includes the Sabbath practice. How did we miss this?

He then, continues with a section titled "The Mosaic rites" *(9:1)* and you well know that is the Old Testament. He calls it the "first covenant" yet he parallels the new covenant as Messiah is our High Priest now replacing the Levite order with the ancient order *(not a new one)* of Melchizedek to which Abraham tithed. That was not just a foreshadowing of his tithe to Jesus*(Yahusha)*, it is a testament that Abraham had a Law to follow which is how he was judged righteous and that was under the Order of Melchizedek to which we have returned as it is not new.

The covenant is new indeed but the Law is not. It never has been. Otherwise, there would be no measure in Abraham's day to determine his righteousness with right or Law. It is that ancient Priestly Order of Melchizedek to which we have returned in this new covenant. This largely mirrors the Law of Moses as well as that applicable from the days of Adam, Enoch and Noah and you will find this in the words of our Messiah over and over again. Once these are connected and you understand such, it is impossible to support much of the modern church's view on the Sabbath. Yahuah has always had Law as He is not the God of chaos named Hovah *(which is never part of His name)*.

Then, he explains "Christ's perfect sacrifice" *(9:11)*. He has "obtained eternal redemption for us" *(9:12)*. In other words, we no longer need to sacrifice bulls, goats and calves because He was made our sacrifice and on what day? The Feast Sabbath of the Passover, Abib 15 known as the first day of Unleavened Bread. The same day Isaac was to be offered in sacrifice by Abraham was the day of His crucifixion and the Weekly Sabbath was His resurrection. Yes, He rose on Sabbath or Saturday not the 1st day of the week and we will fully test that in an entire chapter. That does not abandon the Sabbath, just animal sacrifices we no longer have to offer. Some also ridicule that to teach Sabbath is to teach the reinstitution of animal sacrifices. That is fraud and we know of no one who teaches such. Hebrews is very clear Messiah's blood is sufficient.

Both testaments or covenants are sealed with blood. We now have the eternal blood of Messiah as he continues with "The sufficiency of Christ's sacrifice" *(10:1)*. He replaced our need to sacrifice animals for atonement. He never abolished His Sabbath. Some will then say they keep Sabbath every day. However, the Bible calls that behavior lazy as Sabbath rest is only one day per week and never redefined. It is a sanctified, set apart and holy day once in each week and only once. Otherwise, what one is doing is marginalizing this day by equating it with the other 6 days which is not Bible ever. Such a line is an attack on the sanctity of the Sabbath undermining it's value.

We are reminded that He has put His laws into our hearts, and in our minds He wrote them *(10:16)*. This is a promise from the Old Testament *(Jer. 31:33-34)* for the new covenant to come which still has basis in the Old only it deepens in application for us. We do not just have the Torah to read, it is now embedded in our hearts and written in our minds. This should be evident in our lives yet the modern church tells us His law passed. How can it pass when it is further entrenched in our hearts and minds? Are they reading? It sounds like another Gospel because it is.

He did not develop amnesia in setting forth new covenant nor should we in this ludicrous programmed mindset. He does not say He changes His Laws. This is a further affirmation of His Law taken to a new level for believers as we now have them installed in our hearts and written in our minds. That's a deeper commitment to the law not lawlessness which is the definition of sin. This includes the Sabbath rest. Our sins and iniquities will no longer be remembered and there is no more offering needed for sin. This is not license to sin however as to even think in such manner is sin. In fact, he even addresses that willful sin has no more sacrifice to cover it. Yes, scripture has always defied the modern doctrine of "once saved, always saved." One can certainly lose their salvation.

Hebrews progresses in explaining faith using Old Testament patriarchs and the ultimate encouragement to run the race that is set before us. If the patriarchs are such an example, why are we then to forget what they practiced and stood for? However, this entire book embeds the Sabbath as part of the New Testament practice in foundation and yet the church has mostly lost it. Some may find that hard to believe yet the church, Catholic and Protestant, also lost the name of God, YHWH, Yahuah which is right there in Hebrew over 6,800 times yet replaced now in modern translations with generic titles instead. How could the church lose the name of their God? The same way it lost the Sabbath.

In the end of the Book of Hebrews, it is affirmed that "Jesus*(Yahusha)* is the same yesterday, and to day and for ever" *(13:8)*. We quote that but do we understand it? John 1 and others tell us Messiah was present and participated in Creation in the beginning. He always was and will be God *(Elohim)*. We also know the Father says He changes not *(Mal. 3:6)*. He follows this with this warning and it pertains to everything he just discussed in this entire book including the Sabbath practice this writer continued. The only change he records is we no longer need animal sacrifices because Messiah is our sacrifice and His blood is sufficient forever. Every pastor knows this but do we know that Sabbath was not abandoned?

Hebrews 13:9 KJV

Be not carried about with divers and strange doctrines. For it is a good thing that the heart be established with grace:; not with meats, which have not profited them that have been occupied therein.

He again affirms Jesus*(Yahusha)* is our sacrifice on the altar replacing the sacrifice or meats but He is still Lord of the Sabbath and we celebrate and honor Him on His day especially. Many apply this warning against diverse and strange doctrines as meaning the Old Testament practice yet that is not strange in any sense to the Bible. It is familiar and the very foundation for the New Testament. Who is still sacrificing animals at this point however? The Pharisees are, not the ekklesia. However, the ekklesias were still keeping the Sabbath and the Feasts throughout the New Testament all the way to the end of Revelation. Any church teaching against Hebrews is representing "strange doctrine." That's a flash forward but even going backwards in this passage from Chapter 4 to Chapter 3, we observe the very same message in Hebrews. If you are not keeping the Sabbath, according to the New Testament, you are operating in unbelief.

Hebrews 3:18-19 KJV
And to whom sware he that they should not enter into his rest, but to them that believed not? So we see that they could not enter in because of unbelief.

Hebrews is defining the Sabbath rest as that of believers and those who do not partake act as unbelievers. There is no debating this refers to the 7th Day Sabbath as it defines it multiple times tying this to Creation, David and the 7th Day. Even Messiah's sermon in which it refers took place on the 7th Day Sabbath as does David's Sabbath Psalm and the topic is Sabbath. Any so-called scholar telling you that does not say such, can't read. The Sabbath is the foundation of this entire sermon. This is only one such reference and we peruse many more.

How about Revelation which may be unfolding in our age but still has not completely come to pass? That is well after Messiah's ascension, in a future context even still and yet the English is very plain. If we believe the Bible, then all doctrines must be fully supported by such and not by mere fragments out of context. We will prove on this topic the church's position generally is only that.

Revelation 22:14 KJV
*Blessed are **they that do his commandments**, that they may have right to the tree of life, and may enter in through the gates into the city.*

What is John doing telling us to keep or do His commandments even in the Last Days? Does he not know Sabbath passed away and was redefined? He does not nor does any Apostle and that should bother the church to teach otherwise. You will never find a teaching in context in the entire Bible which abandons the Biblical Sabbath. The End Times and the Garden have always tied together as has the Sabbath from beginning to end. Genesis is still alive and breathing the true Gospel and always will as the Gospels tell us *(John 1)*. The Sabbath is the 4th Commandment and His Commandments have always included it. We will test this including Messiah's supposed new ones.

> ***Revelation 14:12-13 KJV***
> *Here is the patience of the saints: here are **they that keep the commandments of God, and the faith of Jesus**. And I heard a voice from heaven saying unto me, Write, Blessed are the dead which die in the Lord from henceforth: Yea, saith the Spirit, that **they may rest from their labours; and their works do follow them**.*

The faith of Jesus *(Yahusha)* has always included the Commandments. He tells us in John 15 in very great detail in fact as well as other places that if we love him, we keep His commandments. As it is included as the 4th Commandment mentioned, this passage again invokes the Sabbath rest. At the same time, this is one of those passages which tells us we actually do perform works even on the Sabbath and generally. We all know faith without works is dead. Building a relationship requires effort. Salvation has never been a simple prayer in scripture but relationship.

Most of us then hear these refer to Messiah's New 2 Commandments and we will cover those as well in an entire chapter with charts. Those 2 represent the 10 of Moses all the same and in fact, those are not even reading in context as they represent the greatest 2 as Messiah answers the Pharisees who attempt to entrap and He affirms there are 10 in the same passage. Even the 2 He chooses are not new but are part of the Law of Moses which He is quoting here. This is what happens, and it permeates modern theology, when one only extracts a fragment out of context. They will not understand the Bible.

One cannot break either of the 10 Commandments in keeping these 2 as they are the greatest. If we were to tell you, you are the greatest servant, does it then mean we are saying no one else serves? No one would ever interpret this that way yet many in the church do with that passage. As we provide a chart of this, we will also test what Law Noah represented because he most certainly had the Law as well or could not be judged righteous without such and you will find it is the same as Abraham, Moses and Messiah. Jesus *(Yahusha)* also defines End Times believers as keeping the Sabbath in the very end.

> ### Matthew 24:20-21 KJV
> *But pray ye that your flight be not in the winter,* **neither on the sabbath day***: For then shall be* **great tribulation***, such as was not since the beginning of the world to this time, no, nor ever shall be.*

The Biblical Sabbath observance limits how far one can travel on the Sabbath. Here we have Messiah Himself invoking this in the End Times at the time of the Great Tribulation. That has not happened yet and thus, He says the Sabbath will still be kept at that point by believers. Otherwise, there would be no need to mention it. Those demanding to be shown where exactly Messiah affirmed the Sabbath in continuance just got it right there with several more coming. They just simply are not reading because it does not fit their paradigm. It is time we mold our thinking to the Bible rather than attempting the opposite. Jesus *(Yahusha)* was not silent on this in the slightest.

> ### Mark 2:27-28 KJV
> *And he said unto them,* **The sabbath was made for man***, and not man for the sabbath: Therefore the Son of man is* **Lord also of the sabbath***.*

> ### Matthew 12:8 KJV
> *For the Son of man is* **Lord even of the sabbath day***.*

> ### Luke 6:5 KJV
> *And he said unto them, That the Son of man is* **Lord also of the sabbath***.*

Somehow, it is characterized that Messiah never even spoke of the Sabbath but just ignored it and of course, broke it. Both are absolutely false and horrible scholarship of the illiterate kind. He made the

Sabbath as according to John 1, He was there participating in Creation as a Creator. That is why He is Lord of the Sabbath. This is not a new declaration but from the beginning. He did not nor does any scripture ever say He created the Sabbath in the time of Moses as even Moses disagrees with that declaring it a Creation concept on the 7th Day. He is, always has been and always will be Lord of the Sabbath. If He is our Lord, then we should be keeping His Sabbath of which He is Lord.

How can anyone claim He came to declare Himself Lord of the Sabbath only to abolish it? How could they say He changed the day and practice even when not a single scripture ever says so and He says He will not change it. Whomever did is not representing Him on this topic. The Sabbath was made for man, for Adam and all who come after him. Are you a human? This is addressing you and we are told to reject the day He made for us to rest? In 6 days, He created all that is, and on the seventh, He made a day for you and us. This also verifies the Creation account most certainly required 24-hour days not pods of time nor portions but full days as Sabbath is certainly defined as such.

Now, it is time to understand what Hebrews was discussing when Messiah preached His Sabbath sermon. Here it is. We have all at least heard the words of Jesus*(Yahusha)* when He beckons us to come and rest in Him. If we remain weary and heavy-laden, it is likely because we have lost His Sabbath in fact. We all need this rest and anyone wrestling with depression especially, start keeping His Sabbath. This is very falsely characterized as either when we die or on the Day of Judgment of which neither are in this passage but the Sabbath most certainly is and is the context here. Did you know what day it was that He was preaching this? You guessed it, He was preaching on the Sabbath about the Sabbath.

> **Matthew 11:28-30; Matthew 12:1a KJV**
> *Come unto me, all ye that labour and are heavy laden, and **I will give you rest**. Take my yoke upon you, and learn of me; for I am meek and lowly in heart: and **ye shall find rest unto your souls**. For my yoke is easy, and my burden is light. At that time Jesus went on the sabbath day...*

So many even guru evangelists out there today are attempting to provide programs for you to find rest for your soul when the Bible already lays out that rest and we act oblivious. Those are counterfeits and none will work as His Sabbath which cannot be replaced. The chapter break serves to disconnect this but this is why we must read the Word in context and understand it does not originally have such breaks. These are great in order to locate scriptures but we must be mindful these are not always disconnected but many times, a continuation in thought.

In this case, there is no doubting that because verse 12:1 begins with "at that time." What time? The time in which He just said what He said in 11:28-30. It is the same time and it is the Sabbath. On the Sabbath, Messiah says come and rest in Me. He is specifically speaking of the Sabbath rest as He is Lord of the Sabbath and Hebrews 4 just told us so. For those claiming it is such a chore and burden to keep His Sabbath, what did He just say? His yoke is easy and His burden is light. He is talking about the Sabbath and already answered your question 2,000 years ago. We even complain desiring such reprieve which He already installed for us yet we ignore it. Somehow that is then framed as His fault. The peace missing in many of our lives will be found in keeping His Sabbath. It is a blessing and not a curse.

This is beautiful in any sense but for any church to misrepresent this and disconnect this from the Sabbath is committing fraud. We are aware they characterize this as after the Day of Judgment when we are all with Him yet that is not His context at all nor is He discussing after we die which is another topic that greatly needs understanding. Again, we just received clarity from Hebrews, scripture, and no scholar can overcome that. He also is not speaking of Salvation in this passage and any church preaching that our lives become rosey and perfect once we say a prayer, is guilty of absolute negligence. Many who have followed such cultish behavior have been extremely disappointed and turned off to the Word even worse than if they never said the prayer in the first place.

Congratulations, these churches just fulfilled prophecy leading the lambs to slaughter and literally teaching them to break the 3rd commandment taking Yahuah's name in vain. There will be a stern judgment for those churches. In attempting to become seeker-friendly, they change the Word and that comes with a very heavy penalty. Conviction from the Holy Spirit is not seeker-friendly and if your church is absent that, you fit the verse of having a form of Godliness and denying the power thereof *(2 Tim. 3:5)*.

He is speaking of the Sabbath rest on His Sabbath of which He is Lord. Being Lord of the Sabbath means He is Lord of Rest. He tells you He wants to give you rest in Him yet the church comes up with every excuse possible even ridiculing His own words to attempt to avoid this practice which He says He made for you. Is it really that difficult to rest in Him for one day every week? We have found it a blessing not a curse and no chore. It is certainly not bondage but freedom. Messiah has a gift for you every week called the Sabbath. Will you partake in His rest or reject His gift to you?

However, let us all deal with the facts. The church generally agrees with 9 of the 10 Commandments. They do not wish for you to kill, steal, commit adultery, serve other gods, take His name in vain, dishonor parents, bear false witness, covet, nor include idols in worship generally. Certainly, there is clarity needed on some of these in definition but even still, generally, the church is fine with these 9 commandments. However, oddly, the church takes issue with one − the 4th Commandment, remembering and keeping the Sabbath holy. Rest for a day in Him.

We know, we must be absolutely satanic to suggest one keep a day of rest in the presence of the Creator. What a terrible deed for those in your church as well as others actually spend a full day willingly in the presence of Jesus*(Yahusha)*. How could we lead people to do so? We do not, the Bible does and after reading this book, you will know this.

As for Paul being used largely to bolster such claim with fragments, we will fully dismantle this thinking and prove Paul kept and taught the Sabbath. He is greatly misrepresented by most churches because they are following the same Pharisee leaven which began 2,000 years ago according to Peter who warned us Paul was already taken out of context even in those days *(2 Pet. 3:15-17)*.

We will cover the Law of Sin and Death from Paul and you will discover that is an opposite law at odds with Yahuah's Law. Paul never calls Yahuah's Law the Law of Sin and Death and demonstrates very clearly over 20 times in Romans 7 and 8 this distinction yet most churches are telling us Paul taught against a Law he kept and supported. Paul even called the Law good, holy and just *(Rom. 7:12)* and a delight *(Rom. 7:22)*. He was no hypocrite and we will address the Paul haters who have then taken the church's poor assessment and used it to claim Paul's writings should be disregarded.

This is ridiculous and we will prove he was an Apostle and certainly was not what some claim as the son of perdition. That claim is illiterate and solely based on unfounded ridicule and by the way, the term in this sense requires one to read Paul to even understand this son of perdition as essentially the beast. So he rebuked himself? Peter warned of this "willing ignorance" in our era that would deny Creation *(Sabbath is a Creation on the 7th Day)*, the Flood *(Sabbath also included)* and the deity of Messiah *(Lord of the Sabbath)* and he ends this warning endorsing Paul *(2 Pet. 3:1-17)*. This prophecy is coming to pass in our day not only with the Sabbath but with the Anti-Paul Movement and poorly constructed, unscriptural doctrines such as the Serpent Seed, Gap Theory, Alternate Creation Theory, etc. Their origin is not the Bible. Test them.

We will even demonstrate historically the Early Church kept the Sabbath and on Saturday following the example of Messiah and His Apostles. You have likely heard the term "When in Rome, do as the Romans do." Well, did you know the origin of that term actually refers to Rome's changing the Sabbath to Sunday? That is what one would do in Rome, practice on Sunday instead of the Biblical Saturday Sabbath. Did you know it was observed on Saturday and Rome changed it not Messiah nor His Apostles nor the Early Church even?

We will provide even Popes' words that admit such as well as history. It does not say you cannot meet on Sunday which you can meet everyday according to scripture as you will find the Apostles doing so other days but the Sabbath always remained Saturday. There is not a single scripture that ever says otherwise and we are still to observe it. We will cover the very many in the New Testament as well as Old which prove this.

The Sabbath has always been the 7th Day and no Apostle ever changed that nor would they have the authority as Jesus*(Yahusha)* remains Lord of the Sabbath and it's origin is Creation not Moses and that is according to Moses even. Jesus*(Yahusha)* would have to change it and He did the opposite, He kept it in example and still keeps Sabbath in Heaven to this day. He taught it and told us it would not pass away yet many of us in ministry teach it did pass. Who is right? The Son of Yahuah or your denomination? Why would seminaries teach against what Jesus*(Yahusha)* taught? You must present them with that question and after reading this, you will have ample support from scripture to verify this fully.

In his famous Sermon on the Mount, Jesus*(Yahusha)* reinforces the 10 Commandments from the Law of Moses specifically and directly dealing with 4 of them in detail as well as other portions of the law in which he is really invoking Moses in each. We have a chapter on this. How can we be told that His quoting Moses is somehow passing new Law? This passage is used to claim He established new law yet He is merely representing what we call the Old which is not Old at all. He even begins this sermon with this:

> ***Matthew 5:17-20 KJV***
> ***Think not that I am come to destroy the law, or the prophets:***
> ***I am not come to destroy, but to fulfil.*** *For verily I say unto you, **Till heaven and earth pass, one jot or one tittle shall in no wise pass from the law, till all be fulfilled**. Whosoever therefore shall break one of these least commandments, and shall teach men so, he shall be called the least in the kingdom of heaven: but whosoever shall do and teach them, the same shall be called great in the kingdom of heaven. For I say unto you, That except your righteousness shall exceed the righteousness of the scribes and Pharisees, ye shall in no case enter into the kingdom of heaven.*

When did "I did not" become "I did?" There is no other way to read this and yet the church generally is telling us it says the opposite of what any person can clearly read and understand for themselves. The prophets wrote the Old Testament yet many from the pulpit marginalize their writings as passed away but here you have Messiah's endorsement and you will never find an Apostle who says they passed. Not even Paul does as he even preached from it and lived it.

Yes, Messiah will fulfill the law in the end. When does it expire if so? When Heaven and Earth pass which happens on the Day of Final Judgment and not before. He says, and that is all that matters, not one letter *(it's never jot which is illiterate but iota, the Greek "i")* of the Law will pass until that Day of Final Judgment. How can denominations teach otherwise? More so, what so-called scholar chooses to debate with the Son of Yahuah? He says what He says and no scholar can reinterpret what is very obvious here. They do so to fit their doctrines forcing the Bible to comply with men's illiterate positions. No thank you.

If you are reading this before that day of Judgment, that means it applies to you still and no church can abolish it as no pope, apostle, theologian nor pastor have such authority to change the Word. He also fulfilled the Sabbath and the Law when He came as the word fulfill means He kept it fully and even He tells us He would not abolish it. He did not so how can any denomination usurp His authority which remains with Him? If you are a pastor teaching men to break His commandments, he addresses you as well and wisdom would take heed.

Also, this passage rebukes Pharisees and is not calling them righteous which would be inconsistent. Their false appearance of righteousness is what He addresses. He is rebuking legalism which we will discuss. Keeping the Sabbath is not legalism but freedom. That is what our Messiah says and even His brother James *(Yacob, actually)*.

In our journey, we have learned to research beyond what is called tradition and though much remains good, there is doctrine intertwined which has no origin in the Bible and must be tested and exposed. Those worried about such test as a so-called lack of faith are confused and faith misplaced as the Bible is what we are to have faith in. Any doctrine that does not match the Bible, is simply a useless doctrine of men.

Though you will find fragments, which no doubt some are already recalling, one must review the full case of the Sabbath from scripture and we will deal with virtually all of them. If you have not, and you did not in seminary nor sitting in a church pew in most cases, you have a responsibility to know what the Bible says on this topic. This book will restore this for many and again, test it with scripture and then, go test what you call doctrine as well. Any good doctrine will always pass the test of scripture. Otherwise, we hold onto the good and out with the bad if we are following the Bible *(1 Th. 5:21)*.

Let us take a look at this English word fulfill. What does it mean? Here is what Merriam-Webster's Dictionary defines:

**ful·fill | \ fu̇(l)-ˈfil also fə(l)- **
1a: to put into effect : EXECUTE
He fulfilled his pledge to cut taxes.

Does this mean his cutting taxes means no more cutting taxes? Are we to now be taxed in full because he fulfilled cutting them? Would that even make sense? That is what we are being told with this erroneous definition that fulfill means to abolish which is actually the very opposite. Messiah tells you when they pass away, different words certainly not fulfill and that has not happened yet. He executed or performed the Law and if He didn't, he sinned or was lawless. He put it into effect in His life as our example, an example much of the church seems to wish to abolish. He did not.

> *b: to meet the requirements of (a business order)*
> *Their order for more TVs was promptly fulfilled.*

Are we to interpret this as since TVs were delivered, there is to be no more TV? Do the TVs then pass away since they were delivered? In fact, no one else on earth can ever have a TV delivered again because this person got theirs? We know better but this is how they are applying this scripture backwards by redefining this word in error.

> *c: to measure up to : SATISFY*
> *She hasn't yet fulfilled the requirements needed to graduate.*

If Messiah measured up to and satisfied the Law, would this ever be interpreted that his rising to such measure then abandons the Law up to which measure he lived? Because this girl graduated does no one else ever graduate? In other words, believers were to be righteous before Him but no longer? Does that support anything in the whole of scripture?

> *d: to bring to an end*
> *she came to install herself and fulfill her time at the house*

Perhaps this one definition could be attempted for abandoned but it would be a complete misunderstanding to claim this brought an end to the house. The house still stands, just her time in the house was fulfilled. There is no application here to meet what many pastors are teaching on the Sabbath and the Commandments. She fulfilled her time in the house and left just as Messiah did for that matter in a sense. That would not change the Law nor did it and He was not a liar.

2a: to develop the full potentialities of
He has a lot of talent, but he hasn't really fulfilled his potential.

To develop the full potential of the Law certainly could not mean to abolish it. Once this person fulfills his potential, does the potential he is living up to as a measure disappear? No one else is to bother to live up to their potential because this one man did? Is there any logic which would progress in such fashion? No, the measure does not disappear and if he stops living up to such measure, it would be said he no longer lives up to his potential because the measure remains. How have we learned to take such a constant with such historicity and throw it out the window?

b: to convert into reality
a sense of the failure of life to fulfill its ultimate expectations

Making the Law a reality by being the first man to completely live it as sinless could not possibly mean to abolish it. Are we really to believe that if Adam would have fulfilled the Law in completeness, he would have abolished it then? How would he even be judged righteous? Against what? Did Enoch who did so much of his life? Was the Law abolished because he was righteous? Was it abolished because Noah lived righteous or Abraham? No. None of those were as perfect as Messiah but they kept the law in righteousness and that does not abolish it.

The notion that He would abandon the very rules that define righteousness is illogical in every sense especially when to be lawless, as some churches even teach, is to literally teach sin. Sin is lawlessness. Without law, there can no longer be sin as it is not an attribute but an antithesis. Find where scripture tells us to be lawless. You will not. If only the likes of John MacArthur could actually read the Bible, they would not rail against the Sabbath ignorantly as they do. They have no case and we will obliterate it here not with debate but with scripture in context and in overwhelming abundance. They have no debate.

Also, did not Yahuah write especially the 10 Commandments and part of the Law with His very finger? Are we to believe that Jesus*(Yahusha)* rebelled against Yahuah's law? Heaven forbid! He says He represented the Father and did nothing He did not see the Father doing *(John 5:19, 6:38, 14:31)*. Would Yahuah's own writing ever be temporary? Not using logic. Messiah said He kept Yahuah's commandments *(John 15:10)*.

These scholars are not thinking through the ramifications of such lofty doctrine but they are pleasing their mentors, the Pharisees, and who cares what they think. We call out MacArthur especially because he preaches very strongly against the Sabbath yet all from the doctrines of men and scripture out of context in poorly managed fragments. He is a good man and we do not believe his intent is to harm but it does harm and he needs to be addressed. He is not representing Messiah in doing so but instead picking a debate with Him.

The very measure of sin is breaking His Law. Remove that measure, which He does not, and you are living in the Law of Sin and Death not His Law. Yes, we are redeemed from that negative law not His law from which no redemption is required. The modern church literally represents the satanic bible's commandment of "do what though wilt" when they attempt to abolish His Commandments and claim there is no longer Law. If you love Him, you will keep His commandments *(John 15:10, Matt. 19:17-19, 1 Tim. 6:14, 1 John 5:3, Jas. 1:22)*. If you do not keep His commandments, well, you fill in the blank...

> *3archaic : to make full : FILL*
> *her subtle, warm, and golden breath … fulfills him with beatitude*

Making the Law full means it's still there. It's full, complete. One does not fill a glass and call it empty using reason. It does not then disappear as it is still there. All other glasses are also not deemed full because this one glass was filled.

Some respond with the Law must be abolished because no man can keep it. Scripture does not agree. All have sinned and fallen short of His glory *(Rom. 3:23)* yet the person who wrote that, the Messiah before him and the New Testament community continued to keep and teach the law though all imperfect except Jesus*(Yahusha)*. Everyone in the Old Testament fell short as well. The Bible does not redefine them as hopeless and never says to stop living up to His measure because man is imperfect. We are not excused. Salvation is also an Old Testament concept and they were saved then, even Gentiles as we will address, the "stranger among you" is included in the blessings and curses of the Law many times. Grace, in fact, is very strongly rooted in the Old Testament and any teaching of a Gospel of Grace that does not begin with the story of Adam and Noah, is incomplete.

Daniel predicted in the last days, in our era knowledge would increase. If we are not keeping up with this increasing knowledge, we render our ministries impertinent. This includes restoring knowledge once known but somehow obscured especially by the Dark Ages. Today, a regular person can go onto resources like Blue Letter Bible and become a sort of Hebrew expert legitimately. They wouldn't be able to speak it necessarily, nor does modern Israel who speaks Yiddish not Ancient Hebrew as most linguists represent as well, but they can research word for word almost and acquire understanding that we did not even have available 20 years ago except through years of study and very expensive resources.

We are taught in seminaries to compare parallel passages in modern translations which all say very close to the same thing. The world would and does call that confirmation bias and unfortunately, they would be accurate. There is actually little to be gained by such exercise typically. However, a layman can conduct research of the highest scholars in minutes and many are as they dig deeply into the original Hebrew and Greek. Most pastors do not. This should redefine the role of Pastor to refrain from attempting to wear so many hats and instead focus on proving things out as 1 Thessalonians 5:21 tells us.

It is incredible that the number 1 concern we hear from viewers and readers is they cannot get their pastors to take the time to even consider research, increasing knowledge and biblical cases. That is sad and irresponsible. Understand we have many pastors and even clergy who follow all or parts of our research and do not fit such category. It does not mean they agree with everything nor is that expected but learning does not end when you receive a degree or title, it begins at that point.

This book is a great start and observe the methodology. Anyone can conduct this research effectively. Content is far more important than building buildings and creating programs. People have stumbling blocks and we have the responsibility to teach them so they can overcome. In this age, your church will become obsolete very quickly if you are not keeping up no matter how pretty your building nor how broad your infrastructure.

It's not about reading a book and quoting a modern scholar who is relying on antiquated thought because they haven't researched nor kept up. There is also nothing to be gained from quoting the occult philosophers, histories, movies and even outright occult religious practices we have heard from the pulpit far too often.

In fact, in the recent Hollywood movie "Faith Under Fire," the former Nephilim impersonator, Dean Cain, formerly Superman, plays the role of the pastor of a small church. When a conflicted parishioner confronts him with his doubts, he proceeds to quote Robert Frost, the Beatles, and other absolute nonsense without even using scripture that would actually assist the person's understanding. He seemed uncomfortable with the little scripture he shared even from the pulpit but right at home in quoting the occult. Hollywood knows nothing of scripture and no, it is not a good thing that they are making so-called Christian films nor should the church be attempting to infuse modern Hollywood, Nephilim, pop culture into it's content.

Just look at the movie Noah where they actually used the Gnostic account and they do not even apologize for it. However, big name scholars supported the movie in ignorance because they do not even know the account. They are Kabbalists and occultists who have nothing of value to add to society as Yahuah has always rejected them before the Flood, at Babel, in Sodom and today. We must know things for ourselves and there is not a single denomination who has cornered the market on increasing knowledge but instead most shun it. Imagine what Daniel would say about that. We too, do not know everything and we are trying to keep up. However, that which we have researched, and this topic exhaustively, we know.

Once one has truly examined the full case of what the Bible has to say about the Sabbath, it is impossible to conclude that Messiah, the Lord of the Sabbath, was confused or went against His own promise and abandoned the Sabbath. The thinking He would declare Himself Lord of the Sabbath only to abolish it makes no sense.

It is equally illogical to deduce Paul nor any Apostle preached to abolish that which they kept and taught. This thinking characterizes our Messiah as a hypocrite as well as His Apostles who are found dozens of times in the Gospels and even in the Book of Acts keeping the Sabbath. Acts mostly occurs after Jesus*(Yahusha)* ascended to Heaven. Were the Apostles disobedient and in rebellion to continue to keep the Sabbath and the Law after Messiah's ascension? How is it that they did not know He abolished the Sabbath? Did they not know better than any modern theologian or pastor? Are we not to follow their and His example rather than being told to abandon that which they practiced and taught? That thinking is another Gospel from what Paul preached and that is called church doctrine in most churches today. This is the strong delusion already at work.

This is one of the core issues of our day. This book will unravel one of the key elements of the Dark Ages and strong delusion in which we are warned for our time. Many wonder what the delusion will be. It is already here and has been for centuries. The Dark Ages never ended. For the order which arose out of such chaos is that of further profound ignorance of scripture. Today, the church generally, does not know the Word and has little commitment to it as this topic will attest. This includes many scholars, theologians and seminarians. Their commitment is to church doctrine untested and not the pure meat of the Word.

In fact, some request our Statement of Faith in which we respond, it's called the Bible – all of it. We believe in being true to the Word and it's original intent not the traditions of men. Anyone who believes they can sum the Bible's doctrine up into one sentence or a paragraph has an incredibly shallow position. That is a vain attempt. Placating such vanity is the very definition of foolishness.

Today's message is Sabbath rest in Him. Even in light of recent world events, we need His rest more than ever. One of the best scriptures timely for this new era in which the world has entered is found in Isaiah.

ISAIAH 26:20-21 KJV

Come, my people, enter thou into thy chambers, and shut thy doors about thee: hide thyself as it were for a little moment, until the indignation be overpast.
For, behold, the Lord cometh out of his place to punish the inhabitants of the

earth for their iniquity: the earth also shall disclose her blood, and shall no more cover her slain

The Sabbath rest is one of the most beautiful practices imaginable and we need it more today than in any period in history since the Flood as those days of Noah are returning. A day of refueling which mankind needs most. You will never be able to put on your full armor without it. A day in tune with Jesus *(Yahusha)* and Yahuah.

When we all restored this practice in our lives, it truly set us free. Some of us fought this for years. Revelation began to come alive in reading scripture and He began to speak as we had never experienced before in many years of ministry. We were too busy for Him thinking we were doing His work. However, He wants you, your love and devotion, your time and your adherence to His ways. Many wish to tell Him how to conform to theirs. You are not that important and that is a perfect example of the kind of blasphemy the beast system represents found in many churches today. The Gospel is not about you, it is about Him. You benefit but you are not the topic. This is still about relationship not church nor organization.

No, we are not Seventh-day Adventists nor Messianic either. We just believe the Word and we would love nothing more than for you to restore this in your life as well. We do not mix words and we offer a very direct approach which we will continue. That is the true definition of love as you love no one whom you will not rebuke.

Imagine, The Creator wants to know you personally because you matter to Him. He wants you to live with Him forever. His Word is brilliant, concise and preserved but also very clear you must be in relationship *(Matt. 7, John 15)*. In order to live it, you will find yourself eventually keeping the Sabbath according to scripture.

You can debate the day, the time it begins, whether one can drive, how far, and strain gnats on whether electricity is creating fire all you wish. We have no interest in such gnat straining and useless debate as the Sabbath is not about legalism though many in the church attempt to characterize it as such as well as works they say. Step back and think about that. They are telling you the day in which you are to rest according to scripture is work. Huh? Follow your conviction. You can read, understand and apply the Word for yourself.

One can scoff and ridicule but they will never truly pursue a real relationship with Him without spending time with Him no matter how one interprets this. This time will always lead to the Sabbath as it is one of the very foundational principles that define a true walk with Him which defines the End Time remnant believer. Is that you? This is what the Bible says and it matters not how a popular pastor feels about that. You may be a pastor who has never heard this and it is time that you do because you do not know the New Testament fully if you do not understand the Sabbath. If you think that statement is wrong, we dare you to review this Biblical case and try to disprove it as even this introduction is something you cannot truly dispute.

This introduction already opens our case with only New Testament scripture you will notice, and there is far more thus an entire book for this position. It's right there and has been all along. Even reading the New Testament in context and in full will only lead to such conclusion. We challenge all to review this case and execute a complete trial of the Word. You will likely find as we have, the Sabbath is New Testament Doctrine to the end and the New Testament Church should still be keeping it according to the Word and our Messiah said so.

Are we demanding everyone keep what are framed by many as the 614 laws in the Law of Moses or else? These hypocrites do not even realize they are quoting Pharisees not Bible and trying to apply the Pharisee paradigm as the measure to then criticize one simply saying we should keep His Sabbath and follow the Bible. It is the same ridicule they attempt with Paul and it is Pharisee leaven. We do not entertain such fraudulent debate steeped in a false paradigm from the beginning.

All have sinned and you will not keep the Law 100% if you are human and you are in very good company as every patriarch and Apostle was as well. They attempt to create a straw man argument that few teaching Sabbath would ever even espouse as supposedly their position that it is not. It is a fraudulent way to operate and should not be found in the ministry yet you will find scholars leveling such in debate and there is nothing to debate regarding this. We all sin and repent and He forgives.

We should strive not to sin. Is that really that difficult? Is it a satanic aim to tell people what scripture says, that we should all strive for excellence?

We should focus our lives on building true relationship with Him. It is all that matters and your sole purpose for being. However, the church's embracing of the actual satanic commandment "do what though wilt" is unacceptable and unbiblical. There must be Law and there is. It matters not whether they like it. He does and it is His measure for righteousness.

If the Sabbath were insignificant, why is it mentioned 137 times in the Bible? If Messiah had done away with it, why is it observed by the disciples after His ascension? *(Acts 2:1-4, 13:14-16,13:42-44,18:4, 1 Cor. 7:19, 11:1)* Why did the early church keep it as well? If it was temporary, why does scripture profess the Sabbath is forever in your generations for a perpetual and everlasting covenant by a statute forever? *(Ex. 31:13, 16, Lev. 16:31, 24:8)* Why did Jesus*(Yahusha)* say he did not come to abolish it? *(Matt. 5:17-20)* In fact, why does He declare Himself "Lord of the Sabbath" *(Mark 2:28)* only to abolish it which He says He would not? *(Matt. 5:17-20)* Why would He create a day for man and then eliminate that day altogether? *(Mark 2:27)*

For this is the Day of Rest created for man *(Mark 2:27)* to rejuvenate in the presence of our Creator. He knows we need that and without it, we will never have the needed fuel nor will we ever apply our full armor. *(Eph. 6:11-13)* This is never a suggestion but in Israel, to defile this day in many references, would mean death *(Ex. 31:14-15, 35:2)*. On this day, we are to conduct no work not even cooking, nor to indulge in our own pleasure but to focus on Him in a state of rest *(Ex. 35:3, Lev. 23:3, Deut. 5)*. Even when Yahuah rained manna from Heaven, He refrained and rested on the seventh day *(Ex. 16:26)*. He even provided double provision on the sixth to ensure everyone could keep His Sabbath. How could something matter so much to Him in those days and yet be called nothing today?

Did Messiah void the law? No *(Matt. 5:17-20)*. Did Paul? No *(Rom. 3:31, 2:13, 7:12, 7:22)*. Did Luke? No *(Acts 24:14, 25:8)*. Paul's responses to gnostic teachings and Pharisees are never repudiating the law which he says is holy, just and good. His context is one of application of the law which is not the Pharisee nor gnostic way of additives and leaven.

It is time to restore His Sabbath in your life. It is certainly better to operate within His Law rather than lawlessness which is sin in any era. May we all restore His ways in our lives. Yah Bless.

Wherefore the Lord said, Forasmuch as this people draw near me with their mouth, and with their lips do honour me, but have removed their heart far from me, and their fear toward me is taught by the precept of men:
                                                                    –Isaiah 29:13 KJV

This know also, that in the last days perilous times shall come. For men shall be lovers of their own selves, covetous, boasters, proud, blasphemers, disobedient to parents, unthankful, unholy, Without natural affection, trucebreakers, false accusers, incontinent, fierce, despisers of those that are good, Traitors, heady, highminded, lovers of pleasures more than lovers of God; Having a form of godliness, but denying the power thereof: from such turn away.
                                                                  –2 Timothy 3:1-5 KJV

Strong's Concordance Numbers in parentheses

šabāṭ
šeḇeṯ
שׁבת

shabbâth

(H7676*) intermission, i.e (specifically) the Sabbath:—(+ every) sabbath. Verb. (H7673*) to repose, i.e. desist from exertion; used in many implied relations (causative, figurative or specific):——(cause to, let, make to) cease, celebrate, cause (make) to fail, keep (sabbath), suffer to be lacking, leave, put away (down), (make to) rest, rid, still, take away. (H7674*) rest, interruption, cessation:—cease, sit still, loss of time. (H7675*) properly, session; but used also concretely, an abode or locality:——place, seat.

Chapter 1 | What is the Sabbath?

The Sabbath is a Biblical reprieve for the soul – a time of refueling one's spirit, soul and body. It is an intermission or break within the week for one day. We do not exert ourselves – no work as we cease. We celebrate and keep the Sabbath rest. We are lacking in activity, leave the world system for a day, and we are rid of our worries that are taken away. These definitions certainly capture the Sabbath and the final one is very interesting as we will explore in the end Yahuah's seat on Earth.

Nothing else can replace His Sabbath. Messiah did not replace it either but beckons us to come and enter into His rest every week as that is His context. He desires to give us rest. This is clearly interpreted and understood in Hebrews 4 that we examined in our Introduction. When the Bible offers such interpretation of Messiah's words, there is no theologian who can overrule it and reinterpret differently. They would have to change the Bible.

However, do we understand what the Sabbath is? Do many even know what they are rejecting without Biblical investigation but simply trusting men's opinions not Biblically based? We assure you seminaries have not conducted this due diligence and we dare any seminary to review this case in full even in attempt to disprove. They will not do so with fragments out of context. This is too much Bible to overcome with such an approach. It is time we demand more of church leadership who has sunken into willing ignorance *(2 Pet. 3)* especially regarding the Sabbath. What do we know about the Sabbath?

Genesis 2:2-3 KJV
*And on the **seventh** (שביעי: sh^{e}bîy'îy) day God ended his work which he had made; and he **rested** (שבת: shâbath) on the seventh day from all his*

*work which he had made. And God blessed the **seventh** (שביעי: sh^ebîy ʿy)*
*day, and sanctified it: because that in it he had **rested** (שבת: shâbath) from*
all his work which God created and made.

We all know Yahuah created the Heavens and the Earth and all within 6 days. On the 7th day, He rested. Was He tired or is there more significance to this rest? Why is this important and what is it?

The Sabbath is a Free Gift to Mankind

> ### Mark 2:27-28 KJV
> *And he said unto them, **The sabbath was made for man**, and not man for the sabbath: Therefore **the Son of man is Lord also of the sabbath**.*

Man was not created for the Sabbath. He was created on the 6th day and then, on the 7th, man was given an eternal gift called the Sabbath day of rest. It is a Creation and was made or created. That is much more than a commandment. That is what Messiah says. Yes, Yahuah rested on the 7th day of Creation but not alone and we will cover the progressive history of Sabbath from the beginning. However, that 7th Day was made for man. It was not made for Yahuah, it was made for us – Adam initially and all who would follow. Yes, Adam was man and there was no other Creation of man in scripture except His female counterpart who was made from Adam's rib. If you know what an Indian-giver is, then you understand Yahuah is not one. He does not give us gifts to take them away. The Sabbath is not a new concept in the days of Moses. It has been since the 7th day as we will fortify in the next chapter.

There are some who will tell you that they agree the Sabbath was created then but then they will tell you even though Yahuah created it for man, He neglected to tell Adam about it even in the Garden of Eden. Follow the logic. He creates a day of rest for man specifically and notice Jesus*(Yahusha)* does not specify only for Hebrews but all men generally. We do all realize that Adam, Enoch, Noah nor Abraham were Jews or really, Yahudim which is that actual Bible word never Jew.

We all know Adam, Cain and Abel, Enoch, Noah, Abraham and the patriarchs of our faith generally knew especially to sacrifice animals yet we then forget that Biblical purpose of such takes place on the Weekly Sabbath and the 7 Biblical Feasts not arbitrary days. In practicing such they were most certainly keeping especially the Sabbath and even some Feasts which have such history long before Israel. We will cover this more in the next chapter with examples. Moses agrees with Messiah when he tells Israel Yahuah has given them the Sabbath. However, let us be clear, Messiah says man not just Hebrews, and even Exodus includes Gentiles.

> *Exodus 16:29 KJV*
> *See, for that* **the LORD hath given you the sabbath**...

The Sabbath is a Sign of Covenant with Yahuah

Are we in covenant with Yahuah? Yes, it is a New Covenant but still a pact with Yahusha and Yahuah in which we have an end to fulfill as it is not a one-way covenant. It is new yet in basis in what we call the Old. We will prove this includes the Sabbath overwhelmingly. How can we be confident we know Him? Matthew 7 is very clear even Christians will be told "depart from me for I never KNEW you." Again, Sabbath is not salvation but it is part of knowing Him as we love Him, thus we keep His commandments. This is a relationship with our Creators.

Exodus tells us the Sabbath is a sign of covenant between us and Yahuah forever. According to Yahuah, the purpose of keeping it is so that we may know that He is Yahuah who sanctifies it. Those are His words and He wrote this portion of the Law with His own finger and said this Law has no end as it is throughout your generations. We will firmly prove this was for Gentiles as well as Hebrews. The Book of Hebrews clarifies using this same language as not keeping the Sabbath after Messiah's ascension is called a sign or example of unbelief. This also means the Sabbath is the sign of belief.

> *Exodus 31:13 KJV*
> *Speak thou also unto the children of Israel, saying, Verily my sabbaths ye shall keep: for it is a sign between me and you throughout your generations; that ye may know that I am the LORD that doth sanctify you.*

Ezekiel repeats this twice. Yahuah said the Sabbath is for us to know Him. This is part of relationship and the same is said by Messiah in Matthew 11:28-30 according to its interpretation in Hebrews 4 as we observed. How do we know Him? We keep His ways not ours. His way is the Sabbath and there is never a scripture which abandons such.

Ezekiel 20:12 KJV

Moreover also I gave them my sabbaths, to be a sign between me and them, that they might know that I am the LORD that sanctify them.

Ezekiel 20:19-20 KJV

I am the Lord your God; walk in my statutes, and keep my judgments, and do them; And hallow my sabbaths; and they shall be a sign between me and you, that ye may know that I am the Lord (YHWH) your God (Elohim).

Not only is the Sabbath hallowed for all ages, forever, it is a sign of our relationship with Yahuah that we know who He is and He says He sanctifies us on the Sabbath. Why would anyone calling themselves His follower not desire such sanctification? It is also a sign of His Creation. Literally, every 7th day, we are celebrating His works of Creation. It reminds us weekly, just how awesome and powerful He is. For those thinking we don't need this, why is man always forgetting how omnipotent He is? We doubt and question because we don't keep His Sabbath. This is the willing ignorance in which Peter refers *(2 Pet. 3)*.

Jubilees 2:1

Write the complete history of the creation, how in six days the Lord (Yahuah) ALMIGHTY finished all His works and all that He created, and kept Sabbath on the seventh day and hallowed it for all ages, and appointed it as a sign for all His works.

Jubilees 2:17-18

And He gave us a great sign, the Sabbath day, that we should work six days, but keep Sabbath on the seventh day from all work.

New Covenant is still covenant. It is an agreement between the Father, Son and us. Messiah was part of Abraham's covenant as well as Moses' covenant. Isaac was the son of covenant – the miracle child who foreshadows the coming of Messiah. Yahusha is within that covenant and actually even followed the dates being born on the same day as Isaac and his sacrifice also occurred on the same day Isaac was offered and of course, Abraham was stopped. He already existed in Heaven *(John 1)* but had not come to Earth yet in human form and it is foretold that he will arrive within Abraham, Isaac and Jacob's seed even *(Gen. 12:3, 22:17-18; Ps. 72:10)*. Again, we have the interpretation of this in the New Testament as Paul writes Genesis is specifying one seed here.

Galatians 3:16 KJV

Now to Abraham and his seed were the promises made. He saith not, And to seeds, as of many; but as of one, And to thy seed, which is Christ.

However, not only did Moses well know this as he wrote Genesis, but Moses most certainly wrote specifically of Yahusha. That is what He says in His own words.

John 5:46 KJV

For had ye believed Moses, ye would have believed me: for he wrote of me.

The New Covenant remains part of "all ages," "forever," "perpetual generations" and thus includes the Sabbath as it must. When you truly consider the church's position on this it unravels and the language surrounding the topic begins to appear very childish. The complaining and bickering that the Sabbath is such a chore to consider because we are just too important and busy sounds like a two-year old demanding their own way over that of their parents that anyone one observing can clearly see is better for the child. The child cannot see it and they throw a tantrum demanding their own way. Are we in this for ourselves or for Him? Is Sabbath a burden?

The Sabbath is a Delight To Us and Yahuah

> *Isaiah 58:13-14 KJV*
>
> *If thou turn away thy foot from the sabbath, from doing thy pleasure on my holy day; and call the sabbath a delight, the holy of the Lord, honourable; and shalt honour him, not doing thine own ways, nor finding thine own pleasure, nor speaking thine own words: Then shalt thou delight thyself in the Lord; and I will cause thee to ride upon the high places of the earth, and feed thee with the heritage of Jacob thy father: for the mouth of the Lord hath spoken it.*

The Sabbath is a delight for us and for Yahuah. However, it is about His pleasure and His delight not ours. There are those who attempt to debate this with weak debate because they want some of their own pleasure still on Sabbath. That's still two-year old territory as anyone can read this and it is plain. We do not seek our own pleasure on this day as Isaiah is very clear. The delight is in Yahuah and Yahusha not ourselves. He desires to take care of us and nurture this relationship and He says He does so through His Sabbath. We show respect for His ways and Honor to Him which gives Him pleasure and it becomes a delight for us. That is not our delight from our own pleasure but His. The Gospel is about Him not us and Hebrews told us that Gospel in the New Testament after His ascension, includes the Sabbath.

This is simple to understand. However, the two-year old mentality throwing the tantrum does not see it. Don't be the two-year old like much of the modern church. Let us all mature into the meat of the Word. It seems the church's focus remains on teaching and encouraging the very minimum of salvation rather than offering meat in the slightest. They love their 6-week series on Love which is absent rebuke thus not love in the complete sense. They want to tell us about Grace yet ignoring the greatest stories of Grace from the Old Testament especially Noah which also includes salvation which is not even a new concept in the New Testament but mentioned many times in the Old even for Gentiles.

Moses tells us this is about Yahuah's delight as well and He delights in you when you keep His commands or your part of the covenant. How could we ever decide His delight changed into an absolute assault on His Sabbath and His Law? He never participates in such so why do we?

Deuteronomy 30:10 KJV
***The LORD your God will delight in you if you obey his
voice and keep the commands and decrees written in this
Book of Instruction****, and if you turn to the LORD your God with all
your heart and soul.*

Realize, this is the same as Yahusha's supposed 1st New Commandment which is certainly not new and still includes His Sabbath. King David was coined "a man after his *(Yahuah's)* own heart." This was not about perfection as David was not perfect. However, do we understand the context of what it means to be a man after His *(Yahuah's)* own heart? Do we not all desire to have such related about us?

1 Samuel 13:13-14 KJV
And Samuel said to Saul, Thou hast done foolishly: ***thou hast not kept
the commandment of the Lord thy God****, which he commanded
thee: for now would the Lord have established thy kingdom upon Israel for
ever. But now* ***thy kingdom shall not continue: the Lord hath
sought him a man after his own heart****, and the Lord hath
commanded him to be captain over his people, because* ***thou hast not kept
that which the Lord commanded thee****.*

King Saul was in covenant with Yahuah. He heard His voice through the Prophet Samuel and he chose not to obey Him and for selfish reason. That is no different for those of us trying to justify not keeping His Sabbath really as we follow the ways of Saul when we do so. However, why is David called "a man after his own heart?" This is because David kept His commandments including His Sabbath that you will find plaster his writings. David got it. Saul did not. For those claiming one has to become perfect and never sin in any sense in order to be called such, David was not perfect either yet still called such. In Acts, Luke affirms this understanding after Messiah's ascension. How do we not understand as Luke did today? He fully defines what David did in order to earn such accolades. If we desire the same to be said of us, then we must do the same.

Acts 13:22 KJV

And when he had removed him, he raised up unto them David to be their king; to whom also he gave their testimony, and said, **I have found David the son of Jesse, a man after mine own heart, which shall fulfil all my will.**

What is His will? Do we not know it populates the pages of all of His Word – Old and New? Are we seeking His will? Then, we will find it in the writings He inspired. We will not find it in church doctrine on this topic. We find it in the Psalms of David many times over as he understood relationship with Yahuah. In fact, what did David do when he sinned? Saul just doubled down on his position stiff-necked and unrepentant which is why he was removed. David repented. David was a man after His *(Yahuah's)* own Heart because he loved Yahuah's Law including His Sabbath in which he writes extensively. How can the modern church have turned into Saul, a man after his own pleasure, rather than David, a man after His *(Yahuah's)* own heart?

Psalm 1:2 KJV

But his delight is in the law of the LORD; and in his law doth he meditate day and night.

Psalm 40:8 KJV

I delight to do thy will, O my God: yea, thy law is within my heart.

Psalm 112:1 KJV

Praise the LORD! How joyful are those who fear the LORD and delight in obeying his commands.

Psalm 119:16 KJV

I will delight myself in thy statutes: I will not forget thy word.

Psalm 119:47 KJV

And I will delight myself in thy commandments, which I have loved.

Psalm 119:70 KJV

Their heart is as fat as grease; but I delight in thy law.

Psalm 119:77 KJV

Let thy tender mercies come unto me, that I may live: for thy law is my delight.

Psalm 119:174 KJV

I have longed for thy salvation, O LORD; and thy law is my delight.

You will find most of the time these same Old Testament themes are carried into the New Testament as the Biblical practice remained and did not change. Despite the uneducated opinion of many seminaries, Paul never preached against the Law nor the Sabbath. He reinforced it. We will cover this in an entire chapter and don't worry, we will not rely on one fragment though this is certainly in context of what Paul taught.

Romans 7:22 KJV
*For **I delight in the law of God** after the inward man:*

Paul is quoting and applying the Old Testament because that is his same practice. He had no authority to abolish Messiah's message nor change anything. He was one who lived the Commandments and the Law and he taught it. Many misunderstand Paul which Peter warned was already happening 2,000 years ago *(2 Pet. 3:15-16)*. Peter's warning should be posted on every scholar's wall as they should remember this every time they use Paul especially in fragments. Is that really what Paul said? Typically, it is not as these fragments have been taught in a paradigm not in context.

In fact, in reading Romans 7 and 8 alone, this explains the contrast between the Law of Sin and Death which is NOT Yahuah's Law under any circumstance but the opposite and the Law of Life in Yahusha Messiah which we will cover in detail is the same as that of Moses. Paul delights in the law of Elohim after the spirit which he defines as the Law of Life not the Law of Sin and Death which is of the flesh. With the proper perspective, Paul is actually easy to understand.

The Sabbath is Holy, Sanctified and Set Apart

Is any other day of the week set apart, sanctified and holy? Only the 7th Day Sabbath has such definition. Sunday never does in scripture either. Does Yahuah sanctify something as firm as a day of the week from Creation and then trash it as unimportant? In His Commandment He wrote with His finger, He begins with remember to keep the Sabbath holy. Is that where we are in history? Have we forgotten that which He said to remember? We already covered the New Testament says so.

Exodus 20:8-10 KJV
Remember the sabbath day, to keep it holy. *Six days shalt thou labour, and do all thy work: But the seventh day is the sabbath of the Lord thy God: in it thou shalt not do any work, thou, nor thy son, nor thy daughter, thy manservant, nor thy maidservant, nor thy cattle, nor thy stranger that is within thy gates:*

Deuteronomy 5:12-13 KJV
Keep the sabbath day to sanctify it, *as the Lord thy God hath commanded thee. Six days thou shalt labour, and do all thy work: But the seventh day is the sabbath of the Lord thy God: in it thou shalt not do any work, thou, nor thy son, nor thy daughter, nor thy manservant, nor thy maidservant, nor thine ox, nor thine ass, nor any of thy cattle, nor thy stranger that is within thy gates; that thy manservant and thy maidservant may rest as well as thou.*

Exodus 35:2-3 KJV
*Six days shall work be done, but on the seventh day there shall be to you **an holy day**, a sabbath of rest to the LORD: whosoever doeth work therein shall be put to death. Ye shall kindle no fire throughout your habitations upon the sabbath day.*

Leviticus 23:2-3 KJV
*Six days shall work be done: but the seventh day is the sabbath of rest, an **holy convocation**; ye shall do no work therein: it is the sabbath of the Lord in all your dwellings.*

Nehemiah 9:14 KJV
*And madest known unto them **thy holy sabbath**, and commandedst them precepts, statutes, and laws, by the hand of Moses thy servant:*

The Sabbath is a holy day to be set apart as different and sanctified. It is always the 7th day of the week in ALL of scripture to Revelation. This is the cornerstone of the week in worship of Yahuah not Sunday though one can meet every day. It has never changed which we will fully address in this position. Paul says the same thing and we have designated an entire chapter to understanding Paul.

The Sabbath is an Example of Belief

Observing His Sabbath is anchored throughout the New Testament as we will cover over multiple chapters of content and already began in our Introduction in strong position. Again, Hebrews defines such observance as belief and failure to enter this rest or Sabbath is defined as unbelief. This is after Messiah's ascension and the Sabbath remained according to the Bible. Do we believe it or do we prefer man's doctrines? Our churches should be following the Bible rather than the doctrines of men. Most are not on this topic. We also covered Hebrews calls the Sabbath part of the Gospel in the New Testament thus our Gospel must include it or it is another Gospel the Apostles did not preach.

> **Hebrews 4:9-11 KJV (After Messiah's Ascension Sabbath Remains)**
> **There remaineth therefore a rest [Sabbath] to the people of God.** *For he that is entered into his rest [Sabbath], he also hath ceased from his own works, as God did from his. Let us labour therefore to enter into that rest [Sabbath],* **lest any man fall after the same example of unbelief.**

Neglecting the Sabbath is Pollution

> **Isaiah 56:2 KJV**
> *Blessed is the man that doeth this, and the son of man that layeth hold on it;* **that keepeth the sabbath from polluting it,** *and* **keepeth his hand from doing any evil.**

One will observe like David and Paul, the prophets endear the Commandments, the Law and the Sabbath. It was not about their desiring to be saved though as that is a selfish aim of the modern church. Their intent was please Him and not to pollute His ways. That is quite a warning. Those not keeping the Sabbath are polluting the Creation of the 7th Day. When you are keeping the Sabbath, you do not perform evil. You are setting aside a pure and holy day in which the parameters make it extremely difficult for any evil to even enter the picture for at least that day. You are not out in the world, not behaving like them and not even paying attention to them for a day each week. The therapy value of that alone is momentous. However, when you do not, you are a target for such evil and easy prey. Why would we paint a target on our backs rather than retracting back into the shadow of His wings?

Those Keeping His Sabbath Will Be Blessed

> **Jubilees 2:27b-28**
> *...for it is a holy day and a blessed day. And every one who observeth it and keepeth Sabbath thereon from all his work, will be holy and blessed throughout all days like unto us.*
>
> **Jubilees 2:32**
> *And the Creator of all things blessed this day which He had created for a blessing and a sanctification and a glory above all days.*

Not only is the Sabbath a blessed day, those who observe it will be holy and blessed. Abraham understood this as did all of the patriarchs of our faith. This is a day of blessing and sanctification, being set apart for Him. It defines the believer in the beginning and in the end. In our era, this is one of the most important topics, not your salvation.

Sabbath is the Fourth Commandment

> **Exodus 20:8-10 KJV**
> **Remember the sabbath day, to keep it holy.** *Six days shalt thou labour, and do all thy work: But the* **seventh day is the sabbath of the LORD thy God:** *in it* **thou shalt not do any work,** *thou, nor thy son, nor thy daughter, thy manservant, nor thy maidservant, nor thy cattle,* **nor thy stranger** *that is within thy gates:*

Notice the stranger within your gates or Gentiles also were to keep the Sabbath even since the Exodus. That is not new in the New Testament. They are included in abiding by the Law as well multiple times. This Fourth Commandment is the one that the church seems to take issue. Generally, the other 9 seem palatable to them but do not dare tell the church it is supposed to rest for a day in the presence of Yahuah. Step back and think about that and it is quite revealing. One cannot claim to follow Yahuah while ignoring large portions of His Word and ways. We are to remember the Sabbath and keep it holy and this commandment does not pass at least until the Day of Judgment. If your church denomination is attempting to overrule Messiah *(Matt. 5:17-18)*, ask why.

Sabbath is the 7th Day of the Week

As we just witnessed in Exodus 20, the Commandment is to keep Sabbath the 7th day of the week. However, it is clear we are to work the other 6 days. Those cults out there claiming to keep the Sabbath every day are branded as lazy by the Bible *(2 Th. 3:10)*. There is no scripture which says to rest every day of the week.

The Creation account *(Gen. 2:2-3)* explains as well the Sabbath is the 7th day of the week. The question remains is this the Saturday we call the 7th day today? We will vet that in an entire chapter. The significance of the Sabbath is the fact that of the 7 days of the week, it is set apart and holy. It is unique and different and no other day is ever given it's honor especially not Sunday, the 1st day of the week, which can never replace the 7th day Sabbath. No scripture supports that and no church has authority to change what the Lord of the Sabbath only can change and did not. For He rose on the Sabbath on the 7th Day not on the 1st Day of the week even according to scripture which we examine.

The Sabbath is Forever

Sabbath is forever in your generations for a perpetual and everlasting covenant by a statute forever. We all know what this means yet when we do not believe scripture or change it to say what we want, such concepts become blurry. However, one could not view more clarity than the plain language of these passages.

> *Exodus 31 KJV*
>
> *13 Speak thou also unto the children of Israel, saying, Verily **my sabbaths ye shall keep: for it is a sign between me and you throughout your generations; that ye may know that I am the LORD that doth sanctify you.***
>
> *16 Wherefore the children of Israel shall keep the sabbath, to **observe the sabbath throughout their generations, for a perpetual covenant.***
>
> *Leviticus 16:31 KJV*
>
> *It shall be a **sabbath of rest** unto you, and ye shall afflict your souls, **by***

a statute for ever.
Leviticus 24:8 KJV
***Every sabbath** he shall set it in order before the LORD **continually**, being taken from the children of Israel **by an everlasting covenant**.*

Some would then level that this is only the Old Testament. Certainly, the New Testament does not say the Sabbath is forever. They would be wrong again. Messiah Himself set an expiration date for the Sabbath and the Law at the day when Heaven and Earth pass on the Day of Final Judgment and not before. Even then, He does not say it passes away as He merely states it will still be around until then. How could any church say it already passed when Messiah says it did not and would not? They do not represent His words on this topic.

Matthew 5:17-18 KJV
***Think not that I am come to destroy the law, or the prophets: I am not come to destroy, but to fulfil.** For verily I say unto you, **Till heaven and earth pass, one jot or one tittle shall in no wise pass from the law, till all be fulfilled**.*

The Sabbath Cannot Change

The Sabbath was NEVER abolished, replaced or changed by anyone with such authority and we will cover the history in this writing so you can observe this for yourself. Matthew recorded Messiah's very profound words saying the Law and the Sabbath, not one letter of it, would pass until the end. Paul endorses this in doctrine and never the opposite.

Romans 3:31 KJV
Do we then make void the law through faith? God forbid: yea, we establish the law.

How can Paul's saying Elohim forbid that the Law is made void be interpreted as the Law is void? There is no new law as you will find Messiah quotes Moses as does Paul. As he once again invokes the Prophet Jeremiah *(31:33)* quoting and applying Old Testament doctrine, Paul tells us that even those who do not know there is a law will be judged by the Law of Yahuah. Sin is only defined by breaking Yahuah's Law. Yahuah is no respecter of persons in that all will be judged by the same Law. Only doers of the Law will be justified yet we are told Paul believed the opposite which is illiterate. Paul says Gentiles after Messiah's ascension will follow the Law as it is written in their hearts and they show it's work. This relationship is for everyone who will embrace it Hebrew or Gentile either one. There is no differentiation by race. This is the same as the Old Testament as well as the "stranger among us" was to abide by the same Law in blessings and curses as Israel. Those are Gentiles.

Romans 2:10-15 KJV

But glory, honour, and peace, to every man that worketh good, to the Jew first, and also to the Gentile: For there is no respect of persons with God. For as many as have sinned without law shall also perish without law: and as many as have sinned in the law shall be judged by the law; (For not the hearers of the law are just before God, but the doers of the law shall be justified. For when the Gentiles, which have not the law, do by nature the things contained in the law, these, having not the law, are a law unto themselves: Which shew the work of the law written in their hearts, their conscience also bearing witness, and their thoughts the mean while accusing or else excusing one another;)

Notice how Jeremiah whom Paul quotes knew the coming New Covenant and well defines a deeper commitment to Yahuah's Law not the lawless environment preached by the modern church. Paul did not preach that and it is another Gospel. In this great love story, He will forgive their sin and remember it no more as they repent. Understand that requires our keeping the Law that is now written in our hearts and minds. It is impossible to then preach we forget about it. From the least to the greatest of them really refers to Gentiles as well as Hebrews.

Jeremiah 31:31-36 KJV

Behold, the days come, saith the LORD, that I will make a new covenant with the house of Israel, and with the house of Judah: Not according to the covenant that I made with their fathers in the day that I took them by the hand to bring them out of the land of Egypt; which my covenant they brake, although I was an husband unto them, saith the LORD: But this shall be the covenant that I will make with the house of Israel; After those days, saith the LORD, I will put my law in their inward parts, and write it in their hearts; and will be their God, and they shall be my people. And they shall teach no more every man his neighbour, and every man his brother, saying, Know the LORD: for they shall all know me, from the least of them unto the greatest of them, saith the LORD: for I will forgive their iniquity, and I will remember their sin no more. Thus saith the LORD, which giveth the sun for a light by day, and the ordinances of the moon and of the stars for a light by night, which divideth the sea when the waves thereof roar; The LORD of hosts is his name: If those ordinances depart from before me, saith the LORD, then the seed of Israel also shall cease from being a nation before me for ever.

However, most miss this in this passage. Jeremiah, as Paul, says the Law will not need to be taught in the same manner because again, it will be written in our hearts. How is this accomplished? The Holy Spirit came and indwells us. He is most certainly continuing to guide us in the ways of Yahuah. However, just as Messiah assigned a benchmark date on when the Law would continue until at least the Day of Judgment, Jeremiah also defined such indefinitely. He says if Yahuah's ordinances, the Law, depart before Yahuah, then the seed of Israel will cease from being a nation before Him. Some misread this as the land called Israel which is impertinent. Israel is a people and always has been named for their progenitor, Jacob who was renamed Israel. It is his name and a lineage not a land. His nation remains today scattered within three regions mainly from which they will return *(Is. 11)*. However, these peoples are all over the world today in every country. Also, there have always been Gentiles among them who are grafted into the Kingdom just as Paul explains and we will cover. Notice the difference in reviewing this as a passage as opposed to a fragment.

Romans 7:9-13, 22, 25 KJV
For I was alive without the law once: but when the commandment came, sin revived, and I died. And the commandment, which was ordained to life, I found to be unto death. For sin, taking occasion by the commandment,

deceived me, and by it slew me. Wherefore the law is holy, and the commandment holy, and just, and good. Was then that which is good made death unto me? God forbid. But sin, that it might appear sin, working death in me by that which is good; that sin by the commandment might become exceeding sinful.
22 For I delight in the law of God after the inward man:
25 I thank God through Jesus Christ our Lord. So then with the mind I myself serve the law of God; but with the flesh the law of sin.

We will cover this in full later in this book. However, Paul demonstrates a wrestling with sin that is missing from most sermons as they forget that sin is lawlessness or breaking the Law. Paul and Jeremiah are very similar in their view on this. Imagine, Paul was raised a Pharisee as his father was likely of Pharisee blood even and his mother a Benjamite. He says he was raised without the Law yet he certainly was raised by Pharisee law.

What he is doing here is rebuking Pharisee law and placing it where it belongs as Messiah defined it as against His Commandments or Law *(Mark 7:9)*. He expresses a wrangling with sin in which we can all relate. He reaffirms Yahuah's Law is holy, just and good yet many pastors are teaching the opposite of what he believed and said, contrary to the Bible. They learn this in seminaries and they do not test it with scripture typically. Does the Law of Yahuah bring death? He says Elohim forbid! It is sin or lawlessness or breaking the Law which works death. In fact, Paul ends this chapter with thanking Yahuah and Yahusha for the Law of Elohim that he serves. The Law of Sin and Death is never Yahuah's.

Luke offers this same clarity as he and the Apostles of Acts kept and taught the Law. This includes the Sabbath. Again, this is Paul speaking.

Acts 24:14 KJV
But this I confess unto thee, that after the way which they call heresy, so worship I the God of my fathers, believing all things which are written in the law and in the prophets:

How can Paul be said to abolish that which he followed and taught? He even said he did not break the Law of the Yahudim yet we are taught in seminaries he completely redefined the Old Testament ways with new law. This would make Paul a hypocrite and set him at odds with Messiah's teachings. He was no hypocrite and never went against Yahusha. Anyone can assess what Paul taught and you will find all 10 commandments essentially within as well as other portions of the Law of Moses. Also remember, Luke, the writer of a Gospel, wrote that.

He said he continues to worship the same Elohim including His same law and the teachings of the prophets. Do we all realize that is the Old Testament Law Paul just endorsed there? However, notice what was happening 2,000 years ago because this is the origin of these church lines. It is the Pharisees who were attempting to frame Paul in ignorance because he preached Yahusha. They wanted to mischaracterize Paul as breaking the Law. He did break their interpretation of law that is backwards and it is a good thing that he did. Messiah broke their law as well and then explained how their law is against His Law *(Mark 7:9)*. It is they who were taking his words out of context which Peter warned.

2 Peter 3:15-16 KJV

And account that the longsuffering of our Lord is salvation; even as our beloved brother Paul also according to the wisdom given unto him hath written unto you; As also in all his epistles, speaking in them of these things; in which are some things hard to be understood, which they that are unlearned and unstable wrest, as they do also the other scriptures, unto their own destruction.

That is the strange doctrine and strong delusion in which permeates the church today generally and that is how they forgot the Sabbath, the name of YHWH and much more. If Paul continued preaching from and endorsing the Old Testament, how can any pastor claim he spoke against it and abolished the prophets' writings?

Acts 25:8 KJV

While he answered for himself, Neither against the law of the Jews, neither against the temple, nor yet against Caesar, have I offended any thing at all.

As we have opened this topic, we will cover Paul in an entire chapter.

Let us review his actual words and understand what they say in context.

Sabbath Is Written In Stone By the Finger of Yahuah

The rule for keeping Sabbath to remember it and not forget is literally etched in stone. Not just by some stone mason or whomever, it was forged by the very finger of Yahuah. Before dismissing the Sabbath, one should consider the significance of such act by Yahuah. This is the only portion of all of scripture literally written by His own hand. Certainly, He inspired the rest but this is from Him directly. He cared so much about the order of His Creation and how we conduct ourselves on His Earth that He set rules in place.

These commandments originate in the beginning which we will prove out in the next chapter. Did He wait 2,000 years to give His Law? The Law defines what is right the standard for judging one as righteous. If Enoch, Noah and Abraham are judged as righteous as they were, how can such judgment take place without right or Law by which to determine such. How can Yahuah leave the world lawless which is the very definition of sin for the first 2,000 years? The answer is simple – He could not or He would not be right or righteous and He is.

We have dedicated a whole chapter to how to keep the Sabbath. However, first let us understand it's historicity. Is the Sabbath truly since Creation? Is this something we can prove? Was it only practiced in the time of Moses through the prophets? We will break this down systematically and by the end of this book, it is likely most questions will be satisfied. The answers may not agree with some church doctrine but they will originate in the only doctrine that matters – the Bible.

And he gave unto Moses, when he had made an end of communing with him upon mount Sinai, two tables of testimony, tables of stone, written with the finger of God
—Exodus 31:18 KJV
(Cf. Ex. 34:28; Dt. 4:13, 10:4 specify Yahuah wrote the
10 Commandments Himself which includes the Sabbath)

Origin of the
SABBATH

And now, O Father, glorify thou me with thine own self with **the glory which I had with thee before the world was.**

John 17:5 KJV

Chapter 2 | Origin of the Sabbath

And on the seventh (שביעי: sh^ebîy'îy) day God ended his work which he had made; and he rested (שבת: shâbath) on the seventh day from all his work which he had made. And God blessed the seventh (שביעי: sh^ebîy'îy) day, and sanctified it: because that in it he had rested (שבת: shâbath) from all his work which God created and made.

Sabbath is the 7th day of the week or what we call Saturday today. That cannot be debated. The Catholic Church especially and many Protestants pick up control lines, that they moved the Sabbath from it's ordered day of Saturday *(7th Day, which they admit)* to Sunday, the 1st Day of the week because that is when Yahuah said "Let there be Light" and began Creation. In other words, since the Sabbath was not even created yet on the 1st Day for 6 more days, they are hoodwinking us into believing first, they had such right to move a Creation observance, which they did not. They wish for us to celebrate Sabbath before it even existed as that reason requires complete fraud. If you want to celebrate the 1st Day of Creation, you don't rest and it's not the Sabbath.

Second, we are now to observe the Sabbath on the day He first worked instead of the day He rested and set apart and sanctified for us to rest. Observe the 1st Day of Creation and you cannot Sabbath as it did not exist even in concept on Day 1. Does that make any logical sense? Sabbath did not originate on Sunday but Saturday, the 7th Day and it cannot change as it is a Creation. We will vet the day through history as well in a whole chapter and prove it remains Saturday.

They will then say Messiah rose on Sunday, therefore, He changed it.

However, we will fully expose this fraudulent thinking of inept scholars who practice willing ignorance as very clearly in the Gospels, Messiah rose when it was the Biblical Sabbath or the 7th Day *(Saturday)* still on the Bible calendar which we will explore in an entire chapter. The Roman calendar is wrong and meaningless in this regard and this is where they deceive as the Roman Sunday does not correlate to the Biblical Sunday in whole. Thus, He changed nothing for Sabbath in time but further entrenched it being crucified on the Feast Sabbath and resurrecting on the Weekly Sabbath which was still Saturday on the Biblical calendar. We prove this in great detail with chart and you will learn the Biblical Day has never been set on the Roman Calendar nor the Lunar one.

However, there is a far more profound meaning to Sunday *(1st Day)* replacing the Saturday Sabbath *(7th Day)* in the week. It turns out in an ancient context, Sunday is the ancient day in which satan tempted Eve and man fell. It is the day sin entered the world for both man and angels. It was the first day to be corrupted on the week calendar as the birth of evil and sin. What better day to defile His Sabbath and teach people to break the law or sin by definition, than the very day in which sin originated. In an ancient weekly context, perhaps we should really call it "Sinday." Again, this does not mean your church cannot meet then as the Apostles met every day but every 7th-Day Sabbath still remained set apart for them in practice through Revelation. No church can change that. Only the Lord of the Sabbath can and He did not. In order to make such claim, they must prove Messiah said so. He did not.

Jubilees 3:17

*And after the completion of the seven years, which he had completed there, seven years exactly, and in the **second month, on the seventeenth day** (of the month), **the serpent came** and approached the woman, and the serpent said to the woman, "Hath God commanded you, saying, Ye shall not eat of every tree of the garden?"*

According to the Temple Calendar kept at Qumran by the exiled Temple Priests who continued such practice, the 17th Day of the Second Month is Sunday. Notice, even satan knew better than to defile the Sabbath then. He waited til the next day. What better day for him to convince the church to commemorate in the stead of the 7th-Day

Sabbath on Saturday? Indeed, this battle originates in the early days of man. The church has usurped Messiah's authority as Lord of the Sabbath and moved it to the day in which satan successfully coerced the fall of man and sin entered the world both from him and Adam and Eve.

That very day, the 17th of the 2nd month, is also the exact day that Yahuah closed the door to the ark *(Gen. 7:13-16, Jub. 5:23)* and the fountains of the great deep erupted and windows of heaven poured *(Gen. 7:11, Jub. 5:24)* at the beginning of the Flood. Thus, it is Judgment Day in ancient times for Angels, First Man and Pre-Flood Man. That's Sunday and in these senses of worship, they are not a positive reference. Of course, there are Sunday Feasts and the day itself is fine but to move His Creation Sabbath on the weekly calendar from Saturday to the day in which satan tempted Eve and the day in which the Flood erupted is the opposite of foundation in scripture. It requires willing ignorance *(2 Pet. 3)* and no one can defend it.

Research this topic even a little on the internet and you will find especially Catholic propaganda which claims the Sabbath is not even mentioned in early Genesis. A so-called scholar writes of this and there are several. They cannot be so illiterate of scripture can they? What they are doing is only rendering the English completely missing that the Hebrew word for Sabbath *(שבת: shâbath)* is right there twice in Genesis 2 and even the word *sh^ebîy'îy* leads to the same root – the 7th-Day Sabbath. Moses, Hebrews and even Messiah affirm this was the 7th Day and most certainly not the 1st Day. It remained after Messiah's resurrection with the Apostles keeping it 85 times in the Book of Acts *(see Chart p. 353)* alone still on Saturday *(7th Day)* and throughout the New Testament even to Revelation. We will cover many of these and you will never find one passage that changes the 7th-Day Sabbath to Sunday or any other day.

Why is this important? Do days matter to Yahuah? Isn't He forgiving enough to understand when we mix up His calendar and claim His Word says so? Actually, no, not without repentance. He is clear His people perish for lack of knowledge *(Hos. 4:6; Job 36:12; Prov. 5:23, 10:21)*. Live in that realm and one will perish as one could not express a lack of relationship with Him in a greater manner. The only definition of such action is rebellion which is equated to witchcraft in scripture *(1 Sam. 15:23)*. His ekklesia is not brain dead rooted in less than an elementary understanding of scripture. One who chooses that path is not interested in relationship with Him.

We are all learning and He will meet us where we are but we will continue in relationship with Him or we no longer fit the definition of salvation in Matthew 7 nor John 15 in His words. This is why many "Christians" will be told on Judgment Day "I never knew you: Depart from me, ye that work iniquity." Iniquity is sin or breaking His Law. Thus, He says depart from me because you do not know Me and work against My Law. Realize, the Day of Judgment has not happened yet thus His Law remains or at least so He says. What pastor has more weight than the words of Messiah? Sabbath is not salvation but it is a sign of those who are saved. As we note in our Introduction, Hebrews 4 is clear, those who do not enter into His Sabbath that remains the 7th Day after Messiah's ascension, are an example of unbelief. That's what the Bible says. If your denomination does not, it is better to stick with the Word.

They have gone to great lengths to hide the Sabbath. However, we are supposed to accept the reasoning that He created it but then hid it until Israel over 2,000 years later and then, after 1,700 or so years abolished it. When such lines are created in the Christian world and Pharisee Land to justify the doctrines of men, they are worse than satanists. No one would lend credibility to the satanist but we follow these men as if they know things we do not. Unfortunately, rigorous testing proves they do not many times. They know their paradigms – they do not know Bible.

In fact, one of our viewers caught the publishers of a revised publishing of R.H. Charles' translation in 1917 by the Society for Promoting Christian Knowledge from London edited by W. O. E. Oesterley and G. H. Box. This organization remains very influential today as the largest in Christian publishing house in the U.K. calling themselves "the oldest Anglican mission agency" yet what they did to Jubilees as evidenced from their online publishing on the SacredTexts' version was fraud.

This is supposedly to be patterned after Charles' original 1903 release. However, they actually went in on this topic and changed a word in fraud to attempt to claim Yahuah hid the Sabbath from Adam. We didn't catch that either in our initial publishing of Jubilees but this viewer did and we now corrected it in our edition. They took the word "bidden" from R.H. Charles' initial publishing and changed it to "hidden." Talk about blatant outright fraud. Notice how this changes this doctrine to the opposite from a command to a secret. Is that not Catholic doctrine they forced into the text in complete fraud?

> ### *Jubilees 2:18 (1917 Republishing of R.H. Charles Translation)*
> *And all the Angels of the Presence, and all the Angels of Sanctification, these two great classes--He hath* **hidden** *us to keep the Sabbath with Him in heaven and on earth.*
>
> ----------
>
> ### *Jubilees 2:18 (1903 Original by R.H. Charles)*
> *And all the Angels of the Presence, and all the Angels of Sanctification, these two great classes--He hath* **bidden** *us to keep the Sabbath with Him in heaven and on earth.*

That is a large, purposeful deception trying to change what Jubilees says which we prove in The Book of Jubilees: The Torah Calendar, that book was kept as Torah by the Temple indisputably. That is another case one must review before concluding. Most pastors have not. Thus, they brazenly changed Torah. Yahuah had "bidden" or commanded the angels to keep the Sabbath with Him not just in heaven but on Earth from the beginning as this is the Creation narrative. Adam was on Earth and Earth was keeping the Sabbath too but they changed it to "hidden" instead as they were hiding the truth to cover up their fallacious view. They likely thought they could get away this as the Dead Sea Scrolls were not discovered for 30 more years. This is fraud perpetrated by an Anglican church group who couldn't just publish the words but had to commit propaganda changing a letter in English in which would never be supported by the Hebrew and this is no typo. It is a lawless action of the lawless attacking His Sabbath – a standard Catholic practice.

This is not the only time such has happened which is why we all must prove all things as there is deception within the ranks of especially leadership in seminaries who follow Pharisee leaven and have been assaulting the Word for centuries. The modern church is guilty of several counts of such even with what they accept as canon such as replacing the actual, literal name of YHWH over 6,800 times in translation again in fraud. Why would any so-called scholar want you and us to forget the name of our God? Even worse, this is well known now in modern times yet they keep cranking out Bibles that continue such false paradigm.

One much debated topic regarding Sabbath is it's origin. When does the Bible say it began? That is the authority in which no scholar can overrule yet they have tried. Frankly, no one needs to be a scholar to read the Bible and understand it for themselves yet many times, it is scholars who are challenged in understanding and it is very difficult for them to learn.

This will not bode well for the modern church in the days of increasing knowledge that Daniel predicted. They render themselves obsolete. This is very problematic for much of the church who tends to ignore scripture in order to conclude the Sabbath did not start until the time of Moses in observation. That is illiterate of scripture just as Peter warned they would become "willingly ignorant" of Creation *(includes Sabbath)*, the Flood *(includes Sabbath)* and the Deity of Messiah *(Lord of the Sabbath)*. As we said in our introduction, we do not sugarcoat nor placate illogical scholarship and we will prove that is what that view represents.

How can we say with certainty that the Sabbath originated at Creation? We all know Genesis 2 but those scholars try to ignore it. "Maybe it didn't mean Sabbath," they defend, when it said Sabbath twice in Hebrew. "Maybe it just meant rest." This is why we read in context cross-referencing multiple scriptures not as fragments but in context for all. The sanctified holy rest day is always Sabbath. We have already reviewed Genesis 2 and Jubilees 2:18 that specifically identifies the practice of keeping the Sabbath since the 7th Day of Creation. Thus we know what Genesis meant. We see this interpretation affirmed by Moses as the 7th Day of Creation as the origin of the Sabbath not his time. We do realize he also wrote Genesis 2, don't we?

Exodus 20:11 KJV

For in six days the Lord made heaven and earth, the sea, and all that in them is, and rested the seventh day: wherefore the Lord blessed the sabbath day, and hallowed it.

Not only did Moses say the 7th Day was blessed and hallowed at Creation and not during His time but he explains it was made or a

Creation itself. This is a track in research we can thoroughly follow and vet. Does the Sabbath have consistent historicity throughout the ages? We know Genesis 2 defines it's origin on the 7th Day of Creation. However, some scholars attack that and claim it does not say what it clearly says. We can prove this out indisputably over time.

Sabbath From the Beginning in Heaven and on the Earth

You will note we reference the very well documented Book of Jubilees in this Sabbath pursuit. The Sabbath is a large part of this book just as the rest of Torah. If you are not familiar with this book, we fully test it in our publishing of The Book of Jubilees: The Torah Calendar. You can download that in eBook free at BookOfJubilees.org or purchase in print. You will learn this book was kept as Torah in the Temple documented in writing and quoted by Messiah and the Apostles for significant doctrine.

Jubilees 2:30

And they shall not bring in nor take out from house to house on that day; for that day is more holy and blessed than any jubilee day of the jubilees: on this we kept Sabbath in the heavens before it was made known to any flesh to keep Sabbath thereon on the earth..

The Angels kept Sabbath from the beginning first. Then, it was made known to man. Did this take 2,000 years though? That certainly does not seem to make sense. However, Jubilees is not silent on this.

Jubilees 2:20-23

And I have chosen the seed of Jacob from amongst all that I have seen, and have written him down as My firstborn son, and have sanctified him unto Myself for ever and ever; and I will teach them the Sabbath day, that they may keep Sabbath thereon from all work." And thus He created therein a sign in accordance with which they should keep Sabbath with us on the seventh day, to eat and to drink, and to bless Him who hath created all things as He hath blessed and sanctified unto Himself a peculiar people above all peoples, and that they should keep Sabbath together with us. And He caused His commands to ascend as a sweet savour acceptable before Him all the days. . . There (were) two and twenty heads of mankind from Adam to Jacob, and two and twenty kinds of work were made until the seventh day; this is blessed and holy; and the former also is blessed and holy; and this one serves with that one for sanctification and blessing.

Many assume the Bible was only written to Israel especially the Old Testament. However, Gentiles are included throughout even in the Exodus account as keeping the same Law as Israel. No Gentile nations did nor do they now. The reason the people of Israel are so precious is because just as Jubilees expresses, they are the first nation to enter covenant with Yahuah as a nation. Man, even villages had done so before but not an entire nation. This does not demean nor replace what the patriarchs had with Yahuah prior especially the Sabbath. Notice the former Sabbath before Moses, was also blessed and holy and the two serve as the same for sanctification and blessing. This means the Sabbath practice was not new nor did it change in the days of Moses. This is clear evidence that Adam to Jacob kept the same Sabbath as the children of Israel. Yes, Adam kept the Sabbath. He knew sacrifices and taught his sons Cain and Abel.

In fact, Jubilees takes this even further in recording not only this detail, but that Sabbath is hallowed for all ages. We live in all ages still.

Jubilees 2:1

And the Angel of the Presence spake to Moses according to the word of Yahuah, saying: Write the complete history of the creation, how in six days Yahuah Elohim finished all His works and all that He created, and kept Sabbath on the seventh day and hallowed it for all ages, and appointed it as a sign for all His works.

In fact, the Biblical Feasts and Sabbaths are practiced together throughout scripture. Jubilees defines the timeline for Shavuot which is the same for the Sabbath as both are Creation concepts. This passage fortifies the continuation in observance for thousands of years since the very beginning. Again, however, we just learned prior that Adam is specifically documented as keeping the Sabbath the same as Jacob. No scholar can debate that logically.

Jubilees 6:15-22a

And He gave to Noah and his sons a sign that there should not again be a flood on the earth. He set His bow in the cloud for a sign of the eternal covenant that there should not again be a flood on the earth to destroy it all the days of the earth. For this reason it is ordained and written on the heavenly tables, that they should celebrate the feast of weeks in this month once a year, to renew the covenant every year. And this whole festival was celebrated in heaven from the day of creation till the days of Noah-twenty-six jubilees and five weeks of years: and Noah and his sons observed it for seven jubilees and one week of years, till the day of Noah's death, and from the day of Noah's death his sons did away with (it) until the days of Abraham, and they ate blood. But Abraham observed it, and Isaac and Jacob and his children observed it up to thy days, and in thy days the children of Israel forgot it until ye celebrated it anew on this mountain. And do thou command the children of Israel to observe this festival in all their generations for a commandment unto them: one day in the year in this month they shall celebrate the festival. For it is the feast of weeks and the feast of first-fruits: this feast is twofold and of a double nature: according to what is written and engraven concerning it celebrate it. For I have written in the book of the first law...

Adam to Noah observed these laws and they were lost for about two centuries from Noah's death to Abraham. Abraham kept these statutes until Jacob's sons, in the day of Moses, lost it for less than 80 years. In thousands of years, the Earth has only seen a 300-year window of someone not keeping His Sabbath and Feasts. Again, Israel was the first nation to do so as a nation. These are individuals and villages prior. Adam to Jacob kept this commandment of Shavuot and they kept Sabbath as well. In fact, Shavuot is a Sabbath – a special Feast Sabbath commemorating the Sabbath of Creation and the Covenant. Shavuot requires a "holy convocation" in which *"ye shall do **no servile work**."* That is a Sabbath *(Lev. 23:21, 23:3)*.

Adam had Law. If He did not, how could he sin? Sin is transgression of the Law by definition according to John. Without Law, one cannot judge sin. Notice as well, John is writing after Messiah's ascension that the Law remains. Again, if John had no Law, how could he call anything sin or lawless? How can a church function on such an incomplete foundation as to claim that the Law passed away and also, that it only existed during the days of Moses to Jesus *(Yahusha)*? How can they say He then abolished that Law which we will prove He preached, kept and said He would not abolish?

1 John 3:4 KJV
Whosoever committeth sin transgresseth also the law: for sin is the transgression of the law.

Adam had commandments and Law according to 2nd Esdras. This is a book quoted by Messiah Himself according to the 1611 KJV in which it is published. We will quote books Messiah quoted. Why is your denomination not doing so? For detail on that book, you can download our publishing of 2nd Esdas: The Hidden Book of Prophecy at 2Esdras. org or purchase in print.

When Adam sinned, death entered the world. He would not have died if he never sinned. However, what is sin? Transgression of the Law. This is what Paul was talking about when he speaks of the Law of Sin and Death which we will cover is an opposite law which entered in contrast to the Law of Life which even Adam knew. Also, those in the days after the Fall, were given the same Law which we will find in the days of Enoch, Noah, Abraham, Moses and Messiah to present. Yahuah defines right and wrong and why on Earth would He ever redefine that?

2 Esdras 3:7-8 KJVA
And unto him you gave commandment to love your way, which he transgressed, and immediately you appointed death in him, and in his generations, of whom came nations, tribes, people, and kindreds out of number. And every people walked after their own will, and did wonderful things before you, and despised your commandments.

Adam had commandments before and after the Fall. Esdras also defines Adam's sin just as John does as Adam transgressed Yahuah's Statutes. Sin can only be defined as such and Adam had Law including the Day of Rest from the 7th Day of Creation. One cannot ignore this.

2 Esdras 7:11 KJVA

Because for their sakes I made the world: and when Adam transgressed my Statutes, then was decreed that now is done.

It is rather uneducated for a scholar to claim there was no Law in the days of Adam yet then preach that Adam sinned. It is as if they forget the definition of sin. This is because they represent a paradigm not the Bible. That paradigm loses foundation on the very basics.

Enoch Kept the Sabbath

Enoch, the 7th generation from Adam, great grandfather of Noah kept the Sabbath. First, Enoch knew the Law and what sin was which is lawlessness. He even defines it as transgressing the Law.

1st Book Of Enoch 106:14 [Book of the Noah]

[Enoch to Methusaleh (Noah's Grandfather)]
And behold, they commit sin and transgress the law…

Scholars will then demand to know exactly which Law Enoch kept. However, not only do we already know that track, Enoch visited Heaven and there, he was shown the mysteries of the Angels. We know that included the Sabbath as Angels have kept Sabbath since Creation. We also know from Jubilees, Moses received the Creation account from the Heavenly Tablets related by the Angel of the Presence who kept such record in Heaven from the beginning. Enoch reviewed those same tablets. There is no disconnecting any of this. For those claiming the Bible does not say Moses got that from an Angel, read Luke and Paul who said he did *(Acts 7:53; Gal. 3:19)*. They are both quoting the Book of Jubilees. Do we believe the Bible?

1st Book Of Enoch 106:19 [Book of the Noah]

[Enoch to Methusaleh (Noah's Grandfather)]
For I know the mysteries of the Holy Ones, for the Lord showed them to me and made them known to me, and I read them in the Tablets of Heaven.

We know Genesis clearly establishes that Enoch was so righteous in his walk with Yahuah that Yahuah took him. How is it that he could be judged righteous? He just told you he knew the whole of law from the Heavenly Tablets which is the same Law given to Moses on Mt. Sinai. However, Enoch does not stop there. He also discusses the Sabbath in prophecy in the End Times even. The righteous in the end will fulfill or keep the Sabbath in peace. In this prophecy, the whole world will be tilled by the righteous and that is after the Day of Final Judgment.

1st Book Of Enoch 10:17-18 [Book of the Watchers]

And now all the righteous will be humble, and will live until they beget thousands. And all the days of their youth, and their sabbaths, they will fulfill in peace. And in those days the whole earth will be tilled in righteousness and all of it will be planted with trees; and it will be filled with blessing.

Some scholar would then scoff that this does not mean Enoch knew of the Sabbath in his time. Here is a direct reference for said scoffer. Enoch knew the WHOLE Law of time including every aspect of it especially the Sabbath which he mentioned in the previous verse.

1 Enoch 79:2

And he showed me the whole law for these, for every day, and for every time, and for every rule, and for every year, and for the end thereof, according to its command, for every month and every week.

Enoch also mentions the Garden of Righteousness *(1 Enoch 32:3-4)* in which Adam was taken. He well knew the definition of righteousness. Adam could not reside in that realm with Yahuah's Holy of Holies without keeping His Law and especially Sabbath. The High Priest in the Temple in the days of Solomon forward, would die in Yahuah's presence if he were in sin. Adam would have as well. He could not break the Sabbath there.

Noah, His Sons and Their Sons Kept the Sabbath Until Noah's Death

Jubilees 7:20-21 [Noah to his 3 sons. The Law of Noah]
And in the twenty-eighth jubilee Noah began to enjoin upon his sons' sons the ordinances and commandments, and all the judgments that he knew, and he exhorted his sons to observe righteousness, and to cover the shame of their flesh, and to bless their Creator, and honour father and mother, and love their neighbour, and guard their souls from fornication and uncleanness and all iniquity. For owing to these three things came the flood upon the earth, namely, owing to the fornication wherein the Watchers against the law of their ordinances went a whoring after the daughters of men, and took themselves wives of all which they chose: and they made the beginning of uncleanness.

How do we bless the Creator? We keep His Sabbath and Law. Where did Noah get these ordinances? From Enoch who got them from the Heavenly Tablets – the same tablets in which Moses received the Law as well which included the Sabbath. In other words, Noah has the same Law as Enoch that is the Law from the beginning which is the same as that of Moses.

Jubilees 7:38-39 [Origin of The Law of Noah]
For thus did Enoch, the father of your father command Methuselah, his son, and Methuselah his son Lamech, and Lamech commanded me all the things which his fathers commanded him. And I also will give you commandment, my sons, as Enoch commanded his son in the first jubilees: whilst still living, the seventh in his generation, he commanded and testified to his son and to his sons' sons until the day of his death. "

At the end of this chapter, we provide a chart that takes these laws in comparison and also includes the supposed 2 new commandments of Messiah. Of course, those scholars have clearly never even read the Law of Moses nor can they read a paragraph because Messiah answers the Pharisees who ask which is the greatest commandment. They mean from the Law of Moses. Messiah quotes the 1st commandment from the Law of Moses in answer to their question and even gives them a second Law also from the Law of Moses to basically sum up all 10 into 2. He did not change anything, He quoted what already existed and there is nothing new about these Laws. Also, as with Moses, Noah's covenant for all of mankind is forever. If you are man and not Nephilim, you remain under Noah's covenant. Moses did not change it nor did Messiah.

Genesis 9:12 KJV

*And God said, This is the token of the covenant which I make between me and you and every living creature that is with you, **for perpetual generations**: I do set my bow in the cloud, and it shall be for a token of a covenant between me and the earth.*

When you still see the rainbow in the sky, understand this covenant remains beyond His promise not to Flood the Earth. He changes not *(Mal. 3:6)*. Jesus*(Yahusha)* mirrored this in Hebrews 13:8. Noah's precepts remain in Moses' Law and Messiah's Law of Life especially including His Sabbath of which He is Lord. At the end of this chapter, we have compiled a comparison chart for all of these Laws throughout time.

Job Kept the Sabbath

Job lived after the Flood and before Torah was written according to most scholars. He was judged perfect and upright. This required Law. In his time, that would be the same as the Law of Noah that included the Sabbath from the Heavenly Tablets shown to his grandfather Enoch.

Job 1:1 KJV

There was a man in the land of Uz, whose name was Job; and that man was perfect and upright, and one that feared God, and eschewed evil.

Additionally, Job also somehow knew how to sacrifice burnt offerings. When was he doing so? The same as all patriarchs on the Sabbath and the Feasts.

Job 1:5 KJV

And it was so, when the days of their feasting were gone about, that Job sent and sanctified them, and rose up early in the morning, and offered burnt offerings according to the number of them all: for Job said, It may be that my sons have sinned, and cursed God in their hearts. Thus did Job continually.

Job links this practice of covering sin with that of Adam. Once again, Job as well knew the Sabbath and the Law before Moses.

Job 31:33 KJV

If I covered my transgressions as Adam, by hiding mine iniquity in my bosom

It even appears Job understand the concept of no work on the Sabbath. He mentions accomplishing rest as a worker on a His day.

Job 14:5-6 KJV

Seeing his days are determined, the number of his months are with thee, thou hast appointed his bounds that he cannot pass; Turn from him, that he may rest, till he shall accomplish, as an hireling, his day.

What day does a hireling or employee rest? This day is Sabbath. Job knew of the Sabbath and he was righteous thus he kept it. That is not an assumption; it is fact. He could not be called righteous without such.

Abraham Kept the Sabbath

Genesis expresses Abraham obeyed Yahuah and kept His charge, commandments, statutes and laws.

Genesis 26:5 KJV

Because that Abraham obeyed my voice, and kept my charge, my commandments, my statutes, and my laws.

However, Abraham too received this restored knowledge of Noah and Enoch. In addition to learning that Hebrew is the original language of Creation, we learn Abraham possessed writings of his forefathers. His father was a pagan idol worshipper so he did not write these nor did he know Hebrew. These books such as the Book of Enoch most certainly included the Sabbath.

Jubilees 12:25-27

And Yahuah Elohim said: "Open his mouth and his ears, that he may hear and speak with his mouth, with the language which hath been revealed"; for it had ceased from the mouths of all the children of men from the day of the overthrow (of Babel). And I opened his mouth, and his ears and his lips, and I began to speak with him in Hebrew in the tongue of the creation. And he took the books of his fathers, and these were written in Hebrew and he transcribed them, and he began from henceforth to study them, and I made known to him that which he could not (understand), and he studied them during the six rainy months.

Jacob Observed the Sabbath

In the case of Jacob, we have a very specific passage that identifies his sacrificing on Sivan 7. On the ancient calendar found in Qumran among the exiled Temple Priests, Sivan 7 is a Saturday Sabbath. He later celebrates on Sivan 15 the Feast of Weeks, Shavuot/Pentecost that falls on a Sunday on the Bible calendar. Thus, the 7th is a Saturday Sabbath.

Jubilees 44:1 (Sabbath Offering Specifically)

And Israel took his journey from †Haran† from his house on the new moon of the third month, and he went on the way of the Well of the Oath, and he offered a sacrifice to the Elohim of his father Isaac on the seventh of this month.

Sacrifices Before Moses?

Adam, Enoch, Noah, Abraham and Job knew to sacrifice animals for a sin offering. However, the thinking that that represents an arbitrary practice is illiterate. When does one sacrifice as such? On the Sabbath and certain Biblical Feast Days. The patriarchs most certainly continued the Sabbath and some Feasts especially as that is when these sacrifices occur. For those claiming all Feasts began with Moses that Jubilees proves wrong, they still have a massive challenge as that only leaves Sabbaths for such sacrifices. However, we have dates on some of these sacrifices thus we know what they celebrated in some cases. How is it that this knowledge has been lost in the church for a hallow control line?

Adam Covered His Shame

Adam was exiled from the Garden of Eden and he sacrificed to cover his sin the same day. In quick observation, this was the new moon of the 4th month. If correct on the Qumran calendar kept by the exiled Temple Priests, this is the 11th day of the 4th month on a Saturday Sabbath. Regardless, this was a special purpose but how did Adam know to sacrifice for atonement? He had Law. We have already established that Law is similar to that of Enoch, Noah, Abraham and Moses.

To say these forefathers were righteous but had no Law is inept as there would be no measure by which to judge righteousness and lawlessness is the very definition of sin. To say they sacrificed whenever for whatever is nonsense as these specifically occur on Feasts and Sabbaths especially. This is not a disconnected Law nor is it in the New Testament. Messiah was there at Creation and He created the Sabbath thus is Lord of it. He knew all these patriarchs yet we are told that He came to redefine right and good that existed from Creation. Imagine that thinking and where it must originate. For Messiah to abolish right and good would be to sin creating lawlessness. Why on Earth would He ever redefine good and right so that you and I can sin? That is literally what the church is generally teaching.

> ### Jubilees 3:32
> *And on the new moon of the fourth month, Adam and his wife went forth from the Garden of Eden, and they dwelt in the land of 'Eldâ, in the land of their creation.*
>
> ### Jubilees 3:26-27
> *And He made for them coats of skin, and clothed them, and sent them forth from the Garden of Eden. And on that day on which Adam went forth from the garden, he offered as a sweet savour an offering, frankincense, galbanum, and stacte, and spices in the morning with the rising of the sun from the day when he covered his shame.*

However, The Book of Jubilees: The Torah Calendar expresses a timeline that suggests Adam kept the Sabbath especially in the Garden of Eden. The notion that he could enter the very Holy of Holies of Yahuah and break His law is unfounded. However, even deeper, if

Yahuah's Holy of Holies was not keeping the Sabbath yet He did, we can all just throw out the entire Bible as those scholars are doing in their undermining ignorance, because Yahuah allowed His laws to be broken with no consequence in His presence for all those years. This thinking is illiterate of scripture. However, then when Adam sins later, he is exiled. That is known as the first sin and first time Yahuah's Law had been broken in history. However, the modern view claims there was sin before there was sin in the Garden even. This thinking is an attack on Yahuah's righteous judgment, His ways and His Creation. It is completely oblivious to who He is. They do not know Him.

Cain and Abel Knew To Sacrifice

We read the story of Cain and Abel and we typically focus only on Cain's murder. However, how is it that scholars miss that they somehow knew how to sacrifice? Adam taught them the Law. Why would they sacrifice without purpose requiring Law? How is it that scholars forget this completely? They seem unable to even interpret that Cain offered vegetables and with the wrong heart and his sacrifice was rejected. However, the proper offering was animals of Abel and of course, he gave with the right heart as well. This literally defines the sacrifice of atonement as that of the blood of animals later replaced with Messiah's blood that is sufficient for all sacrifices forever.

> ### *Genesis 4:3-5 KJV*
>
> *And in process of time it came to pass, that Cain brought of the fruit of the ground an offering unto the LORD. And Abel, he also brought of the firstlings of his flock and of the fat thereof. And the LORD had respect unto Abel and to his offering: But unto Cain and to his offering he had not respect. And Cain was very wroth, and his countenance fell.*

What day was it that they were offering such? The Bible does not say but what we know is this is the sacred practice on the Sabbath and the Feasts. As they brought their First Fruits, it could be Shavuot perhaps but we have no track on that. Of course, that would be a Feast Sabbath even still. It is likely a Sabbath as Adam would have taught and Jubilees already told us Adam kept the Sabbath and his generations to Noah were aware of it as well. Adam lived 930 years. He passed this knowledge to Cain and Abel and we know in the days of his grandson Enos, the world began to call upon the name of Yahuah *(Gen. 4:26)* in worship. Again, Adam taught them.

Many assume Adam was evil and there is no evidence he ever sinned after he was tricked in the Garden. He made the conscious decision to willfully sin no doubt. However, Adam only ate the fruit after he saw the love of his life do so. He knew she would fall and would no longer be with him if so. His eating the fruit is the greatest love story. However, he chose her over Yahuah and that was a mistake. This is why the serpent, declared as "that old serpent, called the devil, and satan" in Revelation *(12:9, 20:2)*, was more subtle and cunning than any other created. He was able to place Adam in a position where he knew Adam would chose sin. However, Adam atoned and remained righteous after by all accounts. We now know Adam knew and practiced the Law.

Enoch's Offerings in the Garden of Eden

Jubilees 4:25
And he (Enoch) burnt the incense of the sanctuary, (even) sweet spices, acceptable before Yahuah on the Mount.

Jubilees 8:19
And he knew that the Garden of Eden is the holy of holies, and the dwelling of Yahuah, and Mount Sinai the centre of the desert, and Mount Zion--the centre of the navel of the earth: these three were created as holy places facing each other.

How would Enoch know the incense that would be burnt thousands of years later in the sanctuary? It also matches Adam's sacrifice of atonement as well. The Garden of Eden is the original and permanent Holy of Holies and continues to function in the same manner just as it did in the days of Adam. Enoch is still there as that is where Jubilees says he resides still *(Jub. 4:23)* and Genesis never says he was relocated into Heaven but Messiah is clear no man ascended into Heaven before Him *(John 3:13)*. Jesus(Yahusha) was not wrong.

However, the Book of Enoch also indicates that Enoch somehow knew what frankincense and myrrh were as well as their purpose before the

Flood and before he entered the Garden. If you follow a map of Enoch's journey, he was in the Far East when he saw the incense trees not the Middle East as he left there earlier from Sinai. Additionally, if he lived in the Middle East previously, how would he even know what frankincense was? It does not grow there natively.

1 Enoch 29.2

And there I saw Trees of Judgment, especially vessels of the fragrance of incense and myrrh, and the trees were not alike.

Noah Sacrificed Making Atonement

Jubilees 6:1-3

And on the new moon of the third month he went forth from the ark, and built an altar on that mountain. And he made atonement for the earth, and took a kid and made atonement by its blood for all the guilt of the earth; for everything that had been on it had been destroyed, save those that were in the ark with Noah. And he placed the fat thereof on the altar, and he took an ox, and a goat, and a sheep and kids, and salt, and a turtle-dove, and the young of a dove, and placed a burnt sacrifice on the altar, and poured thereon an offering mingled with oil, and sprinkled wine and strewed frankincense over everything, and caused a goodly savour to arise, acceptable before Yahuah.

This is right after Noah exits the ark. Noah either came from an area that had frankincense or he would have had to have found it on top of that mountain in which the ark rested which is unlikely. This proves the Biblical frankincense does not originate in Ethiopia nor Yemen as one has no significant mountains and neither are East of Shinar (Iraq) where Noah landed. However, Noah knew to sacrifice and this particular offering of animals and spices was similar to the temple worship thousands of years later. This took place on the Day of Covenant Renewal called in Hebrew Shavuot, the Feast of Weeks or Pentecost in Greek. Noah was keeping the Feast as his sacrifices always had specific timing to such. Again, Shavuot is a Feast Sabbath, a holy convocation *(Lev. 23:21, 23:3)* in which one is to perform no servile work or Sabbath.

Jubilees 7:2-3

And he made wine therefrom and put it into a vessel, and kept it until the fifth year, until the first day, on the new moon of the first month. 3 And he celebrated with joy the day of this feast, and he made a burnt sacrifice unto the Lord, one young ox and one ram, and seven sheep, each a year old, and a kid of the goats, that he might make atonement thereby for himself and his sons.

Noah also celebrated the first day of Abib, the first month, that is the true "Head of the Year" or Rosh Hashanah that is never in the Fall in the Bible. As this is the first day of the Bible year, it is also celebrated in Moses' time *(Deut. 16:1)*.

Abraham Offers On Sabbaths

Consistent with Genesis and Torah, the Book of Jubilees records with more detail, dates in which Abraham as well offered burnt offerings on Feast Days and Sabbaths.

Jubilees 13

4: And he built an altar there, and he offered thereon a burnt sacrifice to the Lord, who had appeared to him.

8-9: And it came to pass in the first year, in the seventh week, on the new moon of the first month, that he built an altar on this mountain, and called on the name of the Yahuah: "Thou, the eternal Elohim, art my Elohim." And he offered on the altar a burnt sacrifice unto Yahuah that He should be with him and not forsake him all the days of his life.

16: And it came to pass in the forty-first jubilee, in the third year of the first week, that he returned to this place and offered thereon a burnt sacrifice, and called on the name of Yahuah, and said: "Thou, the most high Elohim, art my Elohim for ever and ever."

Jubilees 14

11: And he built there an altar, and sacrificed all these...

19: And the day passed, and Abram offered the pieces, and the birds, and their fruit-offerings, and their drink-offerings, and the fire devoured them.

Jubilees 15:1-2

And in the fifth year of the †fourth† week of this jubilee, in the third month, in the middle of the month, Abram celebrated the feast of the first-fruits of the grain harvest. And he offered new offerings on the altar, the first-fruits of the produce, unto Yahuah, an heifer and a goat and a sheep on the altar as a burnt sacrifice unto Yahuah; their fruit-offerings and their drink-offerings he offered upon the altar with frankincense.

Jubilees 16:22-24

And during these seven days he brought each day to the altar a burnt-offering to Yahuah, two oxen, two rams, seven sheep, one he-goat, for a sin-offering, that he might atone thereby for himself and for his seed. And, as a thank-offering, seven rams, seven kids, seven sheep, and seven he-goats, and their fruit-offerings and their drink-offerings; and he burnt all the fat thereof on the altar, a chosen offering unto Yahuah for a sweet smelling savour. And morning and evening he burnt fragrant substances, frankincense and galbanum, and stacte, and nard, and myrrh, and spice, and costum; all these seven he offered, crushed, mixed together in equal parts (and) pure.

This passage takes place on the Feast of Tabernacles on the Feast Sabbath. Also, even Isaac's sacrifice was timed with the 1st Day of Unleavened Bread that is also a Feast Sabbath. A full review of the time stamps in Jubilees 17:15-18:12 reveals Abraham left with Isaac on the 12th of Abib. He arrived, built an altar and began to offer Isaac in sacrifice on the third day that is Abib 15, the 1st Day and Sabbath of Unleavened Bread. We will prove later this is the same day Messiah was sacrificed as well executing the covenant.

Jubilees 18:12

Abraham lifted up his eyes and looked, and, behold, a single ram caught [in a thicket] by his horns, and Abraham went and took the ram and offered it for a burnt-offering in the stead of his son.

Abraham also observed Shavuot, also a Sabbath. Where did Abraham learn all of these things?

Jubilees 21:8-10

And thou wilt offer the fat of the sacrifice of thank-offerings on the fire which is upon the altar, and the fat which is on the belly, and all the fat on the inwards and the two kidneys, and all the fat that is upon them, and upon the loins and liver thou shalt remove together with the kidneys. 9 And offer all these for a sweet savour acceptable before Yahuah, with its meat-offering and with its drink-offering, for a sweet savour, the bread of the offering unto Yahuah, 10 And eat its meat on that day and on the second day, and let not the sun on the second day go down upon it till it is eaten, and let nothing be left over for the third day; for it is not acceptable [for it is not approved] and let it no longer be eaten, and all who eat thereof will bring sin upon themselves; for thus I have found it written in the books of my forefathers, and in the words of Enoch, and in the words of Noah.

Abraham says Enoch and Noah observed these sacrifices and that's how he learned them from their writings. This is a reference to the Book of Enoch that includes the Book of Noah. This is the ancient practice not a new one in his time and long before Moses.

Isaac Sacrificed on the Feasts

Jubilees 22:3

And in those days Ishmael came to see his father, and they both came together, and Isaac offered a sacrifice for a burnt-offering, and presented it on the altar of his father which he had made in Hebron.

Jubilees 22:23

And he built an altar there, which Abraham his father had first built, and he called upon the name of YHWH, and he offered sacrifice to the Elohim of Abraham his father.

Not only does Isaac call upon the name of Yahuah as he knew and used it even pronouncing it, but he continued Abraham's practices which were learned from the writings of Enoch and Noah which originated in the Heavenly Tablets from Creation.

Jacob Observed Sabbath and Feast Offerings

Earlier we covered a specific weekly Sabbath in which Jacob sacrificed and observed. However, he also kept the Feasts that Abraham kept. This passage even denotes that these are the ancient rituals from the former days.

Jubilees 32:27

And he celebrated there yet another day, and he sacrificed thereon according to all that he sacrificed on the former days...

Jubilees 32:5-6

This was his offering, in consequence of the vow which he had vowed that he would give a tenth, with their fruit-offerings and their drink-offerings. 6 And when the fire had consumed it, he burnt incense on the fire over the fire, and for a thank-offering two oxen and four rams and four sheep, four he-goats, and two sheep of a year old, and two kids of the goats; and thus he did daily for seven days.

These references are specific to the Feast of Tabernacles' Sabbath. Before we covered the Weekly Sabbath and Jacob observed Shavuot as well. These patriarchs were steeped in the Law long before Moses received it. The thinking that errs is that because Moses received it, it must have been new and for the first time. That is the false foundation to this paradigm in which most scholars are entrench. Some gain this from a misreading of Nehemiah especially.

Nehemiah 9:13-14 KJV

Thou camest down also upon mount Sinai, and spakest with them from heaven, and gavest them right judgments, and true laws, good statutes and commandments: And madest known unto them thy holy sabbath, and commandedst them precepts, statutes, and laws, by the hand of Moses thy servant:

It is assumed that because this was "made known to them" that Israel is the first to ever know of the Sabbaths and Feasts. That is an illiterate stretch in understanding of "made known to them" which has nothing to do with the previous eras. In fact, Enoch also wrote that while in Heaven the Angels "made them known to me." That is before the Flood and the very same language even. It does not say no one before them knew it. That is simply not there in this passage nor any. However, we have already produced overwhelming evidence that is unfounded. This does not say only Israel knew of the Sabbath and that track is well paved at this point. Israel was the first nation to keep the Sabbath not person.

Israel was given the commandments because they were lost for the previous 80 years or so not because they had never been observed in all of time. With the Sabbath, they are even told to remember it, to keep it holy. You remember that which you forgot so the terminology is a match to the true history we have covered. It is extremely poor scholarship of propaganda not Bible interpretation to say the Sabbath was unknown before Moses. In fact, that pattern is even identified in the Book of Jubilees as Israel was prophesied to forget again just as they did in the end days of Egypt during Moses' lifetime and just as the sons of Noah had forgotten it before. Man keeps forgetting. Thus, Yahuah tells us to remember. Even today, we have largely forgotten it again.

Jubilees 6:34

And all the children of Israel will forget, and will not find the path of the years, and will forget the new moons, and seasons, and sabbaths, and they will go wrong as to all the order of the years.

The Sabbath in origin is a Creation. Yahuah did not create it only to forget it and He tells us to remember it because mankind forgets it. What other part of Creation are we to forget? Which passed away?

Have you ever noticed that rainbows still appear in our modern sky? The Bible says they represent covenant with Noah and mankind that Yahuah would never flood the Earth again. Yahuah continues to publish a reminder that covenant remains to this day. However, if it passed away with Moses's Law and if not, in the time of Messiah's ascension, then why is it still there in the sky? Does this mean now Yahuah can flood the Earth again and His promise passed away? The thinking is ludicrous yet this how the church applies the Law of Life in Yahusha Messiah. They cut off all that was before it as if it never existed and even call it bondage in ignorance. No Apostle including Paul ever called the Law of Moses bondage. They claim everything began anew as if the rest of the Bible is meaningless. Worse, they teach us to live lawless, the definition of sin.

In summation, the origin of the Sabbath is the 7th Day of Creation. We have compiled a chart that compares these Laws throughout the ages on the next pages. You will find the Law of Adam and the Heavenly Tablets is the Law of Enoch is the Law of Noah is the Law of Abraham is the Law of Moses is the Law of Life in Yahusha Messiah.

Law Comparison Chart:

(Enoch to Noah to Abraham)	(Derives from Law of Noah)	(Derives from Law of Moses)
Law of Noah *Jub. 7:20*	**Law of Moses** *Ex. 20*	**Law of Messiah** *Matt. 5, 22*
1 *Bless their Creator*	**1** *No other gods before me*	**1** *Love Yahuah with all heart, soul, and mind (Matt. 22:37)*
2 *Bless their Creator*	**2** *No graven images*	**2** *No idols (Matt. 4:10). Love Yahuah with all heart, soul, and mind*
3 *Bless their Creator*	**3** *No taking Yahuah in vain*	**3** *No taking Yahuah in vain (Matt. 5:33-34) Love Yahuah with all heart...*
4 *Bless their Creator*	**4** *Remember the Sabbath, keep it holy*	**4** *I will give you Sabbath. (Matt. 11:28). Love Yahuah with all heart...*
5 *Honor father and mother*	**5** *Honor father and mother*	**5** *Honor father and mother (Luke 18:20) Love neighbor as yourself*
6 *No killing (7:26) Love their neighbour.*	**6** *No killing*	**6** *No killing (Luke 18:20) Love neighbor as yourself*
7 *Cover shame of flesh, Guard souls from fornication Love their neighbour.*	**7** *No adultery*	**7** *No adultery (Matt. 5:27-28) Love neighbor as yourself*
8 *Guard souls from uncleanness and all iniquity. Love their neighbour.*	**8** *No stealing*	**8** *No stealing (Luke 18:20) Love neighbor as yourself*
9 *Guard souls from uncleanness and all iniquity. Love their neighbour.*	**9** *No bearing false witness*	**9** *No bearing false witness (Luke 18:20). Love neighbor as yourself*
10 *No envy (7:26) Love their neighbour. Guard souls from uncleanness and all iniquity.*	**10** *No coveting*	**10** *No envy (Luke 12:15). Love neighbour as yourself*

Law of Enoch = Law of Noah
Before and After the Flood

Jubilees 7:38

For thus did Enoch, the father of your father command Methuselah, his son, and Methuselah his son Lamech, and Lamech commanded me all the things which his fathers commanded him.

Law of Abraham = Law of Noah
Up Until Moses

Genesis 26:5 KJV

Because that Abraham obeyed my voice, and kept my charge, my commandments, my statutes, and my laws.

Jubilees 12:27 KJV

And he took the books of his fathers, and these were written in Hebrew and he transcribed them, and he began from henceforth to study them, and I made known to him that which he could not (understand), and he studied them during the six rainy months.

Law of Messiah = Law of Moses
Old and New Testaments

Matthew 22:40 KJV

On these two commandments hang all the law and the prophets.

Matthew 5:17-18 KJV

Think not that I am come to destroy the law, or the prophets: I am not come to destroy, but to fulfil. For verily I say unto you, Till heaven and earth pass, one jot or one tittle shall in no wise pass from the law, till all be fulfilled.

Messiah's Eternal Fire = The Law
Day of Judgment – Same Law

2 Esdras 13 KJVA

4 And whensoever the voice went out of his mouth, all they burnt, that heard his voice, like as the earth fails when it feels the fire. 38 ...and he (Messiah) shall destroy them without labor, by the law which is like unto fire... (Cf. Rev. 1:16, 2:16, 12:17, 14:12, 19:15, 21, 22:14; 1 John 2:3-4, 3:22-24, 5:2-3; 2 John 1:6; Matt. 5:17-18)

The Law is The Law From Beginning to the End

Come unto me, all ye that labour and are heavy laden, and
I will give you rest.

the GOD culture
יהוה

Take my yoke upon you, and learn of me: for I am meek and lowly in heart: and
ye shall find rest unto your souls.
For my yoke is easy, and my burden is light.
At that time Jesus went on the sabbath day...

Matthew 11:28-30; Matthew 12:1a KJV

Chapter 3 | Messiah Kept the Sabbath

1 John 2:3-7 KJV
*And hereby we do know that **we know him, if we keep his commandments**. He that saith, **I know him, and keepeth not his commandments, is a liar**, and the **truth is not in him**. But whoso **keepeth his word, in him verily is the love of God perfected**: hereby **know we that we are in him**. He that saith he abideth in him ought himself also so to **walk, even as he walked**. Brethren, I write **no new commandment unto you**, but **an old commandment which ye had from the beginning**. The old commandment is the word which ye have heard from the beginning.*

Do we know Him? Want to understand Matthew 7 when Messiah will tell some Christians to depart from me because He never knew them. This is how we know Him. We keep His commandments just as Matthew 7 says as well. Which commandments? We will explore the supposed 2 new commandments that are exact quotes from the Law of Moses in answer to the question: what is the greatest commandment from the Law of Moses? There is nothing new about His reasserting the Law of Moses with the two most important commandments. We are to follow the example of our Messiah. John is clear this included the old commandments, not just from Moses' era but the beginning and that certainly means the Sabbath. Did we read that? Did John just call the modern church liars and the truth not in them? Why would he use such strong language? Many will read this book and take offense as we do the same as John. The fact is one cannot teach this without rebuke of the modern church as it proves to operate in obvious willing ignorance.

We know how He walked and we are to imitate that. He kept the Sabbath on the 7th Day of the week every week. John continues in expressing a "new commandment" that you love your brother which is not new in any sense. It was not new when Messiah invoked it either but originates in the Law of Moses *(Lev. 19:18: to the Hebrew, 34: to the Gentile)* and really before that. However, what one cannot do is claim he just abolished the so-called old commandments as instead, he just reinforced them which we see routinely throughout the New Testament. What do we see Messiah doing throughout His life and ministry? For starters, we know His custom was to keep the Sabbath.

> ***Luke 4:16 KJV***
> *And he came to Nazareth, where he had been brought up: and, **as his custom was, he went into the synagogue on the sabbath day**, and stood up for to read.*

Yahusha declared His purpose on Sabbath. As His custom was to keep the Sabbath, He did so all of His life up until that point. That custom never changes in any scripture including today. He ascended to Heaven and what is Heaven's custom? We learned from the Heavenly Tablets, they have always kept Sabbath since the beginning and for all ages.

How can we forget Messiah came from Heaven and already practiced the Sabbath for thousands of years? We have already established Heaven's practice over time. Messiah was there and returned there.

> ***John 1 KJV***
> ***1-3: In the beginning was the Word**, and the Word was with God, and the **Word was God**. The same was in the beginning with God. **All things were made by him; and without him was not any thing made that was made**.*
> *10:...He was in the world, and **the world was made by him**, and the world knew him not.*
> *14:...And **the Word was made flesh, and dwelt among us**,*

(and we beheld his glory, the glory as of the only begotten of the Father,) full
of grace and truth.

When we speak of ancient doctrine of Heaven, we cannot forget Messiah was there from before the First Day of Creation and that is His culture. He did not come to us representing anything He did not already see the Father doing. There is no separating His deeds from the Father and no way He disregarded the Father's commandments.

John 5:19 KJV

Then answered Jesus and said unto them, Verily, verily, I say unto you, The
Son can do nothing of himself, but what he seeth the Father do: for what things
soever he doeth, these also doeth the Son likewise.

He did not come representing His own will but that of the Father. The Father wrote His will with His finger and we are ignoring it and claiming He did too. He did not.

Matthew 12:50 KJV

For whosoever shall do the will of my Father which is in heaven, the same is
my brother, and sister, and mother.

In fact, if He abolished the Law, He would be a liar. Not only did He say the Law cannot pass, not one letter of it, until the Day of Judgment but He told us if He did not do the works of the Father, don't even believe Him. The church has defined Yahusha as someone He is not and they attack who He is. They are not debating with us, they are ridiculing His own words and acts. These are His words. What exactly are we reading if not His words?

John 10:37 KJV

If I do not the works of my Father, believe me not.

Matthew 5:17-18 KJV

Think not that I am come to destroy the law, or the prophets: I am not come to
destroy, but to fulfil. For verily I say unto you, Till heaven and earth pass, one

jot or one tittle shall in no wise pass from the law, till all be fulfilled.

Matthew 24:33-35 KJV

So likewise ye, when ye shall see all these things, know that it is near, even at the doors. Verily I say unto you, This generation shall not pass, till all these things be fulfilled. Heaven and earth shall pass away, but my words shall not pass away.

Abraham shared this culture and Messiah even said so. In fact, Abraham is saved as he has the same promise of salvation even from the Old Testament that you and I have. The realization of his salvation will occur at the same time as ours on the Day of Judgment and not before. Yes, we are saved for certain when we enter and continue in relationship with Him. However, that remains a future context even for us New Testament believers.

John 8:56 KJV

Your father Abraham rejoiced to see my day: and he saw it, and was glad.

Messiah kept the same commandments as Abraham, Moses and Adam. They are the same from the Heavenly Tablets. You don't even have to go to the Book of Enoch to see this though. He said so.

John 15:10 KJV

If ye keep my commandments, ye shall abide in my love; even as I have kept my Father's commandments, and abide in his love.

This is before His death and resurrection and no "new law" has been enacted. He is talking about the Law of Moses that is the same from Adam and from Heaven where He originates. Somehow scholars play willingly ignorant and forget that we have the Father's commandments well recorded. Messiah kept the Law. He says He did and if He did not, He is a sinner or lawbreaker. Notice this is how He abides in Yahuah's love. It is also how we abide in His love. There is no other way to please Him. There is no other way to love Him. There is no other way to know Him. If we do not know Him, we will be told to depart on Judgment Day. This matters immensely.

Some try to challenge John 1 which we just covered because of the Westcott and Hort manuscripts created in fraud in the 1800s. They admit in their letters they intended to attack the deity of Messiah and change the Bible and they did. This is the source of the modern NIV, NLT, and many other bibles including those used by the Jehovah's Witnesses and INC's Moffat Translation. These are missing scriptures and they attempt to attack the deity of Messiah. However, one cannot. Messiah said He was Elohim from the beginning in His own words many times.

> ***Colossians 1:15-17 KJV***
> *Who is the image of the invisible God, the firstborn of every creature:* **For by him were all things created, that are in heaven, and that are in earth, visible and invisible, whether they be thrones, or dominions, or principalities, or powers: all things were created by him, and for him: And he is before all things, and by him all things consist.**
> ***Hebrews 1:1-2 KJV***
> *God, who at sundry times and in divers manners spake in time past unto the fathers by the prophets, Hath in these last days spoken unto us* **by his Son,** *whom he hath appointed heir of all things,* **by whom also he made the worlds;**

Can you create? Do you have such powers? We are not talking about a craft project or building a house because you do so with elements He already created. Can you create something from nothing? Even Angels cannot create as there is no scripture which says so. They were cheerleaders at Creation not participants *(Job 38:4)* and they were created the first day *(Jub. 2:1-2)*. Jesus*(Yahusha)* is the Creator with Yahuah, the Father. This is exclusive to their power and no one else. Even the Holy Spirit was present at Creation but no role is specified. However, the Son is right there creating along with the Father. Again, He said so Himself calling Himself Elohim as only Elohim created in the beginning. Elohim is plural and there were two – the Father and the Son together.

> ***John 17:5 KJV***
> *And now, O Father, glorify thou me with thine own self with* **the glory**

which I had with thee before the world was.
John 17:24 KJV
*Father, I will that they also, whom thou hast given me, be with me where I am; that they may behold my glory, which thou hast given me: for **thou lovedst me before the foundation of the world***.

For those questioning our use of Jubilees in this book which vets perfectly as scripture even as such, read The Book of Jubilees: The Torah Calendar where we conduct a thorough Torah Test in which is passes. However, these doctrines from John, Paul, and the writer of Hebrews *(perhaps James/Jacob, brother of Yahusha)* have no firm anchor to the modern Old Testament canon that never specifies the Messiah to come as a Creator. They each originate in this sense directly and indisputably from the Book of Jubilees which Messiah also quoted multiple times including John 8:56 that we just covered which is a quote of this specific scenario of Abraham rejoicing at the coming Messiah, the eternal plant of righteousness from his seed. We also see twice in John, Messiah said He was before the world was.

> ***Jubilees 16:26***
> *And he (Abraham) blessed his Creator who had created him in his generation, for He had created him according to His good pleasure; for He knew and perceived that from him would arise the plant of righteousness for the eternal generations, and from him a holy seed, so that it should become **like Him who had made all things***.

However, this is not strange doctrine as not only does it align with the New Testament but really Genesis has always represented the two Creators as it says US, OUR and OUR. He wasn't talking to Angels who can't create anyway as man is not made in their image after their likeness nor were they there until the first day. The word God in Hebrew is Elohim which is plural. Messiah was there when the Sabbath was created. Wow!!!

> ***Genesis 1:26A KJV***
> *And God said, Let **us** make man in **our** image, after our likeness:*

The next day, Elohim created the Sabbath which is why Messiah said He was Lord of the Sabbath. He always has been and He always will be. This was not a new declaration. He was there and He created thus He created the Sabbath. Yet, we are told He then violated His own Creation. We are told He broke it as well which is a lie. Those churches are actually defining Him as a sinner.

> *Mark 2:27-28 KJV*
> *And he said unto them, The sabbath was made for man, and not man for the sabbath: Therefore* **the Son of man is Lord also of the sabbath.**
> *Matthew 12:8 KJV*
> *For* **the Son of man is Lord even of the sabbath day.**
> *Luke 6:5 KJV*
> *And he said unto them, That* **the Son of man is Lord also of the sabbath.**

He made the Sabbath for man alongside the Father and He well knew that was it's purpose. He knew it was not the other way around. Understand what He is saying here. If the Sabbath is made for man at Creation, it does not pass away as long as man exists. He remains Lord of the Sabbath and the Sabbath remains.

Again this is no mystery throughout His ministry as He kept the Sabbath. He taught and healed especially on the Sabbath as that was His custom. One simply cannot remove the Sabbath from His narratives that are there many times over. Here are just some examples:

> *Mark 1:21 KJV*
> And they went into Capernaum; and straightway **on the sabbath day he entered into the synagogue, and taught.**
> *Mark 6:2 KJV*
> And **when the sabbath day was come, he began to teach in the synagogue**
> *Luke 13:10 KJV*
> And he was **teaching in one of the synagogues on the sabbath.**

A Message from the Lord of the Sabbath.
Matthew 11:28-30; Matthew 12:1a KJV
Come unto me, all ye that labour and are heavy laden, and I will give you rest. *Take my yoke upon you, and learn of me; for I am meek and lowly in heart: and ye shall find* **rest unto your souls.** *For my* **yoke is easy, and my burden is light. At that time Jesus went on the sabbath day**...

As we dissected in the Introduction, Hebrews 4 interprets Matthew 11:28-12:1 as a Sabbath sermon indisputably given on the Sabbath Day. He said come unto me and I will give you Sabbath. As we are to walk as He walked, how can we ignore that He walked, taught and performed miracles especially on this specific day of the week – the Saturday Sabbath. There is no separating Him from His Sabbath He even invokes among the Pharisees. Don't worry, we have a whole chapter coming in which we will prove Messiah NEVER broke the Biblical Sabbath but the Pharisee Sabbath which He rebuked.

John 7:22 KJV
Moses therefore gave unto you circumcision; (not because it is of Moses, but of the fathers;) and ye on the sabbath day circumcise a man.

Notice, Messiah is pointing out that circumcision began before the Law of Moses. He then invokes the Sabbath as He well knows both precede Mt. Sinai in practice. The Pharisees did not. Their focus starts in Israel because they were never a part of the Old Testament at least not as Hebrews as they are the Samaritans who defiled the Temple exiling the Temple Priests to Qumran where the Biblical practice continued while the Temple from then forward was defiled and ungodly. Messiah was clear on this and we will cover many such passages. They have never known the Bible and today we call them the Rabbis of modern Judaism.

Messiah's 2 "New" Commandments

Did Jesus*(Yahusha)* make new Law? Did He abolish the entire Old Testament and Old Covenant? Is that the way in which scripture ever operates? We are told Messiah scrapped the 10 Commandments and replaced them with 2 Commandments of His own. He just made up new Law because well, He felt like it we imagine. Yes, that is cynical and with good reason. These who say this are among the most illiterate of scholars. There is no way they can read this passage and interpret with this language. Yet, they do. Let's examine.

> **Matthew 22:34-36 KJV**
> *But when the Pharisees had heard that he had put the Sadducees to silence, they were gathered together. Then one of them, which was a lawyer, asked him a question, tempting him, and saying, Master, which is the great commandment in the law?*

The start of Messiah's setting "New Law" is an answer to the question, what is the greatest commandment. This was from a Pharisee lawyer and notice many lawyers are Pharisees today. His aim was to trip up Messiah with a trick question. He was prepared to prove this was not the Messiah. Amazingly, we are told Messiah answered this question with new Law? However, He is being asked about the greatest commandment in the framework of the Law of Moses. Prior to this engagement you can further see the Pharisees wished to entangle Jesus*(Yahusha)* so they could exploit His answer in some way. We see this every day on our YouTube Channel and we are not Him but do our best.

> **Matthew 22:15 KJV**
> *Then went the Pharisees, and took counsel how they might entangle him in his talk.*

Messiah has just answered the Pharisees earlier in this passage as well as this was becoming confrontational. Notice He did not back down. He did not turn the other cheek. He crushed their debate telling them exactly what we often repeat of Pharisees or modern scholars. You err not knowing the scriptures nor the power of Elohim. These have a form of Godliness and deny the power thereof *(2 Tim. 3:5).*

> **Matthew 22:29 KJV**
> *Jesus answered and said unto them, Ye do err, not knowing the scriptures, nor the power of God.*

Now, let us review His response. What is the greatest commandment? He responds with the 1st commandment that He says is the 1st Commandment. Wait a minute... The church is telling us this is "New Law" but He quoted the 1st commandment from the Law of Moses answering which is the greatest commandment. This is the most illiterate of positions and many scholars land on this because they only know their paradigm and they err not knowing the scriptures just as the Pharisees. They are following Pharisee leaven not the Bible.

> **Matthew 22:37-38 KJV**
> *Jesus said unto him, Thou shalt love the Lord thy God with all thy heart, and with all thy soul, and with all thy mind. This is the first and great commandment.*

He says this is the 1st Commandment and yes, He meant from the Law of Moses. Here it is in multiple forms that offer the same language Messiah is quoting. How could anyone call themselves a scholar and claim that His quoting the Law of Moses is somehow setting new law? .

> **Exodus 20:3 KJV**
> *Thou shalt have no other gods before me.*
> **Deuteronomy 11:13 KJV**
> *And it shall come to pass, if ye shall hearken diligently unto **my commandments which I command you this day, to love the LORD your God, and to serve him with all your heart and with all your soul,***
> **Deuteronomy 13:3 KJV**
> *Thou shalt not hearken unto the words of that prophet, or that dreamer of dreams: for the LORD your God proveth you, to know whether ye love the LORD your God with all your heart and with all your soul.*
> **Joshua 22:5 KJV**
> *But take diligent heed to do the commandment and the law, which Moses the*

*servant of the LORD charged you, to love the LORD your God, and to walk
in all his ways, and to keep his commandments, and to cleave unto him, and
to serve him with all your heart and with all your soul.*

He then offers a bonus in understanding when he invokes the Law of Moses yet again as the 2nd greatest commandment.

Matthew 22:39-40 KJV

And the second is like unto it, Thou shalt love thy neighbour as thyself. On these two commandments hang all the law and the prophets.

This one is later quoted by Paul twice *(Rom. 13:9, Gal. 5:24)* and James *(2:8)* and really John as well which we already covered. They are certainly quoting Messiah. However, this too originates in the Law of Moses in exact language.

Leviticus 19:18 KJV

Thou shalt not avenge, nor bear any grudge against the children of thy people, but **thou shalt love thy neighbour as thyself**: *I am the LORD.*

Notice, Moses didn't say this, Yahuah did. Messiah is quoting Yahuah's words from the Law of Moses. That's not new but over 1,500 years old at that point. What exactly are these scholars of? Not the Bible.

Messiah clearly observed the Sabbath. He taught and healed on the Sabbath many times and we could cover abundant such scriptures. The accusation from many scholars leveled at Him is that He then broke His Sabbath. They are repeating Pharisees who are upset because He broke their Sabbath laws in which they added to it and did not understand the tone and tenor of the Law. Messiah did.

In the next chapter, we will fully test this. Messiah could not break the Law or He would have sinned which He did not. They can't have it both ways. They need to think through such allegations because they are undermining scripture in their poor understanding. However, they wholly ignore the fact that Messiah was a Creator and created the Sabbath. He does not abolish that which He created and He told us in Matthew 5:17-18 He would not yet they say He did. We will test this.

Messiah's 2

He Said:

Matthew 22:37-38 KJV
Jesus said unto him, Thou shalt love the Lord thy God with all thy heart, and with all thy soul, and with all thy mind. This is the first and great commandment.

Moses Wrote:

Exodus 20:3 KJV
Thou shalt have no other gods before me.

Deuteronomy 11:13 KJV
And it shall come to pass, if ye shall hearken diligently unto my commandments which I command you this day, to love the LORD your God, and to serve him with all your heart and with all your soul,

Moses wrote the words of Yahuah here.
Messiah uses the same language.

NOT NEW LAW!
Messiah Quoted Yahuah From Moses

"New" Commandments?
Are these really new?

He Said:

Matthew 22:39-40 KJV

And the second is like unto it, Thou shalt love thy neighbour as thyself. On these two commandments hang all the law and the prophets.

Moses Wrote:

Leviticus 19:18 KJV

Thou shalt not avenge, nor bear any grudge against the children of thy people, but thou shalt love thy neighbour as thyself: I am the LORD.

He quotes the 1st Commandment and says it is the 1st Commandment. That is not exactly setting new law.

If the entire law and Old Testament hangs or rests on these 2 Commandments, then they are not new. They are very ancient to be such foundation.

One cannot break either of the 10 Commandments without breaking these 2 Greatest Commandments.

NOT NEW LAW!
Messiah Quoted Yahuah From Moses

Why Heal, Teach And Let Your Serving Disciples Eat On The SABBATH?

Wherefore it is lawful to do well on the sabbath days.
Matthew 12:12 KJV

Chapter 4 | Did Messiah Break the Sabbath?

Knowing that Messiah kept the Sabbath as His custom was, there are those scholars and especially seminaries that teach that Messiah then broke the Sabbath. Understand in doing so they just undermined Messiah as an outlaw who sinned. This leads to the undermining of all of scripture as if He sinned, He was not perfect and sinless. One would think every scholar would consider that but they are too entrenched in paradigms from the doctrines of men to even see what the Bible very clearly states. Did Messiah break the Sabbath? Heaven forbid. They are not reading and comprehending in the slightest. Let's review.

What they seem oblivious too is the accusers of Messiah are the Pharisees who claim he broke their expanded interpretation of His Sabbath. Who knew Sabbath better, Him or the Pharisees whom He rebukes many times over? How can any scholar side with Pharisee accusations against Messiah? He taught and healed on the Sabbath and often. Was this unbiblical? No.

Luke 13:10-13 KJV

And he was teaching in one of the synagogues on the sabbath. And, behold, there was a woman which had a spirit of infirmity eighteen years, and was bowed together, and could in no wise lift up herself. And when Jesus saw her, he called her to him, and said unto her, Woman, thou art loosed from thine infirmity. And he laid his hands on her: and immediately she was made straight, and glorified God.

This is awesome! Jesus*(Yahusha)* healed this woman but it was the Sabbath. Exactly! That is a day of healing even. The question is why don't Pharisees know that? He will correct them and they are powerless.

> **Luke 13:14 KJV**
> *And the ruler of the synagogue answered with indignation, because that Jesus had healed on the sabbath day, and said unto the people, There are six days in which men ought to work: in them therefore come and be healed, and not on the sabbath day.*

The righteous indignation of the ignorant and unrighteous is what scholarship placates and treats as Gospel in this passage. How dare you heal on the Sabbath. Wouldn't the point and focus be the miracle that just occurred to any normal person? What kind of idiot rebukes the Son of Yahuah for healing someone ever? What kind of church places his accusation above Messiah's brilliant answer? It is as if they stop reading right there and then, make accusation that He broke the Sabbath. No, He deals with a jealous Pharisee who can't heal and has no power. He stepped on the man's pride. He just pulled the foundation out from underneath this Pharisee's righteousness and proved the Pharisee Sabbath is not His practice. He heals on the Sabbath and He always has. For a Pharisee to not know this, means they do not know Yahuah nor His Son. Yet these scholars use that guy's words to ridicule our Savior.

> **Luke 13:15-17 KJV**
> *The Lord then answered him, and said, Thou hypocrite, doth not each one of you on the sabbath loose his ox or his ass from the stall, and lead him away to watering? And ought not this woman, being a daughter of Abraham, whom Satan hath bound, lo, these eighteen years, be loosed from this bond on the sabbath day? And when he had said these things, all his adversaries were ashamed: and all the people rejoiced for all the glorious things that were done by him.*

When Jesus*(Yahusha)* calls someone a hypocrite, it means they are a hypocrite. Scholars following this hypocrite then, make themselves hypocrites. He begins in defining work that is permissible on the Sabbath. You loose your ox and take him out for water. He needs water and Sabbath is not a day of starving nor even fasting *(no, that is not Bible but*

Catholic illiteracy). Your ox is allowed to drink. The Pharisees of course knew this and practice it as do all. No one locks their ox in the stall and leaves him to thirst and starve for a day because it's Sabbath. It just doesn't work that way. That shepherd would not be breaking the Sabbath and Messiah is telling us neither did He. The Sabbath Law never intended for your animal to thirst and starve just as it does not prohibit healing those in need.

Really, Rabbi Wrong, you think you have the authority to stop this woman from being released from her sickness after 18 years of bondage? Should she not be loosed as well like the ox to rid her suffering? Should we leave her to thirst and starve and pain? At least in this instance the Pharisees felt ashamed. They knew He was right and they were wrong. Yet how is it that scholars cannot seem to read this? Instead, they take the narrative backwards to the accusation that is proven wrong and the Pharisees even admit such. However, they apply Pharisee doctrine disproven as their doctrine claiming this proves Jesus broke the Sabbath. Yet, He did not.

He teaches us of the Sabbath over many accounts and here, He, the Son of Yahuah, says it is lawful to do well on the Sabbath days. He means it is permissible and always has been to heal on the Sabbath. In fact, He encourages such and the Apostles continued this not because they are law-breaking bandits but they are still following the Law as the Law has never said not to heal on the Sabbath. The Pharisees just showed us their lack of understanding and instead of learning from this, modern scholars read this from the perspective of a Pharisee rather than learning the lesson that in this case, even they learned.

Matthew 12:12 KJV
Wherefore it is lawful to do well on the sabbath days.

We will put this in context. By the pool of Bethesda, there sat a crippled man awaiting a healing miracle. But it is Sabbath, so he will just have to wait, right? Even the sound of that rings false and illogical. The Bible has never said such. Only Pharisee doctrine is so illiterate and uncaring. Messiah exposes this again and restores the Biblical Sabbath.

John 5:2 KJV

Now there is at Jerusalem by the sheep market a pool, which is called in the Hebrew tongue Bethesda, having five porches.

John 5:5–9 KJV

And a certain man was there, which had an infirmity thirty and eight years. When Jesus saw him lie, and knew that he had been now a long time in that case, he saith unto him, Wilt thou be made whole? The impotent man answered him, Sir, I have no man, when the water is troubled, to put me into the pool: but while I am coming, another steppeth down before me. Jesus saith unto him, Rise, take up thy bed, and walk. And immediately the man was made whole, and took up his bed, and walked: and on the same day was the sabbath.

Now, it's time to celebrate the miraculous healing power of Jesus *(Yahusha)*. Is that not how any sane person would respond to a man crippled for 38 years, now walking? It would be insane to then argue with the miracle would it not? The Pharisees do and modern scholars take their side claiming Messiah just broke the Sabbath. That is illiterate.

John 5:5 KJV

The Jews therefore said unto him that was cured, It is the sabbath day: it is not lawful for thee to carry thy bed.

"Get back down there, cripple. What are you doing walking? You are not allowed to walk, it's Sabbath." Their issue is more with the carrying of his bed as we are not to carry burdens on the Sabbath. That is certainly Sabbath Law but this man was just healed from impotence for over 30 years. Messiah told Him to take His bed for a specific purpose. He is proving to the Pharisees they do not understand scripture. Their legalistic interpretation is wrong. If a man is healed, he is allowed to carry his bed leaving his place of bondage. Messiah commanded this in fact. This is not breaking the Sabbath. However, this time, the Pharisees are not ashamed. They desire people follow their traditions over the Bible. Modern scholars follow their way not that of the Bible on this topic and several others. They are not our saviors and we must prove all things for ourselves *(1 Th. 5:21)*. Test everything.

John 5:16-17 KJV

And therefore did the Jews persecute Jesus, and sought to slay him, because he had done these things on the sabbath day. But Jesus answered them, 'My Father works hitherto, and I work.'"

They were so beholden to their interpretation and expansion of the ways of Sabbath that they were already seeking to kill Jesus*(Yahusha)* because of this. Law that is not even Law. The tenor and tone of the Sabbath has never denied someone healing. It has never denied your animal the right to food and drink. It has never denied a man who was just healed to relocate his existence. Those are Pharisee ways of reading the Law in legalism and bondage. That is not His Law which is freedom.

They are not Heaven's and Messiah represents the proper way to read and understand the Word. He is not breaking the Sabbath here. He is not leading a rebellion against the Law of Yahuah. If He did, He would have sinned and He did not. Instead He further tells us He and the Father work on the Sabbath. However, they work good just as the Temple Priests work good but it's still work. It has always been permissible and this is not a new declaration.

However, what did Messiah just do here? He works as Yahuah works. The Pharisees knew exactly what He meant. He was equating Himself as Elohim. For those saying He never said He was Elohim, He does many times. Again, the Pharisees understood this. Their accusation here is He broke the Sabbath. It is a false accusation that He already proved. He is not saying I am Elohim, therefore, I can do whatever I want. You will find several pulpits espousing such. He is saying the Sabbath has never required the sick to continue to be sick. It has never required your animal to starve. It has never required legalism over miracles and a man who is crippled can even relocate his bed from his place of bondage. He is proving the Pharisees do not know His Sabbath, nor Yahuah nor Him.

John 5:18 KJV

Therefore the Jews sought the more to kill him, because he not only had broken the sabbath, but said also that God was his Father, making himself equal with God.

Jesus *(Yahusha)* then explains that not only does He feel this way and read the Word this way, so does the Father. He is only doing what the Father does meaning this is the way it has always been. He is exploiting their weakness in not knowing the scripture and the tone and tenor of His Law which they add to and misinterpret most of the time. Their interpretations turn Torah against Torah He says *(Mark 7:9)*. Scholars are following doctrine rebuked by Messiah Himself.

John 5:19 KJV
Then answered Jesus and said unto them, Verily, verily, I say unto you, The Son can do nothing of himself, but what he seeth the Father do: for what things soever he doeth, these also doeth the Son likewise.

This conversation continues as they hate what He represents – the authentic, pure Word in it's origin. This is because they change it so that it looks different in their age. They add to it with their leaven as He warns many times. They usurp the throne of Yahuah and alter His relationship into a legal document to which they keep adding. Worse, they are not even in covenant with Him as He is not their God. Just as laws in many nations today that are of Pharisee origin not Bible, they continue to multiply the regulation in order to enslave mankind. They do not even believe Torah and the rest of scripture.

John 5:46-47 KJV
For had ye believed Moses, ye would have believed me; for he wrote of me. But if ye believe not his writings, how shall ye believe my words?

Pharisees do not believe Moses or Torah? What? They sing Torah! Torah! Torah! to this day. They appear to worship the Torah even. This is only in appearance. They do not know nor believe Torah and Pharisees *(modern Judaism)* has no understanding nor authority to represent the Word. They represent Talmud not Torah. What part of Torah as well were they not reading having already rejected even in the 1st Century? The Book of Jubilees which Messiah and the Apostles quote for significant doctrine and the exiled Temple Priests in Qumran/ Bethabara label it as Torah and apply it so. Review our Torah Test on that book for yourself because you will never learn that from these scholars who follow Pharisees.

In fact, Jesus *(Yahusha)* takes this even deeper on the Sabbath to prove His point. Realize He is a Creator there at Creation and He is Lord of the Sabbath. Sabbath is a day of rest even from Creation. However, He reaches down in the dirt and molds clay into what is likely an eyeball or parts thereof as He "made the clay." He, then, fully heals the blind man who opens his eyes. This may well have been a Creation as that is power He possesses. We can only speculate on that but what we do know is He was proving it is lawful to do good on the Sabbath. This blind man did not have to watch *(pun intended)* his miracle pass by.

John 9:14 KJV
And it was the sabbath day when Jesus made the clay, and opened his eyes.

As they read, some are already objecting with this next story out of context. The disciples were hungry on the Sabbath Day as they were about ministry. Are they really any different from the ox Messiah discussed before? Are they not allowed to eat? Were they supposed to starve yet your ox is not? Messiah explains this with historical precedence that these scholars do not even bother to read it seems. They again cut off the story and stop before He teaches. They are certainly not Bible scholars when they do so.

Matthew 12:1-2 KJV
At that time Jesus went on the sabbath day through the corn; and his disciples were an hungred, and began to pluck the ears of corn, and to eat. But when the Pharisees saw it, they said unto him, Behold, thy disciples do that which is not lawful to do upon the sabbath day.

"Ah!!! Gotcha! We caught you lawbreakers who pick and eat corn on the Sabbath." What law did they break? None. They were ministering and they, as the Temple Priests and as David and his men needed to eat, ate the showbread from the Temple. Do the Temple Priests break the Sabbath every Sabbath? Of course not, they are ministering to Yahuah but it is work. It is permissible work on the Sabbath. David and his men were supposed to starve? Just like your ox, there is never any intention of the Sabbath for men to starve. Jesus*(Yahusha)* is exploiting legalism here. He is demonstrating that the Pharisees are only legalistic and do not even understand the tone of the Sabbath. They read the words but they do not know what it is about. Yet, the modern church uses their inept interpretations and ignores Messiah's teachings. They turn and ridicule what He says siding with Pharisees. It is time we all put them in the seat of the Pharisee where they belong and rebuke them.

Matthew 12:3-5 KJV

But he said unto them, Have ye not read what David did, when he was an hungred, and they that were with him; How he entered into the house of God, and did eat the shewbread, which was not lawful for him to eat, neither for them which were with him, but only for the priests? Or have ye not read in the law, how that on the sabbath days the priests in the temple profane the sabbath, and are blameless?

What David did was lawful and never truly forbidden on the Sabbath as man's need to survive outweighs a letter of the Law. They had a right to eat above the commandment. This is not new as the Temple Priests break the Sabbath every week if one assesses this the Pharisee way. The Bible way says they did not break the Sabbath nor did David nor did the disciples.

Matthew 12:6-8 KJV

But I say unto you, That in this place is one greater than the temple. But if ye had known what this meaneth, I will have mercy, and not sacrifice, ye would not have condemned the guiltless. For the Son of man is Lord even of the sabbath day.

Messiah really goes for it then. He is teaching them a lesson and He is clarifying He is Elohim. Literally, they are talking to the one who will judge all of these actions and He is telling us all how He judges. He judged David guiltless in this act of eating the showbread, the Temple Priests guiltless in working on the Sabbath, the man who waters his cattle guiltless and the disciples who satisfied their hunger while about ministry on the Sabbath, guiltless. That is not breaking the Sabbath. It is teaching the Sabbath and it's original intent over Pharisee application of the Law in legalism. In fact, He goes to great lengths to teach His Sabbath throughout the Gospels yet these same Pharisee-loving scholars, will tell you He did not even teach it but just broke it. That is illiterate as they place themselves in the seat of the scornful Pharisee.

He declares He is greater than the Temple. You do realize the gravity of that right? Yes, He says He is Elohim many times. We know He was a Creator that means He is Elohim and He Created the Sabbath. We have the account of Sabbath from the horse's mouth – the Lord of the Sabbath. Instead, we ignore what He says Sabbath is and use Pharisee doctrine to ridicule His own words. Let's look at His words in context.

Matthew 12:9-12 KJV

And when he was departed thence, he went into their synagogue: And, behold, there was a man which had his hand withered. And they asked him, saying, Is it lawful to heal on the sabbath days? that they might accuse him. And he said unto them, What man shall there be among you, that shall have one sheep, and if it fall into a pit on the sabbath day, will he not lay hold on it, and lift it out? How much then is a man better than a sheep? Wherefore it is lawful to do well on the sabbath days.

Where in all of the Old Testament do we ever find that one cannot heal on the Sabbath? It is not there. It's an assumption that healing is work. However, healing is mercy not work. This is what Messiah is clearly demonstrating. It is Pharisee doctrine because Pharisees don't heal people. In fact, they harm them. However, they wish to stop you from healing someone on the Sabbath and they tried to entrap Him once again.

Is a man not better than a sheep that he too is entitled healing and deliverance even on the Sabbath? Messiah, the Judge of all, says it is lawful to do well on the Sabbath days.

The next arena most modern scholars will attempt mischaracterization is that of the Sermon on the Mount where many of them claim He established new Law. We will examine this next.

The Sermon On the Mount

Matthew 5

New Law? Or Reinforcing Moses?

Chapter 5 | The Sermon on the Mount: New Law or Reinforcing Moses?

In His famous Sermon on the Mount from Matthew 5, Jesus *(Yahusha)* is said to have established New Law. This is where He abolishes the old and in with the new we are told. However, that view requires one to ignore the purpose of this entire sermon that He established from the start. After the Beatitudes and encouragement, He begins the Law portion with this thesis.

> ### Matthew 5:17-18 KJV
>
> *Think not that I am come to destroy the law, or the prophets: I am not come to destroy, but to fulfil. For verily I say unto you, Till heaven and earth pass, one jot or one tittle shall in no wise pass from the law, till all be fulfilled.*

He says: "Before I begin my sermon, let me just say I did not come to destroy the Law or the entire Old Testament." He just affirmed the entire Old Testament and the Law as His foundation. Reading in fragments will cause one to miss this. However, He declares: "I came to fulfill the Law and the prophets." We cover the definition of fulfill which never means "passed away" but He kept the Law in full. He will fulfill prophesies but once He does, we don't throw them away and choose never to speak of them again. When is the Law completed however?

He does not leave that to interpretation but spells it out very clearly. The time stamp for the application of the Law is at least until heaven and earth pass. When does that happen? Not until the Day of Final Judgment. Not one letter of the Law, the one in place at this time before this sermon and the one from the prophets and Moses, shall pass away until that point. As we are not there yet, He just said the Law remains and I will not abolish it but fulfill it or keep it as an example for you. He was without sin thus He perfected the Law in observance. He did exactly what He said He would do. However, the church has abolished what He said He would not and He even fixed a date in the future. What does He think of those who are teaching against His own words in this very passage even?

> ### *Matthew 5:19-20 KJV*
> *Whosoever therefore shall break one of these least commandments, and shall teach men so, he shall be called the least in the kingdom of heaven: but whosoever shall do and teach them, the same shall be called great in the kingdom of heaven. For I say unto you, That except your righteousness shall exceed the righteousness of the scribes and Pharisees, ye shall in no case enter into the kingdom of heaven.*

First, he addresses seminaries of the future *(today)* and pastors who follow them in teaching us to break His commandments even the least. He demotes them to the least position in His kingdom. They don't lose their salvation necessarily though it is probable that many such have no relationship with Him. However, those of us who teach His Commandments will be called great in His kingdom to come.

Second, Jesus*(Yahusha)* addresses the Pharisees and tells us not to follow their false righteousness which He rebukes many times. He tells us our relationship must exceed the Pharisees in righteousness or we will not be saved. Pharisees focus on legalism, public giving for a plaque with one's name on it, being seen as righteous but not actually executing righteousness. They are not righteous nor is He saying they are. If they truly were, they would not be used as the benchmark for unrighteous and not saved. A Pharisee can be saved and some were in the New Testament. However, in general, they will not.

Essentially, He is reinforcing His Law that derives from the Old Testament and condemning the modified Law of leaven of the Pharisees. As He continues, Messiah deals basically with 6 Laws of sort. Did He just make up 6 new Laws? Have we really never read of these Laws previously? Are they not in the Old Testament? Again, Jesus*(Yahusha)* is known to teach and explain things that had gotten misinterpreted over the years. He came during the Pharisee era that defiled His Temple.

1. Anger (Matt. 5:21-24)

> *Matthew 5:21-24 KJV*
> *Ye have heard that it was said of them of old time, Thou shalt not kill; and*
> *whosoever shall kill shall be in danger of the judgment: But I say unto you,*
> *That whosoever is angry with his brother without a cause shall be in danger*
> *of the judgment: and whosoever shall say to his brother, Raca, shall be in*
> *danger of the council: but whosoever shall say, Thou fool, shall be in danger*
> *of hell fire. Therefore if thou bring thy gift to the altar, and there rememberest*
> *that thy brother hath ought against thee; Leave there thy gift before the altar,*
> *and go thy way; first be reconciled to thy brother, and then come and offer thy*
> *gift.*

Notice He begins with the first Law here telling us this is the one from the time of old or from the Law of Moses and really previously all the way to Adam. Did Messiah abolish "thou shalt not kill?" Of course not. Moses' Law stands affirmed here. He deepened it in a sense but truly only in interpretation as the Law of Moses also says not to be angry with your brother. That, too, is not New Law.

> ***Exodus 20:13 KJV 6th Commandment***
> ***Thou shalt not kill.***

> ***Leviticus 19:18 KJV***
> ***Thou shalt not avenge, nor bear any grudge*** *against the children*
> *of thy people, but* ***thou shalt love thy neighbour as thyself:*** *I am*
> *the Lord.*

The Law says not to bear a grudge nor avenge and to love your neighbor as yourself. These are not new concepts but Messiah reasserts Yahuah's Law of Moses. Remember, the 10 Commandments and other portions of Law were written by the finger of Yahuah. Even the Prophet Zechariah understood this meaning as well thus this is not new.

> **Zechariah 8:17 KJV**
> *And let none of you imagine evil in your hearts against his neighbour; and love*
> *no false oath: for all these are things that I hate, saith the LORD.*

2. Lust (Matt. 5:27-30)

In terms of adultery, where does it begin? One does not just find themselves in bed with their neighbor and wonder how that happened. It begins with lust. Again, man did not change, that was the same in the days of Moses. In dealing with adultery, Messiah affirms the Law of Moses and then, He expounds on it's meaning from the time of old.

> **Matthew 5:27-30 KJV**
> *Ye have heard that it was said by them of old time, Thou shalt not commit*
> *adultery: But I say unto you, That whosoever looketh on a woman to lust after*
> *her hath committed adultery with her already in his heart. And if thy right eye*
> *offend thee, pluck it out, and cast it from thee: for it is profitable for thee that*
> *one of thy members should perish, and not that thy whole body should be cast*
> *into hell. And if thy right hand offend thee, cut it off, and cast it from thee: for*
> *it is profitable for thee that one of thy members should perish, and not that thy*
> *whole body should be cast into hell.*

He again quotes the Law of Moses to start on adultery. He defines for us the inception of adultery is in lusting after another in one's heart because that is the true seed. This is not a new thought either. In setting the Law, Moses may not have explained it as thoroughly but the mindset is found in the Old Testament thus not new.

> **Exodus 20:14 KJV 7th Commandment**
> *Thou shalt not commit adultery.*

How do we interpret this? Can it be deepened to the point of lust according to the Old Testament? Proverbs in terms of the Commandment itself even regarding adultery, specifies exactly the same as Messiah in understanding. Thus this is not even a new understanding. Let's be clear though. Messiah never said He was going to set new Law but started this sermon on the foundation of the Law and the prophets. Only modern scholars make up their own Gospel in this claiming this must be new Law. It is not.

> ### Proverbs 6:23-25 KJV
> *For the commandment is a lamp; and the law is light; and reproofs of instruction are the way of life: To keep thee from the evil woman, from the flattery of the tongue of a strange woman. Lust not after her beauty in thine heart; neither let her take thee with her eyelids.*

3. Divorce (Matt. 5:31-32)

The highly debated topic of divorce today seems elusive yet the Bible is far clearer and Messiah defines this well. However, this time He clarifies where the thinking comes from that He addresses. He no longer says this thinking comes from olden times but just it has been said. He is expressing that the Pharisees are not teaching the Bible nor do they represent it but they say you can essentially put your wife away for any reason. This has never been the intent of the Law as Moses gives specifics and Messiah gives the same.

> ### Matthew 5:31-32 KJV
> *It hath been said, Whosoever shall put away his wife, let him give her a writing of divorcement: But I say unto you, That whosoever shall put away his wife, saving for the cause of fornication, causeth her to commit adultery: and whosoever shall marry her that is divorced committeth adultery.*

Though He hates divorce, there is a reason in which it is lawful. If your spouse commits adultery, then, that is the only reason in which it is permissible. It does not change His disdain for it nor the sanctity of the institution. However, He offers nothing new but the ancient understanding in which the Law of Moses has always represented. He is addressing those who say things that are the Pharisees who are putting their wives away for arbitrary reasons. That has never been lawful. In fact, Jesus *(Yahusha)* expressed exactly that later in Matthew when He says "from the beginning it was not so."

Matthew 19:7-9 KJV

They say unto him, Why did Moses then command to give a writing of divorcement, and to put her away? He saith unto them, Moses because of the hardness of your hearts suffered you to put away your wives: but from the beginning it was not so. And I say unto you, Whosoever shall put away his wife, except it be for fornication, and shall marry another, committeth adultery: and whoso marrieth her which is put away doth commit adultery.

Deuteronomy 24:1-2 KJV

When a man hath taken a wife, and married her, and it come to pass that she find no favour in his eyes, because he hath found some uncleanness in her: then let him write her a bill of divorcement, and give it in her hand, and send her out of his house. And when she is departed out of his house, she may go and be another man's wife.

Jesus *(Yahusha)* is defining this "uncleanness" specifically as adultery which has always been the case. The Pharisees defiled this understanding. However, this has always been a scriptural understanding even in the Old Testament. Yahuah divorced Israel because she played the harlot and committed adultery. Remember, we are His bride and He is the groom. He defines us as married in that sense. Yahuah hates divorce but He executed it Himself. In the end, the good news is He will forgive and He will take her *(us)* back both Israel and the grafted Gentiles.

Jeremiah 3: 8 KJV

And I saw, when for all the causes whereby backsliding Israel committed adultery I had put her away, and given her a bill of divorce; yet her treacherous sister Judah feared not, but went and played the harlot also.

4. Oaths (Matt. 5:33-37)

Let your yes, be yes and no, be no. This sage wisdom is profound but also not new. The Law of Moses certainly deals with oaths in that it tells us to keep our word as if to Yahuah when we make them. Messiah says don't swear oaths at all. Somehow that is misrepresented as meaning He set New Law. However, Moses never says to make oaths. He only says to keep your word regarding those in which you make. There is no inconsistency here. Is Messiah now saying don't keep your word? Of course not. He did not abolish the Law of Moses but further explained.

> **Matthew 5:33-37 KJV**
> *Again, ye have heard that it hath been said by them of old time, Thou shalt not forswear thyself, but shalt perform unto the Lord thine oaths: But I say unto you, Swear not at all; neither by heaven; for it is God's throne: Nor by the earth; for it is his footstool: neither by Jerusalem; for it is the city of the great King. Neither shalt thou swear by thy head, because thou canst not make one hair white or black. But let your communication be, Yea, yea; Nay, nay: for whatsoever is more than these cometh of evil.*

Though a little different in scope, Moses also says not to swear or take oaths by His name falsely. What was Jesus*(Yahusha)* clarifying then? He is clearly addressing Pharisees who changed such meaning. They swear oaths and have expanded the definition. This is the church system of that age as synagogues were not found in the Old Testament until the Pharisees. They are a Babylonian concept not Bible. However, the Pharisees are also good at demanding oaths to this day. These oaths lead to slavery of sort and Messiah rebuked this. There are even churches who follow this freemasonic, Pharisee doctrine to this day requiring one to take an oath to their church doctrine. Don't do it.

> **Leviticus 19:12 KJV**
> *And ye shall not swear by my name falsely, neither shalt thou profane the name of thy God: I am the Lord.*

> **Numbers 30:2-3 KJV**
> *If a man vow a vow unto the Lord, or swear an oath to bind his soul with a bond; he shall not break his word, he shall do according to all that proceedeth out of his mouth. If a woman also vow a vow unto the Lord, and bind herself by a bond, being in her father's house in her youth;*

5. Revenge (Matt. 5:38-42)

Matthew 5:38-42 KJV

Ye have heard that it hath been said, An eye for an eye, and a tooth for a tooth: But I say unto you, That ye resist not evil: but whosoever shall smite thee on thy right cheek, turn to him the other also. And if any man will sue thee at the law, and take away thy coat, let him have thy cloak also. And whosoever shall compel thee to go a mile, go with him twain. Give to him that asketh thee, and from him that would borrow of thee turn not thou away.

Once again, Jesus*(Yahusha)* is not addressing Moses here as this is not an understanding from olden times but again, what is being said. This is how Pharisees operate and he is addressing them. In Moses' day, the justice system required equal punishment for the crime. If you take someone's eye, your sentence would be to lose the same eye. If you knock out the tooth of your neighbor, then your sentence would be to lose a tooth. Moses never wrote of revenge and he is not being addressed here. Clearly, this had been corrupted into revenge. The sentence under Moses was not evil nor is Messiah calling it that as it was justice.

Also, this is where we get the "turn the other cheek" motto. However, notice what Messiah has done throughout in facing the Pharisees. He did not turn the other cheek, He embraced debate and wiped the floor with them. He called them names such as "brood of vipers," "hypocrites all," "liars," and even the seed of satan. He did so in love and we follow his example not an emasculated phony definition of love which is absent rebuke. That would be impotent. That is the tactic of those who deceive as they attempt to silence their opposition who represents the truth. It is the weakest of positions and not how He applied this.

Also, notice, the Law of Moses is really setting national law on this whereas Messiah discusses what you will do in response not the nation. What is left of Israel, Judaea or 2 tribes and some Levites, is under the Roman Empire's thumb and if one applied this at that time when the national power was gone, there is no protection for them as there was in the time of Moses.

Exodus 21:24-25 KJV

Eye for eye, tooth for tooth, hand for hand, foot for foot, Burning for burning, wound for wound, stripe for stripe.

Leviticus 24:20 KJV

Breach for breach, eye for eye, tooth for tooth: as he hath caused a blemish in a man, so shall it be done to him again.

However, the manner in application of an eye for an eye in which Messiah is addressing is that of revenge. Revenge has always been forbidden in the Law of Moses thus He is not addressing Moses here. These are the doctrines of men from the Pharisees in which He rebukes.

Leviticus 19:18 KJV

Thou shalt not avenge, nor bear any grudge against the children of thy people, but thou shalt love thy neighbour as thyself: I am the Lord.

6. Hate Your Enemy (Matt. 5:43-48)

Does Moses say to hate your enemy? Messiah is not addressing Moses in this passage yet again as Moses does not say that. This again is those who say things not from olden times from the Law.

Matthew 5:43-48 KJV

Ye have heard that it hath been said, Thou shalt love thy neighbour, and hate thine enemy. But I say unto you, Love your enemies, bless them that curse you, do good to them that hate you, and pray for them which despitefully use you, and persecute you; That ye may be the children of your Father which is in heaven: for he maketh his sun to rise on the evil and on the good, and sendeth rain on the just and on the unjust. For if ye love them which love you, what reward have ye? do not even the publicans the same? And if ye salute your brethren only, what do ye more than others? do not even the publicans so? Be ye therefore perfect, even as your Father which is in heaven is perfect.

Frankly, David is a great example of Messiah's words here as King Saul became his enemy attempting to kill him yet even at the opportunity to kill Saul, David refused but loved him instead *(1 Sam. 18)*. The concept is not new to the Bible. It is foreign to Pharisees who do hold grudges and seek revenge even in Messiah's time and still today. However, Moses said not to seek revenge as well as to love your neighbor as yourself.

Leviticus 19:18 KJV

Thou shalt not avenge, nor bear any grudge against the children of thy people, but thou shalt love thy neighbour as thyself: I am the Lord.

Again in Proverbs, we find the writers of the Old Testament well knew how to interpret the Law that agrees with Messiah and in fact, is His origin. There is nothing new about this concept either. We were never supposed to hate our enemy but to love them. Pharisees however, are proven to hate their enemies to death as even evidenced in the Gospels many times.

Proverbs 25:21 KJV

If thine enemy be hungry, give him bread to eat; and if he be thirsty, give him water to drink:

Yahuah told this same to the Prophet Zechariah as well. He did not begin hating these abominations in the New Testament and Yahusha represented this same Law.

Zechariah 8:17 KJV

And let none of you imagine evil in your hearts against his neighbour; and love no false oath: for all these are things that I hate, saith the LORD.

The following chart will serve to assist in visualizing that Messiah's Sermon on the Mount was not setting New Law but reasserting and restoring the Law of Moses which had been manipulated by Pharisee leaven. On the six major topics He addresses, He never once abolishes a single law of Moses. He deepens some but again, a reading of the Old Testament understanding does not disagree with Messiah's interpretation either. We find no credibility in this doctrine of men that claims Messiah established new law in Matthew 5.

How is it we forget He came to us as the Word *(John 1)* and "Messenger of the Covenant?" *(right)* How can the Word abolish itself? What is the

Word? At the time of His coming it was the Old Testament only and it contained the Law and Covenant. How could the embodiment of the Law and Covenant who kept it perfectly be said to then abandon the very measure to which He lived? Abolish Himself? How could any scholar suppose that could ever mean because He lived up to such measure, none of us ever have a measure again? Let us not forget as well Messiah said this same Law in place that He kept would not pass at least until the Day of Final Judgment *(Matt. 5:17-18)*. The very standard by which we are to live is His example yet essentially it has become church doctrine to no longer aspire to live like Him. He was sinless or lawful. The Law He followed was that of Moses or really that written by the finger of Yahuah. This He treasured yet what does this say about a church who represents the opposite of what He treasured and lived.

And it happened, as He spoke these things, that a certain woman from the crowd raised her voice and said to Him, "Blessed is the womb that bore You, and the breasts which nursed You!" But He said, "More than that, blessed are those who hear the word of God and keep it!"

—Luke 11:27-28 KJV

"Behold, I send My messenger, And he will prepare the way before Me. And the Lord, whom you seek, Will suddenly come to His temple, Even the Messenger of the covenant, In whom you delight. Behold, He is coming," Says the LORD of hosts.

—Malachi 3:1 KJV

Sermon on the Mount
Affrimation of the Law of Moses

1. Anger	2. Lust	3. Divorce
(Matt. 5:21-24)	*(Matt. 5:27-30)*	*(Matt. 5:31-32)*
No killing **No anger without cause** **No grudges**	**No adultery** **Looking in lust is adultery** *Looking in lust has always been adultery.*	**Divorce is adultery except in the case of fornication which is uncleanness of the spouse and always has been** *Moses writes the same.*
Exodus 20:13 KJV *Thou shalt not kill.* *Leviticus 19:18 KJV* *Thou shalt not avenge, nor bear any grudge against the children of thy people, but thou shalt love thy neighbour as thyself: I am the Lord.* *Zec. 8:17 KJV: And let none of you imagine evil in your hearts against his neighbour... for all these are things that I hate...*	*Exodus 20:14 KJV* *Thou shalt not commit adultery.* *Proverbs 6:23-25 KJV* *For the commandment is a lamp; and the law is light; and reproofs of instruction are the way of life: To keep thee from the evil woman, from the flattery of the tongue of a strange woman. Lust not after her beauty in thine heart; neither let her take thee with her eyelids.*	*Deuteronomy 24:1-2 KJV* *When a man hath taken a wife, and married her, and it come to pass that she find no favour in his eyes, because he hath found some uncleanness in her: then let him write her a bill of divorcement, and give it in her hand, and send her out of his house. And when she is departed out of his house, she may go and be another man's wife.*
# Not New! *Messiah Reasserts Yahuah's Law of Moses*	# Not New! *Messiah Reasserts Yahuah's Law of Moses*	# Not New! *Messiah Reasserts Yahuah's Law of Moses*

4. Oaths (Matt. 5:33-37)	5. Revenge (Matt. 5:38-42)	6. Hate (Matt. 5:43-48)
No oaths *This is a further clarification. One is never told to take oaths with Moses. However, if you give your word, you are to keep it. Messiah simply says don't take oaths in the first place.*	**Turn the other cheek when smitten** *This is a further clarification. However, we are never to bear a grudge nor avenge in the Law of Moses either. Revenge has always been forbidden.*	**Love Neighbor Love Enemy** *The Law of Moses never says to hate your enemy. He is addressing Pharisee doctrine not Moses. Moses wrote similar and so did Solomon and Zechariah.*
Leviticus 19:12 KJV *And ye shall not swear by my name falsely, neither shalt thou profane the name of thy God: I am the Lord.* *Numbers 30:2-3 KJV* *If a man vow a vow unto the Lord, or swear an oath to bind his soul with a bond; he shall not break his word, he shall do according to all that proceedeth out of his mouth. Zec. 8:17: ...and love no false oath...*	*Leviticus 24:20 KJV* *Breach for breach, eye for eye, tooth for tooth: as he hath caused a blemish in a man, so shall it be done to him again. (Cf. Ex. 21:24) (This refers to equal punishment fitting the crime)* *Leviticus 19:18 KJV* *Thou shalt not avenge, nor bear any grudge against the children of thy people, but thou shalt love thy neighbour as thyself: I am the Lord.*	*Deuteronomy 24:1-4 KJV* *For if ye love them which love you, what reward have ye? do not even the publicans the same? And if ye salute your brethren only, what do ye more than others? do not even the publicans so? Be ye therefore perfect, even as your Father which is in heaven is perfect.* *Cf. Lev. 19:18; Prov. 25:21; Zec. 8:17*
## Not New! *Messiah Reasserts Yahuah's Law of Moses*	## Not New! *Messiah Reasserts Yahuah's Law of Moses*	## Not New! *Messiah Reasserts Yahuah's Law of Moses*

This is NOT New Law!

It is absurd to suggest such and call oneself a scholar.

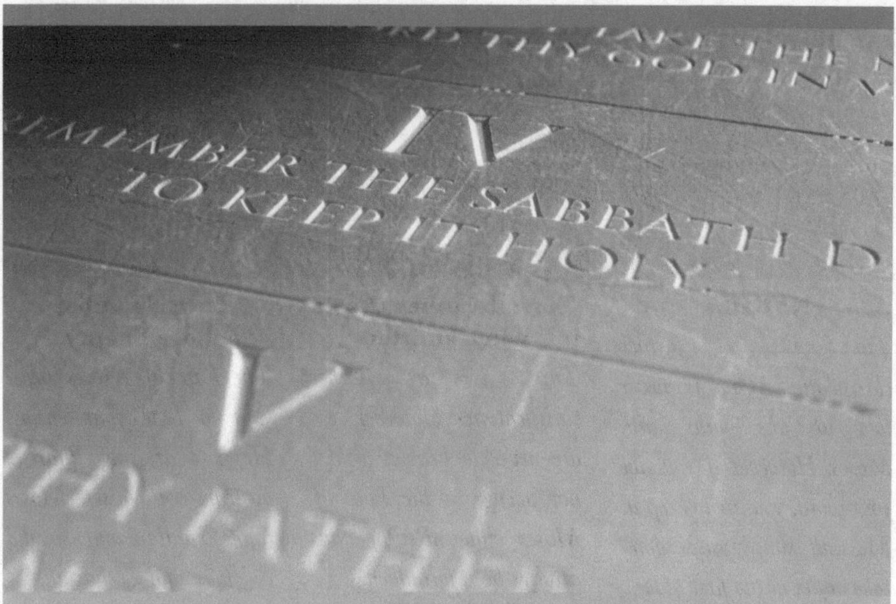

the APOSTLES kept the SABBATH of the OLD TESTAMENT

So did the Gentiles!

Chapter 6 | The Apostles Kept the Sabbath Of the Old Testament

If Messiah had abolished the Sabbath and the Feasts, we will find the Apostles after His ascension abandoning them. Otherwise, it appears they did not get the same message from Jesus *(Yahusha)* as do many modern scholars who seem to desire to make their own Bible not Yahuah's. This is a problem for the church generally when they are ignoring the Biblical practice and precedent standing vehemently against it in obvious ignorance. We will address the Pope and Pharisees in coming chapters as well. Though much is extracted in fragments from Paul which we will deal with in detail next chapter, we find the Apostles and Paul observed and taught the Sabbath and Biblical Feasts according to very abundant scripture over 85 Sabbaths in the Book of Acts alone *(see chart p. 353)*.

You will never find the apostles keeping Christmas nor even Easter though they shoved them in there in fraud as the only 1 time the word Easter appears in scripture, it is the same Greek word always interpreted as Passover not Easter. Indeed, they are willing to fraud and change the Bible and we will address this. Their penalty for doing so is severe. However, as established in the previous, we already know the disciples observed the Sabbath many times during Messiah's ministry on Earth.

Just as it was Jesus' *(Yahusha's)* custom to keep the Sabbath, Luke says the same of Paul. Was Paul now keeping Sunday? Acts is clear and we will cover, the Sabbath remained the 7th Day. In this passage, in addition to establishing a tradition of Paul's keeping Sabbath and on Saturday, the pattern is demonstrated over 3-consecutive Sabbaths that Paul kept and taught.

Acts 17:2 KJV

And Paul, as his manner was, went in unto them, and three sabbath days reasoned with them out of the scriptures

Paul traveled and yet we find him keeping the Sabbath and the Feast Sabbaths all over and with fervor. He was devout. One cannot ignore that Feasts have Sabbaths as well and that is Sabbath observance of a different day but the practice is similar. No Feast Sabbath observance ever changes the Weekly Sabbath and we will cover that in a chapter as well. Both serve to reinforce each other. We are told the Sabbath and the Feasts passed yet that is not what the Bible ever says. Paul and the Apostles followed in the example of Jesus *(Yahusha)* as they must.

Acts 13:13-14 KJV

Now when Paul and his company loosed from Paphos, they came to Perga in Pamphylia: and John departing from them returned to Jerusalem. But when they departed from Perga, they came to Antioch in Pisidia, and went into the synagogue on the sabbath day, and sat down.

What are you doing Paul? Did you not get the memo. You are supposed to keep Sunday now not Saturday, the 7th day. No one would attempt to claim synagogues changed their Sabbath to Sunday and where is Paul teaching? The Sabbath remains Saturday.

Acts 13:16 KJV

Then Paul stood up, and beckoning with his hand said, Men of Israel, and ye that fear God, give audience.

Paul continues with his sermon in Acts 13 where he preaches on the Old Testament largely including Israel in Egypt, Israel in Canaan, Judges, and King David. He, then, moves forward to John the Baptist finishing with Messiah's Resurrection. He melts the Old and the New as all the Apostles do and pastors should be doing as well. There is no wall between the two. They did not have the New Testament yet but preached salvation from the Old as well because it is not a new concept. How often does your pastor preach salvation from the Old Testament? Hebrews even says part of that Gospel should be the Sabbath even.

Acts 13:27 KJV

For they that dwell at Jerusalem, and their rulers, because they knew him not,

nor yet the voices of the prophets which are read every sabbath day, they have
fulfilled them in condemning him.

Paul is talking about the Pharisees. Those who try to characterize him as continuing to teach Pharisaism, are not reading Paul who condemns their practice. He no longer observed their ways. The writings of the prophets are still read every Sabbath even by the Apostles who teach from them. Paul just did that. When they use the term Sabbath in Acts after Messiah's ascension, they link it firmly as the same 7th day as that of Moses. It did not change and they did not practice it differently but the same as Messiah who did the same as Moses. How can anyone claim it changed yet no scriptural support ever says so? They add to the Word.

Every Old Testament patriarch is saved just as any New Testament believer. We all have the promise of salvation if we are in relationship with Him and yes, He is throughout the Old Testament as well just not in the flesh yet. The question is does the Law of Moses save? No, nor did it in the Old Testament either. The Law is not salvation. Sabbath is not salvation. These accompany believers as baptism does. However, they are the signs of relationship and that matters most. If we are in a true relationship with Him, we are saved. If we are not and think we can just say a prayer without progressing into a relationship, we were never saved in the first place. Again, read Matthew 7 and John 15 for Messiah's full definition of salvation. It is not a fragment nor is it about street witnessing with fragments. Discipleship is much more involved.

Acts 13:39 KJV

And by him all that believe are justified from all things, from which ye could
not be justified by the law of Moses.

Does any scripture ever say we are justified by the Law of Moses even in the Old Testament? No. Not if we are reading it properly. Again, the Law is not salvation, relationship is and that has always been the case since Adam. Who is it that teaches that strange doctrine then? The Pharisees. We will cover specific instances from scripture where they claim circumcision and keeping the Law of Moses is salvation. That is never Biblical. They are liars and their doctrine is being obliterated by the Apostles especially Paul constantly as well as Messiah.

> **Acts 13:40-41 KJV**
> *Beware therefore, lest that come upon you, which is spoken of in the prophets;*
> *Behold, ye despisers, and wonder, and perish: for I work a work in your days,*
> *a work which ye shall in no wise believe, though a man declare it unto you.*

The Sabbath day was at the center of their worship and again, this is after Messiah's ascension and they are still inserting the teachings of the prophets and their practice as theirs in continuance. Therefore, unless one can make a case they were in rebellion, which cannot be done, the Apostles were following what He told them. He did not abolish the Sabbath. In fact, even the Gentiles kept the Sabbath.

> **Acts 13:42 KJV**
> *And when the Jews were gone out of the synagogue,* **the Gentiles besought that these words might be preached to them the next sabbath.**
> **Acts 13:44 KJV**
> *And* **the next sabbath day came almost the whole city together to hear the word of God.**

Yes, the Bible says Gentiles kept the Sabbath. Not only does this establish their meeting in synagogues on the Saturday *(7th Day)* Sabbath, but they even requested Paul preach again next week on the same Sabbath they were observing. This pattern is obvious and never changes and proves Paul and the Apostles and even the Gentiles kept the Sabbath. It is illiterate and unscholarly to attempt a counterpoint and ridicule the Bible which should be our foundation not any church doctrine.

> **Acts 15:13 KJV** *[James with Paul and Barnabas]*
> *And after they had held their peace, James answered, saying, Men and brethren, hearken unto me:*
> **Acts 15:18 KJV** *[James with Paul and Barnabas]*
> *Known unto God are all his works from the beginning of the world.*

Acts 15:21-22 KJV

For Moses of old time hath in every city them that preach him, being read in the synagogues every sabbath day. Then pleased it the apostles and elders, with the whole church, to send chosen men of their own company to Antioch with Paul and Barnabas; namely, Judas surnamed Barsabas, and Silas, chief men among the brethren:

Here James*(Yacob)*, the brother of Jesus*(Yahusha)* is preaching once again regarding all of Yahuah's works from the beginning. In other words, Sabbath which is the 7th Day Creation. What does one do on the Sabbath? Since the time of Torah written by Moses, they would read Torah every Sabbath to the people and teach from it. You will once again find the "strangers among them" fully participating as equals according to scripture which we will cover. That is not a new practice in the New Testament either. Throughout Messiah's time we see this affirmed. Now, after His ascension again.

Acts 16:13 KJV [Paul and Disciples in Philippi]

And on the sabbath we went out of the city by a river side, where prayer was wont to be made; and we sat down, and spake unto the women which resorted thither.

The Apostles are teaching and having ekklesia on Sabbath. They did not only do this in the Synagogue as some illiterate scholars attempt in ridicule. They did so outside of the synagogue as well in ekklesia. This is the true practice of the true early ekklesia on Saturday. Who cares what Rome practiced? They are not the early church if they preach another Gospel that Paul and the Apostles never preached. Once again, not just Jews*(Yahudim)* met in the Synagogues practicing the 7th Day *(Saturday)* Sabbath, so did Gentiles or Greeks. They were following the Apostles. Rome was not and proves they are not the Bible practice.

Acts 18:1-4 KJV

After these things Paul departed from Athens, and came to Corinth; And found a certain Jew named Aquila, born in Pontus, lately come from Italy, with his wife Priscilla; (because that Claudius had commanded all Jews to depart from Rome:) and came unto them. And he reasoned in the synagogue every sabbath, and persuaded the Jews and the Greeks. And when Silas and Timotheus were come from Macedonia, Paul was pressed in the spirit, and testified to the Jews that Jesus was Christ.

In confirmation time and time again, Paul and the Apostles are keeping the Sabbath on Saturday. Even a Biblically endorsed ekklesia leader from Rome was also still keeping the Saturday Sabbath. Notice, he was driven out of Rome so whomever is saying Rome is the origin of the early ekklesia is a liar and does not know scripture. They drove out the ekklesia and the practice of changing Sabbath was not among the true ekklesia but the foundation of the blasphemous, anti-Bible Catholic Church. Timothy and Silas join for what is termed as EVERY Sabbath in observance of the Sabbath which remains the 7th day, Saturday. This was not just pocket groups, it was the entire early ekklesia, the real one. Any writing found or any person in that era known as changing the Sabbath to Sunday, was not part of the early ekklesia. They had another religion and followed strange doctrine as they are those who crept in.

Acts 9:31 KJV
Then had the churches rest throughout all Judaea and Galilee and Samaria, and were edified; and walking in the fear of the Lord, and in the comfort of the Holy Ghost, were multiplied.

The passage continues as Peter performs miracles just as Messiah did on the Sabbath. This is the Sabbath on the 7th day and the entire early ekklesia kept it in observance in continuation of the Old Testament Sabbath practice. They invoke the prophets and the observance of Moses as theirs. There is no debating this and the fact that we have a centuries old argument here, is proof of an anti-Bible and anti-Christ so-called church which is the opposite of the Biblical ekklesia. Clearly the Bible practice is foreign to them. Thus, why listen to them at all? Have we not read all of Messiah's warnings especially from Turkey's Synagogue of Satan who say they are Yahudim and are not but do lie *(Rev. 2:9, 3:9)* and where the Catholic Church originated?

We then find the Pope even endorsing the supposed find of the Didache full of Catholic doctrine from the time of the Apostles in about 50-70 A.D. supposedly including the Sunday practice. If that dating is accurate, this document proves they are the Synagogue of Satan as they do not follow the practice of the Biblical ekklesia at the same time in the same area where they are said by Messiah to have operated even. If older dating of 3rd to 4th century, it is still no less damning.

We then find in addition to the Weekly Sabbath, the Apostles continuing to keep the Feast Sabbaths. That is significant as the two cannot be separated. Yahuah commanded Israel to keep the Sabbath and the 7 Biblical Feasts follow in the next sentences. These are all Mo'edim Biblically sanctioned and you will not find Christmas and Easter among them. Though Messiah has come in fulfillment of the Spring Feasts, they, too, have never changed. We no longer offer animal sacrifices because Jesus' *(Yahusha's)* sacrifice covers all sacrifices forever. However, the Apostles continued this observance with the Sabbath after His ascension and they were not in rebellion.

Acts 2:1 KJV

And when the day of Pentecost was fully come, they were all with one accord in one place.

Messiah was born on the Feast of Weeks known in Hebrew as Shavuot *(Shabuot in Ancient Hebrew)* and Pentecost in Greek. We prove this over multiple videos entitled "When Was Jesus Born" and "The Restoration of Shavuot" where we find overwhelming evidence of this especially that Isaac, whom Messiah mirrors in covenant, was born on this day. Christmas, which has pagan origins, is a counterfeit replacement the wrong time of year just as Easter has been paraded as Passover/Unleavened Bread yet it has truly pagan fertility origins, thus the bunnies and eggs. These are not the practices of the early ekklesia but a branch of the Synagogue of Satan.

We have curated a chart that demonstrates Messiah and the Apostles keeping the Weekly Sabbath and Feast Sabbaths. This was an entrenched part of their observance. Next, we will deal directly with the ways in which Paul's epistles are taken out of context as he kept the Sabbath.

Born On, & Died On a Feast Day

New Testament Feasts

Messiah & Apostles Kept the Feasts

Passover/
Unleavened Bread
Matt. 5:17-18, 24, 26:2-19
Mark 14:12-16
Luke 2:41-42, 22:1-20
John 2:13-23, 6:4, 13:1-30
Crucified on 1st Day of
Unleavened Bread as Isaac:
Jub. 18:3
Mark 14:1-12, 15:1, 42-43
Luke 23:54-56

First Fruits
1 Cor. 15:20-23

Shavuot
Born on Shavuot as Isaac:
Jub. 16:12-13, Luke 1:26
Luke 22:27-30
Acts 2:1-4

In Prophecy:
Trumpets
(The Last Trump)
Matt. 24:30-31, 46-51, 25:13

Atonement
(Day of Judgment to Come)
Matt. 10:15, 11:22-24, 12:36
Luke 10:12-14
John 5:22, 12:31, 48

Tabernacles
(New Heavenly Bodies)
Matt. 17:2-3
Luke 9:28-36
Mark 4:30-32

Apostles After Ascension Kept the Feasts

Passover/
Unleavened Bread
Acts 12:3, 20:6-7, 18:20-21
1 Cor. 5:6-8, 11:23-26

First Fruits
1 Cor. 15:20-23
Romans 8:23

Shavuot
Acts 2:1-4; 1 Cor. 16:8

In Prophecy:
Trumpets
(The Last Trump)
1 Cor. 15:50-54
1 Thess. 4:13-18
Rev. 8:6, 10:7, 11:15-19, 16:17-21

Atonement
(Day of Judgment to Come)
Acts 17:31, 24:25
Rom. 2:16, 14:12
1 Pet. 4:5-17, 2 Pet. 2:4-9, 3:7
James 2:13
1 Cor. 1:18, 2 Cor. 5:10
1 John 4:17, Jude 1:6
Rev. 19:15, 20:12-13

Tabernacles
(New Heavenly Bodies)
Rom. 6:5-8, 7:20-25 , 8:28-30
Phil. 3:21
1 Cor 15:35-53
2 Cor. 3:17-18, 5:1-10,
1 Pet. 1:22-23, 2 Pet. 1:13-14
1 John 3:2-3
Revelation 21:1-4

Sabbath New Testament

Messiah & Apostles Kept the Sabbath

Matt. 11:28-30
Matt. 12:1-12
Mark 1:21,
Mark 2:27-28
Mark 6:2
Luke 4:16
Luke 13:10-17
John 5:2-19
John 7:22
John 9:14

Reusrrection:
Matt. 28:1
Mark 1
John 20:1-19
(ALL on Saturday, the 7th Day)

Apostles After Ascension Kept the Sabbath

Acts 9:31
Acts 13:13-44,
Acts 15:13-22
Acts 16:13
Acts 17:2
Acts 18:1-4

Gentiles & Jews Kept Sabbath
After Ascension:
Acts 13:42-44, 16:13, 18:1-11, 9:31
(even outside of the synagogue)

**The Entire Ekklesia Kept
Sabbath After Ascension:
Acts 9:31**
(ALL on Saturday, the 7th Day)

Did Messiah Void the Law? No.

Matthew 5:17-18 KJV

Think not that I am come to destroy the law, or the prophets: I am not come to destroy, but to fulfil. For verily I say unto you, Till heaven and earth pass, one jot or one tittle shall in no wise pass from the law, till all be fulfilled.

Did Paul Void the Law? No.

Romans 7:12 KJV

Wherefore the law is holy, and the commandment holy, and just, and good.

Romans 7:22 KJV

For I delight in the law of God after the inward man:

Romans 3:31 KJV

Do we then make void the law through faith? God forbid: yea, we establish the law.

Did Acts Void the Law? No.

Acts 24:14 (Also, 25:8)

But this I confess unto thee, that after the way which they call heresy, so worship I the God of my fathers, believing all things which are written in the law and in the prophets:

Be ye followers of me,
even as I also am of Christ.
1 Corinthians 11:1 KJV

But we know that the law is good,
if a man use it lawfully;
1 Timothy 1:8 KJV *(Pharisees did not)*

Chapter 7 | Did Paul Hate the Law?

Acts 24:14 KJV (Paul Speaking)
But this I confess unto thee, that after the way which they call heresy, so worship I the God of my fathers, believing all things which are written in the law and in the prophets:
Acts 25:8 KJV (Paul Speaking)
While he answered for himself, Neither against the law of the Jews, neither against the temple, nor yet against Caesar, have I offended any thing at all.

How is it that this guy who says and believes these things could ever be mischaracterized as saying the opposite? The writer of two-thirds of the entire New Testament has been under attack not just by Pharisees whom he is answering here, but by the false church for almost 2,000 years. These same Pharisee accusations turn up in church doctrine as valid when they are based on lies from Biblically proven liars. Then, the "Paul haters" exercise ridicule also accepting this illiterate mindset and they claim Paul's words, two-thirds of the entire New Testament, must be ignored. This is very telling as to the days in which we live. Lies are becoming the espoused truth. Truth is being labeled a lie or "conspiracy theory" or "flat-earthers" or whatever nasty label they can affix to dismiss truth and embrace falsehood. It's time to prove this out and see what emerges as fact and what is fiction.

Paul said twice in these passages from Acts, after Messiah's ascension and being accused by Pharisees, he keeps the Law of Moses and teaches the writings of the prophets. We can observe this many times as he preaches from the Old Testament and observes the Law. Yes, the old one as it's basis doesn't pass away. We know Messiah told us it cannot pass, not one letter of it, at least until the Day of Final Judgment *(Matt. 5:17-18)*.

Galatians1:11-24 KJV

But I certify you, brethren, that the gospel which was preached of me is not after man. For I neither received it of man, neither was I taught it, but by the revelation of Jesus Christ. For ye have heard of my conversation in time past in the Jews' religion, how that beyond measure I persecuted the church of God, and wasted it: And profited in the Jews' religion above many my equals in mine own nation, being more exceedingly zealous of the traditions of my fathers. But when it pleased God, who separated me from my mother's womb, and called me by his grace, To reveal his Son in me, that I might preach him among the heathen; immediately I conferred not with flesh and blood: Neither went I up to Jerusalem to them which were apostles before me; but I went into Arabia, and returned again unto Damascus. Then after three years I went up to Jerusalem to see Peter, and abode with him fifteen days. But other of the apostles saw I none, save James the Lord's brother. Now the things which I write unto you, behold, before God, I lie not. Afterwards I came into the regions of Syria and Cilicia; And was unknown by face unto the churches of Judaea which were in Christ: But they had heard only, That he which persecuted us in times past now preacheth the faith which once he destroyed. And they glorified God in me.

We cannot imagine anyone more sincere and proven than the Apostle Paul save Messiah Himself. Understand at this point, Paul is admitting he used to be a Pharisee in doctrine that he said before but no longer as he follows the doctrines of Messiah that are the opposite according to Messiah Himself *(Mark 7:9)*. We will address this at the end of this chapter with other witnesses saying the same in scripture. He knew Peter which 2 Peter confirms even endorsing Paul's epistles as scripture *(2 Pet. 3:15-16)*. This is also evident in Jerusalem in Acts 13-15. He knew James, the brother of Jesus*(Yahusha)* as well *(Acts 15)*.

When captured by the Pharisees, Paul would invoke the rights in which he was born into such as being a Pharisee by blood in part from his father and the other part Hebrew, the tribe of Benjamin, through his mother. He would be unwise to not bring that up because there are rights that accompany that bloodline. He never said however, that he remained a Pharisee in doctrine and here he says he was no longer a Pharisee in doctrine. His writings are very clearly in rebuke of the

Pharisee paradigm that he well knew. This will be a long chapter of such examples. At the mercy of the Romans, he will exercise his Roman citizenship in which he was born into as a citizen of a Roman "Free City" in Tarsus of Asia Minor *(Modern Turkey)*.

Notice, Pharisees thrived there and throughout Turkey in those days as they were and remain the Synagogue of Satan who say they are Yahudim and are not but do lie *(Rev. 2:9, 3:9)*. Paul, however, was both part Pharisee and part Hebrew in blood. He even invokes the "Jew's religion" or Pharisaism *(modern Judaism)* which at that time, the Pharisees had hijacked the term and step in between the relationship put forth in scripture. They were not representative of the Bible relationship which Paul made clear many times as did Messiah.

The Pharisees were not Yahudim interpreted Jews in fraud as the short form for that word is Yah's not Jews. Those calling themselves scholars apply his rebuke of Pharisee interpretation of the Law of Moses in ignorance. Pharisees represent the opposite of Torah *(Mark 7:9)*. Paul is clear he converted and no longer remained a Pharisee of the "Jew's Religion" in doctrine.

Paul did not teach Pharisee doctrine. We have his words in two-thirds of the New Testament and they most certainly parallel Messiah in his teachings if we read them in context. Paul addressed Pharisaism many times throughout and his writings serve to clarify the distinction between what the Bible says and what Pharisees are teaching and accusing others of not following their interpretations. They did this to Messiah and His disciples many times. How is it that we forget that in reading Paul? We cannot. Peter tells us Paul was being taken out of context already 2,000 years ago. He calls Paul's epistles scripture and elevates him to the status of Apostle writing such. Peter did not endorse a Pharisee.

2 Peter 3:14-17 KJV

Wherefore, beloved, seeing that ye look for such things, be diligent that ye may be found of him in peace, without spot, and blameless. And account that the longsuffering of our Lord is salvation; even as our beloved brother Paul also according to the wisdom given unto him hath written unto you; As also in all his epistles, speaking in them of these things; in which are some things hard to be understood, which they that are unlearned and unstable wrest, as they do also the other scriptures, unto their own destruction. Ye therefore, beloved, seeing ye know these things before, beware lest ye also, being led away with the error of the wicked, fall from your own stedfastness.

This chapter will revisit this in detail. However, let us begin in addressing one of the fragments taken outrageously out of context to render the opposite of what Paul believed and taught. Here is the fragment:

Colossians 2:16 KJV

Let no man therefore judge you in meat, or in drink, or in respect of an holyday, or of the new moon, or of the sabbath days:

When one only reads these words, forgets or doesn't know whom Paul was, and at least acts oblivious as to who the Pharisees were and what they taught, then, they conclude this says we are not to keep the Sabbath. See, it's right there they say. No more holy days, no more Sabbath. Of course, those same hypocrites then celebrate pagan replacements of such most of the time. They are not representing the Word as this fragment is not what Paul just said. Let's review the entire passage but first, who was Paul?

Paul observed the Sabbath many times documented in writing by others as that was his custom just as Messiah that we will prove and after Messiah's ascension. He tells us Messiah Himself spoke to him and he learned from him thus his keeping the Sabbath is in obedience to Jesus' *(Yahusha's)* command. That should not be a surprise as we have covered in abundance. Here is Paul's pattern:

Acts 17:2 KJV

And Paul, as his manner was, went in unto them, and three sabbath days reasoned with them out of the scriptures.

This is a fragment in context as we will cover Paul kept and taught the Sabbath and the Law of Moses. He can be rather complex but the real problem is the same Pharisee nonsense sticking their nose into Paul's words and twisting them. That Pharisee leaven is not only prevalent in the church today but it is entrenched in many church doctrines. They read Paul like they are Pharisees instead of taking his words in context.

Entire doctrines are derived from misreading Paul. Did Paul hate the Law of Moses? That is illiterate.

Romans 7:12 KJV

Wherefore the law is holy, and the commandment holy, and just, and good.

How can any scholar say the man that wrote that is now against the very commandment he says is holy, just and good? It requires what Peter calls in 2 Peter 3 where he deals with the end times paradigm and Paul – "willing ignorance." This is what we are rebuking in this writing proving from abundant scripture, these scholars do not represent the Bible nor Paul. The Bible says Paul delights in the Law of Yahuah.

Romans 7:22 KJV

For I delight in the law of God after the inward man:

What Law is Paul talking about? Paul is quoting Psalm 1:2 as he delights in the law just as David did, the man after Yahuah's own heart. He is delighting in the Law of Moses that is the Law after the spirit not the one after the flesh that he calls the contrary Law of Sin and Death which we will address. Did Paul believe in voiding and abolishing this law in which he delights and says is good, holy and just?

Romans 3:31 KJV

Do we then make void the law through faith? God forbid: yea, we establish the law.

Have we forgotten where faith comes from? We quote it by memory all the time yet what does it say? It comes by hearing the Word. We will cover this in this chapter as it is pertinent to Paul's mindset that originates in the Old Testament as did Messiah's. Now that we remember whom Paul is, we can read the passage in which we began with clarity and understanding. Is Paul saying to abandon that which he delights and preaches, says is good, holy and just and says not to abolish? In addition, to his actually teaching the Sabbath same as the Old Testament, Paul reaffirms all 10 commandments in his writings *(see chart p. 170)*. He did not establish new ones nor did he have such authority.

Did Paul Rebuke the Sabbath Observance of the Bible?

Colossians 2

This is one of the main passages repeated by many scholars in ignorance as they do not know who Paul was nor whom he was responding. For he never rebukes the Law of Moses as a commandment or doctrine of men. We are talking about the Law Yahuah wrote with His very finger and Paul knew this. Why don't scholars know this? Paul begins this letter with a warning of men who beguile with enticing words. Notice, those espousing the Serpent Seed Doctrine based solely on this word beguile are disproven as the Bible use of this word is not sexual.

> ### Colossians 2:4 KJV
> *And this I say, lest any man should beguile you with enticing words.*

He offers encouragement and another warning of those who spoil them through philosophy and vain deceit after their tradition. Messiah rebuked those who operate that way as well in Mark 7 and this is a warning of Pharisees. Their philosophy is filled with vain deceit and leaven in which we were warned many times. However, the church appears to overlook this today and instead gains even doctrine from Pharisees.

> ### Colossians 2:8 KJV
> *Beware lest any man spoil you through philosophy and vain deceit, after the tradition of men, after the rudiments of the world, and not after Christ.*

Now let's dive into some doctrine here. Paul is deep but you cannot forget whom he was when he writes. Pulling out fragments from Paul will lead to deception whether that is one's desire or not.

> ### Colossians 2:9-10 KJV
> *For in him dwelleth all the fulness of the Godhead bodily. And ye are complete in him, which is the head of all principality and power:*

Nowhere does the Old Testament tell us Messiah would not complete us. Instead the Messianic prophesies abound with this exact tone Paul is using. The prophets knew He would be the head of all *(Is. 9:6; Ps. 2:6, 24: 7-10, 68:11, 110:1; Zech. 9:9).* This is not a new declaration from Him nor His Apostles as much of the "New" Testament really originates in the Old.

In these next verses, somehow some scholars tend to read this and then ignore what it says. Paul is not saying circumcision is wrong, nor bad. He is not saying not to do it even. He is saying you are born again. His comparison is using circumcision as a meaningful practice but in a spiritual sense we are circumcised by Him without losing flesh. It does not mean one should not be circumcised and Paul is not speaking to 8-day old children here but adults especially Gentiles who were not raised in that practice. Circumcision is not salvation nor does the Old Testament ever say that it is. Here he even compares it to baptism that also is not salvation but something those are saved do to declare faith.

However, here Paul addresses what we will cover in major detail. He is discussing "Blotting out the handwriting of ordinances that was against us, which was contrary to us, and took it out of the way, nailing it to his cross." Is Paul saying the Law of Moses were ordinances against us and contrary to us? Some see thou shalt not and claim that is contrary to us which is illiterate. As we covered, the Law of Moses according to Paul is NOT contrary to us but a delight, holy, just and good, and NOT made void through faith. He tells us to establish the law yet then writes the opposite? The question is what Law is contrary to us? Not Moses' nor any Law of Yahuah. This Law is the Law of Sin and Death – the Law of the Flesh that is NOT the Law of Moses but the opposite.

Colossians 2:11-15 KJV

In whom also ye are circumcised with the circumcision made without hands, in putting off the body of the sins of the flesh by the circumcision of Christ: Buried with him in baptism, wherein also ye are risen with him through the faith of the operation of God, who hath raised him from the dead. And you, being dead in your sins and the uncircumcision of your flesh, hath he quickened together with him, having forgiven you all trespasses; Blotting out the handwriting of ordinances that was against us, which was contrary to us, and took it out of the way, nailing it to his cross; And having spoiled principalities and powers, he made a shew of them openly, triumphing over them in it.

Paul's telling us to be circumcised spiritually as we will cover, the Apostles, not just Paul, rendered a wise decision not to force adult Gentiles to now be circumcised. Ouch! They removed that stumbling block which the Pharisees were exploiting to confuse people. You will find that was not Paul's doctrine alone either, but that of all of the Apostles as a group. He represented them.

This is the build-up to our fragment taken out of context which is used ignorantly in debate to attempt to say Paul condemned Sabbath-keeping. However, Paul is clearly responding to those who are judging these new Gentile believers. Who is that? The Pharisees. He is responding to the Pharisee Law which he is rebuking. They follow the Law of Sin and Death and of the Flesh. They are contrary to us and their law not Yahuah's. Did they not even judge Messiah and His disciples on the Sabbath erroneously? They screw up the Feasts or holydays, the entire calendar because they follow the moon that is not Biblical. We cover that in an entire chapter. This is what Paul says about Pharisee criticism and accusations accusing the brethren just as their father, the devil does.

Colossians 2:16-17 KJV

Let no man therefore judge you in meat, or in drink, or in respect of an holyday, or of the new moon, or of the sabbath days: Which are a shadow of things to come; but the body is of Christ.

In fact, Hebrews 10 uses this same terminology regarding the animal sacrifices of the Feasts and Sabbaths – "shadow of good things to come." It seems James *(Yacob)* or whomever wrote that was on the same page as Paul. They were not at odds at all. They agreed. Paul is misunderstood. The Feasts foreshadow Messiah's birth, death and resurrection in the Spring and in the Fall, the future End Times of the trumpet sounding *(Trumpets)*, Day of Judgment *(Atonement)* and when we attain our new heavenly bodies *(Tabernacles)*. Paul understood this as did James but neither says their being a shadow means they are abolished. In fact, 3 of the 7 Feasts are not fulfilled in prophecy yet and thus must remain as they are a shadow still of things to come. Paul is saying don't let the Pharisees tell us we aren't keeping the Sabbath correctly. They do not know what they are talking about. He already warned us he was addressing them from the beginning of this chapter. He does so again.

Colossians 2:18-23 KJV

Let no man beguile you of your reward in a voluntary humility and worshipping of angels, intruding into those things which he hath not seen, vainly puffed up by his fleshly mind, And not holding the Head, from which all the body by joints and bands having nourishment ministered, and knit together, increaseth with the increase of God. Wherefore if ye be dead with Christ from the rudiments of the world, why, as though living in the world, are ye subject to ordinances, (Touch not; taste not; handle not; Which all are to perish with the using;) after the commandments and doctrines of men? Which things have indeed a shew of wisdom in will worship, and humility, and neglecting of the body; not in any honour to the satisfying of the flesh.

Is Paul telling us we are not to be subject to ordinances? To any Law? Again, he says the Law is good, holy and just. He is talking about the ordinances that "are against us" in the Law of Sin and Death of the Flesh not the Law of Moses. Are we to be subject to ordinances? Yes, we are. Where do you live if you are not? At what time in any of history has Yahuah not had Law? NEVER! He cannot judge you righteous without right. Paul would never mean that. However, they don't finish the sentence that ends with which law – "the commandments and doctrines of men." You have got to be kidding that one calls themselves a scholar and uses this to claim the Law written by the finger of Yahuah and given to Moses was the commandments and doctrines of men. That is worse than illiterate. Every such scholar should be fired immediately. Paul is not saying that. He is rebuking Pharisee interpretations of the Law of Moses that turn it into the doctrines of men *(Mark 7:9)*. He is fixing their mess and scholars are using this to behave as Pharisees.

The Law of Sin and Death Is Not Moses' Law!

In Romans 7-8, Paul provides a thorough examination in contrast between the Law of Sin and Death which he characterizes as an opposite Law essentially in place since Adam sinned when it entered. It is not Yahuah's Law that he interprets as the Law of Moses equal to the Law of Life in Yahusha Messiah. Those are the same but what they are not is the Law of Sin and Death. When he rebukes the Law of Sin and Death he is clear it is the Law of the Flesh not Yahuah's Law of the Spirit. For clarity's sake, we have included in brackets our interpretation of which Law in which Paul refers because otherwise this can be confusing.

> ### *Romans 7:4-6 KJV*
>
> *Wherefore, my brethren, ye also are become dead to the law **[Sin & Death]** by the body of Christ; that ye should be married to another, even to him who is raised from the dead, that we should bring forth fruit unto God. For when we were in the flesh **[Sin & Death]**, the motions of sins **[Sin & Death]**, which were by the law **[Sin & Death]**, did work in our members to bring forth fruit unto death **[Sin & Death]**. But now we are delivered from the law **[Sin & Death]**, that being dead wherein we were held; that we should serve in newness of spirit **[Law of Life]**, and not in the oldness of the letter **[Sin & Death]**.*

The table tennis match has commenced. Paul will now bounce back and forth from the Law of Sin as this portion is that Law vs. the Law of Moses that is the Law of Life in Yahusha Messiah. One cannot deny that contrast when they read this in context. However, this is one of the worst passages to attempt to pull fragments. One will never understand Paul that way especially not here which you will see. Notice it begins with BUT. It is contrasting back and forth constantly. You will pick up on the pattern as this develops. He clears up he did not just refer to the Law of Moses as the Law of Sin and Death.

> ### *Romans 7:7-10 KJV*
>
> *What shall we say then? Is the law sin **[Sin & Death]**? God forbid. **[No, Law is Life the counter Law is Sin and Death]** Nay, I had not known sin, but by the law: **[Law of Life]** for I had not known lust **[Sin & Death]**, except the law **[Law of Life]** had said, **Thou shalt not covet [Law of Moses = Law of Life]**. But sin **[Sin & Death]**, taking occasion by the commandment, wrought in me all manner of concupiscence. For without the law **[Law of Life]** sin was dead. For I was alive without the law once **[Law of Life]**: but when the commandment came, sin revived **[Sin & Death]**, and I died. And the commandment, which was ordained to life **[Law of Life]**, I found to be unto death **[Sin & Death]**.*

Paul just quoted the 10th Commandment within this passage as the Law of Life. That means Paul says the Law of Moses is equivalent to the Law of Life here. He does not serve a new Law nor did Messiah create one essentially. Of course, Paul reaffirms all 10 Commandments in his writings *(see chart p. 170)*. The New Covenant in basis is the Old. Sin is lawlessness or breaking Yahuah's Law of Life. Paul will clarify this over and over. You will find Paul expressing these two Laws at odds with each other. One either serves one or the other as they are opposites. When he says he was without Law, he means the Law of Life but still that him placed unknowingly under the Law of Sin and Death. That still may appear a bit muddy at first but he is merely warming up here. Follow as he explains and this will open your eyes.

Romans 7:11-13 KJV

*For sin **[Sin & Death]**, taking occasion by the commandment, deceived me, and by it slew me. Wherefore the law **[Law of Life]** is holy, and the commandment holy, and just, and good. Was then that which is good made death unto me? God forbid. But sin, that it might appear sin **[Sin & Death]**, working death **[Sin & Death]** in me by that which is good; that sin **[Sin & Death]** by the commandment might become exceeding sinful **[Sin & Death]**.*

Now the exposition begins in complete comparison in the conflict of two opposing Laws or natures as the KJV titles it. However, Paul calls them Laws. The Law of Sin and Death vs. the Law of Life.

Romans 7:14-20 KJV

*For we know that the law is spiritual **[Law of Life]**: but I am carnal, sold under sin **[Sin & Death]**. For that which I do I allow not: for what I would, that do I not; but what I hate, that do I. If then I do that which I would not, I consent unto the law **[Law of Life]** that it is good. Now then it is no more I that do it, but sin **[Sin & Death]** that dwelleth in me. For I know that in me (that is, in my flesh,) **[Sin & Death]** dwelleth no good thing: for to will is present with me; but how to perform that which is good I find not **[Law of Life]**. For the good that I would I do not: but the evil which I would not, that I do. Now if I do that I would not, it is no more I that do it, but sin **[Sin & Death]** that dwelleth in me.*

Paul is not suggesting the devil made him do it but expressing the contrast between the two Laws and his nature to sin. This will become clearer. So far, he is defining a struggle with his flesh in which we can all relate. We are either serving the Law of Life or that of Sin and Death. Here is the context for this back and forth that will bring things into full focus. In the end, it is not confusing at all but this is not a verse.

Romans 7:21-25 KJV

*I find then a law **[Law of Life]**, that, when I would do good, evil is present with me **[Sin & Death]**. For I delight in the law of God **[Law of Life]** after the inward man **[Law of Life/Spirit]**: But I see another law **[Sin & Death]** in my members, warring against the law of my mind **[Law of Life]**, and bringing me into captivity to the law of sin **[Sin & Death]** which is in my members. O wretched man that I am! who shall deliver me from the body of this death? **[Sin & Death]** I thank God through Jesus Christ our Lord. So then with the mind I myself serve the law of God **[Law of Life]**; but with the flesh the law of sin **[Sin & Death]**.*

Paul delights in the Law of Life, the Law of Yahuah after the Spirit as we all should. He recognizes the war with the Flesh that serves the Law of Sin and Death. This is our true battle and one in which we should all be fully aware. This is why we need our full armor that requires returning to His ways not church doctrine. Paul is misrepresented in saying the Law of Moses is somehow the Law of Sin and Death. However, that is not at all what he explains. There are two laws at work and they are opposites. He rebukes and in a later letter says we have been redeemed from the curse of the Law of Sin and Death. We have but we keep the Law of Life that is the opposite. If you are not, you are not reading Paul. Realize if Paul just said he is at war with the Law of Moses, then, he would be saying he is killing, stealing, etc. That is an insane interpretation yet essentially what many church doctrines hold.

Romans 8:1-2 KJV

*There is therefore now no condemnation to them which are in Christ Jesus, who walk **not** after the flesh **[Sin & Death]**, but after the Spirit **[Law of Life]**. For the law of the Spirit of life in Christ Jesus **[Law of Life]** hath made me free from the law of sin and death **[Sin & Death]**.*

The picture is no longer blurry as Paul expresses the two opposite laws here. If your denomination is claiming the Law of Life or Moses is the one that is Sin and Death, they have no foundation in scripture. That is an opposite Law at work against the Law of Moses he says which is the Law of Life he is referencing which he equates to the Law of Life in Jesus*(Yahusha)* Messiah. Again this is not new in the New Testament but Sirach and 2nd Esdras call the Law of Moses the Law of Life which is likely where Paul acquired the term. Proverbs 13:14 approaches close in concept as well. That as well is not new.

> ### Sirach 17:11 KJVA (Law of Moses is the Law of Life)
> *Beside this he gave them knowledge, and the **law of life** for an heritage.*
> ### 2 Esdras 14:30 KJVA
> *And received the **law of life** which they kept not, which you also have transgressed after them.*

The notion that Paul did not teach and represent the Old Testament is a deep fraud perpetrated by the Catholic Church but really the Pharisees in origin. They were exploiting his words out of context 2,000 years ago. Some will then claim there is no such thing as a Law of Sin and Death in scripture but that as well is not true. Not only did Proverbs allude to it, James shared the same doctrine and really so did Baruch, the scribe for Jeremiah.

> ### Hebrews 7:16 KJV
> *Who is made, not after the law of a carnal commandment, but after the power of an endless life.*
> ### Baruch 4:1 KJVA
> *This is the book of the commandments of God, and the law that endureth for ever: all they that keep it shall come to life; but such as leave it shall die.*

Hebrews' Law of Carnal Commandment cannot be the Law of Life that he endorses and teaches throughout the whole of the Book of Hebrews. It is an opposite Law of the Flesh as he says. For those attempting that he is saying the Law of Life in Jesus*(Yahusha)* Messiah is new, better read because before and after this he says we have the Ancient Priesthood in the Order of Melchizedek. That's not a new order but the one in place at the time of Abraham who tithed to that Law.

Romans 8:3-8 KJV

*For what the law could not do, in that it was weak through the flesh **[Sin & Death]**, God sending his own Son in the likeness of sinful flesh, and for sin, condemned sin in the flesh **[Sin & Death]**: That the righteousness of the law might be fulfilled in us **[Law of Life]**, who walk **not** after the flesh **[Sin & Death]**, but after the Spirit **[Law of Life]**. For they that are after the flesh **[Sin & Death]** do mind the things of the flesh **[Sin & Death]**; but they that are after the Spirit the things of the Spirit **[Law of Life]**. For to be carnally minded is death **[Sin & Death]**; but to be spiritually minded is life and peace **[Law of Life]**. Because the carnal mind is enmity against God **[Sin & Death]**: for it is not subject to the law of God **[Law of Life]**, neither indeed can be. So then they that are in the flesh **[Sin & Death]** cannot please God.*

This is truly revealing as Paul firmly identifies that we serve the Law of Life in Jesus*(Yahusha)* Messiah and not the Law of Sin and Death. To serve that Law is bondage, enmity, and one cannot please Yahuah. It is it's curse that Jesus*(Yahusha)* has redeemed us from which is Death. Through Him we now have eternal life if we are in relationship with Him.

Romans 8:9-11 KJV

*But ye are not in the flesh **[Sin & Death]**, but in the Spirit **[Law of Life]**, if so be that the Spirit of God dwell in you. Now if any man have not the Spirit of Christ, he is none of his. And if Christ be in you, the body is dead because of sin **[Sin & Death]**; but the Spirit is life because of righteousness **[Law of Life]**. But if the Spirit of him that raised up Jesus from the dead dwell in you, he that raised up Christ from the dead shall also quicken your mortal bodies by his Spirit that dwelleth in you.*

We are not sure Paul could be any clearer in his endorsement of the Law of Moses in continuation as the Law of Life in Jesus*(Yahusha)* Messiah. He came right out and quoted it and equated it. He is not serving a new Law in his own words. Anyone can go in and interrupt this ping pong match and yank out a fragment out of context and reframe Paul's words but that is called fraud not Bible interpretation. Paul is teaching the Law here. That cannot be disputed. He kept it and he taught it. He writes of the Law extensively.

Romans 2 KJV

Paul understood that there is no difference in Yahuah's eyes between Hebrew or Gentile when it comes to salvation. As a nation, Israel was special and it's people remain so though they are not in that nation today generally. However, Gentiles labeled as the "stranger among you" had the same salvation, blessings and curses as Israel in the Exodus *(Ex. 12:49; Lev. 16:29, 19:34; Num. 9:14, etc.)*. In fact, Abraham was not even the only Hebrew clan as Joktan's sons from Eber migrated to Ophir but Abraham entered covenant that continued for the people of Jacob/Israel. This is a people not a land.

Romans 2:8-11 KJV

But unto them that are contentious, and do not obey the truth, but obey unrighteousness, indignation and wrath, Tribulation and anguish, upon every soul of man that doeth evil, of the Jew first, and also of the Gentile; But glory, honour, and peace, to every man that worketh good, to the Jew first, and also to the Gentile: For there is no respect of persons with God.

Paul follows the Old Testament protocol as Yahuah spoke to Israel first but also included the "stranger among them" or Gentile. He equates them even from the Exodus thus Zionism has no place in Bible interpretation. He then, reinforces the Law. What Law? The same Law he quotes many times over. You will find all 10 commandments in Paul's teachings as we have charted at the end of this chapter along with Messiah's using all 10 and essentially all 10 appear in End Times prophecy as well. It is rather difficult to claim they all passed away when all 10 of them are being used as doctrine to the end. This position is not supported by the Bible.

Romans 2:12-16 KJV

For as many as have sinned without law shall also perish without law: and as many as have sinned in the law shall be judged by the law; (For not the hearers of the law are just before God, but the doers of the law shall be justified. For when the Gentiles, which have not the law, do by nature the things contained in the law, these, having not the law, are a law unto themselves: Which shew the work of the law written in their hearts, their conscience also bearing witness, and their thoughts the mean while accusing or else excusing one another;) In the day when God shall judge the secrets of men by Jesus Christ according to my gospel.

Who judges all men? Jesus *(Yahusha)* does. That includes those of the Old Testament yet we are told He was not here so they have a different measure. No, they do not nor do we from them. He will judge us all together by the same measure because He never changed it. This measure has always been and will always be. It is the Law. What Law, the Law of Moses in continuation according to Paul. Whether one serves the Law or not, they will be judged by it in the end.

James 1:22 KJV
But be ye doers of the word, and not hearers only, deceiving your own selves.

Look at that, Paul agrees with James *(Yacob)*, brother of Messiah regarding the Law. Some scholars attempt to claim there was a rift between these 2 Apostles over this issue. However, that is also false. It is never in scripture and a very poor assumption inserted haphazardly. Paul too, says to be doers of the word that is the Law, not hearers only.

Was The Law Finished?
The Intent of the Law Has Never Been Salvation

Galatians offers another gross example of Paul taken out of context. Again, we hear of the fragment from one verse but in context, it does not in any way go against Paul's practice and teachings that reinforce the Law. If it does, then Paul would be a hypocrite and he most certainly was no liar. They simply do not read the build up here about Abraham which destroys their thinking and then Paul again saying of those who would abolish the Law and claim it is against His promises: God forbid!

Galatians 3:15-21 KJV
Brethren, I speak after the manner of men; Though it be but a man's

covenant, yet if it be confirmed, no man disannulleth, or addeth thereto. Now to Abraham and his seed were the promises made. He saith not, And to seeds, as of many; but as of one, And to thy seed, which is Christ. And this I say, that the covenant, that was confirmed before of God in Christ, the law, which was four hundred and thirty years after, cannot disannul, that it should make the promise of none effect. For if the inheritance be of the law, it is no more of promise: but God gave it to Abraham by promise. Wherefore then serveth the law? It was added because of transgressions, till the seed should come to whom the promise was made; and it was ordained by angels in the hand of a mediator. Now a mediator is not a mediator of one, but God is one. Is the law then against the promises of God? God forbid: for if there had been a law given which could have given life, verily righteousness should have been by the law.

Paul begins this dissertation with the promise that he is not adding to the Word. Yet, we are then told he adds to the Word. He did not. He begins with Abraham receiving the promise of salvation through Messiah. Yes, that is Old Testament fact. He certainly is not abolishing it but using the Old Testament to teach yet again. Paul is expressing that the Covenant with Abraham was before the Law of Moses and it was, 430+ years before. The Law did not disannul that Covenant rendering it of none effect. It reinforced it as it must. Messiah's is no different.

The inheritance is eternal life or salvation and it was never from the Law of Moses but from the Covenant promise prior and that is true. What is that Covenant promise according to Paul even to Abraham? Messiah is salvation not the Law and He was in the Old Testament as well. Paul is saying the opposite of what some represent. He instead reinforces that Old Testament patriarchs had the same promise of salvation that we have. However, the law is not against the promises of the Covenant but serve them. Paul does not abolish the Law here. He is reinforcing it but clarifying that the Law is not salvation. It never was.

Others throw out Galatians 4:10 yet Paul is telling us there he taught them to observe days, months, times and years. In order to claim he is rebuking that practice, one has to believe he rebuked himself. Instead Paul is rebuking legalism whereby one only focuses on Feasts rather than true relationship with Jesus*(Yahusha)*. The Old Testament says the exact same *(Amos 5:21)*. Also, the Law in which he refers again was not the Law of Moses. He is again discussing the Law of Sin and Death which is contrary to us. We are redeemed from that Law not the Law of Moses.

Does Ephesians say the Law of Life or Moses was abolished. It used the word abolished if that is all one is seeking. However, what was abolished? They are not reading at all. This was just explained in Romans 7-8 as we already know which Law was abolished – the Law of Sin and Death which is NOT the Law of Moses or Life in Jesus *(Yahusha)* Messiah.

> ### *Ephesians 2:14-15 KJV*
> *For he is our peace, who hath made both one, and hath broken down the middle wall of partition between us; Having abolished in his flesh the enmity, even the law of commandments contained in ordinances; for to make in himself of twain one new man, so making peace;*

What does Paul view as the wall of partition that separates us from Him? Not the Law of Moses. The Law of Sin and Death which he expresses as enmity here, in Romans 7-8 and Galatians 4. It is the commandments and ordinances expressed before as "against us" from the Law of Sin and Death in which he refers. This does not abolish the Law of Moses nor does Galatians 4. Let us also rewind a little in this passage for clarity.

> ### *Ephesians 2:8-9-15 KJV*
> *For by grace are ye saved through faith; and that not of yourselves: it is the gift of God: Not of works, lest any man should boast.*

Realize this is the same grace in which Abraham was saved not the Law. Abraham was not saved by the Law nor was Moses nor is anyone in the Old Testament. Only Pharisees say that in scripture and it is rebuked by the Apostles in Acts. Noah found grace in the sight of Yahuah as well and any teaching of the Gospel of Grace without his story is lacking.

Many will also bring up Romans 6:15 but they again are not reading in context. This is the set up for chapters 7-8 which we already covered thus we know what Paul meant. Otherwise, one must believe, and scholars are essentially saying Paul was a hypocrite. He was not.

Romans 6:12 KJV

Let not sin therefore reign in your mortal body, that ye should obey it in the lusts thereof. Neither yield ye your members as instruments of unrighteousness unto sin: but yield yourselves unto God, as those that are alive from the dead, and your members as instruments of righteousness unto God. For sin shall not have dominion over you: for ye are not under the law, but under grace. What then? shall we sin, because we are not under the law, but under grace? God forbid.

What part of God forbid do they not understand? Paul is saying that we do not sin which means we do not break the Law. Yet, he says we are not under the Law. What Law? The Law of Sin and Death is the Law that is sin. One cannot sin while obeying the Law of Moses. What kind of scholar does not know that? We are not under that Law of Sin and Death but under grace. That does not abolish the Law of Moses or Law of Life in Jesus*(Yahusha)* Messiah.

Some will throw out fragment after fragment and we have seen it all on our YouTube Channel. Romans 3:20 for instance tells us no one is justified by the law. The Old Testament has always said that as the Law has never been the promise of salvation but Messiah has always been such promise since Genesis 3:15. Only Pharisees teach that doctrine.

In Romans 14, Paul rebukes the judging of your brother in some choosing to be vegans of sort and others meat eaters, he did not declare all food clean. Even if he had, that does not abolish the Sabbath practice which is well-proven as Paul's practice and he taught it. He also speaks of one man esteeming one day above another and another a different day. What he does not say is never mind about the Sabbath and Feasts that I have taught throughout my ministry. He certainly is not saying you no longer need that bad old Law of Moses so just throw it out yet he kept and taught it as we have proven. These are out of context.

We are then told Peter in Acts 10:12-20 abolished unclean foods rendering all foods clean. Therefore the Law is dead they claim. However, again, they cannot even read as Peter's vision is of unclean foods as a metaphor and he recognizes the fulfillment of that vision in which the unclean foods were representative of Gentiles whom came to him and that is what he was being shown. In the end, his story is not even about food yet we are told he declared all foods clean in utter ignorance because they are reading in fragments and cannot even complete a paragraph.

Let's look at Titus 1:5 which they destroy in ignorance.

Titus 1:5 KJV

Now the end of the commandment is charity out of a pure heart, and of a good conscience, and of faith unfeigned:

Did Paul just say that charity ends the commandments? That is ridiculous. He is saying the completion or fulfillment of the commandment really to love your neighbor as yourself is to apply charity and faith. We could spend several volumes on just how much leaven has been applied to Paul's epistles. It is gross and it is not just in the church but what is called doctrine too often. However, Paul completely addresses many issues of our faith in ways untold from most pulpits. He kept and applied the Law of Moses as that is what he taught. However, one the largest we hear about, is Paul's changing the Law on circumcision. Did he?

Circumcision

The origin of circumcision is not the Law of Moses. Abraham practiced it long before and generations up until Moses' time. Of course, it was continued in the Law of Moses for newborns of 8 days old. Does the Law ever say circumcision is salvation? No. The following is a perfect example of how Pharisees are inept when it comes to interpreting the Word. They were going around Jerusalem telling people, even adult males, that they must be circumcised or they are not saved. They were telling them, this was a requirement for salvation. Again, Moses never said that. They are adding to the Word and this is the problem with Pharisees. They don't know what they are talking about then or now. The relationship of the Word is very foreign to them and they screw it up as in this case.

Acts 15:1-5 KJV (Written by Luke, not Paul)

And certain men which came down from Judaea taught the brethren, and said, Except ye be circumcised after the manner of Moses, ye cannot be saved. When therefore Paul and Barnabas had no small dissension and disputation with them, they determined that Paul and Barnabas, and certain other of them, should go up to Jerusalem unto the apostles and elders about this question. And being brought on their way by the church, they passed through Phenice and Samaria, declaring the conversion of the Gentiles: and they caused great joy unto all the brethren. And when they were come to Jerusalem, they were received of the church, and of the apostles and elders, and they declared all things that God had done with them. But there rose up certain of the sect of the Pharisees which believed, saying, That it was needful to circumcise them, and to command them to keep the law of Moses.

Understand circumcision is not genital mutilation as some would mischaracterize. It is a First Fruit Offering of the flesh of a male child. We even find medically, it is beneficial to most. What we don't find even in the Law of Moses is that circumcision is salvation. It is not. It really is much like baptism in the same sense as it is something one does with their sons at a very early age of 8 days old. Thus the Apostolic leadership had a tough decision to make especially forcing Gentile men to now be circumcised. Ouch!

They render a very wise decision and Paul abides by it. He is not in the leadership at that time though he was praised by them in this meeting. They send Paul and Barnabas out with this message. Anyone claiming Paul then went against the Apostles in his teaching of circumcision is illiterate of scripture because the message he shared is exactly what they decided. Essentially, the Pharisee emphasis on circumcision was wrong in the first place as it is not salvation and the leadership chose to tell the Gentile men to focus on other issues which just so happen to reinforce the Law of Moses which James taught then and Paul also taught. Again, the Pharisees do not understand the Law of Moses. When they say to keep it, they refer to the legalistic application in which they have expanded. The Apostles did not agree with that but what they never do is say not to keep the Law of Moses. It doesn't happen and this passage is certainly not saying so as James then, reinforces the Law of Moses.

Acts 15:13-20 KJV

And after they had held their peace, James answered, saying, Men and brethren, hearken unto me: Simeon hath declared how God at the first did visit the Gentiles, to take out of them a people for his name. And to this agree the words of the prophets; as it is written, After this I will return, and will build again the tabernacle of David, which is fallen down; and I will build again the ruins thereof, and I will set it up: That the residue of men might seek after the Lord, and all the Gentiles, upon whom my name is called, saith the Lord, who doeth all these things. Known unto God are all his works from the beginning of the world. Wherefore my sentence is, that we trouble not them, which from among the Gentiles are turned to God: But that we write unto them, that they abstain from pollutions of idols, and from fornication, and from things strangled, and from blood.

What James just did was reaffirm the Law of Moses picking out the 3rd Commandment most importantly – no idols. He then mentions Yahuah's works from the beginning of the world and that includes the 7th day Sabbath. He then affirms the Biblical diet from the Law of Moses and really long before as those originate with Noah after the Flood. He and the others agreed they should not force especially adult Gentile men to now be circumcised. They agreed that should not become a stumbling block to salvation as it is not salvation. Essentially they are cleaning up another Pharisee mess that you will find Paul especially doing throughout his epistles which Peter endorsed specifically as scripture. Then, James endorses the Sabbath day practice the Apostles continued which has not changed.

Acts 15:21 KJV
For Moses of old time hath in every city them that preach him, being read in the synagogues every sabbath day.

Peter, James and the leadership were pleased with Paul and Barnabas and sent them out as their chief messengers. There are actually those who attempt to claim Paul was never endorsed by the Apostles. That is illiterate of scripture. Others will say Paul represented another Gospel yet he left with letters of endorsement and doctrine that he followed. He was not preaching against the Apostles but representing them and they loved him. For those who have heard that James and Paul has a sort of argument, that is completely fabricated from a misreading of both but scholars incapable of understanding.

Acts 15:22 KJV

Then pleased it the apostles and elders, with the whole church, to send chosen men of their own company to Antioch with Paul and Barnabas; namely, Judas surnamed Barsabas, and Silas, chief men among the brethren:

Some attempt to position Paul as a loose canon out on his own. He was not and a true assessment of his words in context never abolish Law especially the Sabbath which he practiced and taught.

Acts 15:23-26 KJV

And they wrote letters by them after this manner; The apostles and elders and brethren send greeting unto the brethren which are of the Gentiles in Antioch and Syria and Cilicia: Forasmuch as we have heard, that certain which went out from us have troubled you with words, subverting your souls, saying, Ye must be circumcised, and keep the law: to whom we gave no such commandment: It seemed good unto us, being assembled with one accord, to send chosen men unto you with our beloved Barnabas and Paul, Men that have hazarded their lives for the name of our Lord Jesus Christ.

These letters are the writings of the Apostles, not Paul. He represented them and accurately shared their view. Some misread this and claim it just said not to keep the law that is false. It says the commandment to circumcise in application of adult males accepting Messiah. In fact, those saying this scripture just told us not to keep the law need to read the next sentences as they reinforce the Law.

Acts 15:28 KJV

For it seemed good to the Holy Ghost, and to us, to lay upon you no greater burden than these necessary things; That ye abstain from meats offered to idols, and from blood, and from things strangled, and from fornication: from which if ye keep yourselves, ye shall do well. Fare ye well.

Imagine how many men may pass on salvation because they were not willing to be circumcised as adults. It is a big ask and the Pharisees were not trying to help people. They were throwing stumbling blocks in their way to throw a wrench into the works of the viral movement that had begun. This was their desperate ploy in agitation which tactic is classic Pharisee. Abraham did it as an adult but the Law of Moses is to circumcise children of 8 days of age not men. The Apostles were not preaching to 8-day-old children but adults. There is nothing here that abolishes circumcision as the practice for newborn children of 8 days. You will find this practice still very prevalent in many cultures today.

This is further demonstrated in the same fashion by Paul in his letter to the Galatians.

Galatians 2:3-4 KJV

But neither Titus, who was with me, being a Greek, was compelled to be circumcised: And that because of false brethren unawares brought in, who came in privily to spy out our liberty which we have in Christ Jesus, that they might bring us into bondage:

This is not new doctrine but exactly what the Apostles sent Paul out to share. Circumcision is not salvation and no surprise that Titus, a Greek, Gentile, adult male chose not to undergo such pain unnecessarily. Again, this is the Pharisee mess not the Bible's that has never said circumcision is salvation. Of what bondage is Paul speaking? He is talking about the threat of bondage even being handcuffed in speech when there is an enemy in your midst as false brethren unawares or perhaps even more so the threat of bondage they may be seeking if they can find anything to report. Either way, Paul is not calling circumcision bondage and this application is right out of the letters that James and the Apostle leadership provided back in Jerusalem before.

In 1 Corinthians 7:19, Paul also addresses circumcision as impertinent and not a factor in salvation and service. That's not a news flash, it is Old Testament doctrine as well as New. It seems when one quotes Paul these days, things are so distorted by the Anti-Paul movement founded only in ridicule not the Word, they must address this elephant in the room. We gladly do so. The Bible is very clear as to whom Paul was and was no longer. Let's take a look and clear this up now.

You can find many books, blogs and videos on this but this is a statement from the website of BibleReasons.com:

> *"In Acts the Jerusalem Council ruled that Gentile Christians were not required to keep the law of Moses. If Sabbath keeping was required, then it would have been stated by the apostles in Acts 15. Why didn't the apostles force the Sabbath on the Gentile Christians? They would have if it were required."*
> *—BibleReasons.com*

Except, we already showed you the Gentiles also already kept the Sabbath as new believers according to scripture. This website does not represent the Bible on this but scoffing and ignorant ridicule. That is the true root of the problem in scholarship today. They think they are supposed to sit in the seat of the scornful. No decree was necessary, that decree has nothing to do with Sabbath but addressed the Pharisee agitation.

Here we have a very direct rebuke of "Sabbath-keeping" indeed. However, this is false. They seem unable to read. James and the letter sent with Paul with their decision was for the men to focus on tenets right out of the Law of Moses and not new law as we covered. There is no requirement for that to include a new publishing of the whole of law. Using their reason, it is now permissible to kill because thou shalt not kill was not one of the things mentioned either. In fact, the Apostles' decision, which was just about circumcision not a decree of the whole of the law, did not include many things that we find in scripture in their own words including all 10 commandments which appear in Messiah's words, the Apostles after His ascension and even in the End Times *(see chart p. 170)*. One cannot ignore that. One also cannot overlook the fact that just before this in Acts 15:21 in the same chapter, the Sabbath is mentioned in observance just as the Apostles always did including 85 Sabbaths in the Book of Acts alone. How can they miss that? They do not wish to see it. These are deceivers not those representing the Bible.

However, while on this topic, let us address the accusations from the "Paul haters" which has been a growing movement to abolish two-thirds of the New Testament. In fact, since there are endorsements of Paul from Peter, Luke, Messiah, Ananias and the men on the road to Damascus, they go ahead and ridicule them as well because they must be wrong to support Paul. That is baseless ridicule and the Bible says what it says and it does not say what it does not say. Their movement is no worse than the Pharisee crusade against Paul and in fact they are joining their 2,000-year movement to demean Paul. Not on our watch.

Was Paul An Apostle?

Paul identifies himself as an Apostle of Jesus Christ in the first verse of Romans, 1st and 2nd Corinthians, Galatians, Ephesians, Colossians, 1st and 2nd Timothy and Titus. Was he telling the truth? Many go to the 12 Apostles and the definition from Acts to be within the 12 but that is impertinent as Paul never claims to be one of the original 12 Apostles. Paul never claims to be an eyewitness to Jesus*(Yahusha)* other than in His appearances to him after His ascension. They will try to create one false paradigm after another in which to debate but they set a straw man first that is not even accurate. Paul was an Apostle not because he said so but because Luke and Peter said so as well as Messiah Himself. Luke wrote scripture including a Gospel. There is no debating him on this.

Acts 14:14 KJV

*Which when **the apostles, Barnabas and Paul**, heard of, they rent their clothes, and ran in among the people, crying out,*

Peter is attacked for endorsing Paul because 1st Peter and 2nd Peter appear to be written by a different person. However, Peter used scribes and likely used two different scribes. There is no scholar who would claim Peter's epistles are not attributed to Peter. Peter endorses ALL of Paul's epistles as an example of living the Law. He says Paul has wisdom and essentially treats Paul's writings as scripture. This means Paul wrote them before Peter was dead as well placing a timestamp in history. Those who oppose Paul's message and twist his words are called unlearned and unstable just as they are with the scriptures and lead to their own destruction. He warns us they represent the error of the wicked that could lead us away if we do not discern.

2 Peter 3:14-17 KJV

*Wherefore, beloved, seeing that ye look for such things, be diligent that ye may be found of him in peace, without spot, and blameless. And account that the longsuffering of our Lord is salvation; even as **our beloved brother***

Paul also according to the wisdom given unto him hath written unto you; As also in all his epistles, speaking in them of these things; in which are *some things hard to be understood,* which they that are *unlearned and unstable wrest, as they do also the other scriptures, unto their own destruction.* Ye therefore, beloved, seeing ye know these things before, beware lest ye also, being led away with *the error of the wicked,* fall from your own stedfastness.

That qualifies as an Apostle saying Paul was indeed the level of an Apostle writing scripture and performing miracles within such office. There is no scripture that says there will only ever be 12 Apostles but instead, Apostle is an office within the 5-fold ministry of calling just as prophet is *(Luke 11:49; Eph. 4:11; 1 Cor. 12:28).* Neither are of the 12 Apostles nor the Prophets which ended with John the Baptist. However, these remain offices of ministry and Paul certainly operated as an Apostle and never said he was one of the 12 original ones. Paul performed miracles many times according to Luke and had disciples *(Acts 19:1, 20:1).* Paul preached the doctrine of the Apostles *(Acts 16:3-4).*

Ephesians 4:11 KJV
And he gave some, apostles; and some, prophets; and some, evangelists; and some, pastors and teachers;

Paul also calls himself the "Apostle of the Gentiles." He does this multiple times and he says Peter is sent to the Jews but never once does he say he does not minister to Jews nor that Peter does not minister to Gentiles. Both reach both audiences. Paul preached in Synagogues at least 85 times in the Book of Acts alone. Those synagogues had both Jews and Greeks or Gentiles. The notion that Paul had bouncers at the door to weed out Jews from a synagogue is illiterate as would be the case for Peter and Gentiles. That does not change that he was called to the Gentile principally which is fact nor Peter to the Jew principally.

Romans 11:13 KJV
For I speak to you Gentiles, inasmuch as I am the apostle of the Gentiles, I magnify mine office:

Paul exercised humility and was not boastful.

> ### 1 Corinthians 15:9 KJV
> *For I am the least of the apostles, that am not meet to be called an apostle, because I persecuted the church of God.*

This accusation is not new as Paul answers the same in his time *(1 Cor. 9:1-27)*. These are the same Pharisees in spirit who attack Paul. Notice his humility in saying he does not measure up to an Apostle even. He certainly did according to his title but this is humble.

Was Paul a Pharisee, a Hebrew and a Roman?

Paul chased the early ekklesia as he was a Pharisee *(Acts 9)* and that is what Pharisees did and still do to this day using different means including through the Catholic Church. When Paul met Messiah face-to-face and realized he was persecuting him, he turned away from being a Pharisee in practice. Luke wrote of this so this is all recorded by another witness who also called Paul an Apostle. There were witnesses to Paul's encounter on the road to Damascus who were with him and very likely, Luke, who proves very thorough, would have interviewed them at some point and confirmed the story.

Yahusha appeared to Ananias who would minister to Paul. Ananias affirms that he knew Paul was a Pharisee who was hunting the ekklesia previously.

> ### Acts 9:15-16 KJV [Jesus(Yahusha) to Ananias Regarding Paul]
> *But the Lord said unto him, Go thy way: for **he (Paul) is a chosen vessel unto me, to bear my name before the Gentiles, and kings, and the children of Israel: For I will shew him how great things he must suffer for my name's sake**.*

Paul was called a "chosen vessel unto Messiah." Wow!!! Luke wrote this not Paul and he is the writer of a Gospel. Thus one cannot attain a better endorsement than a credible account of Messiah's words not even to Paul but to Ananias who would have confirmed this to Luke and Luke would have affirmed. Paul's calling is undeniable and he was called to the Gentiles not by himself, but by Messiah Himself. Paul was even told of his coming suffering for the Gospel. How can anyone ridicule this man of Yahuah? Ananias told Luke that Paul was filled with the Holy Spirit and the miracles which followed him prove this overwhelmingly. Again, Peter endorsed this as well.

Paul admitted he was a Pharisee previously *(Acts 23:6, 26:5, Phil. 3:5)* by birth in fact. However, he also writes he is from the Tribe of Benjamin *(Rom. 11:1, Phil. 3:5)*. This is simple to understand as we all know it requires 2 parents and one was of Pharisee bloodline, likely his father, and his mother, a Benjamite. Some seem confused that a Benjamite is a Jew yet the Bible says they are. This is easy to resolve yet the "Paul haters" represent this as his lying because they cannot figure out that we all have 2 parents.

Some bellow: "Paul was a ravenous wolf because he was a Benjamite." So was the Prophet Jeremiah. Are they going to call him a ravenous wolf too? In fact, Benjamin was the ravenous wolf and in a positive sense as he was fierce in battle and his lineage remained so throughout the Old Testament fulfilling that prophecy long before Paul.

> **Genesis 49:27 KJV**
> *Benjamin shall ravin as a wolf: in the morning he shall devour the prey, and at night he shall divide the spoil.*

> *"The prediction alludes to the warlike character of the tribe of Benjamin, which was manifested in Ehud the judge (Judges 3:15), and Saul the king of Israel (1 Samuel 11:6-11; 1 Samuel 14:13, 15, 47, 48), who both sprang from Rachel's younger son." – Ellicott's Commentary for English Readers. Pulpit Commentary.*

Paul claims to have been taught by Gamaliel, a Pharisee, and the opposition assumes that is the Levite family from the priestly courses and calls Paul a liar. However, again, they assume without bothering to read Acts even which says Gamaliel is the name of a very prominent Pharisee and this explains why Paul carried a lot of sway as a Pharisee and even as a former practicing Pharisee because of who trained him and his bloodline in part.

> ***Acts 5:34 KJV***
> *Then stood there up one in the council, a **Pharisee**, named*
> ***Gamaliel**, a doctor of the law, had in reputation among all the*
> *people, and commanded to put the apostles forth a little space.*

He then, claims Roman Citizenship *(Acts 22:25-26)*. To this they demand to know where he got the money to purchase such but again they are not reading where Paul was born. This is no different today in many instances. Paul was born in the "Free City" of Tarsus that was a Roman hub in that part of the world in modern Turkey.

> *"It is one of the oldest continually inhabited urban centers in the world,*
> *dating back to the Neolithic Period. After 64 BCE, it was the capital of*
> *the district of Cilicia Campestris… Caesar was so impressed by Tarsus*
> *that he made it tax-exempt and lavished further favors on the city; in*
> *gratitude, Tarsus renamed itself Juliopolis. Caesar also rewarded the*
> *Jews of the region (and, by extension, all Jews who would eventually*
> *live under Roman rule) freedom to practice their religion in thanks for*
> *their support during his struggles with Pompey. His decree, most likely*
> *from 47 BCE, was upheld by Augustus Caesar (r. 27 BCE-14 CE)*
> *and the emperors who succeeded him."*
> *– https://www.ancient.eu/Tarsus/*

Paul did not have to purchase citizenship, he was born a citizen of Rome. That is just fact and has nothing to do with his mixed bloodline. Citizenship is not by blood but location. There is nothing to ridicule and Paul passes every test. All in all, Paul vets as the perfect mixture to minister to Gentiles, Jews, Kings and everyone Messiah called him to reach. His Pharisee bloodline protects him from an environment where Pharisees could not kill him as well as his Roman citizenship that he smartly invokes. He was uniquely qualified for such a time as this and he was chosen by Jesus*(Yahusha)* Himself according to the most credible of witnesses. In a court of law, these scoffers would have their ridicule quickly and easily dismantled.

Some even go so far as to claim Paul is the "son of perdition" which would make him the Beast 2,000 years ago. I guess we missed the whole Tribulation, Day of Judgment, and no more satan thing and pretty much they don't even believe the Bible in saying so. This is illiterate. Where does this term even derive? They are accusing Paul of being the Beast or a form of anti-Christ 2,000 years ago. However, they have to read Paul in order to even understand that the Beast is called the "son of perdition." So is Paul rebuking himself in a future context? Huh? Talk about illiteracy. They are actually saying Paul rebuked himself as the Beast which time proves he was not.

> **2 Thessalonians 2:3-4 KJV**
> *Let no man deceive you by any means: for that day shall not come, except there come a falling away first, and that man of sin be revealed,* ***the son of perdition; Who opposeth and exalteth himself above all that is called God, or that is worshipped; so that he as God sitteth in the temple of God, shewing himself that he is God.***

When exactly did Paul do these things 2,000 years ago? It did not happen and if it did, we are living in a different universe because everything in prophecy would be wrong. It requires one to completely forget most of scripture as you have seen. We can all rest assured Paul was an Apostle affirmed by Luke and Peter. He was a former Pharisee who did not continue to teach their doctrine but very clearly against it being called by Messiah Himself who vouched for him. Paul was a Benjamite of Hebrew blood and that is a Yahudim *(Jew is not a Bible word)*. By birth, Paul was Saul, a Roman citizen of the "Free City" of Tarsus. Yes, Paul was everything he said he was and perfectly suited for the task at hand.

He affirmed all of this by his being in-filled with the Holy Spirit in which he could not be demon possessed and performing miracles and teaching the same doctrines of Messiah. As we have seen in this chapter, in context, Paul is deep but very clearly on the same page as Jesus *(Yahusha)* and the Apostles. He kept and taught the Sabbath and the Law and this becomes evident when one reads Paul in context of passages instead of trying to extract fragments that lead to error.

The so-called "lawless" Paul sure does spend a lot of time on the Law telling us it is good and to keep it. However, what is misunderstood is his rebuke of Pharisees who do not even know Torah or the Law. Here he chastises them for teaching other doctrines that are not his. Who are these? Not Lost Tribes of Israel but Pharisees who pontificate about a lineage they do not even have just as in modern times. The Talmud is full of fables and even written in such format of rambling Rabbis who say nothing and talk in circles. It is one of the most profoundly illiterate writings in history.

Once written down, as at that time it was oral, we now know exactly why Messiah rebuked their traditions as against His commandments *(Mark 7:9)* and why Paul says they tell fables, false genealogies and mainly only raise questions. This is the exact paradigm of thinking in much of scholarship today. Even modern Scientism does the same. Their aim is not to prove anything but to lead one around in circles only to end up where they started or a trail of unanswered questions. This is the tactic of satan, the author of confusion and has no place in the church. Scholars should prove and document and we should require them to do so.

1 Timothy 1:3-11 KJV

As I besought thee to abide still at Ephesus, when I went into Macedonia, that thou mightest charge some that they teach no other doctrine, Neither give heed to fables and endless genealogies, which minister questions, rather than godly edifying which is in faith: so do. Now the end of the commandment is charity out of a pure heart, and of a good conscience, and of faith unfeigned: From which some having swerved have turned aside unto vain jangling; Desiring to be teachers of the law; understanding neither what they say, nor whereof they affirm. But we know that the law is good, if a man use it lawfully; Knowing this, that the law is not made for a righteous man, but for the lawless and disobedient, for the ungodly and for sinners, for unholy and profane, for murderers of fathers and murderers of mothers, for manslayers, For whoremongers, for them that defile themselves with mankind, for menstealers, for liars, for perjured persons, and if there be any other thing that is contrary to sound doctrine; According to the glorious gospel of the blessed God, which was committed to my trust.

Paul is not calling the Old Testament fables of useless genealogies, that is illiterate. He also did not just make an end to all commandments as he says charity is the completion or execution of the Law not the abolishing of it. He is supporting the Law that he says again here is good. He addresses the vain scholar or Pharisee who is double-minded and unstable in all his ways because he has no foundation. The teachings of the Pharisees from that time forward quickly prove, when tested, to fit Paul's rebuke as they do not understand what they are talking about. It is affirmed in their own words that do not match scripture.

Is that the Law's shortcoming? No, it is their lack of understanding and knowledge and in this age, willing ignorance as Peter warned. You have to use the Law lawfully. Pharisees and modern Judaism do not. The righteous obey the Law as they know Jesus*(Yahusha)*. That includes His Sabbath. The law is made for the unrighteous who are lawless *(sinners)* and disobedient. It defines their actions as sin. Without it, one cannot do so which is why they want it abandoned so they can hide or justify their sin. The Bible never does. Paul tells us doctrine without the Law is unsound. Most churches are unsound today as they have no foundation on the solid rock.

This is the Paul known to Messiah, the Apostles and the first ekklesias. The stranger being preached is unidentifiable. This is the Gospel he preached and anyone preaching another Gospel represents strange doctrine that must be tested and rejected. Here Paul says "I preach the Law" and the church says he preached against it. Who is right? His own words far outweigh any modern scholar's opinion.

Paul cannot be against the Law and for it at the same time. He would have to choose and yet he did and lays down his thinking in incredible detail. Those taking the church's erroneous interpretation of what Paul did not teach and treating that as fact in a false paradigm only to use those illiterate interpretations to then redefine Paul as an hypocrite, are following even worse. They wish to abolish Paul then because they know the New Testament teaches the Law yet they simply seem unable to read his words in context for themselves. If the church is right about Paul, then according to scripture, he would be a false prophet. However, the church is grossly missing the mark on Paul and this leaves many in confusion.

Test Paul for yourself. Read him in chapters and not in fragments and test everything he says against the words of Messiah. He passes.

10 Commandments:
New Testament Continuation

The 10 Commandments Cannot Be Separated From the New Testament

During Messiah's Ministry	After Messiah's Ascension	In The End Times
1 *No other gods before me* **Matt. 4:10, 6:24, 22:37-38; Luke 4:8; Rev. 2:4-5**	**Gal. 4:8**	**Rev. 14:7** **Rev. 13:4**
2 *No graven images* **Matt. 4:10, 6:24; Luke 4:8, 16:13-15 Rev. 2:14, 2:21-22**	**Acts 15:20, 17:16, 29; 1 Cor. 5:10-11 , 6:9-10, 10:7, 14, 19, 12:2; Gal. 5:19-20; Eph. 5:5 2 Cor. 6:16; Col. 3:5 1 Th. 1:9; 1 Pet. 4:3 1 John 5:21**	**Rev. 9:20, 13:15, 14:9-10, 21:8, 27, 22:15 Ez. 26:25**
3 *No taking Yahuah in vain* **Matt. 5:33-37**	**Jas. 2:7; 5:12 1 Tim. 6:1**	**Matt. 7:21-23 Ez. 36:23, 39:7**
4 *Remember the Sabbath, keep it holy* **Luke 4:16, 31, 6:5, 23:55-56 Matt. 12:9, 12, 24:20; Mark 1:21, 2: 27-28, 6:2**	**Acts 13:14, 42-44, 15:21, 16:13, 17:1-2, 18:4; Heb. 4; 1 John 2:6**	**Matt. 24:20; Isaiah 66:22-23; Rev. 12:17, 14:12, 21:27, 22:14**
5 *Honor father and mother* **Matt. 15:4-9, 19:19 Mark 7:10, 10:19 Luke 18:20**	**Rom. 1:29-30 Eph. 6:1-3 Col. 3:20; 1 Tim. 5:4; 2 Tim. 3:2**	*No direct reference* **Rev. 12:17, 14:12, 22:14 Ez. 36:23**

This is not intended to be a complete list of all such passages but to demonstrate the 10 Commandments are found in the New Testament in abundance.

During Messiah's Ministry	After Messiah's Ascension	In The End Times
6 *No killing* Matt. 5:21-22, 19:18 Mark 7:21, 10:19 Luke 18:20; John 10:10	Rom. 1:29-30, 13:9 Gal. 5:21; 1 Tim. 1:9 Jas. 2:11; 1 Pet. 4:15 1 John 3:15	Rev. 9:21, 21:8, 22:15
7 *No adultery* Matt. 5:27-28 , 19:18 Mark 10:11-12, 19 Luke 16:18, 18:20 Mark 7:21, Rev. 2:14, 21-22	Rom. 7:2-3, 13:9 Acts 21:25, Rom. 1:29, 2:22 1 Cor. 5:11, 6:9, 18, 10:8 Gal. 5:19; Eph. 5:3; Heb. 13:4 ; 1 Th. 4:3; Jas. 2:11; 2 Pet. 2:14 Jude 1:7	Rev. 9:21, 13:4, 14:8, 17:2, 21:8, 22:15
8 *No stealing* Matt. 19:18; Mark 7:22 , 10:19; Luke 18:20; John 10:10	Rom. 13:9; Eph. 4:28; 1 Pet. 4:15; Rom. 2:21; 1 Cor. 5:10-11, 6:10;	Rev. 9:21 2 Esdras 16:47
9 *No bearing false witness* Matt. 15:19, 19:18 Mark 10:19 Luke 18:20 John 8:44	Acts 5:3-4; Eph. 4:25 Rom. 1:29, 13:9 Col. 3:9; 1 Tim. 4:2 2 Tim. 3:3	Rev. 21:8, 27, 22:15
10 *No coveting* Luke 12:15 Mark 7:22	Rom. 1:29, 7:7-10, 13:9 1 Cor. 5:10-11, 6:9-10 Gal. 5:19-21 Eph. 5:3, 5; Acts 20:33 1 Tim. 6:10, 2 Tim. 3:2 2 Pet. 2:14; Heb. 13:5	*No direct reference* Rev. 12:17, 14:12, 22:14 Ez. 36:23

The 10 Commandments Cannot Pass When Applied After Messiah's Ascension and in the Last Days

THE
END TIMES
SABBATH

Chapter 8 | The End Times Sabbath

In Jesus' *(Yahusha's)* unveiling of the signs of the time of His return, He begins with a warning that we allow no man to deceive us. Unfortunately, the times in which we live are defined by deception even in the church. This is referred to as the "strong delusion" and at the heart of this, is the Sabbath. In this age, this will become the dividing line between the Biblical ekklesia and those who are in danger of being turned away on Judgment Day. The Sabbath is not salvation but those truly seeking relationship with Him will find it. This is important because Messiah invokes the Sabbath practice to the very end times.

If Sabbath passed away, why did Messiah say it will still matter in the End Times? Even in the Great Tribulation, believers will keep His Sabbath and it will matter in practice as this denotes observance. Sabbath includes a rule to limit one's travel on the Sabbath Day.

Isaiah 66:22-23 KJV

For as the new heavens and the new earth, which I will make, shall remain before me, saith the Lord, so shall your seed and your name remain. And it shall come to pass, that from one new moon to another, and from one sabbath to another, shall all flesh come to worship before me, saith the Lord.

When do we get new heavens and a new earth? The Day of Final Judgment. Messiah told us every letter of the Law will remain at least until this day *(Matt. 5:17-18)*. Isaiah is indicating the same in prophecy. On the Day of Judgment, all flesh will come to worship Yahuah on the Sabbath and from one Sabbath to another. Sabbath does not even pass away at that point but will be practiced forever.

Revelation 22:14 KJV

Blessed are they that do his commandments, that they may have right to the tree of life, and may enter in through the gates into the city.

The End Times and the Garden have always tied together as has the Sabbath from beginning to end. The End Times remnant will be found keeping His commandments all the way to the point that they enter into New Jerusalem. This is where we will have access once again, as Adam and Eve once did, to the Tree of Life. However, we will do so keeping His commandments. They are not salvation but they define relationship that is salvation.

Revelation 14:12-13 KJV

Here is the patience of the saints: here are they that keep the commandments of God, and the faith of Jesus. And I heard a voice from heaven saying unto me, Write, Blessed are the dead which die in the Lord from henceforth: Yea, saith the Spirit, that they may rest from their labours; and their works do follow them.

The consistent saints will have the patience to keep the Sabbath rest to the very end. We will observe His commandments that include the Sabbath. It is time to start now. Daniel predicted the Sabbath would be changed and it has been.

Daniel 7:25 KJV

And he shall speak great words against the most High, and shall wear out the saints of the most High, and think to change times and laws: and they shall be given into his hand until a time and times and the dividing of time.

The only Law that is a time is Sabbath. The Beast will change it and his system and religion already has. When one reviews prophecy with intensity, it becomes clear that to be against Sabbath is to support the Beast. The line is being drawn right now. Will we have the patience to follow His ways even when our livelihoods are at stake?

Ezekiel 36:22-28 KJV

Therefore say unto the house of Israel, Thus saith the Lord GOD; I do not this for your sakes, O house of Israel, but for mine holy name's sake, which ye have profaned among the heathen, whither ye went. And I will sanctify my great name, which was profaned among the heathen, which ye have profaned in the midst of them; and the heathen shall know that I am the LORD, saith the Lord GOD, when I shall be sanctified in you before their eyes. For I will take you from among the heathen, and gather you out of all countries, and will bring you into your own land. Then will I sprinkle clean water upon you, and ye shall be clean: from all your filthiness, and from all your idols, will I cleanse you. A new heart also will I give you, and a new spirit will I put within you: and I will take away the stony heart out of your flesh, and I will give you an heart of flesh. And I will put my spirit within you, and cause you to walk in my statutes, and ye shall keep my judgments, and do them. And ye shall dwell in the land that I gave to your fathers; and ye shall be my people, and I will be your God.

The Prophet Ezekiel foretells of the return of the Lost Tribes of Israel in the very End Times. He sanctifies His great name in the end in multiple scriptures even after Gog of Magog's forces are destroyed. At that point of return, Israel will renew covenant and once again, walk in His statutes and keep His Commandments. This includes the Sabbath. We also know that Messiah is our Lord and He is Lord of the Sabbath. He remains Lord to this day and will be in the end and forever. This means He will continue His Sabbath practice in which He is Lord.

> *Mark 2:27-28 KJV*
>
> *And he said unto them, The sabbath was made for man, and not man for the sabbath: Therefore the Son of man is Lord also of the sabbath.*

Believers will not find this foreign because they will keep His commandments because they love Him. Is the Lord of the Sabbath our Lord? Then, we will learn to keep His Sabbath. They will learn that Sabbath is paramount in understanding His ways since Creation and to the end. Even when Israel was given the Law, the Sabbath especially comes with no expiration date but it is to be observed by Israel and the Gentiles among them throughout your generations, for a perpetual covenant, a statute forever, continually, as an everlasting covenant. Can we really overlook such language?

> *Exodus 31:16 KJV*
>
> *Wherefore the children of Israel shall keep the sabbath, to observe the sabbath throughout their generations, for a perpetual covenant.*
>
> *Leviticus 16:31 KJV*
>
> *It shall be a sabbath of rest unto you, and ye shall afflict your souls, by a statute for ever.*
>
> *Leviticus 24:8 KJV*
>
> *Every sabbath he shall set it in order before the LORD continually, being taken from the children of Israel by an everlasting covenant.*

Messiah told us the Law, even 1 letter, does not have an expiration date until at least the Day of Final Judgment. Baruch, the scribe for the Prophet Jeremiah, takes this a step further declaring the Law is forever.

> *Baruch 4:1 KJVA*
>
> *This is the book of the commandments of God, and the law that endureth for ever: all they that keep it shall come to life; but such as leave it shall die.*

The Old Testament prophets well knew the Sabbath had no end. Isaiah speaks of the End Times again as salvation is near to come and Yahuah's righteousness revealed. What does this mean to believers? He says it means it is time to keep the Sabbath. When we do not observe it, we pollute it. Isaiah is not only referencing Israel but he says this is also for the Gentile that is a recurring theme in scripture. Anyone that claims the Sabbath is Jewish, does not know Hebrew nor who a Jew is and certainly does not know the Bible. Just as Paul says many times, the Old Testament has offered this consistently all along. Everyone, even the stranger or Gentile, will be brought to His Holy mountain in the end which is a reference to New Jerusalem.

Isaiah 56:1-8 KJV

Thus saith the Lord, Keep ye judgment, and do justice: for my salvation is near to come, and my righteousness to be revealed. Blessed is the man that doeth this, and the son of man that layeth hold on it; that keepeth the sabbath from polluting it, and keepeth his hand from doing any evil. Neither let the son of the stranger, that hath joined himself to the Lord, speak, saying, The Lord hath utterly separated me from his people: neither let the eunuch say, Behold, I am a dry tree. For thus saith the Lord unto the eunuchs that keep my sabbaths, and choose the things that please me, and take hold of my covenant; Even unto them will I give in mine house and within my walls a place and a name better than of sons and of daughters: I will give them an everlasting name, that shall not be cut off. Also the sons of the stranger, that join themselves to the Lord, to serve him, and to love the name of the Lord, to be his servants, every one that keepeth the sabbath from polluting it, and taketh hold of my covenant; Even them will I bring to my holy mountain, and make them joyful in my house of prayer: their burnt offerings and their sacrifices shall be accepted upon mine altar; for mine house shall be called an house of prayer for all people. The Lord God, which gathereth the outcasts of Israel saith, Yet will I gather others to him, beside those that are gathered unto him.

Many in the church have ignored the Old Testament as if it is impertinent and passed away yet these prophesies and the ways of the Old Testament are still relevant to the very end. They cannot pass away. When it comes to Sabbath, not only is the day critical, but the prophetic time clock appears set on a Sabbath schedule for our coming 1,000-year rest in Him.

2 Esdras 8:52-54 KJVA
For unto you is Paradise opened, the tree of life is planted, the time to come is prepared, plentiousness is made ready, a city is built, and rest is allowed, yes perfect goodness and wisdom. The root of evil is sealed up from you, weakness and the moth is hidden from you, and corruption is fled into hell to be forgotten. Sorrows are passed, and in the end is shown the treasure of immortality.

We are soon to behold the works of Messiah like the world has never seen. He will do this to bring goodness, wisdom and rest or Sabbath to us all. There will be a 1,000-year Sabbath rest in peace with no satan.

2 Esdras 2:34 KJVA
And therefore I say unto you, O you heathen, that hear and understand, Look for your shepherd, he shall give you everlasting rest; for he is near at hand, that shall come in the end of the world.

The Lord of the Sabbath will then destroy satan and we will have everlasting rest in Him. You can have that rest every week right now on His Sabbath. There is a satan now and demons and a world full of those who hate Jesus*(Yahusha)* and even hate you for His sake. Take courage and know that He will give you rest every week even now. You know you need it. This will be restored in our time.

His Law cannot pass. If it does, that would mean there is no way to define sin *(lawlessness)* that appears to the end of Revelation. How does He Judge without Law on the Day of Judgment? Better yet, how is it that anyone calling themselves a scholar has not considered this question and the hypocrisy of claiming there is no Law? This means they teach lawlessness that is the definition of sin. It matters not whether that is their intention, it is what they are teaching. 2nd Esdras defines this in enhanced resolution. We know from Revelation, in the end, Jesus*(Yahusha)* will consume His enemies with a sword from His mouth. What is this sword? Not only is it the flaming sword of His eternal fire, but He destroys His enemies with... the Law.

2 Esdras 13 KJVA

4 And whensoever the voice went out of his mouth, all they burnt, that heard his voice, like as the earth fails when it feels the fire. 38 ...and he (Messiah) shall destroy them without labor, by the law which is like unto fire... (Cf. Rev. 1:16, 2:16, 12:17, 14:12, 19:15, 21, 22:14; 1 John 2:3-4, 3:22-24, 5:2-3; 2 John 1:6; Matt. 5:17-18)

Jeremiah also encourages Israel that it will return but also, that it will face the measure that is the Law in correction and punishment. That is what righteousness is all about.

Jeremiah 46:28 KJV

Fear thou not, O Jacob my servant, saith the LORD: for I am with thee; for I will make a full end of all the nations whither I have driven thee: but I will not make a full end of thee, but correct thee in measure; yet will I not leave thee wholly unpunished.

Most of us recall by memory that His people perish for lack of knowledge. However, have we truly read this in context? What knowledge is it that we lack? The Law.

Hosea 4:6-8 KJV

My people are destroyed for lack of knowledge: because thou hast rejected knowledge, I will also reject thee, that thou shalt be no priest to me: seeing thou hast forgotten the law of thy God, I will also forget thy children. As they were increased, so they sinned against me: therefore will I change their glory into shame. They eat up the sin of my people, and they set their heart on their iniquity.

One pastor stood against us claiming we teach knowledge and he, the spirit. If a pastor does not know we perish from the lack of knowledge and that is the Law even, yet thinks that he is to teach people from his feelings or better said, whatever he feels like teaching, then he is not of Yahuah. He doesn't know Him. Bear in mind, these are prophesies of the very End Times which the church believes but they ignore the part that says His Law will be restored. They were talking about the Law at their time of writing not some new Law.

The Sabbath is a foundational pillar of His Law since Creation and it is applied throughout the End Times as significant to Him. He did not abolish His role and title as Lord of the Sabbath and told us in Matthew 5, He would not. This is the doctrine of the Bible. It is the only doctrine that matters. Our foundation must include His foundation. Otherwise, we are building our house on sinking sand.

When Martin Luther nailed his 95 theses to the door of the Catholic Church in 1517, an awakening began as people realized that church was not following the Bible. The staple of those Dark Ages was the Catholic Church's demand that only they could read and understand the Word yet they proved illiterate. He rebuked them for things like seeking indulgences where men pay for forgiveness of sin like going to a McDonalds Drive-Thru to be absolved. The rich could buy their indulgences in bulk even covering a lifetime of sin. Essentially, the Catholic Church was representing the opposite of the Word.

As much as one must applaud the content of his rebuke, Luther was wrong. You do not protest a Biblically illiterate church yet keep it's foundations built on sinking sand. In Matthew 5, Messiah tells us to set our foundation on the solid rock instead. If you discover after many years your house has a faulty foundation, you do not continue to build up on such because it is already set to fall. The only question is when. The Protestant Church has continued many Catholic illiteracies which are far from the Bible especially in interpretation. The Sabbath is at the very center and part of the Catholic foundation is to profane it.

For this is the calling of our age. That is not our prophecy. This is the time that Moses predicted that we would return to His Law. In Jubilees, which he wrote, Moses offers prophecy of the very End Times in which we are entering. The amazing thing is even if this were written in 150 B.C. as some scholars guess ignorantly, it would still be prophecy and it rings true. That is a sign of inspired scripture further proving it was written when it says. We will begin to study the Laws again and relearn His Commandments and ways in a return to the path of righteousness. This is not a revival, this is a lifestyle that once ignited, never ends.

Jubilees 23:26 [End Times Prophecy]

And in those days the children will begin to study the laws, And to seek the commandments, And to return to the path of righteousness.

We will go back in time and cover the history of Sabbath in the time of transition from the Old to the New Testament. We already covered the New Testament practice to the end that is well documented. However, did the exiled Temple Priests who were connected to Messiah as He was baptized and launched His ministry right there in Bethabara which they still call by it's Muslim name, Qumran, continue the Sabbath just before, during and just after His time? Did the true Biblical ekklesia after the Apostles continue to keep the 7th-Day Sabbath? We will explore these next and expose the powers who oppose His Law and His Sabbath.

*O receive the gift that is given you, and be glad, giving thanks unto him that has called you to the heavenly kingdom. Arise up and stand, behold the number of those that be sealed in the feast of Yahuah: Which are departed from the shadow of the world, and have received glorious garments of Yahuah. Take your number, O Sion, and shut up those of yours that are clothed in white, **which have fulfilled the Law of Yahuah**. The number of your children whom you long for, is fulfilled: beseech the power of Yahuah, that your people which have been called from the beginning, may be hallowed.*

— 2 Esdras 2:37-41 KJVA

SABBATH

150 B.C.
-to-
100 A.D.

in the

DEAD SEA SCROLLS

Chapter 9 | Sabbath in the Dead Sea Scrolls

They shall keep the Sabbath day according to its exact interpretation, and the feasts and the Day of Fasting according to the finding of the members of the New Covenant in the land of Damascus.
−*The Damascus Document, p. 134 [1]*

Where does this exact determination originate? In Torah. Wait a minute, this community before Messiah calls themselves members of a New Covenant. How does that work? Their practices and Law remain the same as Torah that is their source and foundation just as the New Covenant of Messiah. This is evidence the Biblical practice of forming New Covenant does NOT abandon the Old. That thinking is unbiblical and unfounded in all of scripture. Paul never truly says such either.

The Temple Levite Priests from the Sons of Zadok who led the Temple practice since the days of Solomon were exiled into the Wilderness of Judaea. That is historical fact. We have abundant archaeology of their compound which was built similar to the Temple with an inordinate amount of water. This was the Biblical Bethabara where John the Baptist baptized Messiah still oddly called by it's new Muslim name today − Qumran *[chart, end of chapter]*.

This was the Temple Practice continued with Messiah's endorsement as He chose to launch His ministry there and even visited again. Why? The Word was kept there just as the Levite Temple Priests always did. He is the Word *(John 1)*. They were charged with such responsibility by Moses in Deuteronomy 31:24-26 and even by Jacob according to Jubilees 45:16. At that time, there were no printing presses and binderies. There were scroll libraries where they compiled what we would call the Bible today in the Old Testament. This is the only historically proven Bible Canon and no other can compare nor be used in debate. The authority rested with these specific Levites and no one else up until that time.

In 1947, we rediscovered the true, legitimate, historically proven Bible Canon and just as with the Sabbath, the modern church ignores it even buying the illiterate propaganda that Essenes lived in Qumran. However, "The Essene Find" in archaeology is in Ein Gedi, 25 miles South of Qumran *[chart, end of chapter]*. They were not there. Pliny placed them in Ein Gedi right where the treasure trove of archaeology tied to the Essenes was found. There is not a single finger nail of archaeology of Essenes in Qumran and their writings there identify themselves as the exiled Temple Preists, Sons of Zadok, Sons of Aaron, Sons of Levi, and never a single time as Essenes *[chart, end of chapter]*. It is the most illiterate mantra in history though the Anti-Sabbath mantra is similar.

We cover this in detail in the Introduction of our publishing of The Book of Jubilees: The Torah Calendar and 2nd Esdras: The Hidden Book of Prophecy including from the oldest map of Israel dated around the 5th Century or so, all the way up until 1901 labeling Qumran as Bethabara where Messiah was baptized. Israel will take you to the muddy Jordan River today that fails the test of scripture as it is not in the Wilderness of Judaea. Those Pharisees will proudly baptize us in that nasty water while Jesus *(Yahusha)* was baptized in freshwater springs as John operated typically.

However, this community of the exiled Temple Priest leadership continued the Temple Practice there in Qumran/Bethabara. What they kept in their library is what we call Bible Canon for the Old Testament and they included the Book of Jubilees which they defined as Torah. This is the book in that they used for the "exact determination" of the Biblical Calendar for Sabbath and Feasts. There is no other and notice they took their library with them when exiled and the Pharisee library is impertinent as they were ignorant of the true Bible practice when they conquered the Temple and usurped this priestly authority illegally around 165 B.C. or soon after This community is very clear in their writings about this and they identify the Pharisees as Jesus *(Yahusha)* does with scathing rebuke of the very worse kind.

Here is what they recorded regarding the Book of Jubilees:

> *(For Yahuah made) a Covenant with you and all Israel; therefore a man shall bind himself by oath to return to the Law of Moses, for in it all things are strictly defined. As for the exact determination of their times to which Israel turns a blind eye, behold it is strictly defined in the Book of the Divisions of the Times into their Jubilees and Weeks.*
> *—The Damascus Document, 50 A.D. [21]*

The Sabbath is a large part of the Book of Jubilees that was ranked the 6th most abundant of scrolls found there. However, their local community writings demonstrate over and over this community of exiled Temple Priests kept and taught the Sabbath in great detail. They followed Torah in this village from their arrival around 150 B.C. to the time of Messiah and they continued after Messiah according to dating. In fact, about 50 years after Messiah, this writing even identifies Him specifically as it also rebukes the Pharisees whom Yahuah is against:

> *[And chokes prey for its lionesses; and it fills] its caves [with prey] and its dens with victims (ii, i2a-b).*
> *Interpreted, this concerns the furious young lion [who executes revenge] on* **those who seek smooth things** *and* **hangs men alive,** *...* **formerly in Israel. Because of a man hanged alive on [the] tree,** *He proclaims,* **'Behold I am against [you, says the Lord of Hosts']**. *— Commentary on Nahum, P. 505. [1]*

What man was hanged on the tree in which Yahuah responded to the Pharisees who we will prove in that chapter are "those who seek smooth things" in Jerusalem? This is Jesus*(Yahusha)* and though any other writings which would make this connection found there will likely be suppressed or destroyed, this one survives. This community is the bridge between the Old Testament and New Testament practices. They were both.

At the end of this chapter, we provide a chart of the quotes in prophecy that these Temple Priests aligned their community as those who prepare the way in the Wilderness and they specify John the Baptist as a leader who would rise from their ranks. He did and he baptized Messiah there. John is a New Testament figure known as the Great Prophet, the Elijah come again according to Jesus*(Yahusha)* Himself. Therefore, this is a New

Testament community and find and the Pharisees should not be given charge as they are the enemy. This is full-circle, indisputable evidence that the Bible practice of the Old Testament remained in the New Testament. That should be no surprise as the Apostles did the same as we already demonstrated.

When it comes to Sabbath, this community in their local writings, observed this practice right out of Torah that included The Book of Jubilees. They too, as the Old and New Testaments, record the Sabbath is to be observed perpetually or forever.

> *This is the holocaust of every Sabbath in addition to the perpetual holocaust and the corresponding drink-offering. —The Temple Scroll, p. 194 [1]*

As David, these Temple Preists even wrote songbooks for the Sabbath such as *"Hymns for the Sabbath Day" [1-p.379]* and *"Songs for the Holocaust of the Sabbath" [1-p.329]*. Their ranks always included worshippers in voice and instruments but they also include David's Psalms that were found complete and even include additional psalms than what we have in our Bibles today.

> *An Account of David's Poems*
> *XXVII David son of Jesse was wise and brilliant like the light of the sun; (he was) a scribe, intelligent and perfect in all his ways before God and men. YHWH gave him an intelligent and brilliant spirit, and he wrote 3,600 psalms and 364 songs to sing before the altar for the daily perpetual sacrifice, for all the days of the year; and 52 songs for the Sabbath offerings; and 30 songs for the New Moons, for Feast-days and for the Day of Atonement. In all, the songs which he uttered were 446, and 4 songs to make music on behalf of those stricken (by evil spirits). In all, they were 4,050. All these he uttered through prophecy which was given him from before the Most High.*
> *—Apocryphal Psalms (1), p. 313 [1]*

They detail the Sabbath Law *[1-p.38,134,141,157,231,234]*, calendars that include the Sabbath always on the 7th Day of the Week and NEVER the 1st, even some specifically for Sabbaths as well as Priestly Courses, sacrifices *[1-p.541]*, etc. They were submerged in Sabbath doctrine as they should be.

> *[On the sixteenth of it (of the second month): sabbath.]*
> *On the twenty-third of it: sabbath.*
> *[On] the thir[tie]th [of it: sabbath.*
> *On the seventh of the third month: sabbath.*
> *On the fourteenth of it: sabbath.*
> *On the fifteenth of it: Feast of Weeks.*
> *On the twenty-] I I [f]irs[t] of it: sabbath.*
> *–M M T A = A S E C T A R I A N C A L E N D A R (4Q3941-2),*
> *p.222. [1]*

> *Calendars of Priestly Courses*
> *Ca In the first (month) on the fourth (day) is Sabbath ...*
> *On the eighth (day) in it [is Sabbath] ...*
> *On the eleventh (day) in it is Sabbath ...*
> *[On the 14th (day) in it is Passover on the third (day of the week).*
> *On the 15th (day) in it: the feast of the Unleavened Bread on the*
> *fourth (day of the week).*
> *On the 1 8th (day) is Sabbath.*
> *On the 25th (day) in it: Sabbath.*
> *On the 26th (day) in it:] feast of the Gr[ain after the Sabbath.*
> *In the first month] 30 (days). 5*
> *On the second (day) in it: [Sabbath.*
> *On the ninth (day) in it: Sabbath.*
> *On the 16th (day)]*
> *–Calendrical Document C (4Q326), p. 363 [1]*

They read and interpreted "the Book" meaning Torah every Sabbath. However, they did not revise their writings or copy scrolls on the Sabbath.

Frs. 1-2

... and to draw water from a cistern ... the drawing ... [No] man shall take anything from his place on the Sabbath, [from outside the house into it] or from the house outsi[de] ... for him to interpret and read in the Book on the [Sabba]th ...

—4QHalakhah A (4Q251), p. 231 [1]

Fr. 1 i

[No man shall revise the scro]ll of a book reading its script on the day of [Sabbath] ... But they may read and study it. No man shall make plans with his mouth ... [on the day of Sabbath. He shall not talk] about any matter relating to work or wealth or ... on the day of Sabbath. He shall sp[eak no wo]rd apart from speaking holy words as prescribed and from pronouncing blessings of God. He may talk about eating and drink[ing] ...

—4QHalakhah B (40264a), p. 234 [1]

In fact, these Temple Priests offer incredible detail about how they observed Sabbath that largely matches Torah. We know they interpreted the same as Isaiah and Jubilees when they understood that we are not to seek our own pleasure on the Sabbath but His instead. We possess historical confirmation that we do not have to throw out Jubilees and also really Isaiah over this gnat-straining point some have attempted to debate with no position.

Concerning the Sabbath to observe it according to its law No man shall work on the sixth day from the moment when the sun's orb is distant by its own fulness from the gate (wherein it sinks); for this is what He said, Observe the Sabbath day to keep it holy (Deut. v, 12). No man shall speak any vain or idle word on the Sabbath day. He shall make no loan to his companion. He shall make no decision in matters of money and gain. He shall say nothing about work or labour to be done on the morrow. No man shall walk in the field to do business on the Sabbath. He shall not walk more than one thousand cubits beyond his town. No man shall eat on the Sabbath day except that which is already prepared. He shall eat nothing lying in the fields. He shall not drink except in the camp. XI If he is on a journey and goes down to bathe, he shall drink where he stands, but he shall not draw water into a vessel. He shall send out no stranger on his business on the Sabbath day. No man shall wear soiled garments, or garments brought to the store, unless they have been washed with water or rubbed with incense. No man shall willingly mingle (with others) on the Sabbath. No man shall walk more than two thousand cubits after a beast to pasture it outside his town. He shall not raise his hand to strike it with his fist. If it is stubborn he shall not take it out of his house. No man shall take anything out of the house or bring anything in. And if he is in a booth, let him neither take anything out nor bring anything in. He shall not open a sealed vessel on the Sabbath. No man shall carry perfumes on himself whilst going and coming on the Sabbath. He shall lift neither stone nor dust in his dwelling. No man minding a child shall carry it whilst going and coming on the Sabbath. No man shall chide his manservant or maidservant or labourer on the

Sabbath. No man shall assist a beast to give birth on the Sabbath day. And if it should fall into a cistern or pit, he shall not lift it out on the Sabbath. No man shall spend the Sabbath in a place near to Gentiles on the Sabbath. No man shall profane the Sabbath for the sake of riches or gain on the Sabbath day. But should any man fall into water or (fire), let him not be

pulled out with the aid of a ladder or rope or (some such) utensil. No man on the Sabbath shall offer anything on the altar except the Sabbath burnt-offering; for it is written thus: Except your Sabbath offerings (Lev. xxiii, 38). No man shall send to the altar any burnt-offering, or cereal offering, or incense, or wood, by the hand of one smitten with any uncleanness, permitting him thus to defile the altar. For it is written, The sacrifice of the wicked is an abomination, but the prayer of the just is as an agreeable offering (Prov. xv, 8). No man entering the house of worship shall come unclean and in need of washing. And at the sounding of the trumpets for assembly, he shall go there before or after (the meeting), and shall not cause the whole service to stop, XII for it is a holy service. No man shall lie with a woman in the city of the Sanctuary, to defile the city of the Sanctuary with their uncleanness. Every man who preaches apostasy under the dominion of the spirits of Belial shall be judged according to the law relating to those possessed by a ghost or familiar spirit (Lev. xx, 27). But no man who strays so as to profane the Sabbath and the feasts shall be put to death; it shall fall to men to keep him in custody. And if he is healed of his error, they shall keep him in custody for seven years and

he shall afterwards approach the Assembly.
—The Damascus Document, p. 142-143 [1]

These Aaronic, Levite Temple Priests record their history of being exiled by the Hasmoneans and Pharisees multiple times. There is no question what happened and whom they were. Anyone claiming they were Essenes makes themselves appear as fools. Their track from the Temple Priesthood which NEVER included Essenes nor do they use the term even once, is well-preserved and this is archaeology and history that is undeniable. The Book of Maccabees however, is proven a lie.

*Interpreted, this concerns **the Wicked Priest who pursued the Teacher of Righteousness to the house of his exile** that he might confuse him with his venomous fury. And at the time appointed for rest, for the Day of Atonement, he appeared before them to confuse them, and to cause them to stumble on the Day of Fasting, their Sabbath of repose.*
—Commentary on Habukkuk (1QpHab), p.515 [1]

"[For the violence done to Lebanon shall overwhelm you, and the destruction of the beasts] X II shall terrify you, because of the blood of men and the violence done to the land, the city, and all its inhabitants (ii, 17).
Interpreted, this saying concerns the Wicked Priest, inasmuch as he shall be paid the reward which he himself tendered to the Poor. For Lebanon is the Council of the Community; and the beasts are the simple of Judah who keep the Law. As he himself plotted the destruction of the Poor, so will God condemn him to destruction.
*And as for that which He said, Because of the blood of the city and the violence done to the land: interpreted, the city is **Jerusalem where the Wicked Priest committed abominable deeds and defiled the Temple of God**. The violence done to the land: these are the cities of Judah where he **robbed the Poor of their possessions**."*
—Commentary On HABAKKUK, p. 515 [1]

The Priests in Jerusalem at the time of this writing which are being rebuked are the Hasmoneans and Pharisees. This is not debatable nor in question. However, these inhabitants of Qumran are the "sons of

Zadok the Priests" who keep the Law and the Sabbath forever.

> *"Words of blessing. The M[aster shall bless] the sons of Zadok the Priests,*
> *whom God has chosen to confirm His Covenant for [ever]"*
> *– The Blessing of the High Priest, p.388 [1]*

> *"The sons of Zadok are the elect of Israel, the men called by name who shall*
> *stand at the end of days." –The Damascus Document, p. 132 [1]*

Many forget that even though Israel strayed, these sons of Zadok of the Temple did not. They are the ones to follow in order to find The God Culture of the Temple and the Bible. This is why Messiah launched His ministry there at their headquarters at Bethabara which we prove overwhelmingly is Qumran. Every believer should know this because this is a massive deception to hide scripture and the true history of the true ekklesia as well as their practices.

Ezekiel 44:15-16 KJV
But the priests the Levites, the sons of Zadok, that kept the charge of my sanctuary when the children of Israel went astray from me, they shall come near to me to minister unto me, and they shall stand before me to offer unto me the fat and the blood, saith the Lord GOD: They shall enter into my sanctuary, and they shall come near to my table, to minister unto me, and they shall keep my charge.

Ezekiel 48:11 KJV
It shall be for the priests that are sanctified of the sons of Zadok; which have kept my charge, which went not astray when the children of Israel went astray, as the Levites went astray.

In addition to identifying Messiah on the fragment we previously covered, the rest of these are prior to His coming. After John the Baptist was beheaded as a leader of this community, they became a target for the Hasmoneans married to Herod even and the Pharisees who even had a military as well as forts.

"When God engenders (the Priest-) Messiah, he shall come with them [at] the head of the whole congregation of Israel with all [his brethren, the sons] of Aaron the Priests" – The Messianic Rule, p.161 [1]

This Qumran/Bethabara community ties to Messiah especially when some of John the Baptist's disciples chose to follow Jesus*(Yahusha)* physically. The community disappears with no trace or trail and this is because they would have left Judaea with the Lost Tribes of the Southern Kingdom who were being driven out. There was clearly a mass migration into Africa in which Isaiah, Zephaniah and other prophets detail. That is a different topic we cannot prove in this book but if one views our Lost Tribes Series on YouTube, you will learn this connection is firm.

John the Baptist, a Qumran/Bethabara son of Zadok recorded in their writings *[chart, end of chapter]*, declared Jesus*(Yahusha)* right there in Qumran/Bethabara as the son of Yahuah.

John 1:32-42 KJV

*And **John bare record**, saying, I saw the Spirit descending from heaven like a dove, and it abode upon him. And I knew him not: but he that sent me to baptize with water, the same said unto me, Upon whom thou shalt see the Spirit descending, and remaining on him, the same is he which baptizeth with the Holy Ghost. And I saw, and bare record that **this is the Son of God**. Again the **next day after John stood, and two of his disciples**; And looking upon Jesus as he walked, he saith, **Behold the Lamb of God! And the two disciples heard him speak, and they followed Jesus**. Then Jesus turned, and saw them following, and saith unto them, What seek ye? They said unto him, Rabbi, (which is to say, being interpreted, Master,) where dwellest thou? He saith unto them, Come and see. They came and saw where he dwelt, and abode with him that day: for it was about the tenth hour. **One of the two which heard John speak, and followed him, was Andrew, Simon Peter's brother**. He **first findeth his own brother Simon**, and saith unto him, **We have found the Messias**, which is, being interpreted, the Christ. And **he brought him to Jesus**. And when Jesus beheld him, he said, **Thou art Simon the son of Jona: thou shalt be called Cephas, which is by interpretation, A stone. [Peter in Greek]***

What is the continuation of the Qumran community and the scrolls they kept? Did they continue to write? Yes, they did. For some of them became the disciples and even Peter's brother Andrew was one of them originally. This likely indicates Andrew was a Levite which means Peter would have been of the same bloodline. We cannot prove that as not everyone at Qumran had to be a Levite. They followed Jesus*(Yahusha)* leaving Qumran and it is likely many did over time. However, Peter through his brother ties to this Qumran/Bethabara community in continuation. The next Dead Sea Scroll essentially would be titled 1st and 2nd Peter. It was not found there but the trail is obvious. Peter too kept and taught the Sabbath as Qumran did.

Those who remained there would have been chased away by the armies of the Pharisees and Rome in time. They were not Essenes so the standoff at Masada of Essenes and Sicarii who were likely Essene assassins has nothing to do with Qumran. They were already down there in Ein Gedi. At least some of Qumran, and likely all of it, took up their cross and followed Messiah especially after His death and resurrection. This is why their writings seem to disappear after that point. They became part of the New Testament and someone there wrote of Messiah's death.

This is the Old Testament coming alive in the New. The Pharisees are never in the Old Testament except being rebuked as they were Samaritans previously not Hebrews. Their lot came from Modi'in in the territory of Dan taken over by Samaria and Philistines to conquer Judaea and the Temple and they defiled it. They were even buried there not Judaea proving their origin was not Hebrew. This was no revolt; it was a conquest. They exiled the Temple Priests and practice as they replaced the Priesthood leadership with themselves. Messiah rebukes them many times and we provide a chart for these Pharisee fruits as well as all of the characteristics of the Pharisees and Hasmoneans as they appear in these Qumran local writings *(see charts, pp. 288-291)*. You will notice they match Messiah's rebuke.

You will also find Messiah's doctrine is a continuation of the Old Testament practice. His Apostles continue the same after this and again some of them were from Qumran/Bethabara as John the Baptist's former disciples. The reason this entire narrative has been hijacked since these scrolls were found is because it documents the Bible Old Testament Canon. It proves the Catholic Church compiled nothing but added to and deleted books of the Bible usurping Jesus' *(Yahusha's)* throne.

We will now move on to the phase of history called the "early church" which is a very confused mess. We will sift through this as the Bible is clear there is a Synagogue of Satan who say they are Yahudim and are not but do lie *(Rev. 2:9, 3:9)* and men that crept in unawares according to Jude and Paul. There are Nicolaitans, those who follow the way of Core, the doctrine of Balaam and Jezebel. These men have always been at work and they are the founders of what we call the Catholic Church which is not His early church or ekklesia really. Their writings and doctrines prove they have never been a part of His ekklesia. These are the agitators and infiltrators and they have established many denominations that continue to carry their banner especially attacking the Sabbath and undermining the Word.

We will expose this in this writing with abundant scripture as we have already. We must all know Yahuah's ways especially in the age in which we live. The strong delusion in which we were warned is not coming but upon us and centuries old. It truly began in root with this group in 165 B.C. when they conquered and defiled the Temple fulfilling the Psalm 83 prophetic war. They say they are Jews having changed the Bible word Yahudim to remove His name from His people and then they claim to be His people. However, they do not know Him and most of them never will. Even modern Israel cannot be a supposed re-gathering of the Lost Tribes as less than 2% of that nation accepts Jesus *(Yahusha)* as the Messiah. They must re-gather in the vine not in Pharisee leaven and in peace, not the perpetual war stance of modern Israel. This is all being brought into the light in our era and many of us will know the truth and restore His ways.

The following charts document the Dead Sea Scroll position on their identity. It is extremely unscholarly to ignore who they say they are and manufacture that they were a cult of Essenes which they do not say. It is outright fraud. When "The Essene Find" in archaeology which is the next chart is found 25 miles South of Qumran in Ein Gedi and nothing found at Qumran, these scholars make themselves fools. When Pliny the Elder places them in the mountains above Ein Gedi and these same scholars act as if they can't read that, they only offer willing ignorance and propaganda.

Furthermore, the connection to John the Baptist with this Qumran community known as Bethabara in scripture, becomes firmly entrenched when this community identifies itself in prophesy as those who prepare the way for Messiah in the wilderness. They already knew this is where Jesus*(Yahusha)* would launch His ministry. They knew they would play a role and that John would rise from their ranks.

They and John kept and taught the Sabbath. In fact, John's main message was to repent and sin no more. What does that mean? He taught the return to the Law of Moses. He did so with Messiah's endorsement as the Great Prophet even. Why did Jesus*(Yahusha)* not correct John and let people know He came to change the Law? Not only was that not His purpose, He said He would not change the Law.

And they shall teach my people the difference between the holy and profane, and cause them to discern between the unclean and the clean. And in controversy they shall stand in judgment; and they shall judge it according to my judgments: and they shall keep my laws and my statutes in all mine assemblies; and they shall hallow my sabbaths.
–Ezekiel 44:23-24 (Sons of Zadok, Temple Priests)

SONS OF ZADOK = 20 times

From the days of King Solomon, these are the Temple Priests. They are Levites and sons of Aaron both. However, they were given charge of the Temple worship and are the only Biblical keepers of scripture. They never call themselves Essenes but they identify themselves over 100 times and any scholar confusing the two is no scholar. They remained holy according to Ezekiel:

Ezekiel 48:11 KJV
It shall be for the priests that are sanctified of the sons of Zadok; which have kept my charge, which went not astray when the children of Israel went astray, as the Levites went astray.

They remained faithful when exiled from the Temple to Qumran and they will stand again in the End Times.

"The sons of Zadok are the elect of Israel, the men called by name who shall stand at the end of days."
-The Damascus Document, p. 132 [1]

Scripture was found in their library meaning this was Bible canon kept by the Sons of Zadok as was Biblical tradition. Essenes are never mentioned in scripture and never a Biblical tribe nor found in or near Qumran. That is blatant fraud!

Moses in Deuteronomy 31:25-26 KJV (Cf. Jubilees 45:16)
That Moses commanded the Levites, which bare the ark of the covenant of the LORD, saying, Take this book of the law, and put it in the side of the ark of the covenant of the LORD your God, that it may be there for a witness against thee.

"...this concerns the Wicked Priest who pursued the Teacher of Righteousness to the house of his exile..." –Commentary On HABAKKUK, p. 515 |1|

"the city is Jerusalem where the Wicked Priest committed abominable deeds and defiled the Temple of God. The violence done to the land..." –Commentary On HABAKKUK, p. 515 |1|

When groups of scholars make themselves so stupid as to say this group were Essenes, you know they are only offering propaganda.

ESSENES = 0 times

THE ESSENES OF EIN GEDI

"On the west side of the Dead Sea, but out of range of the noxious exhalations of the coast, is the solitary tribe of the Essenes..."
"Lying below the Essenes was formerly the town of Engedi..." "Next comes Masada..." [10]
– Pliny the Elder, Natural History (Book V)

Pliny, a geographer, indisputably located the Essenes in the mountains overlooking Ein Gedi, 25 miles South of Qumran. He even anchors it to Masada just to the South and that is the Southern tip not near Qumran.

This is affirmed in mass scale archaeology called "The Essene Find" in Ein Gedi. This included a very ancient temple identified as a Chalcolithic Temple, c. 4th millennium B.C., which was not built by the Essenes but likely part of their compound in the mountains.

Also, archaeologists discovered a synagogue with many symbols identifying these Essenes as the secret cult throughout history fitting to everything we know about the Essenes who never lived in Qumran.

They were obsessed with peacocks as they worship the Peacock Angel *(Persian)* identified by many as the Nephilim deity known as Asmodeus. They etched swastika on the wall, very prominently display an 8-pointed star of Ishtar on the floor in tile, etc. They even offer what appears a very freemasonic warning on the wall.

There is no actual coherent data placing Essenes in Qumran.

Remnants of a Chalcolithic Temple (4th millennium BCE). [18]

Essene synagogue in Ein Gedi. [18]

Tile mosaic on synagogue floor in Ein Gedi. [18]

Peacock symbols in Ein Gedi synagogue. [18]

JOHN THE BAPTIST
IN QUMRAN?

He Likely Grew Up There *(Luke 1:80)*

Prophecy of John Blessing Messiah

The Blessing of the Prince of the Congregation (100 B.C.) [56] "The *Master (John the Baptist) shall bless the Prince of the Congregation (Yahusha)* . . . and shall *renew for him the Covenant of the Community* that he may establish the *kingdom of His people for ever*, [that he may **judge the poor** with righteousness and] **dispense justice** with {equity to the oppressed} of the land, and that he may walk perfectly before Him in all the ways [of truth], and that *he may establish His holy Covenant* at the time of the affliction of those who seek God. May the Lord raise you up to everlasting heights, and as a fortified tower upon a high wall! [May you *smite the peoples*] with the might of your hand and ravage the earth with *your sceptre*; may you *bring death to the ungodly with the breath of your lips*! ...The *rulers ... [and all the kings of the] nations shall serve you*. He shall strengthen you with *His holy Name* and you shall be *as a [lion*; and you shall not lie down until you have devoured the] prey which naught shall deliver"
—Calendars, Liturgies and Prayers, p. 389-390. [1]

John's Rare Diet Found in Qumran

No, this cannot be the "locust bean" of the Carob tree as the Bible mentions those in Luke 15:16 as the food of swine and does not call them locusts but husks/pods. The Biblical covenant diet included the insect.

Prepare the Way in the Wilderness...

And when these become members of the Community in Israel according to all these rules, they shall separate from the habitation of unjust men and shall go into the wilderness to prepare there the way of Him; as it is written, Prepare in the wilderness the way of..., make straight in the desert a path for our God (Isa. xl, 3). This (path) is the study of the Law which He commanded by the hand of Moses, that they may do according to all that has been revealed from age to age, and as the Prophets have revealed by His Holy Spirit.
–The Community Rule, P. 109. [1]

John baptized Yahusha in Qumran/ Bethabara fulfilling these 2 Qumran prophesies and Isaiah. These exiled Temple Priests knew their community would play such a role. This is the link between the Old and New Testaments.

SABBATH HISTORY
Second Century

The 7 Churches of Revelation in Turkey Speak

Acts 9:31 KJV

*Then had the churches **rest** throughout all Judaea and Galilee and Samaria, and were edified; and walking in the fear of the Lord, and in the comfort of the Holy Ghost, were multiplied.*

εἰρήνη: **eirēnē**: *peace (literally or figuratively); by implication, prosperity:—one, peace, quietness, rest, + set at one again. The KJV translates in the following manner: peace (89x), one (1x), rest (1x), quietness (1x). (Strong's #G1515)*

Acts 18:4 KJV

And he reasoned in the synagogue every sabbath, and persuaded the Jews and the Greeks.

Acts 16:13 KJV

And on the sabbath we went out of the city by a river side, where prayer was wont to be made; and we sat down, and spake unto the women which resorted thither.

Acts 13:42-44 KJV

And when the Jews were gone out of the synagogue, the Gentiles besought that these words might be preached to them the next sabbath. Now when the congregation was broken up, many of the Jews and religious proselytes followed Paul and Barnabas: who, speaking to them, persuaded them to continue in the grace of God. And the next sabbath day came almost the whole city together to hear the word of God.

As we just examined the true early church of the Apostles, we already know they were keeping the Sabbath. Here we have a perfect example that appears to be translated accurately. The ekklesias had rest or Sabbath throughout the region. They were all keeping Sabbath and were edified. They would not be walking in fear of Yahuah otherwise. The comfort of the Holy Spirit also leads to His Sabbath. Peter then goes about healing just as Messiah did on the Sabbath. We also find Gentiles and Jews together observed the Saturday, 7th-Day Sabbath after His ascension and even outside of synagogues. It can only be a lie for one to say the Apostles did not keep the Sabbath. They did so on the 7th Day, NEVER the 1st.

We find Acts 9:31 very interesting as the Greek word used here is interpreted "peace" almost every time it is used and that is often. However, this one time in all 92 of it's uses, the KJV translators chose to use the word "rest." As this appears to be Sabbath, that makes sense and fits the paradigm of that day. The true early church kept the Sabbath and history affirms this as we already covered.

At this point, we have well proven the Bible through the 1st Century A.D. continued the practice of Sabbath on the 7th Day which we will fully vet as Saturday later. We also found the Qumran Community of exiled Temple Priests continued the Sabbath practice throughout the 1st Century as well on the same. They embraced Jesus *(Yahusha)* and even fulfilled prophecy in preparing the way for His coming in the Wilderness as John the Baptist originated there in their community. How then, did it become the 1st Day of the week on Sunday in almost all denominations? The question is did anyone after Messiah and His Apostles who all observed and taught the 7th-Day Sabbath, have the authority to overrule the Lord of the Sabbath? If He told us the Commandments including the Sabbath cannot pass until the Day of Final Judgment *(Matt. 5:17-18)*, then, who usurped his throne to make such a change? He did not. His Apostles most certainly did not. Qumran did not.

You will find the Early Church in continuation kept the Sabbath on the 7th Day originally as well. We will explore portions of history which document this practice and roughly when it shifted and by whom. What you will find is it was practiced by most believers originally patterned after the Apostles on the 7th Day and then, it was first changed in Rome especially to "The Lord's Day" which they call Sunday in absolute ignorance. We will prove in an entire chapter The Lord's Day remains the Saturday Sabbath as He rose on the Sabbath of Saturday NOT Sunday. They are viewing the wrong calendar as He operated on the Bible calendar not the Roman one nor the Pharisee one and the day does not begin at midnight nor is it governed by the moon but the sun according to scripture. We will prove this.

Some churches at that point still continued the 7th-Day Sabbath while satisfying Rome's demand for Sunday worship. In time, Saturday was forgotten and only Sunday was left and for some, Rome had to force it with their military. Is that how the Bible operates? Does Yahuah phase Commandments out as such marginalizing His own writing with His own finger? It certainly does not seem rational. Let's explore as we pick up the history of the Sabbath from the 2nd Century. You will find there is no shift until far later except in Rome who was never a Biblical ekklesia but a political religion that would be installed into absolute power in the days of Constantine "the Not-So-Great." It is the Final Empire rebuked in scripture especially by Daniel 2 and 7 as well as 2 Esdras 11-12. This was already foretold with exceptional accuracy. Also, we will address the Didache claim from the Catholic Church next chapter.

2nd Century: Early Ekklesia Observed the Feasts and Sabbath

Polycarp of Smryna in modern Turkey essentially came from one of the 7 ekklesias from Revelation as a direct follower of John the Apostle. He followed the teachings of the Apostles whom he knew directly. Though we do not have direct writings and references from him, we know that he kept the Sabbath and the Feasts. The first reference from Irenaeus was written contemporaneously with Polycarp's time and attests that these same practices continued until his time later in the 2nd century. Thus, we have a preserved timeline the Sabbath and Feasts were being observed by the early church especially in Turkey throughout the 2nd Century.

Polycarp of Smyrna, 69-155 A.D. (Practice to late 1st Century)

"But Polycarp also was not only instructed by apostles, and conversed with many who had seen Christ, but was also, by apostles in Asia, appointed bishop of the Church in Smyrna…always taught the things which he had learned from the apostles, and which the Church has handed down, and which alone are true. To these things all the Asiatic Churches testify, as do also those men who have succeeded Polycarp down to the present time."
–Irenaeus (120-200 A.D.). [58]

We know Polycarp followed the Apostles' example and that meant it must include the Sabbath and Feasts as they kept them and so did even the Gentiles that were with them. However, the record of Polycarp's death leaves nothing to guesswork. His death occurred on the same Sabbath that Messiah was crucified on the 1st Day of Unleavened Bread which is a Feast Sabbath but His death made it "The Great Sabbath." That is what this is referencing. Additionally, this history affirms that the early ekklesia after the Apostles was keeping the Feasts as well as Sabbath. Irenaeus records that ALL the Asiatic Churches were observing these same practices. Polycarp, like the Apostles before him, was martyred, burned to death, by the Romans for refusing to renounce Messiah.

Polycarp of Smyrna, 69-155 A.D.

*"On the **day of the preparation**, at the hour of dinner, there came out pursuers and horsemen" and **Polycarp was killed "on the day of the great Sabbath at the eighth hour."***
–The Martyrdom of Polycarp, Bishop of Smyrna. [59]

However, there is a direct reference to Polycarp keeping the Saturday Sabbath specifically. The true early ekklesia followed the pattern of the Apostles. The Lord's Day was this Great Sabbath and it was Saturday.

Vita Polycarpi (3rd to early 4th century):

"This work is attributed to Pionius and is dated anywhere from the 3rd to the early 4th century A.D. Many historians view the Vita Polycarpi as a book of legends and fantastic supernaturalism, quoting non-existent documents, and not of any real historical value beyond what was taking place during the 3rd

or 4th centuries. However, many historians view this document as having some historical value, such as in its descriptions of the life and liturgy of the 3rd-century church in Smyrna — as well as Christian interactions with the Jews and pagans. Specifically relevant to this discussion, the Christian community in this region of Smyrna is specifically described, in the Vita Polycarpi, as keeping the Saturday Sabbath in the same manner the Jews — and gathering for Biblical instruction and to celebrate Sabbath as a feast day with their brethren. [68]

As the Feasts are really in tandem in this same ancient debate which is really defiling the Law, Polycarp's successor Polycrates continued these same practices of observing the Feasts and Sabbaths. Again, this originates in the Apostles' teaching and was also confirmed previously by Irenaeus through the end of the 2nd Century. The Roman Church did not. The true ekklesia in Rome from where Aquila and Priscilla were chased out by the Roman Church that would marry the government in just a century were against the Bible and believers from the beginning *(Acts 18:1-4)*. They act as Pharisees because they are Pharisees in origin. They were threatening Polycrates as well which he mentions. This is an absolute endorsement of the Feasts and Sabbath and Biblical practice in continual effect through the end of the 2nd Century at least. It is also a rebuke of the anti-Christ church who was martyring all these men for keeping to the Word. Imagine that.

Polycrates of Ephesus (125-196 A.D.): Letter to Victor, Bishop of Rome.

A question of no small importance arose at that time. For the parishes of all Asia, as from an older tradition, held that the fourteenth day of the moon, on which day the Jews were commanded to sacrifice the lamb, **should be observed as the feast of the Saviour's passover...But it was not the custom of the churches in the rest of the world... But the bishops of Asia, led by Polycrates, decided to hold to the old custom handed down to them**. *He himself, in a letter which he addressed to Victor and the church of Rome, set forth in the following words the tradition which had come down to him.*

__Eusebius records that Polycrates wrote:__ "__We observe the__ __exact day__; neither adding, nor taking away. For in Asia also great lights have fallen asleep, which shall rise again on the day of the Lord's coming, when he shall come with glory from heaven, and shall seek out all the saints. Among these are __Philip__, one of the twelve apostles, who fell asleep in Hierapolis; and his two aged virgin daughters, and another daughter, who lived in the Holy Spirit and now rests at Ephesus; and, moreover, __John__, who was both a witness and a teacher, who reclined upon the bosom of the Lord, and, being a priest, wore the sacerdotal plate. He fell asleep at Ephesus. And __Polycarp in Smyrna__, who was a bishop and martyr; and __Thraseas, bishop and martyr from Eumeneia__, who fell asleep in Smyrna. Why need I mention the __bishop and martyr Sagaris who fell asleep in Laodicea__, or the blessed __Papirius, or Melito the Eunuch__ who lived altogether in the Holy Spirit, and who lies in __Sardis__, awaiting the episcopate from heaven, when he shall rise from the dead? __All these observed the fourteenth day of the passover according to the Gospel__, deviating in no respect, but following the rule of faith. And __I also, Polycrates__, the least of you all, __do according to the tradition of my relatives__, some of whom I have closely followed. For __seven of my relatives were bishops;__ and I am the eighth. And __my relatives always observed the day when the people put away the leaven__. I, therefore, brethren, who have __lived sixty-five years__ in the Lord, and __have met with the brethren throughout the world__, and have gone through every Holy Scripture, am __not affrighted by terrifying words__. For those greater than I have said 'We ought to obey God rather than man'...I could mention __the bishops who were present, whom I summoned at your desire; whose names, should I write them, would constitute a great multitude__. And they, beholding my littleness, __gave their consent to the letter__, knowing that I did not bear my gray hairs in vain, but had always governed my life by the Lord Jesus"
– Eusebius of Caesarea (314 A.D.) [65]

Remember, John recorded Messiah's message to the continuation of the Apostles and they were in Turkey not Rome. Polycrates not only preserves that they keep the Law in the Feasts and Sabbath but he lays out a list of those leaders who do and notice most were martyred as a result. He is listing the 7 ekklesias and demonstrating that they were being pressured and wiped out at least in leadership. So not only did the Apostles keep the Feasts and the Sabbath according to Polycrates but so did his predecessor, Polycarp of Smyrna. He includes: ***"Thraseas, bishop and martyr from Eumeneia," "bishop and martyr Sagaris who fell asleep in Laodicea," "Papirius, or Melito the Eunuch from Sardis."*** They were all keeping the Sabbath and Feasts. Polycrates, then, writes ***his relatives, 7 more bishops*** of the true ekklesia, were observing what he observed. However, then, he invokes a ***multitude of bishops*** who were with him in approval of this letter he wrote to the Roman Church in rebuke as they did not represent the Bible. This is the Biblical ekklesia not the Roman Church who usurped the throne of Messiah.

Even the Church of England, who is not known for Sabbath-keeping, documents that the first ekklesia after the Apostles continued to follow in their ways. This word veneration by the way originates from the Latin word which means "to worship." Anyone telling you their venerating something is not worship is illiterate of definitions and word origins.

> *"The primitive Christians had a great veneration for the Sabbath, and spent the day in devotion and sermons. And it is not to be doubted but they derived this practice from the Apostles themselves, as appears by several scriptures to that purpose." –Dr. T.H. Morer (Church of England). [28]*

Apollinaris also lived around 100 A.D. and part of the same ekklesia group as Polycrates and Polycarp whom we just quoted. He affirms the same as Polycarp and Polycrates. [64] In the same era and region, Theophilus, Bishop of Antioch specifies they were keeping the Sabbath and on the 7th day of the week. He even notes that word Sabbath in Greek means "Seventh." It does not mean "First" ever.

Theophilus, Bishop of Antioch (120-190 AD):

And on the sixth day God finished His works which He made, and rested on the seventh day from all His works which He made. And God blessed the seventh day, and sanctified it; because in it He rested from all His works which God began to create…Moreover, [they spoke] concerning the seventh day, which all men acknowledge; but the most know not that what among the Hebrews is called the "Sabbath," is translated into Greek the "Seventh" (ebdomas), a name which is adopted by every nation, although they know not the reason of the appellation. [66]

Theophilus then applauds those who keep the Law and the Commandments including the Sabbath. He characterizes the prophets as fixed stars that cannot move. The second place is to the righteous who keep that same Law of Moses but the prophets gain first place in his view because he kept the law of Moses even still. Those who abandon the Sabbath and the Law are compared to wandering stars or what James would call double-minded men *(1:8, 4:8)*. This is the ekklesia of the Bible. The origin of the Catholic Church is the opposite known as the Synagogue of Satan who follow strange doctrine. They are rebuked by Messiah and they change the Law and the Sabbath as well as times and seasons as is predicted of the anti-Christ. Which do you desire to serve?

Theophilus, Bishop of Antioch (120-190 AD):

"The disposition of the stars, too, contains a type of the arrangement and order of the righteous and pious, and of those who keep the law and commandments of God. For the brilliant and bright stars are an imitation of the prophets, and therfore they remain fixed, not declining nor passing from place to place. And those which hold the second place in brightness, are types of the people of the righteous. And those, again, which change their position, and flee from place to place, which also are cared planets, they too are a type of the men who have wandered from God, abandoning His law and commandments." [66]

We have seen the pattern in the 2nd Century continued as the First Century emulating the Apostles' example. This is already enough to make the connection. Messiah Himself identified in Revelation, 7 areas in Turkey in which His ekklesia had continued through the Apostles. They appear in the Apostles' epistles as well fortified as His ekklesia. We have the writings of the Bishops of Smyrna and Ephesus that also identify the Bishops of Sardis and Laodicea in the same observance establishing the continued observance of the Sabbath and the Feasts among at least 4 of the 7 ekklesias Messiah mentioned. That is ironclad history of the right peoples.

This is the root of the fallacy in thinking for many scholars. They do not understand who the church is and who it is not and was not. This is why, in this chapter, we will only focus on these succeeding few generations after the Apostles to demonstrate who the ekklesia really was. Messiah names them and so do the Apostles. The true ekklesia of Aquila and Priscilla from Rome were exiled. Whoever that church is still prominent there, is not His ekklesia. This is a typical tactic well proven throughout history of the Synagogue of Satan. They infiltrate, agitate, and conquer from within and if that does not work and they gain enough power, they attack.

In the next chapter, we will continue further into the 3rd Century when things begin to change. We will demonstrate the pivot points where you will find some ekklesias of the East giving into the pressure of the West. Then, Constantine happened and the Synagogue of Satan now had an Empire at it's fingertips.

That list is expanded beyond significantly with 6 more named Bishops, plus 7 more bishops of the family of Polycrates and a multitude of Bishops keeping the Sabbath and Feasts who supported Polycrates letter. Then, there is Theophilus in the same era from Antioch where the first ekklesia outside of Judaea was established also affirming the Sabbath and the Feasts. All of them are continuing the Saturday Sabbath and none had moved it to Sunday. It does not even matter when it moved or by whom, though we will cover that, but that the practices of Messiah and the Apostles continued in the areas Jesus*(Yahusha)* identified as His ekklesia though imperfect.

Rome is impertinent and so is their opinion. They are not His ekklesia and never were. There is no authority beyond this point who can usurp the throne of the Lord of the Sabbath and alter it to another day in observance. The thinking is among the most ridiculous in all of history. No Pope can change the Sabbath nor an Emperor, they are just men with no authority except what they steal. They will answer for that.

I have written to him the great things of my law, but they were counted as a strange thing.   **–Hosea 8:12 KJV**

Sabbath Through the Ages

ENOCH & SONS

Enoch knew of the Sabbath and mentions it by name in 1 En. 10:17. He, at least, learned of it while visiting Heaven from the Heavenly Tablets. 1En. 106:19 [3]

ABRAHAM

From the Books of his forefathers, Abraham learned of the Sabbath and Feasts as Yahuah taught him Hebrew (Jub. 12:27, 6:19). He wasn't inventing those sacrifices but observing the ancient law (Gen. 26:5). [2]

MOSES

From the Exodus Moses reinstituted Yahuah's law (Ex. 20, Jub. 6:19). Continued by the Temple Priest Order, the Sons of Zadok from the days of Solomon through the entire Old Testament. [1]

Angels in Heaven kept Sabbath since Creation. Jub. 2:17-18, 30.

DAY 7

Lost for 217 years from Noah's sons to Abraham

3500 B.C.

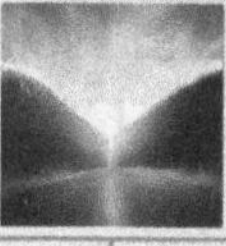

2100 B.C. to 1700 B.C.

7th Generation

2100 B.C.

1700 B.C.

Lost in Moses' days but returned in Moses' days. Less than 80 yrs.

ADAM

Adam was formed of red soil thus he was medium brown. אדמה, adamah: soil (from its general redness)

The Sabbath was made for Adam and man (Mark 2:27-28). He lived in the Garden of Eden in the Holy of Holies of Yahuah. He kept Sabbath. (Jub. 2:20-23, 6:18) [2]

NOAH & SONS

Noah learned the Sabbath and Feasts from his great grandfather Enoch, Methuselah and Lamech (Jub. 7:38). His sons kept this observance of the Law until his death and then, forgot (Jub. 6:18). [2]

ABRAHAM'S DESCENDANTS

Abraham's sons kept the Law and his ancestors continued to practice the Law up until the days of Moses when they began to lose it while in slavery (Jub. 6:19). [2]

All dates are approximate.

Sabbath Is Forever

Ex. 31:13, 16
Lev. 16:31, 24:8

Sabbath and the Feasts were lost 217 years after Noah died and again, less than 80 years in Moses' days. In thousands of years, only a 300-year gap.

Yahusha kept the Sabbath (Matt. 11:28-12:1; Luke 4:16, 13:10; Mark 1:21, 2:27-28, 6:2; John 7:22) He said Sabbath does not pass (Matt. 5:17-18).

Sabbath worship on 7th day continued by the Early Ekklesias derived from the Apostles practice of Saturday. [28]

Constantinople assembled together on the Sabbath, as well as on the first day of the week, which custom is never observed at Rome or at Alexandria. [30]

MESSIAH

EARLY EKKLESIAS

EARLY EKKLESIAS

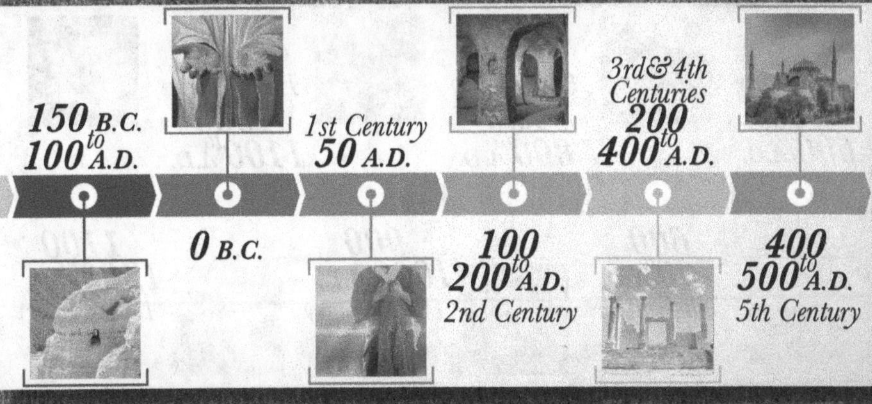

QUMRAN

Sons of Zadok kept the law and Sabbath even when Israel strayed.
Ez. 44:15, 48:11.

The community writings in the Dead Sea Scrolls written by the Sons of Zadok exiled there, are very strict in observing the Sabbath and the Law. Sabbath is mentioned 165 times. — Vermes [1]

APOSTLES

The Apostles are recorded keeping and teaching the Sabbath after Messiah's ascension. (Acts 2:1-4, 13:14-16, 13:42-44, 18:4, 1 Cor. 7:19, 11:1, etc.)

For Israel and the "stranger among you"

SO SAYS TORAH: Ex. 12:49, 20:10, 23:12; Lev. 16:29, 17:12, 18:26, 19:34, 24:16, 24:22, 25:6; Num. 9:14, 15:14-16, 15:26, 15:29-30, 19:10; Deut. 5:14, 31:12; Jos. 8:33, 20:9

EARLY EKKLESIAS

Catholic Council in Laodicea acknowledges Saturday Sabbath observance and attacks it. [29] **366 A.D.**: Egyptian Coptic Church continued Saturday Sabbath both with Sunday as well. [24]

Sabbath Through the Ages

Ireland and Scotland kept the Saturday Sabbath. Moffatt, Princeton. [32]

Church of the East, Kurdistan still keeping the 7th-Day Sabbath on Saturday. Note: 2 Esdras 13 places some Lost Tribes of the Northern Kingdom there. Likely migration of the 7 churches from Turkey as well. [33]

Sabbath prevailed in Wales universally until A.D. 1115 when Rome cracked down. [35]

IRELAND & SCOTLAND   **KURDISTAN**   **WALES**

6th Century
500 to 600 A.D.

8th Century
700 to 800 A.D.

11th Century
1000 to 1100 A.D.

600 to 700 A.D.
7th Century

900 to 1000 A.D.
10th Century

1100 to 1200 A.D.
12th Century

ROME ATTACKS   **INDIA, CHINA, PERSIA, ARMENIA**   **SCOTLAND**

Pope Gregory attacks Saturday Sabbath-keepers as "anti-Christ." [31] Saturday Sabbath lost in Egypt crushed by Pope. [24] However, some were still keeping the 7th Day.

The Saturday Sabbath is recorded in worship among those Christians of India, China, Persia, Armenia, the Abyssinians, the Jacobites, & the Maronites. [33]

Scotland still found keeping the Saturday Sabbath. [34]

All dates are approximate.

1435: "We are informed that some people in different districts of the kingdom, have adopted and observed Saturdaykeeping. It is severely forbidden - in holy church canon... [37]

1668 England: 9-10 churches still keeping Sabbath. 1648: Physician to King James still keeping the Saturday Sabbath. 1664 America: Stephen Mumford migrated keeping Sabbath. [45-48]

America, 1844: Seventh-day Adventist formed. [52] Orient, 1900: In many of the Oriental churches the Sabbath (Saturday) was still observed. [53] China: Taipings observed the seventh day Sabbath. Sweden, 1863: Observing Sabbath. [54]

NORWAY

ENGLAND & AMERICA

U.S., ORIENT CHINA, SWEDEN

13th Century
1200 to 1300 A.D.

16th Century
1500 to 1600 A.D.

18th Century
1700 to 1800 A.D.

1400 to 1500 A.D.
15th Century

1600 to 1700 A.D.
17th Century

1800 A.D. to PRESENT
20th Century

FRANCE

COUNCIL OF TRENT WAR ON SABBATH

ROMANIA, BOHEMIA MORAVIA, U.S.

"The inquisitors. . . [declare] that the sign of a Vaudois, deemed worthy of death, was that he followed Christ and sought to obey the commandments of God." [36]

1563: Council of Trent ruled Tradition is greater than Scripture. Hunted Saturdaykeepers in Holland, Germany, Russia, Sweden, Europe, India, Abyssinia, etc. [38-44]

Sabbatarians hunted in Romania (1760), Bohemia and Moravia (1635-1867). Sabbathkeepers in Pennsylvania thrive. [49-51]

The remnant will be found keeping the Sabbath (Matt. 24:20, Rev. 12:17, 14:12, 22:14, Is. 66:23)

forgetting to REMEMBER the SABBATH

3rd Century to Present

the GOD culture
יהוה

The Assault
from the Catholic Church

Chapter 11 | Forgetting to Remember the Sabbath: The Assault

Jubilees 1:13
And they will forget all My law and all My commandments and all
My judgments, and will go astray as to new moons, and sabbaths, and
festivals, and jubilees, and ordinances.

Jubilees 6:34
And all the children of Yisrael will forget and will not find the path of
the years, and will forget the new months, and seasons, and Sabbaths
and they will go wrong as to all the order of the years.

Anyone not familiar with Jubilees can read our publishing The Book of Jubilees: The Torah Calendar *(free in eBook at BookOfJubilees.org)* where we apply a stringent Torah Test and find this book quoted by Messiah, Peter, John, James, Paul, Luke and even an angel in Heaven. It was kept as, applied as and even called Torah by name and application in the Qumran Scrolls of the exiled Temple Priests. They said it was the source for the exact determination of how to keep Torah and most churches ignore this part of Torah as they follow the Pharisee canon not the one kept by the exiled Temple Priests.

Pharisees are rebuked as changing Torah in Mark 7:9 and in many places, we are warned of their leaven which they infuse to expand scripture in interpretation. We have had 2,000 years of that which a reading of this Book of Jubilees exposes. This means The Book of Jubilees was not only in the original Bible canon in history kept by the only Biblical keepers of canon until the time of Messiah, but Torah even. If you have not vetted and read this book for yourself, you are ineligible to render an opinion on it's inspiration and looking up a blog by a Pharisee is not research. Sure, they hate the book and we prove why. It exposes them. The legitimate Temple Priests, sons of Zadok in Qumran quote it as Torah and it tests as such. Your denomination has not conducted such a test we assure you. Ridicule is not testing.

He knew Israel and even the modern church doctrine in our age would forget what He and His Word say on the matter. Even in Noah's time, after his death, his sons also forgot. This was renewed in the time of Abraham and then, at the earlier time of Moses, it was forgotten again. This amnesia is not accidental however. It is a rebellious position of which we are warned many times. Man does not wish to be told to keep Law. He wants liberty to even sin whenever he wishes. We have been dealing with this human nature since the Garden of Eden and today it is only becoming more profound.

Imagine an entire church system that teaches us to be lawless as if that is freedom yet it is bondage. Freedom is His Law. This literally means to teach us to sin. It justifies such sin even in the salvation doctrine that does not derive from scripture when we are told once saved, we are always saved. Put that in layman's terms. Anyone hearing that not in the church knows exactly what is being said there. You can do whatever you want and nothing surrenders your salvation. The problem is you cannot. If we choose to live in sin or lawless, we are under the Law of Sin and Death which is the opposite of Yahuah's law.

We begin to see a pattern of another religion here in the 2nd Century. It is possible the Didache, if accurately dated to 50-70 A.D., may even precede this and prove the Synagogue of Satan originates in Turkey as that is the church being rebuked there in Revelation. However, this is evidence of a different religion not that of the Bible. It may parade as such but from it's foundations, it never was. In admitting that his church, the false church not that of the Bible, is a stranger to Bible practices such as the Sabbath and Feasts 100 years after the Apostles is unimaginable. Tertullian, admits that believers should remain solemn to the Sabbath and Feasts. However, his admission of guilt proves the church in which he was within, which would become known as the Catholic Church, is not a Bible ekklesia. He is at least lamenting the straying from the Word.

Tertullian, 155 A.D.

"By us who are strangers to Sabbaths, and new moons, and festivals, once

acceptable to God, the Saturnalia, the feasts of January, the Brumalia, and Matronalia, are now frequented; gifts are carried to and fro, new year's day presents are made with din, and sports and banquets are celebrated with uproar; oh, how much more faithful are the heathen to their religion, who take special care to adopt no solemnity from the Christians." –De Idolatria [63]

Tertullian just gave us the origin of what we call Christmas as Saturnalia is it's origin observed in the Catholic Church in practice replacing His Shavuot the wrong time of year with a counterfeit that include orgies. There are no Biblical Feasts in January. These are pagan.

The Didache (Διδαχή) [69]

In 1873, the Catholic Church discovered a lost writing in a church in Turkey. The Didache was referenced by Athanasius of Alexandria in 373 A.D. Some date the writing 50-70 A.D. claiming it was written before the Book of Revelation and it has prophecy it claims may be the origin of such. Most scholars date the writing to the first or early second century and some as late as the 3rd or 4th. In other words, they have no clue as to the true origin of this document. What they do not realize is the earlier the dating, the more damning this find would be for the Catholic Church.

In assessing this 17-page document, if it is dated to the time of the writing of the New Testament, it proves the origin of the Synagogue of Satan from Revelation. It certainly is not scripture, is not written as scripture and let us not forget the Catholic Church never canonized it thus it has no such importance in content. However, in a time where the ekklesia was keeping the 10 commandments including the Sabbath, the Didache renders the commandments omitting three extremely important Commandments that are very telling. It is missing the Sabbath, not taking Yahuah's name in vain and honoring one's parents. It does not include no graven images directly in it's commandments but does indicate not to eat food sacrificed to idols and a rebuke of idolatry with it. Then, the Didache separates from scripture adding to "confess your sins in church" which is a doctrine of men not Bible. It continues with Catholic baptism, fasting, ointment, and eucharist rituals that also are not truly from the Bible. It even renders repetitive prayers such as praying the Lord's Prayer three times daily. The Bible rebukes such vain repetitions. However, this is not intended to offer a full review as there would be much more. The final element that explains why they omit the 4th Commandment to keep the Sabbath, is the order to gather together each Sunday rather than the Biblical Saturday.

Let us not forget that not only are the original 7 ekklesias from Revelation in Turkey, but so are the Synagogue of Satan and Nicolaitans whose doctrines Jesus*(Yahusha)* hates. We have the track of the Biblical ekklesias and they continued the Sabbath and the Feasts in Turkey as a group and individually in such accounts. Anyone not doing so is not from the original ekklesia but something else as Jude and Paul warned.

Jude 1:4 KJV

For there are certain men crept in unawares, who were before of old ordained to this condemnation, ungodly men, turning the grace of our God into lasciviousness, and denying the only Lord God, and our Lord Jesus Christ.

Galatians 2:4 KJV

And that because of false brethren unawares brought in, who came in privily to spy out our liberty which we have in Christ Jesus, that they might bring us into bondage:

This odious stench in the nostrils of Yahuah brings the ekklesia into bondage not the law. Their sin posture of lawlessness is the bondage of which Paul speaks. Jude says they turn grace into lasciviousness or sexual perversion and this is that of the harlot of Babylon just as Israel played the harlot in serving other gods.

The fact that the Didache does not represent this affirmed practice proves it is the opposite of the Bible. It offers many Catholic foundations. If it were written at the time of the New Testament, then it proves Catholic origins in the Synagogue of Satan. If later, it is no less damning as it proves against scripture in any era. Either way, follow the Didache and those who follow it through history and you will find the false church not the Bible ekklesia. This is the thinking that begins to take over the narrative many times through force of course.

3rd and 4th Centuries. Orient and Most of the World

Much of the remainder of this history was compiled by the Seventh-Day Adventists largely. They have done well in their record keeping. We will cover The Lord's Day over two chapters proving out the timing which is not Sunday and the practice which is also not Sunday as Jesus' *(Yahusha's)* Day has always remained the 7th-Day Sabbath in which He is Lord which is also when He resurrected thus He did not move it.

The Apostles and early ekklesia knew this and if the Catholic Church did not and does not, it merely proves they have no connection to the original ekklesia. These references begin to expose the agenda of the Catholic Church to eradicate the Sabbath in profanity. Athanasius defends them but enemies of the Sabbath are growing. He records the Asian ekklesias continuing the Saturday practice. They are not "Judaizers" but represent the authentic observance from the Apostles. Labels do not change that.

> *"The ancient Christians were very careful in the observation of Saturday, or the seventh day. . .It is plain that all the Oriental churches, and the greatest part of the world, observed the Sabbath as a festival. . . . Athanasius likewise tells us that they held religious assemblies on the Sabbath, not because they were infected with Judaism, but to worship Jesus, the Lord of the Sabbath; Epiphanius says the same."* –Antiquities of the Christian Church. [29]

> **Council of Laodicea:** *"From the apostles' time until the council of Laodicea, which was about the year 364, the holy observation of the Jews' Sabbath continued, as may be proved out of many authors; yea, notwithstanding the decree of the council against it."* –John Ley, 1640. [29]

> *"Christians shall not Judaize and be idle on Saturday, but shall work on that day; but the Lord's Day they shall especially honor, and, as being Christians, shall, if possible, do no work on that day. If, however, they are found Judaizing, they shall be shut out from Christ."*
> –Catholic Church Council in Laodicea, 364 A.D. [29]

In Egypt, we continue to observe the pattern of the 7th-Day Sabbath but unlike the Asian ekklesia which the Apostles founded, they had now blended with the Sunday practice erroneously termed the Lord's Day which remains Saturday not Sunday as well. That entire erroneous doctrine originates in only one mention in all of scripture in which John was clearly invoking the Saturday Sabbath.

> ***Egypt:*** *"Let the servants (of the Lord) work five days; On the Sabbath (Sabbaton/ Saturday) and the Lord's day (kyriakE/ Sunday) let them rest for the church that they may be instructed in piety. The Sabbath because God Himself rested on it when He completed all the creation. The Lord's day because it is the day of the resurrection of the Lord."*
> *—Coptic Orthodox Statute 75. [25]*
>
> ***Egypt:*** *. . . Let them who will be baptized fast on the preparation (paraskeue) of the Sabbath (Sabbaton/Saturday). And (de) on the Sabbath (Sabbaton/ Saturday), when they who will be baptized have assembled in one place by the direction (gnome) of the bishop, let them all be commanded to pray and bend their knees . . . – Coptic Orthodox Statute 45. [26]*
>
> ***Egypt:*** *Athanasius himself, who was a chief Egyptian delegate at Nicea, in his canons dated around A.D. 366 points out the necessity of observing both days.*

This is what the Bible calls "lukewarm" and Jesus*(Yahusha)* will spit those out of His mouth. This kind of watering down will become the staple of the so-called church which will infuse many strange doctrines, idol worship, elevate Mary to the status of the ancient goddess, etc. This is what happens when one's foundation is built on sinking sand. However, even in the midst of all of this, history continues to witness the Saturday Sabbath observance. However, that must be crushed in the view of the Catholic Church. They would defile and profane that Sabbath and the Law at any cost even unto death. The true question is what is the root of that kind of thinking? We all know it is not the Bible.

This is when Constantine rises to power and establishes the Holy Roman Empire infusing government and church. This would give them the power to eradicate the Sabbath or so they thought. They fail in this through history and still today. They will never eradicate it.

"This controversy lasted almost two centuries, until Constantine intervened in behalf of the Roman bishops and outlawed the other group." –R. L. Odom, Sunday in Roman Paganism. [67]

5th Century. Constantinople

History now exposes the stronger encroachment of the Catholic ideology into Turkey. Constantine had to conquer the area, move the Roman seat of power there and declare the Catholic religion as the state in order to carry out this agenda. He declared Sunday as the Sabbath by law. This would lead to the persecution of the original ekklesia as to keep the Biblical Sabbath was to break the law generally. Pressure would be applied until they acquiesced. Essentially, this next generation after Constantine already infused worship on both days that will not last.

"The people of Constantinople and almost everywhere, assemble together on the Sabbath, as well as on the first day of the week, which custom is never observed at Rome or at Alexandria." –Sozomen, Ecclesiastical History. [30]

"Almost all churches throughout the world celebrate the sacred mysteries on the Sabbath of every week, yet the Christians of Alexandria and at Rome, on account of some ancient traditions, refuse to do this."—Socrates, Ecclesiastical History. [81]

Notice Socrates and Sozomen knew that Sabbath was Saturday, the 7th Day and Sunday was simply the first day of the week not Sabbath. This has never truly been in question. The assault however, will ramp up and no Catholic can truly defend this.

"Down even to the fifth century the observance of the Jewish Sabbath was continued in the Christian church."—Ancient Christianity Exemplified. [71]

6th Century.

Expanding on the Sunday Law, Pope Gregory assaulted those who keep the 7th-Day Sabbath labeling them "the prophets of Antichrist" for not working on the 7th Day. In other words, it was unlawful to keep the true Sabbath now. It was not enough to oppose it in the arena of ideas. He had to shove it down everyone's throat. He represented the opposite of the Bible in complete Anti-Christ form.

> ### Rome:
> *"About 590, Pope Gregory, in a letter to the Roman people, denounced as the prophets of Antichrist those who maintained that work ought not to be done on the seventh day." –James T. Ringgold. [31]*

Meanwhile, following the patterns in Egypt, one can see the progression that leads to forgetting the Sabbath.

> *"It seems possible that Sabbath observance among the Copts in Egypt and Ethiopia may have passed through three stages:*
> **0-325 A.D.: 7th Day Sabbath on Saturday Only:**
> *"1) Only the seventh-day Sabbath observed-from apostolic times until the Council of Nicea;"*
> **325 A.D.-525 A.D.: 7th Day Sabbath on Saturday and Lord's Day on Sunday:**
> *"2) Sunday and the seventh-day Sabbath both observed-from the Council of Nicea until perhaps a century or two later; and..."*
> **525 A.D. Abandon the 7th Day Sabbath on Saturday, Sunday Only:**
> *"3) only Sunday designated as a day of public worship-a practice still observed today." –Sabbath Observance From Coptic Sources, Bishai, The Johns Hopkins University. [24]*

Notice, the original ekklesia in Turkey is silenced at this point. They were likely chased out or killed. Many wonder what happened to them. It is most likely they migrated deeper into Turkey into the area of modern Kurdistan that is the location of some of the Northern Kingdom Lost Tribes of Israel. As with the Lost Tribes, the history becomes fuzzy as the victors who write history are the Synagogue of Satan. However, Christians who were reading the Bible were still figuring out for themselves that the Biblical Sabbath remained Saturday, the 7th day. The reality for every Pope is they will never succeed in eradicating it.

7th Century. Scotland and Ireland

"It seems to have been customary in the Celtic churches of early times, in Ireland as well as Scotland, to keep Saturday, the Jewish Sabbath, as a day of rest from labour. They obeyed the fourth commandment literally upon the seventh day of the week." —Professor James C. Moffatt, D.D., Professor of Church History at Princeton. [32]

Just when they thought they had squashed the Sabbath, there it crops up again on the other side of Europe. The Bible says what it says.

8th Century. India, China, Persia [33]

"Widespread and enduring was the observance of the seventh-day Sabbath among the believers of the Church of the East and the St. Thomas Christians of India, who never were connected with Rome. It also was maintained among those bodies which broke off from Rome after the Council of Chalcedon namely, the Abyssinians, the Jacobites, the Maronites, and Armenians." —Schaff-Herzog, The New Encyclopedia of Religious Knowledge, art. Nestorians.

People in several other parts of the East began to awaken to the Biblical Sabbath position. This is an example of truth. No one forced them to do so. They studied the Word and learned it says the Sabbath remains at the center of our worship.

10th Century. Church of the East. Kurdistan

"The Nestorians eat no pork and keep the Sabbath. They believe in neither auricular confession nor purgatory." —Schaff-Herzog, The New Encyclopedia of Religious Knowledge, art. Nestorians. [33]

Again, a Lost Tribes area, formerly Assyria, Kurdistan continues to keep the Sabbath on the Biblical 7th Day of Saturday. This is the likely transfer from Turkey though they may have been included in such worship all along.

11th Century. Scotland

They held that Saturday was properly the Sabbath on which they abstained from work. —Celtic Scotland. [34]

It is rather impossible for the Catholic Church to assume people are unable to count to 7. It is not so difficult to determine that the 7th Day never changed and impossible to prove the Sabbath moved to Sunday except by man's hands who had no such authority.

12th Century. Wales

"There is much evidence that the Sabbath prevailed in Wales universally until A.D. 1115, when the first Roman bishop was seated at St. David's. The old Welsh Sabbath-keeping churches did not even then altogether bow the knee to Rome, but fled to their hiding places."
—Lewis, Seventh Day Baptists in Europe and America. [35]

Where in the Bible does it say to bow our knee to any church, any Pope nor anyone but Messiah? Where does it say go into all the world and conquer? Those are satan's fruits which follow the Synagogue of Satan not followers of the Bible.

13th Century. Waldenses of France

"The inquisitors. . . [declare] that the sign of a Vaudois, deemed worthy of death, was that he followed Christ and sought to obey the commandments of God." —History of the Inquisition of the Middle Ages, H.C. Lea. [36]

The commandments include the Sabbath. Who gives the Catholic Church the authority to kill those who keep the Biblical practice instead of profaning it as they do? Not the Bible. The Inquisition is a blatant exercise in Nephilim doctrine never supported by scripture. It is definitive evidence the Catholic Church has operated in satan's fruits which continues to spread it's disease across the world.

15th Century. Norway

1. "We are informed that some people in different districts of the kingdom, have adopted and observed Saturdaykeeping. It is severely forbidden - in holy church canon - one and all to observe days excepting those which the holy Pope, archbishop, or the bishops command. Saturdaykeeping must under no circumstances be permitted hereafter further than the church canon commands. Therefore, we counsel all the friends of God throughout all Norway who want to be obedient towards the holy church to let this evil of Saturdaykeeping alone; and the rest we forbid under penalty of severe church punishment to keep Saturday holy." –Catholic Provincial Council at Bergen. 1435. [37]

Why is it so important to stop us from keeping Saturday? If the Catholic Church were honest and Bible believing, it could never engage in murder and persecution on such levels. One would think they would be happy that people are at least keeping what they believe the Bible says. If their motive were pure, they would not need to kill anyone ever over such issue. They would win in the arena of ideas. This demonstrates just how weak their position has always been and remains. It is time to obliterate their illiterate and evil stance once and for all. Enter the overtly satanic Council of Trent that caused the Catholic Church to declare their evil intentions elevating the Pope and their tradition above Yahuah.

16th Century. Council of Trent

"On the 18th of January, 1563, the Council of Trent ruled that Tradition is greater than Scripture, after a powerful speech by the Archbishop of Reggio, in which he said that the fact that the Church had changed the Fourth Commandment clearly proved that Tradition was greater than Scripture." –H.J. Holtzman, Kanon und Tradition, 1859 edition, p. 263. [38]

Holland and Germany: *Babara of Thiers, who was executed in 1529, declared: "God has commanded us to rest on the seventh day." –T.J. Van Bragt. [39]*

Russia: *"The accused [Sabbathkeepers] were summoned; they openly acknowledged the new faith, and defended the same. The most eminent of them, the secretary of state, Kuritzyn, Ivan Maximow, Kassian, archimandrite of the Jury Monastery of Novgorod, were condemned to death, and burned publicly in cages, at Moscow, Dec. 27, 1503."*
–(Council, Moscow, 1503). H. Sternberf. [40]

Sweden: *"This zeal for Saturdaykeeping continued for a long time; even little things which might strengthen the practice of keeping Saturday were punished." –Bishop Anjou. [41]*

Europe: *About the year 1520 many of these Sabbathkeepers found shelter on the estate of Lord Leonhardt of Lichtensein, "as the princes of Lichtenstein held to the observance of the true Sabbath."*
–History of the Sabbath, J.N. Andrews. [42]

India: *"The famous Jesuit, Francis Xavier, called for the Inquisition, which was set up in Goa, India, in 1560, to check the 'Jewish wickedness' (Sabbathkeeping)." –Adeney, The Greek and Eastern Churches. [43]*

Abyssinia: *"It is not therefore, in imitation of the Jews, but in obedience to Christ and His holy apostles, that we observe that day."*
–Abyssinian legate at court of Lisbon, 1534. [44]

The pattern continues throughout the 17th, 18th and 19th centuries to present as people are reading and understanding the Catholic position has always been illiterate and easily proven so.

17th Century
England: *"Here in England are about nine or ten churches that keep the Sabbath, besides many scattered disciples, who have been eminently preserved."*
–Stennet's letters, 1668 and 1670. [45]

Dr. Peter Chamberlain: *Dr. Peter Chamberlain was physician to King James and Queen Katherine. The inscription on the monument over his* *grave says Dr. Chamberlain was "a Christian, keeping the commandments of God and the faith of Jesus, being baptized about the year 1648, and keeping the seventh day for the Sabbath above thirty-two years." [46]*

America: *"Stephen Mumford, the first Sabbathkeeper in America came from London in 1664."*
–History of the Seventh Day Baptist General Conference by Jas. Bailey. [47]

England: *"It will surely be far safer to observe the seventh day, according to the express commandment of God, than on the authority of mere human conjecture to adopt the first." –John Milton. [48]*

18th Century
Romania (1760): *"Joseph II's edict of tolerance did not apply to the Sabbatarians, some of whom again lost all of their possessions."*
–Jahrgang 2, 254. [49]

Bohemia and Moravia: *"The condition of the Sabbatarians [from 1635 to 1867] was dreadful. Their books and writings had to be delivered to the Karlsburg Consistory to become the spoil of flames."*
–Adolf Dux, 1880. [50]

America: *"But before Zinzendorf and the Moravians at Bethlehem thus began the observance of the Sabbath and prospered, there was a small body of German Sabbathkeepers in Pennsylvania."*
–Rupp's History of Religious Denominations in the United States. [51]

19th Century to Present
America: *The Seventh-day Adventist movement was formed around 1844.*

Orient: *"In many of the Oriental churches the Sabbath (Saturday) was still observed like Sunday, while in the West a large number, by way of opposition to Jewish institutions, held a fast on that day."*
–History of the Christian Church, George Park Fisher. [52]

China: *"The Taipings when asked why they observed the seventh day Sabbath, replied that it was, first, because the Bible taught it, and second, because their ancestors observed it as a day of worship."*
—A Critical History of the Sabbath and the Sunday. [53]

Sweden: *"We will now endeavor to show that the sanctification of the Sabbath has its foundation and its origin in a law which God at creation itself established for the whole world, and as a consequence thereof is binding on all men in all ages." —The Evangelist, 1863. [54]*

The following is a quote from a Catholic magazine, The Catholic Mirror: "The Catholic Church for over 1,000 years before the existence of a Protestant, by virtue of her divine mission, changed the day [of worship] from Saturday to Sunday. . . . In the Old Testament, reference is made 126 times to the Sabbath, and all these texts conspire harmoniously in voicing the will of God commanding the seventh day to be kept, because God Himself first kept it, making it obligatory on all as 'a perpetual covenant.' Nor can we imagine any one foolhardy enough to question the identity of Saturday with the Sabbath or seventh day, seeing that the people of Israel have been keeping Saturday from the giving of the law 2514 BC to the present . . . Examining the New Testament from cover to cover critically, we find the Sabbath referred to 61 times. We find, too, that the Savior invariably selected the Sabbath (Saturday) to teach in the synagogues and work miracles. The four Gospels refer to the Sabbath (Saturday) 51 times. . . . Hence the conclusion is inevitable . . . that of those who follow the Bible as their guide, the Israelites and the Seventh-day Adventists, have the exclusive weight of evidence on their side, whilst the biblical Protestant has not a word in self-defense for his substitution of Sunday for Saturday. . . . They have ignored and condemned their teacher, the Bible . . . and they have adopted a day [instituted and] kept by the Catholic Church." —Official publication of Cardinal Gibbons and the Papacy in the United States, published in Baltimore, Maryland, September 1893. [55]

So how have we so easily forgotten what is abundant and clear in the Old and New Testaments? Author Peter Henlyn captures the unapologetic Catholic leadership attitude. They hate the Bible.

For thus Rutilius Claudius, having before upbraided them for the Circumcision and other ceremonies; doth thus deride them for their Sabbaths.

Latin: *Radix stultitiae, cui frigida Sabbata cordi, Sed cor frigidius religione sua. Septima quaque dies turpi damnata veterno, Tanquam lassati mollis imago Dei. Caetera mendacis deliramenta Catastae, Nec pueros omnes credere posse reor. Atq; utinam nunquam Iudaea subacta fuisset Pompeii bellis, imperioque Titi. Latius excisae gentis contagia serpunt, Victoresque suos natio victa premit.*

English: *Vain men, by whom their sluggish Sabbaths are So priz'd, yet have an heart more sluggish far: Who each seventh day to their old sloth devote; Of their tired God, a true, but lazy note. Other the dotages of that lying Sect, Me thinks no child should credit, or respect. O would Judea never had been won By Pompey's armies, or Vespasian's son! Their superstition spreads itself so far, That they give Laws unto the Conqueror.*

Nor were the Sabbaths entertained only in Rome itself. Some, in almost all places of their Empire, were that way inclined; as Seneca most rightly noted.

Latin: *Eo usque sceleratissima gentis consuetudo invaluit, ut per omnes jam terras recepta sit, & victi victoribus leges dederunt.*

English: *"So far, saith he, the custom of that wretched people hath prevailed amongst us, that it is now received over all the world; and the conquered seem to prescribe laws unto the victors."*

—The History of the Sabbath, Peter Heylyn, 1636. [56]

The assault on the Sabbath by the Catholic Church is among the most evil of actions in history. The office of Pope has usurped the throne of Yahusha and demands their ways above His ways. In fact, they have outright declared for centuries that when the Bible disagrees with the Pope, the Pope must be right and infallible. Clearly, they do not read the Bible such as Romans 3:23. How could His people do so? The Catholic Church's foundation has never been set on the Bible. They quote and change it in interpretation as Pharisees and in outright fraud even changing scripture at times. The brazen audacity of such Popes will earn them a special judgment indeed. They know this and they embrace it and understand, they wish you to share their fate. Will you follow an unbiblical position of man or the Bible itself?

How To Keep The
SABBATH

Chapter 12 | How to Keep the Sabbath

The Bible Sabbath is not about legalism. Those who seek such evidence in scripture will only find the Pharisee Sabbath leads to legalism and bondage. His Sabbath is freedom but He and Paul rebuked the Pharisee manipulation that is against His commandments *(Mark 7:9)*. "Thou shalt not" is never bondage unless we view such as children who do not wish to be given any boundaries. As parents, we all know that those limits protect our children and are for their benefit. Why would we forget that when our Heavenly Father shows love to us in the same manner?

First and foremost, we cannot forget to remember the Sabbath. We must keep it holy, sanctified and set apart from the other 6 days of the week. We will address when the Sabbath Day begins and affirm that it is Saturday and not Sunday in forthcoming chapters though you have probably already received enough historical and Biblical reference to support that.

> **Exodus 20:8 KJV**
> *Remember the sabbath day, to keep it holy.*

We have broken down the Sabbath into 12 precepts in which we have compiled a chart at the end of this chapter for quick reference.

1. NO WORK

> **Exodus 20:10**
> *But the seventh day is the sabbath of the LORD thy God: in it thou shalt not do any work, thou, nor thy son, nor thy daughter, thy manservant, nor thy*

maidservant, nor thy cattle, nor thy stranger that is within thy gates:

We are not to conduct nor participate in any work on the 7th-Day Sabbath as it is a day of rest for our souls. However, it is the only day of the week set apart and sanctified as the day of rest. Anyone resting the other 6 days is labeled lazy by the Bible. We do not get to choose when we keep His day. He is Lord of the Sabbath and think so is to usurp His authority as Lord of the Sabbath. No one can keep the Sabbath any other day. Again, this is not just Old Testament, the New Testament refers to us as an example of unbelief if we are not entering into His rest. The writer of Hebrews and the Apostles did and so should we.

Hebrews 4:9-11 KJV

There remaineth therefore a rest to the people of God. For he that is entered into his rest, he also hath ceased from his own works, as God did from his. Let us labour therefore to enter into that rest, lest any man fall after the same example of unbelief.

The exiled Temple Priests in Qumran were adamant about observing the Sabbath not in legalism like the Pharisees nor bondage but in the freedom of His true rest. There is no remedy in modern times that can replace it.

"Concerning the Sabbath to observe it according to its law. No man shall work on the sixth day from the moment when the sun's orb is distant by its own fulness from the gate ; for this is what He said, Observe the Sabbath day to keep it holy (Deut. v, 12)."
"He shall say nothing about work or labour to be done on the morrow."
*"No man shall profane the Sabbath for the sake of riches or gain on the Sabbath day." –**The Damascus Document, p. 141-143. [1]***

Note we removed the commentary injection in Geza Vermes' translation in parentheses that claimed "when the sun's orb is distant by its own fulness from the gate" as to mean sunset. That is fraud and misrepresentation as this occurs twice daily – once at sunrise and once at sunset. The sun is equidistant in both instances. Regarding the start of the Biblical day, this passage is not specifying which it means but we will cover other portions of the Dead Sea Scrolls that do along with abundant scripture one cannot truly debate. The Book of Jubilees weighs in in complete agreement with Torah as it always affirms many times with clarification and revelation we have lost over the years.

Jubilees 2:29 (Excerpt)

Declare and say to the children of Israel the law of this day both that they should keep Sabbath thereon, and that they should not forsake it in the error of their hearts; (and) that it is not lawful to do any work thereon which is unseemly...

Jubilees 50 (Excerpt)

8-9: Six days wilt thou labour, but on the seventh day is the Sabbath of Yahuah your Elohim. In it ye shall do no manner of work, ye and your sons, and your men-servants and your maid-servants, and all your cattle and the sojourner also who is with you. 8 And the man that doeth any work on it shall die:

12: And every man who doeth any work thereon...

2. NO COOKING

Exodus 35:3 KJV

Ye shall kindle no fire throughout your habitations upon the sabbath day.

Some question what this means. However, it is clear not to kindle fire period but especially for cooking as that is how one would prepare food in that age. Today, we have gas and electric and you turn a knob or push a button. However, understand the point of this is for you to take no thought of yourself for the Sabbath. You prepare your food the day before. All your meals should already be ready so you do not have to even think about cooking or yourself really. There is a long list of foods that you can prepare the day before or even order the day before to have cold the next day. For us, we love things like sandwiches that are already made, pasta already mixed, pizza, salad already mixed, etc. We, many times, will cook up some eggs scrambled or omelets the day before but sometimes, we just have boiled eggs or cereal. There are many options even pastries, muffins, and pandesal if you are in the Philippines (masarap!). You can always pick up rotisserie chicken which is still good cold the next day or in the Philippines lechon manok. A list of snacks that are already prepared is massive as well. It is really just a matter of planning and preparation. Once you get used to it, it is no burden at all. In fact, we now live from "one Sabbath to another" as Isaiah mentioned as we look forward all week to the Sabbath rest. For us we stay away from unclean foods more because the Creator told us they were not good to eat. Of course, no blood.

Some Pharisees will tell you, you cannot use electricity because that is work. They are legalistic and in bondage because they do not understand the reason for the Sabbath. Can you use a fan or air conditioning for instance? Some of us live in tropical areas that certain times of the year especially are unbearable without at least a fan. Using that fan or even AC or heat for those in the Northern Regions certain times, in no way violates the tone of the Law. Yahuah does not wish for you to have a heat stroke nor freeze. He desires that you are comfortable for the Sabbath and more importantly that there are no distractions. Being too hot or too cold can be a distraction. Use your electric. However, we do not cook or prepare foods that day. We do not even warm them. Some are OK with microwaves. We do not use them as it is cooking. Follow your conviction as the Holy Spirit will guide you. The Dead Sea Scrolls written by the Temple Priests and Jubilees agree.

> *"No man shall eat on the Sabbath day except that which is already prepared. He shall eat nothing lying in the fields. He shall not drink except in the camp."*
> **—The Damascus Document, p. 141-143. [1]**

Jubilees 2:29 (Excerpt)
...and that they should not prepare thereon anything to be eaten or drunk. and (that it is not lawful) to draw water, or bring in or take out thereon through their gates any burden, which they had not prepared for themselves on the sixth day in their dwellings.

Jubilees 50 (Excerpt)
9: Ye shall do no work whatever on the Sabbath day save that ye have prepared for yourselves on the sixth day, so as to eat, and drink, and rest, and keep Sabbath from all work on that day, and to bless Yahuah your Elohim...
12: ...and whoever lighteth a fire... or slaughtereth a beast or a bird, or whoever catcheth an animal or a bird or a fish

3. NO BUYING / SELLING

We always make sure we have things like water deliveries, any errands, any monies owed anyone are paid and delivered on Friday. Again, this way, we do not need to put any thought into our own needs. Sure, we eat but as we covered, it's prepared already so we just grab and eat. Again, this is not difficult but it becomes habit. For those beginning the Sabbath observance, don't beat yourself up in minutiae. You will learn. The point is to begin and grow from there. You will improve your planning and it will become second nature. Even if you slip at that point, you ask forgiveness and see that you plan better next time.

In the days of Nehemiah, Israel was really straying from this observance. They would become too busy to rest. Merchants were arriving Friday all night long in order to begin selling their wares and commodities first thing in the morning. Nehemiah was so serious about keeping the Sabbath because he knew his nation was in trouble. He closed the gates but not just in the early a.m. when Sabbath begins which we prove later, but he would close them the night before so the vendors could not even get into the city until Sunday. That is truly the only way to have stopped them and some still sold fish and goods from outside the wall.

Nehemiah 13:15 KJV
In those days saw I in Judah some treading wine presses on the sabbath, and bringing in sheaves, and lading asses; as also wine, grapes, and figs, and all manner of burdens, which they brought into Jerusalem on the sabbath day: and I testified against them in the day wherein they sold victuals.

Once again, as they were the Sons of Zadok from the Temple and Moses wrote Jubilees, both agree with the Bible.

"He shall make no loan to his companion. He shall make no decision in matters of money and gain. He shall say nothing about work or labour to be done on the morrow. No man shall walk in the field to do business on the Sabbath."

"No man shall profane the Sabbath for the sake of riches or gain on the Sabbath day."

–The Damascus Document, p. 141 [1]

Jubilees 50:8 (Excerpt)

...that he will set out on a journey thereon in regard to any buying or selling:

4. NO WORK FOR OTHERS

Not only are we not to work but we are not to do anything that requires another to work even those in our households. We don't go to restaurants. Yes, some will serve if you have a gathering but that is permissible on the Sabbath if they are volunteers. However, if they are paid workers, that is not permissible. We have also found that when we have even had workers on our house, etc., they have always been understanding of the rule not to work on Saturday. You set the observance and people will follow. Family will likely be your largest challenge.

Exodus 20:10 KJV

But the seventh day is the sabbath of the LORD thy God: in it thou shalt not do any work, thou, nor thy son, nor thy daughter, thy manservant, nor thy maidservant, nor thy cattle, nor thy stranger that is within thy gates:

"He shall send out no stranger on his business on the Sabbath day."
*"No man shall profane the Sabbath for the sake of riches or gain on the Sabbath day." –**The Damascus Document, p. 141-143 [1]***

Jubilees 50:7 (Excerpt)

In it ye shall do no manner of work, ye and your sons, and your men-servants and your maid-servants, and all your cattle and the sojourner also who is with you.

Really, for these first 4 thus far, they all boil down to no work. If you do not like the negative of do not, then apply it is as rest. Rest yourself, allow others to rest and rest from cooking. You can sum them up in one word so it is not hard to understand – REST.

5. NO PERSONAL PLEASURE

Especially among Pharisees and Messianics who largely follow Pharisees, there is a doctrine that having spousal relations on the Sabbath brings a double blessing. Of course, there is not a single scripture that supports that. The tone of the Sabbath in reason already tells us this day is about His pleasure not ours. Do we gain pleasure from pleasing Him? Of course we do. However, that's His pleasure and we are pleasuring in Him not ourselves. The Sabbath has always been interpreted this way as evidenced in Isaiah. He knew how to read and apply Torah.

> ### Isaiah 58:13 KJV
> *If thou turn away thy foot from the sabbath, from doing thy pleasure on my*
> *holy day; and call the sabbath a delight, the holy of the Lord, honourable; and*
> *shalt honour him, not doing thine own ways, nor finding thine own pleasure,*
> *nor speaking thine own words:*

The debate then begins to enter mindless ridicule as they will say it doesn't mean the Weekly Sabbath. The problem is there is no other day of the week that is called Sabbath nor that is called His holy day. The notion is illiterate but they just don't want to give up their "double blessing" which is Rabbi babble, not Bible. Let them go argue with themselves. Isaiah is clear and the Sons of Zadok who ran the Temple applied this the same way as we have their writings.

> *"No man shall lie with a woman in the city of the Sanctuary, to defile the city*
> *of the Sanctuary with their uncleanness."*
> **–The Damascus Document, p. 141-143 [1]**

Then, there is the Book of Jubilees which affirms the very same interpretation as the Prophet Isaiah, the Temple Priests and once again, that was written by Moses who wrote Torah so he kinda knew what he meant just as he knew what happened at Sinai..

> **Jubilees 2:29 (Excerpt)**
> *"...that it is not lawful to do any work thereon which is unseemly, to do thereon their own pleasure,"*
> **Jubilees 50:7 (Excerpt)**
> *"...whoever desecrateth that day, whoever lieth with (his) wife or whoever saith he will do something on it,"*

They wish to throw out The Book of Jubilees over this one so-called discrepancy in the Law. Talk about gnat straining and downright illogical. However, this thinking does not just come from Isaiah, the Sons of Zadok Temple Priests and Jubilees but this is a doctrine right out Torah in which they are overlooking. When Adam and Eve were taken into the Garden there was no sex in the Garden. Adam knew Eve and she conceived Cain well after the Garden exile that Jubilees dates to over 50 years later. The Garden has Yahuah's Holy of Holies and you do not have spousal relations there. If so, you die in His presence. This is evidenced in the Mt. Sinai encounter and very obviously the same tone in keeping the Sabbath.

> *Exodus 19:14-15 KJV*
> *And Moses went down from the mount unto the people, and sanctified the people; and they washed their clothes. And he said unto the people, Be ready against the third day: come not at your wives.*

Husbands, you have 6 other days of the week to take care of that. You can refrain one day per week. No one can overrule Jubilees as scripture over this point as it affirms scripture. In fact, if Jubilees said that you receive a "double blessing" for doing this on the Sabbath, that would be a problem as that would be against the Bible even Torah. It is time to let that go Messianics as you have lost the debate.

6. NO CARRYING

Notice how we are breaking this down into 12 precepts but essentially most of these stem from work of some kind. If you are carrying things, that is work. If you have a gathering on the Sabbath in which you need to setup chairs and tables, try to do so the day before. It is lawful to do good on the Sabbath and that is ministry so no one can condemn that. However, remember the tone of the day and try to stay at rest even in service as best you can because this is typically a planning issue.

Jeremiah 17:21 KJV

Thus saith the Lord; Take heed to yourselves, and bear no burden on the sabbath day, nor bring it in by the gates of Jerusalem;

The Qumran Scrolls from the Temple Priest take this a step further in interpretation. They even say that if you are rearing a child, don't carry it on the Sabbath. That can be difficult and not an issue we would call a sticking point but that is their interpretation. Clearly, they are saying to train your child as well to keep Sabbath as that is really the true meaning of that. It fits the tone of Sabbath and we would encourage it. Again, these are not about condemnation and legalism but interpretations of how to rest one day per week. They are not debate points as that is for the foolish. We believe your family and even your child will be blessed to have such boundaries established. No doubt a newborn cannot understand this and you need to do what you need to do. It does not give an age and it is obvious you cannot leave a newborn in the crib all day without picking them up at least some. However, you can limit that and train them over the years. There are also other ways to adapt your setup to accommodate such as having them in a safe room gated and you can be next to them comforting them without picking them up at times.

"No man shall take anything out of the house or bring anything in. And if he is in a booth, let him neither take anything out nor bring anything in."
"He shall lift neither stone nor dust in his dwelling. No man minding a child shall carry it whilst going and coming on the Sabbath."
"No man shall assist a beast to give birth on the Sabbath day. And if it should fall into a cistern or pit, he shall not lift it out on the Sabbath."
–The Damascus Document, p. 141-143 [1]

Jubilees really explains the purpose of this. It is not about moving boxes or whatever. It is about not taking thought for yourself. Yahuah does not need anything on the Sabbath. He does not need your box and whatever is inside, is not for Him likely. He wants you and your attention. That is what this is about. Also, this is another planning issue in which we simply take care of moving things the day before or they wait a day mostly. Jubilees will also explain and we will cover at the end of the chapter what this warning of being put to death means.

> **Jubilees 2:29 (Excerpt)**
> *...or bring in or take out thereon through their gates any burden, which they had not prepared for themselves on the sixth day in their dwellings.*
> **Jubilees 50:8 (Excerpt)**
> *...and whoever taketh up any burden to carry it out of his tent or out of his house shall die.*

7. NO MONEY MATTERS

Of course, we work to acquire money or alternatives in barter of sort. Exodus has always said not to focus on money matters. However, the Dead Sea Scrolls really explain this so we can all understand how it was interpreted by the Temple Priests who had the continuance in observance in their practices since Moses.

> **Exodus 20:10 KJV**
> *But the seventh day is the sabbath of the LORD thy God: in it thou shalt not do any work, thou, nor thy son, nor thy daughter, thy manservant, nor thy maidservant, nor thy cattle, nor thy stranger that is within thy gates:*
>
> *"He shall make no loan to his companion. He shall make no decision in matters of money and gain. He shall say nothing about work or labour to be done on the morrow. No man shall walk in the field to do business on the Sabbath."*
> *"He shall send out no stranger on his business on the Sabbath day."*
> *"No man shall profane the Sabbath for the sake of riches or gain on the*

Sabbath day." –The Damascus Document, p. 141-143 [1]

Jubilees really supports this as this is really working. Again, we are to have no distractions as best we can align as we rest for the day. If we are even thinking about money matters, we are not focused on Him.

8. NO EXTENDED TRAVEL

Moses said let no man leave his place on the Sabbath. How was this interpreted? Messiah addressed this as well in an End Times context when people will be forced to flee. He invokes the Sabbath from Moses as we will still be keeping it in the End Times. Acts is still set on the Sabbath observance from the Old Testament as it mentions "a Sabbath day's journey." When you calculate the distance, Luke meant the distance one is allowed to travel on the Sabbath just as Messiah is saying the same.

Exodus 16:29 KJV

See, for that the Lord hath given you the sabbath, therefore he giveth you on the sixth day the bread of two days; abide ye every man in his place, let no man go out of his place on the seventh day.

Matthew 24:20 KJV

But pray ye that your flight be not in the winter, neither on the sabbath day:

Acts 1:12 KJV

Then returned they unto Jerusalem from the mount called Olivet, which is from Jerusalem a sabbath day's journey.

What happens if you travel far? You will need to buy gas and end up breaking other Sabbath precepts. You would have to plan food the day before and also, you would likely need to pack the car. The point is to rest. Can one travel to minister or participate in such on the Sabbath? It is lawful to do good on the Sabbath day. Today, we have cars, motorcycles, etc. However, in the time of the Qumran community, the Temple Priests put a distance on this journey. Obviously, in the same amount of time, we can travel faster and a farther distance. Just remember, the point is to keep Him at the center without distraction. You know whether that journey is a distraction and even necessary that day. Some even attend a gathering at church or other regularly on Saturday and that is generally doing good thus lawful. However, you know when you are over the line. Conditions have changed in modern times. Just limit your travel on the Sabbath. For those who take public transportation, that would be buying and selling and requiring someone else to work for you. This does include riding on a ship in Jubilees.

> *"He shall not walk more than one thousand cubits beyond his town."*
> *"No man shall walk more than two thousand cubits after a beast to pasture it outside his town."*
> **—The Damascus Document, p. 141-143 [1]**

> **Jubilees 50:12 (Excerpt)**
> *... or goeth a journey... or rideth on any beast... or travelleth by ship on the sea...*

9. NO WORK FOR ANIMALS

The earth kept the Sabbath from the beginning as we demonstrated. There are even some animals who have been observed in the wild resting on Saturday very oddly. Your animals are your responsibility and they should keep the Sabbath with you. Messiah made it clear that the Bible practice has always included feeding and watering your animals as that is permissible work on the Sabbath. You can minimize that today though with automatic feeders and the like.

> **Exodus 23:12 KJV**
> *Six days thou shalt do thy work, and on the seventh day thou shalt rest: that thine ox and thine ass may rest, and the son of thy handmaid, and the stranger, may be refreshed.*

> *"No man shall walk more than two thousand cubits after a beast to pasture it*

outside his town. He shall not raise his hand to strike it with his fist. If it is
stubborn he shall not take it out of his house."
–The Damascus Document, p. 141-143 [1]

Jubilees 50:12 (Excerpt)
... or rideth on any beast... and whoever striketh or killeth anything

10. NO PLANNING

As we have discussed, planning is essentially work thus this is covered in Exodus as well but not in direct reference. The Dead Sea Scrolls manifest the Temple practice and Jubilees offers Moses' clarity himself. If we are planning, we are not focused on Him.

"He shall say nothing about work or labour to be done on the morrow."
–The Damascus Document, p. 141-143 [1]

"No man shall make plans with his mouth ... [on the day of Sabbath. He
shall not talk] about any matter relating to work or wealth or ... on the day
of Sabbath."
–4QHalakhah B, 40264a. DSS, p. 234 [1]

Jubilees 50:8 (Excerpt)
...or whoever saith he will do something on it...

11. NO VAIN / IDLE WORD

In order to remain focused on Jesus*(Yahusha)*, we are to speak His words and not our own. We do not complain, murmur, curse, show anger or even attempt conversations about us, our accomplishments, etc. We speak holy words and blessings. With those in your household, this is the day you can teach them.

Isaiah 58:13 KJV
If thou turn away thy foot from the sabbath, from doing thy pleasure on my

holy day; and call the sabbath a delight, the holy of the Lord, honourable; and shalt honour him, not doing thine own ways, nor finding thine own pleasure, nor speaking thine own words:

"No manshall speak any vain or idle word on the Sabbath day."
–The Damascus Document, p. 141-143 [1]

"He shall sp[eak no wo]rd apart from speaking holy words as prescribed and from pronouncing blessings of God."
–4QHalakhah B, 40264a. DSS, p. 234 [1]

12. MEDITATE & WORSHIP

For number 12, let's address what we do on the Sabbath. Once again, for those worried about the "thou shalt nots," reframe it as thou shalt rest. All of these are positive as this is about rest for your soul as Messiah taught. This is not a day of sleep and laziness. You can lounge and read and watch teaching videos, study, worship, pray and rest physically. However, this is not about a day of "slumming it" in focus. That would be about us. We affix our attention to Him, His Word and His ways.

Joshua 1:8 KJV

This book of the law shall not depart out of thy mouth; but thou shalt meditate therein day and night, that thou mayest observe to do according to all that is written therein: for then thou shalt make thy way prosperous, and then thou shalt have good success.

Psalm 1:2 KJV

But his delight is in the law of the Lord; and in his law doth he meditate day and night.

1 Timothy 4 KJV

1-2: Now the Spirit speaketh expressly, that in the latter times some shall depart from the faith, giving heed to seducing spirits, and doctrines of devils; Speaking lies in hypocrisy; having their conscience seared with a hot iron;

15: Meditate upon these things; give thyself wholly to them; that thy profiting may appear to all.

"[No man shall revise the scro]ll of a book reading its script on the day of [Sabbath] ... But they may read and study it."
–4QHalakhah B, 40264a. DSS, p. 234 [1]

The Sabbath is appointed by Yahuah as a sign for all His works of Creation. We celebrate His Creation on the same cycle in which He created – 7 days. We observe as He did on the 7th day of rest not the first which is a day of work on that same Creation clock.

Jubilees. 2:1

Write the complete history of the creation, how in six days Yahuah Elohim finished all His works and all that He created, and kept Sabbath on the seventh day and hallowed it for all ages, and appointed it as a sign for all His works.

This is our test as believers as Hebrews 4 defines those not entering this rest on the Sabbath as an example of unbelief. The Sabbath is a sign of covenant relationship with the Father and Son. It is not salvation. However, those in love and relationship with Him keep His commandments according to the New Testament. We see in Israel that a man would be put to death for not keeping the Sabbath. In Israel, this meant physical death when it was a nation. However, in clarification, they were a nation in covenant with national laws framed within such. The true intent is spiritual death according to Jubilees and Qumran.

Jubilees 2:27-28

*And whoever profaneth it shall surely die, and **whoever doeth thereon any work shall surely die eternally,** that the children of Israel may observe this day throughout their generations, and not be rooted out of the land; for it is a holy day and a blessed day. And every one who observeth it and keepeth Sabbath thereon from all his work, will be holy and blessed throughout all days like unto us.*

Recipe For REST

01 — NO WORK

Ex. 20:10
Damascus Doc., p. 141
Heb. 4:9-11
Jub. 2:29, 50:8,12

In order to keep the Sabbath holy, the first tenet is to do no work on this day each week for the entire 24 hours.

02 — NO COOKING

Ex. 35:3
Damascus Doc., p. 141
Jub. 2:29 Jub. 50:9, 12

We are not to create fire to cook on the Sabbath. We prepare our meals the previous day. This way we take no thought for our own maintenance.

03 — NO BUYING / SELLING

Neh. 13:15
Damascus Doc., p. 141
Jub. 50:8

We are not to engage in commerce neither buying nor selling. Nehemiah closed the gates the night before so no one could enter to sell the next morning.

04 — NO WORK FOR OTHERS

Ex. 20:10
Damascus Doc., p. 142
Jub. 50:7

Our children, maids, or anyone in our households are not to work on the Sabbath. We are to do nothing that requires another to work on our behalf.

05 — NO PERSONAL PLEASURE

Is. 58:13
Damascus Doc., p. 142
Jub. 2:29, 50:7

Though a delight, Sabbath is for His pleasure not ours. We are not to engage in our own personal pleasure for ourselves. Celebrate Creation not re-creation.

06 — NO CARRYING

Jer. 17:21
Damascus Doc., p. 142
Jub. 2:29, 50:8

As it requires work, we are not to lift any burden on the Sabbath including children.

12 Sabbath Precepts

07 — NO MONEY MATTERS

Ex. 20:10
Damascus Doc., p. 141

Our focus even in thought should not be on our own finances, debts and investments on the Sabbath. Only Him.

08 — NO EXTENDED TRAVEL

Ex. 16:29
Matt. 24:20
Damascus Doc., p. 141
Jub. 50:12

Though we may congregate on the Sabbath and it is always permissible to do good on the Sabbath, our travel should be limited. This takes focus away from Him.

09 — NO WORK FOR ANIMALS

Ex. 23:12
Damascus Doc., p. 142
Jub. 50:12

Animals are not to work on the Sabbath either. They keep it too.

10 — NO PLANNING

4QHalakhah B 40264a. DSS p. 234 [1]
Jub. 50:8

"No man shall make plans with his mouth" on the Sabbath Day. This day is about Him. Everything is to be planned even for Sabbath prior.

11 — NO VAIN / IDLE WORD

Is. 58:13
Damascus Doc., p. 141

We are not to waste words on the Sabbath as it is His day. No complaining, anger, nor vanity. We do not reflect on us but Him in word and deed on this day.

12 — MEDITATE & WORSHIP

Jos. 1:8
Ps. 1:2
1 Ti. 4:15
Jub. 2:1

We read, study, watch teaching videos, worship, congregate, etc. on the Sabbath. Celebrate His works of Creation weekly.

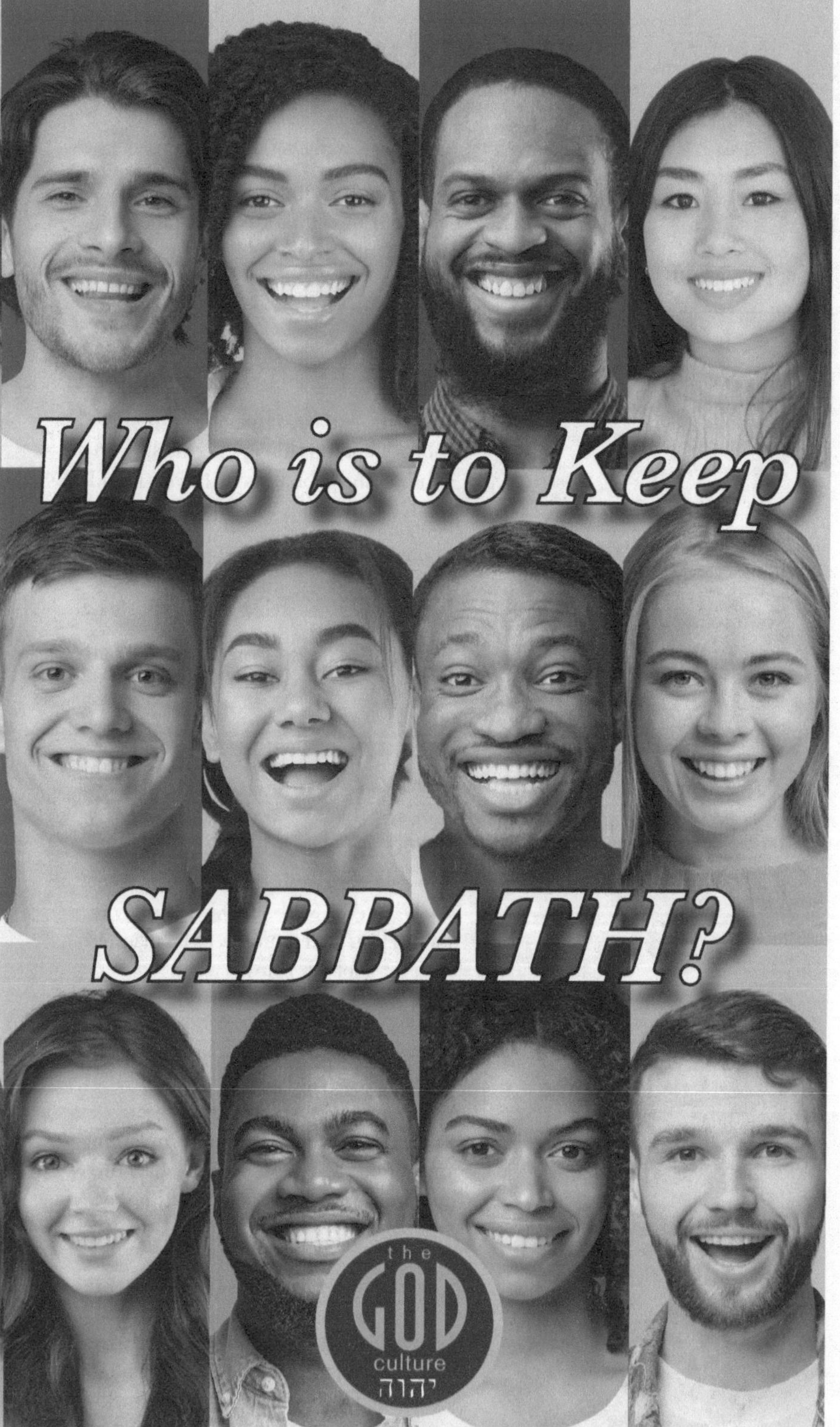
Who is to Keep
SABBATH?
the
GOD
culture
יהוה

Chapter 13 | Who Is to Keep Sabbath? Not a Jewish Tradition

Before even addressing this question, history must be corrected and understood. Those calling themselves "Jews" today are Pharisees by historic definition even from their own sources whether direct bloodline Pharisees or simply in religious doctrine. After the 2nd Temple was destroyed around 70 A.D., the Pharisees changed their practice eliminating especially the Second Temple rituals.

"Henceforth Jewish life was regulated by the teachings of the Pharisees; the whole history of Judaism was reconstructed from the Pharisaic point of view, and a new aspect was given to the Sanhedrin of the past. A new chain of tradition supplanted the older, priestly tradition (Abot i. 1). Pharisaism shaped the character of Judaism and the life and thought of the Jew for all the future. True, it gave the Jewish religion a legalistic tendency and made "separatism" its chief characteristic; yet only thus were the pure monotheistic faith, the ethical ideal, and the intellectual and spiritual character of the Jew preserved in the midst of the downfall of the old world and the deluge of barbarism which swept over the medieval world."
–Jewish Encylopedia [60]

"The Pharisees (/ˈfærəsiːz/; Hebrew: פְּרוּשִׁים Pərūšīm) were a social movement and a school of thought in the Levant during the time of Second Temple Judaism. After the destruction of the Second Temple in 70 CE, Pharisaic beliefs became the foundational, liturgical, and ritualistic basis for Rabbinic Judaism."–Wikipedia [61]

"Pharisees: făr' ə səz (פְּרוּשִׁים; φαρισαῖοι). One of the most important

251

of the Jewish sects of the late intertestamental and NT periods, determining
thereafter the character of reconstituted Judaism."
–Bible Gateway, Encyclopedia Of The Bible [62]

This should not be a surprise in the church, as again, even Judaism's own history records that modern "Jews" rose from Pharisaism and that is their foundation. A Rabbi in the 1st Century is a Pharisee and they still call themselves Rabbis today as they remain Pharisees. Pharisees evolve their doctrines in any time as they apply leaven that is an expanding agent. Thus there is no such thing as a Pharisee religion that would remain the exact same in 2,000 years but the foundation is obvious and recorded. Messiah did not call Himself Rabbi though some did refer to him as such and eventually he rebuked it and said to call no man Rabbi nor Father *(Matt. 23:8-9)*. He did not wish to be confused with a Pharisee or even a Catholic Priest that is very revealing as to what He saw in the future. When you read his scathing rebukes of Pharisees which we have curated into a chart in the chapter on "The Pharisee Sabbath," you quickly realize why the distancing existed.

Understand, there is no mention of the Pharisees and Sadducees in the Old Testament. This is because they did not exist in Judaea until about 165 B.C. when the Hasmoneans of Modi'in came into Judaea as foreigners conquering the nation and the Temple. They installed their priests from Samaria that would make up the Sanhedrin. They were not there in Judaea in any Old Testament book. Samaritans are rebuked and they are mentioned as such but they are not Hebrews.

Pharisees: (Heb. פרושים, Perushim), a Jewish religious and political party or
sect during the Second Temple period which emerged as a distinct group shortly
after the Hasmonean revolt, about 165–160 b.c.e. –Encyclopedia.com [83]

A new unbiblical order would control the Temple fulfilling the Psalm 83 war where David prophesied of this exact event. No other can fit and this is not a future event to us today as there is no Temple since and though scripture prophesies it's rebuilding, it does not condone it nor does Yahuah command it nor need it. The third Temple will be built for the Beast who declares he is God there and will rule the Earth largely from Jerusalem which Revelation 11 calls "spiritual Sodom and Egypt" in our time.

We know you do not hear this in most churches because these same Pharisees control seminaries and allegiance to Zionism is taught and demanded of most of your pastors and leadership. As we have covered, the legitimate Temple Priests were exiled to Qumran as in recorded history and they continued the Temple practice which is why Messiah chose to launch His ministry there and not at the Temple in Jerusalem. When He made His way to Jerusalem in the end, He well knew He was not welcomed in that Temple anymore as Yahuah was not either because He is not the God of the Pharisees. They plotted and sought and succeeded setting up the sacrifice of the Son of Yahuah even in the Temple. How could they possibly know Him?

That alone should cause a scholar to awaken. Most will not. Therefore, the paradigm we see in religion today is that of Pharisaism by a new name as Judaism. This is a religion rebuked by Messiah in Mark 7 and many other places against His commandments or anti-Torah. We cannot forget nor overlook this when understanding the religious paradigm of our day. Pharisaism or modern Judaism is not built on a Biblical foundation. It is an infusion that looks nothing like the Biblical relationship as it is against His Commandments but it mingles deceptively.

Many Rabbis will claim the Sabbath is a Jewish Feast only and not for the Gentile. That is illiterate and they clearly have never truly read the Torah that identifies Gentiles as the "stranger among you" many times. This stranger or Gentile had the same Law and relationship with Yahuah as did the Israelites who never called themselves the non-Hebrew word Jew. They were and are the Yahudim inclusive of Gentiles from the very Exodus and even in the time of Abraham. How can anyone calling themselves a Bible scholar not know this?

Leviticus 16:29 KJV
*And this shall be a **statute for ever** unto you: that in the seventh month, on the tenth day of the month, ye shall afflict your souls, and do no work at all, **whether it be one of your own country, or a stranger that sojourneth among you**:*

Exodus 12:49 KJV
**One law shall be to him that is homeborn, and unto the
stranger that sojourneth among you**.
Leviticus 17:12 KJV
Therefore I said unto the children of Israel, No soul of you shall eat blood,
neither shall any stranger that sojourneth among you *eat
blood.*
Leviticus 18:26 KJV
*Ye shall therefore keep my statutes and my judgments, and shall not commit
any of these abominations;* ***neither any of your own nation, nor
any stranger that sojourneth among you:***
Leviticus 19:34 KJV
But ***the stranger that dwelleth with you shall be unto you as
one born among you, and thou shalt love him as thyself***; *for
ye were strangers in the land of Egypt: I am the LORD your God.*
Numbers 9:14 KJV
And if a ***stranger shall sojourn among you, and will keep
the passover unto the LORD***; *according to the ordinance of the
passover, and according to the manner thereof,* ***so shall he do***: *ye shall have*
***one ordinance, both for the stranger, and for him that was
born in the land***.
Numbers 15:29 KJV
***Ye shall have one law for him that sinneth through
ignorance, both for him that is born among the children of
Israel, and for the stranger that sojourneth among them***.
Numbers 15:26 kjv
And it shall be ***forgiven*** *all the congregation of the children of Israel,* ***and
the stranger that sojourneth among them***; *seeing all the people
were in ignorance.*

The blessings and curses that appear in the Law have always applied
to the Gentile as well. They were not under a different Law nor were
they to be lawless. The fact is no Gentile nations ever entered covenant
as a nation that makes Israel special. The patriarchs did but they are
generally, a family or small group of people. None of the patriarchs
before Abraham/Eber were Hebrews. None before Jacob/Israel were

Israelites whom we call "Jews" inappropriately. The word "Jew" is never a Bible word of Ancient Hebrew, Greek, Aramaic, Latin, Old French, Old German nor Old English origin. Neither had a "J" until the Ashkenazi migration into Europe who claimed to be Jews replacing the connotation with a non-Hebrew word in fraud. The "J" originates in their Yiddish language in which they infused and perhaps Persian ultimately. Infusing is what they have always done. They did not want Yahuah's name in theirs because they are not Yah's which is the only short rendering for the word and Yah is found 45 times on a standalone basis in scripture. However, Gentiles were saved and they had Law.

This is not one fragment out of context but an overwhelming doctrine not typically taught today yet it is right there abundant in scripture. The Pharisees do not want us to know they are not Hebrews as they represent the Synagogue of Satan who say they are Yahudim and are not but do lie *(Rev. 2:9, 3:9)*. The church largely wants you to believe Israel was replaced by the Gentile "in the time of the Gentiles." Both are equally false and represent strange doctrine to the Bible which records Gentiles keeping the Law in relationship and even being saved long before Jesus *(Yahusha)* ever became flesh. Understand He is their salvation as well just as He is ours. That has never changed. There is no salvation through the Law but only in Him from the beginning. The Bible has never said otherwise. Keeping His Law and the Sabbath is a sign of our covenant with Him, it is not salvation nor ever has been.

Some confuse passages like this one found in Jubilees. However, once again, when one only reads in fragments forgetting the context, they will never understand. This appears to say only Israel is to keep the Sabbath. However, we have well documented the Sabbath was kept from Adam to Abraham to Moses with about 300 years of non-observance only. We did so using the Book of Jubilees which identifies this pattern and cannot say the opposite here and it does not. The only NATION/People who has entered covenant is Israel. No other nation has on record but some within have as evidenced in scripture just not their entire nations. That is what this is saying not that only Israel has ever kept the Sabbath that would be against what Jubilees already said twice and in great detail. Unfortunately, we live in a time, where scholarship as a paradigm will read only this fragment and attempt to use it in debate to defend their

Biblical illiteracy. We can all see through this as we "prove all things."

Jubilees 2:31

And the Creator of all things blessed it, but He did not sanctify all peoples and nations to keep Sabbath thereon, but Israel alone: them alone He permitted to eat and drink and to keep Sabbath thereon on the earth.

It is rather unimaginable that Moses could be so clear yet so ignored. Here is an extremely direct passage that the Covenant was not just for Israel but those that stand with them and even other Gentiles who are not with them that day. That is all encompassing and clear that ALL Gentiles still had His Law to follow and if they did, they would be called His. That is not new in the New Testament.

Deuteronomy 29:12-15 KJV

That thou shouldest enter into covenant with the LORD thy God, and into his oath, which the LORD thy God maketh with thee this day: That he may establish thee to day for a people unto himself, and that he may be unto thee a God, as he hath said unto thee, and as he hath sworn unto thy fathers, to Abraham, to Isaac, and to Jacob. Neither with you only do I make this covenant and this oath; But with him that standeth here with us this day before the LORD our God, and also with him that is not here with us this day:

The Covenant and the Law were never just for Israel solely. That is a Pharisee claim that the Old Testament is only written to the Jew. It is arrogant illiteracy of scripture especially when the only "Jews" in the Bible are rebuked mostly. Isaiah very strongly espouses this same doctrine that Gentiles can and will be saved. The relationship that Israel had which does not belong to the Pharisees unless one becomes a true believer, was always available to the Gentile.

Isaiah 49:6 KJV

And he said, It is a light thing that thou shouldest be my servant to raise up the tribes of Jacob, and to restore the preserved of Israel: I will also give thee for a light to the Gentiles, that thou mayest be my salvation unto the end of the earth.

One could read this until the end when the Earth is made new or the ends of the Earth in territory either way. However, Isaiah is speaking to you whether Hebrew or Gentile in the Old Testament. In the next chapters, he becomes more profound and specific. Not only is he clear that all are to keep the Sabbath and those who do will be blessed, but Isaiah sets forth a timeline for those keeping the Sabbath in Israel's re-gathering. In our age, that still has not happened and remains prophecy. We can look to the future that believers will be keeping His Sabbath. If you are not, you are polluting it even in our age.

Isaiah 56:1-8 KJV

Thus saith the Lord, Keep ye judgment, and do justice: for my salvation is near to come, and my righteousness to be revealed. Blessed is the man that doeth this, and the son of man that layeth hold on it; that keepeth the sabbath from polluting it, and keepeth his hand from doing any evil. Neither let the son of the stranger, that hath joined himself to the Lord, speak, saying, The Lord hath utterly separated me from his people: neither let the eunuch say, Behold, I am a dry tree. For thus saith the Lord unto the eunuchs that keep my sabbaths, and choose the things that please me, and take hold of my covenant; Even unto them will I give in mine house and within my walls a place and a name better than of sons and of daughters: I will give them an everlasting name, that shall not be cut off. Also the sons of the stranger, that join themselves to the Lord, to serve him, and to love the name of the Lord, to be his servants, every one that keepeth the sabbath from polluting it, and taketh hold of my covenant; Even them will I bring to my holy mountain, and make them joyful in my house of prayer: their burnt offerings and their sacrifices shall be accepted upon mine altar; for mine house shall be called an house of prayer for all people. The Lord God, which gathereth the outcasts of Israel saith, Yet will I gather others to him, beside those that are gathered unto him.

Paul says this very same thing though overlooked. He knew there was no difference between Gentile and Hebrew in Yahuah's sight. This is not new but he knew it was an Old Testament theme as well. Some misread the English here as saying Jesus*(Yahusha)* just ended the Law. That is not what this says. He is the end of the Law means He completes it and He told us in Matthew 5:17-18 it will not pass at least until the Day of Final

Judgment. Paul knew this as well and was saying no different.

Did Moses say there is salvation through the Law? No. Did Paul say that is what Moses said? No. Paul is clarifying over paragraphs not fragments. He affirms that. Paul knew Moses was right that we are to be righteous. Did he not just open up with many are ignorant of Yahuah's righteousness? He certainly is not placing Moses in that category and to say so as a scholar is inept and demonstrates no foundation in scripture whatsoever. In setting the context, he is rebuking one's own righteousness that is a staple of Pharisee doctrine he rebukes. They believe the Law of Moses is salvation. Paul and the whole of scripture does not agree with the Pharisees.

Romans 10:3-13 KJV

For they being ignorant of God's righteousness, and going about to establish their own righteousness, have not submitted themselves unto the righteousness of God. For Christ is the end of the law for righteousness to every one that believeth. For Moses describeth the righteousness which is of the law, That the man which doeth those things shall live by them. But the righteousness which is of faith speaketh on this wise, Say not in thine heart, Who shall ascend into heaven? (that is, to bring Christ down from above:) Or, Who shall descend into the deep? (that is, to bring up Christ again from the dead.) But what saith it? The word is nigh thee, even in thy mouth, and in thy heart: that is, the word of faith, which we preach; That if thou shalt confess with thy mouth the Lord Jesus, and shalt believe in thine heart that God hath raised him from the dead, thou shalt be saved. For with the heart man believeth unto righteousness; and with the mouth confession is made unto salvation. For the scripture saith, Whosoever believeth on him shall not be ashamed. For there is no difference between the Jew and the Greek: for the same Lord over all is rich unto all that call upon him. For whosoever shall call upon the name of the Lord shall be saved.

Here we have another passage where reading a small fragment produces strange doctrine. Moses knew that Jesus*(Yahusha)* was salvation even then. That has never changed. Here is especially what is overlooked. Where does faith come from according to Paul? Hearing by the word of Yahuah *(Rom. 10:17)*. What Word is Paul reading? The New Testament is not written yet mostly. He is talking about the Old Testament. He finds faith in reading it and so will we. That is also called the Law of Moses. There is no separating the Law from Paul. He kept and taught it.

Romans 10:16-17 KJV

But they have not all obeyed the gospel. For Esaias saith, Lord, who hath believed our report? So then faith cometh by hearing, and hearing by the word of God.

How can any scholar read this and not see that Paul just affirmed the writings of the Prophets saying we should obey them? He does not say Moses was wrong but just refocus your thinking from what the Pharisees are teaching you. The Law is not salvation. However, it is still valid. We find especially all 10 Commandments in Paul's preaching *(see chart p. 170)*. He is not creating new Law, he quotes Moses. He does not view Moses as bad nor the Law of Moses that Yahuah wrote with His finger as we have shown several scriptures where he endorses the Law and teaches it.

For what is the fire that emanates from the mouth of Messiah that consumes His enemies on Judgment Day or in the end when He is the end of the Law as Paul is discussing above? The Law.

2 Esdras 13:10-11 KJVA

But only I saw that he sent out of his mouth, as it had been a blast of fire, and out of his lips a flaming breath, and out of his tongue he cast out sparks and tempests, And they were all mixed together; the blast of fire, the flaming breath, and the great tempest, and fell with violence upon the multitude, which was prepared to fight, and burnt them up every one, so that upon a sudden, of an innumerable multitude, nothing was to be perceived, but only dust and smell of smoke: when I saw this, I was afraid.

2 Esdras 13:38 KJVA

...and he (Messiah) shall destroy them without labor, by the law which is like unto fire... *(Cf. Rev. 1:16, 2:16, 12:17, 14:12, 19:15, 21, 22:14; 1 John 2:3-4, 3:22-24, 5:2-3; 2 John 1:6; Matt. 5:17-18)*

You will find Messiah at the end of the Law. He will still be applying it on the Day of Judgment in the end just as He said.

Gentiles and Jews Observed the Saturday, 7th-Day Sabbath

According to the only source that matters, the Bible, Gentiles as well as Jews *(Yahudim)* observed the Sabbath on the 7th Day continuing the Old Testament practice. We demonstrated this in abundant Old Testament scripture from Torah. That remains in the New Testament.

Acts 18:4 KJV

And he reasoned in the synagogue every sabbath, and persuaded the Jews and the Greeks.

Acts 9:31 KJV

*Then had the churches **rest** throughout all Judaea and Galilee and Samaria, and were edified; and walking in the fear of the Lord, and in the comfort of the Holy Ghost, were multiplied.*

Acts 13:42-44 KJV

And when the Jews were gone out of the synagogue, the Gentiles besought that these words might be preached to them the next sabbath. Now when the congregation was broken up, many of the Jews and religious proselytes followed Paul and Barnabas: who, speaking to them, persuaded them to continue in the grace of God.And the next sabbath day came almost the whole city together to hear the word of God.

In fact, the New Testament ekklesia kept the Sabbath outside of synagogues thus no one can attempt to say Paul only preached to Jews on Sabbath because of the Old Testament practice. It was the New Testament observance as well continued as fact. Scripture says so; if your denomination does not, ask them to produce their authority to rewrite scripture.

Acts 16:13 KJV

And on the sabbath we went out of the city by a river side, where prayer was wont to be made; and we sat down, and spake unto the women which resorted thither.

After Messiah's ascension, we see the Apostles keeping at least 85 documented Sabbaths in the Book of Acts alone *(chart on p. 353)*. We curated a chart later but in Acts 17, there are 3 consecutive Sabbaths observed by the Apostles, there are 78 consecutive Sabbaths in which Paul preached in a synagogue on Saturday in Acts 18:5 alone and singular Sabbaths in Acts 23:13, 13:43, 16:11 and 18:1. These are mostly gatherings of both Gentiles and Jews*(Yahudim)* and there is no differentiation in the 7th-Day Sabbath observance. How exactly can anyone claim they did not keep the Sabbath when it is right there in Acts 85 times in writing? They do not represent the Bible in the slightest. That is profound, willing ignorance and it is called church doctrine in most denominations.

The other thing we find is that the Sabbath and Feasts are commanded forever for both Israel and the Gentile. We have already viewed this in Lev. 16:29 but this is Bible doctrine many times.

> ### *Leviticus 23 KJV - 7 Biblical FEAST DAYS*
> *14 ...it shall be a **statute for ever throughout your generations in all your dwellings**.*
> *21   ...it shall be a **statute for ever in all your dwellings throughout your generations**.*
> *31 ...it shall be a **statute for ever throughout your generations in all your dwellings**.*
> *41 ...It shall be a **statute for ever in your generations**...*

Therefore, not only is the Sabbath not a Jewish mo'edim as they are not Hebrews anyway, but Gentiles have always partaken and they received the same command that this is a statute forever throughout your generations in ALL your dwellings. This includes all of us. It does not matter if you are in a Sabbath-keeping nation as none truly are even in Israel who keeps the Pharisee Sabbath not the Bible Sabbath. This day of rest was made for mankind and there were no Jews then. The patriarchs were not Hebrews until Abraham/Eber. This is a paradigm we have accepted but it strays far from the Bible paradigm which sees Hebrews and Gentiles the same. The Sabbath is for everyone.

The Track of the Pharisee

the pharisee SABBATH

Chapter 14 | The Pharisee Sabbath: The Track of the Pharisee

Ye do the deeds of your father. Then said they to him, We be not born of fornication; we have one Father, even God. Jesus said unto them, If God were your Father, ye would love me: for I proceeded forth and came from God; neither came I of myself, but he sent me. Why do ye not understand my speech? even because ye cannot hear my word. Ye are of your father the devil, and the lusts of your father ye will do. He was a murderer from the beginning, and abode not in the truth, because there is no truth in him. When he speaketh a lie, he speaketh of his own: for he is a liar, and the father of it.

Why these "knock-down, drag-out" confrontations with Pharisees? Why did Jesus*(Yahusha)* not turn the other cheek but engaged them and crushed them in debate making them appear as fools and even calling them such? Why does He rebuke their interpretation of His Commandments as wrong including Sabbath? Notice these accusers and liars answer Messiah claiming He is an illegitimate child. They are quick to accuse, and they care not what the actual truth is which is the same with their teachings then and now. Does that not sound familiar today? They seek debate points and attempt to win debate as if that is a remote representation of truth. It is not. They, generally, did not repent after demanding the death of the very Son of Yahuah.

What makes the church think they are now the foundation of the Bible religion when they are exposed by Messiah Himself so many times in so many different ways? Why does the church not realize they are not Levites nor even mentioned in Jerusalem in the entire Old Testament? Many scholars have lost track of the enemy and thus, lost their bearings.

They truly need to fix that foundation in order to begin addressing the Word coherently. The Sons of Zadok led the Temple worship and they were not Pharisees. There was not one Pharisee among them. That party did not exist until 165 B.C. in Jerusalem and they are rebuked by the exiled Temple Priests for expelling them from the Temple and usurping the Priesthood. Many scholars look to these false imposters for guidance especially on Ancient Israel yet they are not experts in anything but deception and pretending. We will maintain Jesus' *(Yahusha's)* attitude toward them as they have never changed. Any scholar or theologian who does not, is not acting like Jesus *(Yahusha)*.

He responds and proclaims they are of their father the devil and ultimately, they pursue his lusts. Can you imagine a more damning review of the Pharisees? The dilemma is this is one of many where Jesus *(Yahusha)* builds a characterization of this group in which no one can argue. They are liars like their father. It's like the joke: How can you tell a liar is lying? His mouth is open. That's essentially His quote.

Why do we find such severe language regarding Pharisees in the New Testament? At the end of this chapter, we have compiled a chart of some of these direct rebukes from Messiah Himself and then, from the Qumran Community *(pp. 288-291)*. They are many. Why would He choose to use such strong terms such as "brood of vipers," "hypocrites all," "of your father the devil," "liars," "murderers," and more. We offer the passages so one can confirm. However, a picture begins to come into focus based on these rebukes.

He tells us why. They have changed the Word with their interpretations into the opposite of Torah *(Mark 7:9)* and that was 2,000 years ago. What makes us think that ever changed? Messiah is the Word and you better believe He does not respond to one changing it with anything but righteous anger. He is operating righteously and in love as Jesus *(Yahusha)* did not sin ever even in calling them these names. If you are not recognizing and using this same language as Messiah, you are likely unaware or not operating in love.

They work hard to appear righteous but they pray and give to be seen. This is more dangerous than satanism as they represent the opposite of the Bible while pretending to represent it. They want their plaque of recognition to appear righteous. The problem is, inside, they are rotten to the core. They prey on widows and the poor, function as thieves, accusers, liars, murderers, and stand in the way of knowledge. Imagine the ones usurping the right to teach actually impeding learning. Their actions lead people to Hell Messiah says. Are we reading the Bible or just the portions we want to hear?

We can see a full demonstration of this today in a company or billionaire who founds a charity. The non-profit is supposed to be doing good work yet instead it is merely a front to funnel monies without their paying taxes. They enable these so-called charities to advance their agendas that behind the scenes can be very evil ultimately undermining the fabric of society. Why? This is the Pharisee way and it is more prevalent and far better funded today than it was then. Jesus*(Yahusha)* does not only deal with them in those days but He places them in prophecy as having a large role in the End Times against His ekklesia. They are the physical form of the principalities and powers of darkness in His words for in them, Satan has a Synagogue of followers.

Revelation 2:9 KJV

I know thy works, and tribulation, and poverty, (but thou art rich) and I know the blasphemy of them which say they are Jews, and are not, but are the synagogue of Satan.

Revelation 3:9 KJV

Behold, I will make them of the synagogue of Satan, which say they are Jews, and are not, but do lie; behold, I will make them to come and worship before thy feet, and to know that I have loved thee.

How can any scholar read these passages and then forget that this "Synagogue of Satan" not only operated in the days of Messiah but until the End Times? How can we not heed His many warnings?

There are far more subtle rebukes as well especially in Paul's epistles. One just needs to understand whom Paul is addressing because he is careful in his time not to call them out by name. However, Paul rebukes ignorance and certain doctrines especially those from Moses that are not Moses' view. One needs to understand Paul would never go against Moses and Torah. He is not being argumentative with Torah and for someone calling themselves a scholar to say that he is, is among the most illiterate of any view.

The question remains since Messiah calls them out even in an End Times context in Revelation 2:9 and 3:9 as the Synagogue of Satan who say they are Yahudim and are not but do lie, how has the church lost track of them? Why is this not being taught and exposed regularly? Much of the church does not know what happened to the Pharisees as Messiah was clear they do not disappear but instigate to the very end. We are in a spiritual battle.

Ephesians 6:11-18 KJV

Put on all of God's armor so that you will be able to stand firm against all strategies of the devil. For we are not fighting against flesh-and-blood enemies, but against evil rulers and authorities of the unseen world, against mighty powers in this dark world, and against evil spirits in the heavenly places. Therefore, put on every piece of God's armor so you will be able to resist the enemy in the time of evil. Then after the battle you will still be standing firm. Stand your ground, putting on the belt of truth and the body armor of God's righteousness. For shoes, put on the peace that comes from the Good News so that you will be fully prepared. In addition to all of these, hold up the shield of faith to stop the fiery arrows of the devil. Put on salvation as your helmet, and take the sword of the Spirit, which is the word of God. Pray in the Spirit at all times and on every occasion. Stay alert and be persistent in your prayers for all believers everywhere.

Our enemy is spiritual – principalities and powers of darkness. However, Jesus*(Yahusha)* identifies a group in which they operate and the church not only does not know who these are today, they place this group on a pedestal as if they know Torah and even the land of Israel. However, they are strangers in that land and strangers to Torah. They do not know it nor understand it. They did not somehow gain such understanding and yet still reject Him to this day. How can we even know whom to resist if we do not know our enemy? Also, how can we not see in yet another passage Paul is teaching righteousness yet scholars are telling us he did not believe in having any Law by which to judge?

There are churches who only focus on salvation as if it is the only topic in the Bible yet where is our belt of truth? Do we know the truth? Our body armor, the most important part is righteousness not salvation. Only the helmet is salvation. One does not enter the battlefield only wearing a helmet. What kind of denomination or mega-church dares to leave people so vulnerable? For shoes, we put on peace. Then, we have a shield of faith that we attain from hearing the Word of Yahuah. When Paul wrote this, much of the New Testament was not even at his disposal. He is talking about reading the Old Testament as well and not just focusing on 12 fragments about your own salvation. That would not denote a warrior but one entering the fight naked of protection. The bigger question is how can the modern church lead the lambs to slaughter so?

Who were the righteous priests who lead Israel in the ways of Yahuah? The Sons of Zadok. Even when Israel strayed, they kept His charge.

Ezekiel 44:15-16 KJV

But the priests the Levites, the sons of Zadok, that kept the charge of my sanctuary when the children of Israel went astray from me, they shall come near to me to minister unto me, and they shall stand before me to offer unto me the fat and the blood, saith the Lord GOD: They shall enter into my sanctuary, and they shall come near to my table, to minister unto me, and they shall keep my charge.

These were not Pharisees. They were exiled to the Wilderness of Judaea replaced by Pharisees in the Temple. We have well covered this. What have we heard from most pulpits on this? Crickets... We can track them to Qumran and we have now even found their scroll library of scripture and many writings of which they identify themselves and their practices that match those of the true Temple Priests. They prophesy of Messiah and they play a role in the launch of His ministry directly linking the Old and New Testaments and to the End Times. There were no Pharisees nor Essenes among them and they, too have much to say about the Hasmoneans and their priests – the Pharisees. We have also curated a chart on their rebukes of Pharisees and Hasmoneans and it is incredible how similar their words are to those of Messiah as well as how abundant these negative references *(pp. 288-291)*. Every believer should know and understand this.

However, as we demonstrated last chapter, we can track the Pharisees very easily. They are not even hidden. The language may be a bit obscured but Pharisaism became Modern Judaism. The same Pharisee Rabbis are now called Jewish Rabbis. When one quotes a 1st century Rabbi, they are embracing Pharisees. When one quotes 2nd century Rabbis calling themselves Jews, they are still accepting Pharisaism. Even in the Bible, one can observe how Pharisees are called Jews yet they were never Yahudim. Of course, they changed the word to a non-Hebrew word proving they are not even Hebrews. However, they assimilated into the connotations of the culture but remained foreigners forcing their ways into the life and practices of Judaea.

John the Baptist on Pharisees and Saduccees

Matthew 3:7 KJV

But when he saw many of the Pharisees and Sadducees come to his baptism, he said unto them, O generation of vipers, who hath warned you to flee from the wrath to come? Bring forth therefore fruits meet for repentance: And think not to say within yourselves, We have Abraham to our father: for I say unto you, that God is able of these stones to raise up children unto Abraham. And now also the axe is laid unto the root of the trees: therefore every tree which bringeth not forth good fruit is hewn down, and cast into the fire.

Messiah shares John's exact language, "generation of vipers" in Matt. 12:34, 23:33, Luke 3:7 and in John 15 he lays out a very similar message regarding bearing good fruit. Remember, John was from Qumran/ Bethabara as well. Notice the similarities in the view of John, Messiah and the Qumran/Bethabara Priests as they were all on the same page. No wonder modern Pharisees attempt to obscure who lived in Qumran by claiming they were Kabbalistic Essenes in complete fraud with no archaeology and not a single reference to support such claim. In Qumran, many of their names and titles for Pharisees and Hasmoneans are the same including the "sons of darkness," "sons or lot of Belail*(satan)*," "those who seek smooth things," "wicked priest(s)," etc.

Is this true? Is there a group of men who represent such evil? We should know our enemy. Certainly, we wrestle with principalities and powers of darkness but here we have a specific cult who are their pawns. Once again, when Paul mentions we wrestle with spiritual powers, he was not marginalizing this group in whom he was well familiar. He rebuked them many times as well. However, when have we heard this from the pulpit? Why has the church forgotten who they are even listening to them to form church doctrine?

Pharisees Generally Will Not Enter the Kingdom of Heaven

Matthew 5:20 KJV

For I say unto you, That except your righteousness shall exceed the righteousness of the scribes and Pharisees, ye shall in no case enter into the kingdom of heaven.

Even a Pharisee can be saved as some were in the New Testament. However, when a group in the Bible is used as the benchmark for not entering the Kingdom of Heaven, we should all take note. This scripture is scolding them for being unrighteous not for espousing such as they attempt to appear so but are not. We don't listen to such a group, certainly don't treat them as if they know the Bible nor accept them as even capable of speaking the truth which they do not represent. How can one who Messiah says fails the standard of Heaven then become our standard even in so-called "respect?" They offer nothing deserving of respect. We either believe the words of Jesus*(Yahusha)* or we do not. Shame on the church for losing the enemy and allowing them within.

Pharisees are not just generally destined to Hell, they impede others from entering the Kingdom. This is why we have the basic message of salvation even redefined in ludicrous, impotent terms in order to lead the lambs to slaughter.

Matthew 23:13 KJV

But woe unto you, scribes and Pharisees, hypocrites! for ye shut up the kingdom of heaven against men: for ye neither go in yourselves, neither suffer ye them that are entering to go in. Woe unto you, scribes and Pharisees, hypocrites! for ye devour widows' houses, and for a pretence make long prayer: therefore ye shall receive the greater damnation. Woe unto you, scribes and Pharisees, hypocrites! for ye compass sea and land to make one proselyte, and when he is made, ye make him twofold more the child of hell than yourselves.

Ask yourself, should we be following them? They will not escape the damnation of Hell as a group though some have been and will be saved. As Paul, they cannot remain Pharisees though. We can follow their fruit.

Matthew 23:33 KJV

Ye serpents, ye generation of vipers, how can ye escape the damnation of hell?

Pharisees Add to the Word

We are warned time and time again not to give heed to the leaven of the Pharisees and you will find Sadducees, Herod and the scribes of that time also included in these rebukes. Note, their scribes are not those of the Old Testament but also replacements as their entire order is and Herod is an Edomite not an Israelite. These are the enemies spelled out in Psalm 83 that would attack and conquer the Temple and they executed that in 165 B.C. They have made themselves the enemies of the Bible and Jesus*(Yahusha)*. They have changed the entire Word but here are just a few misrepresentations they offer in scripture. This has only expanded in depth and scope since in the past 2,000 years.

Matthew 16:6 KJV

Then Jesus said unto them, Take heed and beware of the leaven of the Pharisees and of the Sadducees.

Mark 8:15 KJV

And he charged them, saying, Take heed, beware of the leaven of the Pharisees, and of the leaven of Herod.

Luke 12:1b KJV

...he began to say unto his disciples first of all, Beware ye of the leaven of the Pharisees, which is hypocrisy.

Hypocrisy is Pharisee doctrine indeed as Jesus*(Yahusha)*

rebuked it as such many times directly. When some of the Apostles did not quite understand this, Messiah then clarifies beware the leaven of the Sanhedrin – all of them. You don't separate Pharisees and Sadducees. They both make up the Sanhedrin and neither represent the Biblical Priesthood but are imposters. The same tactic is used today in propaganda so that we will get wrapped up into taking a side yet there is no side such as with Left and Right in politics. They both represent the same Sanhedrin and all of them generally, are pursuing the ways of the Pharisees and usually after their own gain and reputation not ours and certainly not Yahuah's.

Matthew 16:11-12 KJV

How is it that ye do not understand that I spake it not to you concerning bread, that ye should beware of the leaven of the Pharisees and of the Sadducees? Then understood they how that he bade them not beware of the leaven of bread, but of the doctrine of the Pharisees and of the Sadducees.

Paul knew this and though he is careful not to call out Pharisees by name who had already imprisoned him and were already attempting to kill him, he rebukes the same leaven. We all know whom he is talking about and that he left that same paradigm where he hunted believers before as one of them. He defines this as the leaven of malice and wickedness. Add hypocrisy to this and you have three of the outright rebukes of Pharisees found multiple times in scripture. These are their attributes certainly not those of the Law of Moses in true application. He follows Messiah's lead in this. You overcome such leaven with sincerity and truth. Again, Pharisees do not represent either and that is a direct rebuke repeated multiple times as well.

1 Corinthians 5:6-8 KJV

Your glorying is not good. Know ye not that a little leaven leaveneth the whole lump? Purge out therefore the old leaven, that ye may be a new lump, as ye are unleavened. For even Christ our passover is sacrificed for us: Therefore let us keep the feast, not with old leaven, neither with the leaven of malice and wickedness; but with the unleavened bread of sincerity and truth.

As Paul endorses the Feast of Unleavened Bread NOT Easter, he teaches even a little leaven, leavens or causes the whole lump to expand. In other words, the bread of the word, is expanded into something else. Messiah said this renders the word of none effect and against His Commandments *(Mark 7)*.

Galatians 5:8-9 KJV

This persuasion cometh not of him that calleth you. A little leaven leaveneth the whole lump.

There are even specific examples but this is not limited to a few topics. These are flat-out rebukes of all Pharisee doctrine. Of course, there is some truth mixed in as they claim it based on Torah but we know the end result. For instance, the Pharisees fast often but that is not a commanded Biblical ritual often. Yes, there are times of fasting but the Pharisees made it a routine that is not holy as they have no foundation in purpose and Yahuah rejects every one of their fasts just as He did Cain's sacrifice. The disciples were not breaking Biblical rules, they were not observing Pharisee additives or leaven and neither should we.

Fasts: Matthew 9:14 KJV

Then came to him the disciples of John, saying, Why do we and the Pharisees fast oft, but thy disciples fast not?

Pharisees added to purification rituals with water and Messiah rebuked them for that as well. In fact, He says their traditions themselves are a transgression of the Commandments or Anti-Torah.

Washing Hands: Matthew 15:2-3 KJV

Why do thy disciples transgress the tradition of the elders? for they wash not their hands when they eat bread. But he answered and said unto them, Why do ye also transgress the commandment of God by your tradition?

Pharisees also do not honor their parents as the Commandment says. They changed it into the opposite rendering the Commandment of

NONE EFECT or useless. How is that even possible? Look at today's culture where many throw their parents into nursing homes in many cases without necessity. Then, they forget them and do not truly honor them much of the time. We are to honor our parents and yet our culture today appears to follow Pharisee leaven rather than the Bible. For just watch the Disney Channel for a while and you will see the root of this as they undermine parents as foolish and incapable. This is our culture – a Pharisee culture. You will find Pharisee leaven lines the halls of Disney.

Dishonoring Parents: Matthew 15:2-3 KJV

For God commanded, saying, Honour thy father and mother: and, He that curseth father or mother, let him die the death. But ye say, Whosoever shall say to his father or his mother, It is a gift, by whatsoever thou mightest be profited by me; And honour not his father or his mother, he shall be free. Thus have ye made the commandment of God of none effect by your tradition.

There are so many more in which we could spend an entire book on the many ways in which Pharisees are called out in scripture. Instead, we compiled this into charts at the end of this chapter *(pp. 288-291)*. A full view of their characterization materializes an evil cult in which we were warned in that time and still today.

Pharisees Represent Ancient Unbiblical Doctrine

Matthew 9:17 KJV

Neither do men put new wine into old bottles: else the bottles break, and the wine runneth out, and the bottles perish: but they put new wine into new bottles, and both are preserved.

Though much of the church represents that this passage refers to the Old Testament which Messiah just endorsed four chapters early and throughout His ministry, this is a direct reference to Pharisee doctrine NOT the Old Testament or Torah that they do not follow.

However, so-called scholars actually take that Pharisee paradigm and attempt to apply it to those who keep the Sabbath and the Law. They will even bark; "Do you sacrifice?" James said Messiah's blood covered all sacrifices. How could a New Testament scholar be so absurd as to even ask? They bellow: "Do you obey all 614 commandments?" The Bible only gives 10. Only the Pharisees would claim 10 equals 614. How could any so-called scholar not realize that is leaven that they apply to those keeping the Bible practice using the false Pharisee measure of ignorance? They act like Pharisees. Certainly the Bible offers additional detail in the days of Moses later as to how to apply the 10 Commandments. However, they cover everything period. They always have and they always will.

The same scholars will claim Jesus*(Yahusha)* replaced the 10 Commandments with 2 which is illiterate as those 2 are direct quotes from the Law of Moses not new. However, He answers Pharisees who attempt to entrap Him. He answers from the Law of Moses the 1st Commandment in exact language and part of the Law of Moses that tells us to love our neighbor as ourselves also truly covering at least 5 of the commandments in tone. Neither are new but these 2 sum up, He says, the whole of the Law which rests on those 2 principles. That does not sound so complicated as to bark about 614 Laws does it? You cannot break either of the 10 Commandments without breaking the 2. You also cannot break any of the additional detail of Torah in Law without breaking the 10 Commandments. Only Pharisees use such clarity and detail to create bondage and only scholars acting like Pharisees accuse one following the Bible as operating against Jesus'*(Yahusha's)* wishes. What a world in which we live. These are Pharisees generally not scholars as that is the true root of their training evidenced in their actions.

Pharisees Have No Spiritual Discernment

Matthew 9:34 KJV
But the Pharisees said, He casteth out devils through the prince of the devils.
Matthew 12:24 KJV
But when the Pharisees heard it, they said, This fellow doth not cast out devils, but by Beelzebub the prince of the devils.

Can you imagine the gall of a group standing against the Son of Yahuah? It is far worse than opposing Him, they had to portray Him as being associated and working with the devil. Can you imagine a more inept interpretation. Yahuah sends His Son in the flesh and they don't just reject Him, they put Him on trial and find Him guilty. Guilty of what? Guilty of breaking their false and phony interpretation of the Bible. Could one not be more clueless than to arrest the very Son of Yahuah who created them and claim Him guilty of transgressing their laws? He is the Law. Everything He did represents the Law. They are against the very Law they claim to espouse.

Matthew 15:12-14 KJV

Then came his disciples, and said unto him, Knowest thou that the Pharisees were offended, after they heard this saying? But he answered and said, Every plant, which my heavenly Father hath not planted, shall be rooted up. Let them alone: they be blind leaders of the blind. And if the blind lead the blind, both shall fall into the ditch.

Once again, we could spend an entire book just on this topic. What we know about Pharisees is they are dangerous. Their doctrines represent the opposite of Torah more than satanism does as they represent the true evil. Their fruit shall be uprooted as they are the blind leading the blind. Many have heard and use that idiom without even realizing that came from Jesus*(Yahusha)* and he was talking to the Pharisees – the blind. They are leading us into a ditch and right now, the modern church generally is following without question. You do not have to.

The Pharisees Are Murderous

This would be quite an accusation if it did not come from the lips of Messiah Himself. Many times, the Gospels speak of the murderous tendencies of the Pharisees toward Messiah but so does Acts and Paul speaks of the same. Paul would know because he used to be a Pharisee in doctrine carrying out their wishes in punishing true believers and followers of Jesus*(Yahusha)*. Are we really to listen to these murderers?

Matthew 12: 14 KJV

Then the Pharisees went out, and held a council against him, how they might destroy him.

Matthew 23: 34-25 KJV

Wherefore, behold, I send unto you prophets, and wise men, and scribes: and some of them ye shall kill and crucify; and some of them shall ye scourge in your synagogues, and persecute them from city to city: (Note: there were no synagogues in the Old Testament. That is a Pharisee building and system.) That upon you may come all the righteous blood shed upon the earth, from the blood of righteous Abel unto the blood of Zacharias son of Barachias, whom ye slew between the temple and the altar.

Luke 22:2 KJV

And the chief priests and scribes sought how they might kill him; for they feared the people.

John 7:1 KJV

After these things Jesus walked in Galilee: for he would not walk in Jewry, because the Jews sought to kill him.

The Jews are Pharisees in these contexts. They are not Yahudim nor were they ever. However, when they conquered Judaea, Jerusalem and the Temple, they now called themselves Yahudim. Again, the word Jew never belongs in the Bible as it is never a Bible word. Scholars should know these things yet we find few that seem to understand.

Matthew 26: 3-4 KJV

Then assembled together the chief priests, and the scribes, and the elders of the people, unto the palace of the high priest, who was called Caiaphas, And consulted that they might take Jesus by subtilty, and kill him.

Why did the Pharisees seek to kill the Son? He told us in the Parable of the Landowner that their true intend is to kill Him and seek His inheritance. This is why they did not stop with Him even. They continued to hunt, imprison and murder His followers. They wanted His inheritance. His inheritance is His people. They want you. This is why they agitate, infiltrate and conquer from within the church. They desire His inheritance. They want people to follow their ways instead of

His ways. His ways lead to freedom and theirs to bondage where they engorge themselves with riches and high esteem undeserved.

Matthew 21:33-38 KJV (Parallel in Mark 12)

Hear another parable: There was a certain householder, which planted a vineyard, and hedged it round about, and digged a winepress in it, and built a tower, and let it out to husbandmen, and went into a far country: And when the time of the fruit drew near, he sent his servants to the husbandmen, that they might receive the fruits of it. And the husbandmen took his servants, and beat one, and killed another, and stoned another. Again, he sent other servants more than the first: and they did unto them likewise. But last of all he sent unto them his son, saying, They will reverence my son. But when the husbandmen saw the son, they said among themselves, This is the heir; come, let us kill him, and let us seize on his inheritance.

The first servants are the prophets whom they killed and the Son is Jesus*(Yahusha)*. Some scholar will read this fragment and claim: "See, He wasn't even talking about Pharisees." Well, if one reads to Verse 45, it says *"And when the chief priests and Pharisees had heard his parables, they perceived that he spake of them."* Yes, the Pharisees knew He was talking about them. How can we have a church today that greatly ignores all of these exchanges? Are they not there to teach us? They wish for us to focus on an emasculated love absent rebuke. This way we would never rebuke.

In fact, Jesus*(Yahusha)* even knew they would have Him killed on the Sabbath – the Feast Sabbath of the first day of Unleavened Bread. We will prove that timeline in the next chapter. It follows the sacrifice of Isaac whom foreshadowed Messiah not the Passover Lamb who does not. That is another Pharisee false paradigm.

Matthew 23:29-34 KJV

Woe unto you, scribes and Pharisees, hypocrites! because ye build the tombs of the prophets, and garnish the sepulchres of the righteous, And say, If we had been in the days of our fathers, we would not have been partakers with them in the blood of the prophets. Wherefore ye be witnesses unto yourselves, that ye are the children of them which killed the prophets. Fill ye up then the measure of your fathers.

Jesus*(Yahusha)* knew they would kill him and on the Sabbath day. They held their peace or in other words, he shut them up but He knew this would be the case. Even on the Sabbath, they wanted to kill Him for breaking it that He did not. Remember, He did not break the Biblical Sabbath but the Pharisee observation that He was exposing as wrong.

Mark 3:4 KJV

And he saith unto them, Is it lawful to do good on the sabbath days, or to do evil? to save life, or to kill? But they held their peace.

John 5:18 KJV

Therefore the Jews sought the more to kill him, because he not only had broken the sabbath, but said also that God was his Father, making himself equal with God.

The Pharisees Do Not Represent the Law (Torah)

We covered earlier when the disciples were hungry going about ministry on the Sabbath, they picked and ate. This has always been lawful. Notice several times He says have you not read the law or don't you know the Law or even better, you do not know the Law. Who would ever wish to listen to this group's interpretation of anything. Not only is their Bible slanted, their history, geography, migration patterns and even modern DNA interpretation are all steeped in fraud as that is all they represent. It is incredible that one requires their interpretation to match the Bible before they will believe it. However, theirs' will never match the Bible and one will never understand viewing through their spectacles.

Matthew 12:2 KJV

But when the Pharisees saw it, they said unto him, Behold, thy disciples do that which is not lawful to do upon the sabbath day. But he said unto them, Have ye not read what David did, when he was an hungred, and they that were with him;

Matthew 12:5 KJV

Or have ye not read in the law, how that on the sabbath days the priests in the temple profane the sabbath, and are blameless?

Not only do Pharisees not know the Law, they do not even keep it. They claim whatever they want. Messiah exposed them and their ways. Singing and dancing to "Torah! Torah! Torah!" does not equate to practicing or understanding it. How can any scholar attempt to condemn one actually keeping the Law using this false Pharisee paradigm as the measure for such? They are Pharisees in their thinking as they are condoning their practices. Messiah did not nor did Paul or any Apostle. Here we see their murderous tendency as well.

John 7:19 KJV

Did not Moses give you the law, and yet none of you keepeth the law? Why go ye about to kill me?

Pharisees Are Pawnbrokers and Bankers

Remember, when Jesus*(Yahusha)* turned over the tables in the Temple. Those were not vendors on their steps, this was the Pharisee practice and it remains so today. This too, as many of their doctrines, originate in Babylon not the Bible where usury is forbidden especially to the Hebrews. This is definitive proof they are not Hebrews.

Matthew 23:16-17 KJV

Woe unto you, ye blind guides, which say, Whosoever shall swear by the temple, it is nothing; but whosoever shall swear by the gold of the temple, he is a debtor! Ye fools and blind: for whether is greater, the gold, or the temple that sanctifieth the gold?

To this day, we hear the mantra of the rebuilding of the Temple. This is something Yahuah never commanded in our age. We do not need it but scripture does say it will be built for the Beast to declare he is God and he will rule from Jerusalem. No Lost Tribes have returned before that as they return in peace and that will be the worst time in Israel's history. Many Christians jump aboard the bandwagon, even Trump. However, this is more propaganda of the inept. Messiah made it clear, the importance of a physical temple is no more. We don't need it. These

Pharisees swear by it in those times and they continue to do so. They will tell you in Messianic circles the Temple will be rebuilt and sacrifices will be renewed.

This is illiterate to the Gospel in which Hebrews especially tells us there is never need for sacrifice of animal blood ever again as Messiah's blood is sufficient for all of time. There will be no more renewal of animal sacrifices. There will be no more Temple. His Holy of Holies remains in the Garden of Eden. This will be opened to man again and we will eat of the Tree of Life according to Revelation. New Jerusalem will encompass the Garden as well where the Tree of Life will be in the midst of the Garden still that will be in the midst of New Jerusalem.

Pharisees Are Compared to Vipers and Produce Evil Treasure

The Dead Sea Scrolls take this even further comparing Pharisees to vipers, spiders, serpents, and dragons *(see chart pp. 288-291)*. Messiah and we saw John the Baptist, a Qumran/Bethabara Priest, referred to them as the same.

> ### *Matthew 12:34-35 KJV*
> *O generation of vipers, how can ye, being evil, speak good things? for out of the abundance of the heart the mouth speaketh. A good man out of the good treasure of the heart bringeth forth good things: and an evil man out of the evil treasure bringeth forth evil things.*
>
> ### *Matthew 12:38-39 KJV*
> *Then certain of the scribes and of the Pharisees answered, saying, Master, we would see a sign from thee. But he answered and said unto them, An evil and adulterous generation seeketh after a sign; and there shall no sign be given to it, but the sign of the prophet Jonas:*
>
> ### *Matthew 23:33 KJV*
> *Ye serpents, ye generation of vipers, how can ye escape the damnation of hell?*

Pharisees Are Hypocrites

As we have curated a comprehensive chart at the end of this chapter, here are just a few examples of Jesus*(Yahusha)* classifying the Pharisees as hypocrites. This is a theme throughout. They worship in vain teaching only the doctrines of men. This is a perfect definition of much of the modern church today who is following Pharisees. This topic of the Sabbath and the Law is a great example of their not even possessing the ability to read scripture and comprehend as they are set in a false Pharisee paradigm with Pharisee foundation.

Matthew 15:7-9 KJV

Ye hypocrites, well did Esaias prophesy of you, saying, This people draweth nigh unto me with their mouth, and honoureth me with their lips; but their heart is far from me. But in vain they do worship me, teaching for doctrines the commandments of men.

Matthew 16:3 KJV

And in the morning, It will be foul weather to day: for the sky is red and lowring. O ye hypocrites, ye can discern the face of the sky; but can ye not discern the signs of the times?

Matthew 22:18 KJV

But Jesus perceived their wickedness, and said, Why tempt ye me, ye hypocrites?

Matthew 23:13 KJV

But woe unto you, scribes and Pharisees, hypocrites! for ye shut up the kingdom of heaven against men: for ye neither go in yourselves, neither suffer ye them that are entering to go in.

Pharisees Devour Widows and the Poor

The Bible, even the Old Testament, places emphasis on caring for widows, orphans and those who need assistance. The Pharisees are defined by Messiah as devouring widow's houses. How do you do that? You impose estate tax of crippling amount making their inheritance from their husband's estate far smaller. This is theft and a routine practice of many governments today of which they are not entitled and operating against scripture. They are following Pharisee law and Pharisees even take credit for writing the first constitutions. This is why they evolve and are added to with thousands upon thousands of changes and alterations. The entire governmental structure that follows such chaotic evolution is Pharisee in origin. This is extortion and excess.

> ***Matthew 23:14 KJV***
>
> *Woe unto you, scribes and Pharisees, hypocrites! for ye devour widows' houses, and for a pretence make long prayer: therefore ye shall receive the greater damnation.*
>
> ***Matthew 23:25 KJV***
>
> *Woe unto you, scribes and Pharisees, hypocrites! for ye make clean the outside of the cup and of the platter, but within they are full of extortion and excess.*

Pharisees Are Unclean and Self-Righteous

Are we to follow the unclean and self-righteous who only serve their own interests? We all know the answer in scripture is no. However, the modern church does.

> ***Matthew 23:25-28 KJV***
>
> *Woe unto you, scribes and Pharisees, hypocrites! for ye make clean the outside of the cup and of the platter, but within they are full of extortion and excess. Thou blind Pharisee, cleanse first that which is within the cup and platter, that the outside of them may be clean also. Woe unto you, scribes and Pharisees, hypocrites! for ye are like unto whited sepulchres, which indeed appear beautiful outward, but are within full of dead men's bones, and of all uncleanness. Even so ye also outwardly appear righteous unto men, but within ye are full of hypocrisy and iniquity.*
>
> ***Luke 7:29-30 KJV***
>
> *And all the people that heard him, and the publicans, justified God, being baptized with the baptism of John. But the Pharisees and lawyers rejected the counsel of God against themselves, being not baptized of him.*
>
> ***Luke 7:39 KJV***
>
> *Now when the Pharisee which had bidden him saw it, he spake within himself, saying, This man, if he were a prophet, would have known who and what manner of woman this is that toucheth him: for she is a sinner.*

You will also notice history tells us ancient Catholics fasted twice a week. This is a Pharisee doctrine that Messiah rebuked as well. The Catholic Church is set on a Pharisee foundation not the Bible. This is why you find Persian roots there just as in Pharisaism. They are the same infusion with other religions specifically Persian/Babylonian. Yahuah has always rejected this infusion. Anyone claiming to "Christianize" anything is illiterate of Yahuah's ways. You do not adapt pagan practices and rename them. You avoid them and follow His ways already set forth for thousands of years. He did not change *[Mal. 3:6]* and neither does Jesus*(Yahusha)* *[Heb. 13:8]*.

Luke 18:9-14 KJV [The Pharisee and the Publican]

And he spake this parable unto certain which trusted in themselves that they were righteous, and despised others: Two men went up into the temple to pray; the one a Pharisee, and the other a publican. The Pharisee stood and prayed thus with himself, God, I thank thee, that I am not as other men are, extortioners, unjust, adulterers, or even as this publican. I fast twice in the week, I give tithes of all that I possess. And the publican, standing afar off, would not lift up so much as his eyes unto heaven, but smote upon his breast, saying, God be merciful to me a sinner. I tell you, this man went down to his house justified rather than the other: for every one that exalteth himself shall be abased; and he that humbleth himself shall be exalted.

John 8:37-47 KJV

I know that ye are Abraham's seed; but ye seek to kill me, because my word hath no place in you. I speak that which I have seen with my Father: and ye do that which ye have seen with your father. They answered and said unto him, Abraham is our father. Jesus saith unto them, If ye were Abraham's children, ye would do the works of Abraham. But now ye seek to kill me, a man that hath told you the truth, which I have heard of God: this did not Abraham. Ye do the deeds of your father. Then said they to him, We be not born of fornication; we have one Father, even God. Jesus said unto them, If God were your Father, ye would love me: for I proceeded forth and came from God; neither came I of myself, but he sent me. Why do ye not understand my speech? even because ye cannot hear my word. Ye are of your father the devil, and the lusts of your father ye will do. He was a murderer from the beginning, and abode not in the truth, because there is no truth in him. When he speaketh a lie, he speaketh of his own: for he is a liar, and the father of it. And because I tell you the truth, ye believe me not. Which of you convinceth me of sin? And if I say the truth, why do ye not believe me? He that is of God heareth God's words: ye therefore hear them not, because ye are not of God.

John 12:42 KJV

Nevertheless among the chief rulers also many believed on him; but because of the Pharisees they did not confess him, lest they should be put out of the synagogue: For they loved the praise of men more than the praise of God.

Matthew 6:5 KJV

And when thou prayest, thou shalt not be as the hypocrites are: for they love to pray standing in the synagogues and in the corners of the streets, that they may be seen of men. Verily I say unto you, They have their reward.

Pharisees are Called Fools

This is not our word but that of Jesus*(Yahusha)* Himself as well as the exiled Temple Priests in Qumran/Bethabara. Why do we not show love in using the word fool? Better read scripture. Messiah never sinned and He uses the word to rebuke Pharisees and we do as well.

Matthew 23 KJV

17: Ye fools and blind: for whether is greater, the gold, or the temple that sanctifieth the gold?

19: Ye fools and blind: for whether is greater, the gift, or the altar that sanctifieth the gift?

Luke 11:40 KJV

Ye fools, did not he that made that which is without make that which is within also?

Luke 24:25 KJV

Then he said unto them, O fools, and slow of heart to believe all that the prophets have spoken:

Romans 1:22 KJV

Professing themselves to be wise, they became fools,

Romans 2:17-20 KJV

Behold, thou art called a Jew, and restest in the law, and makest thy boast of God, And knowest his will, and approvest the things that are more excellent, being instructed out of the law; And art confident that thou thyself art a guide of the blind, a light of them which are in darkness, An instructor of the foolish, a teacher of babes, which hast the form of knowledge and of the truth in the law.

Pharisees do not know the Sabbath. As with everything else, they represent a false counterfeit of everything Torah especially the Sabbath which they have changed and defiled just as they did the Temple. They continue to profane the name of YHWH spouting their lies that Abraham did not know His name yet Yahuah told Abraham His name, Abraham pronounced it many times to his family, servants, in prayers and discussions with Yahuah and even with the King of Sodom. He did not hide the name of Yahuah, he used it and that is absolute blasphemy in which He will respond. That is Pharisee doctrine to this day.

Pharisees called their god Lord in Samaria which in Hebrew is the word Ba'al. His name is actually Molech, Melech, Adrammelech or similar which is noted many times. However, they travel around telling us how to pronounce a name they are sworn not to pronounce. Talk about deception. It is their doctrine not to pronounce the name and you better believe they are never going to teach you the appropriate way. However, they removed it from Bibles over 6,800 times typically replacing it with Lord or Ba'al in Hebrew. They call their god Hashem today still and that is a derivative of the same god from 1 Kings, Ashima, the god of the Samaritans which they brought into Samaria when they replaced the Northern Tribes of Israel taken captive into Assyria. These gods remain infused in their religion as well as their doctrines not those of Torah.

Paul told us they were not Israelites even though they were in Israel. Yes, Pharisees did reside in Israel as they conquered it and usurped the Priesthood taking the Temple in theft. Pharisees are not Israelites by blood. However, they call themselves such because they once lived there. They returned to further defile the Land as strangers in modern times.

Romans 9:6-7 KJV

Not as though the word of God hath taken none effect. For they are not all Israel, which are of Israel: Neither, because they are the seed of Abraham, are they all children: but, In Isaac shall thy seed be called.

Pharisee False Teachings Later in the New Testament

This continued in the days after Messiah. The Pharisees did not go away or disappear nor have they today. Today, we call them Jews but they remain Pharisees. Much of the church thinks they are built on their foundation which is unfortunately, true. The modern church has Pharisee roots. However, this is not the Bible root and that foundation remains sinking sand regardless of Martin Luther's protest. He should have started with a fresh foundation of scripture. He did not. The Catholic Church was founded by a likely Pharisee as Constantine was a Flavian in name but not in blood. He and his father were likely of Josephus' adopted Flavian bloodline which is really a Pharisee and Hasmonean bloodline. He was not a Hebrew.

He continued the same Pharisee practice of infusing his false religion from Persia, Mithraism the same as the Samaritans did which were his likely ancestors. If not by blood, he certainly was in practice. The Catholic Church is far more likely a reinstitution of Pharisaism with the New Testament just as the Samaritan Pharisaism entwined the doctrines of Ashima *(Hashem)*, Adrammelech*(Molech/Baal or Lord in English)*, etc. from Persia, Media and Babylon with the worship of YHWH. They follow many of the same patterns such as replacing the name of YHWH over 6,800 times in the Bible. This cannot be done by accident.

> ***Acts 15:1-2 KJV***
>
> *And certain men which came down from Judaea taught the brethren, and said, Except ye be circumcised after the manner of Moses, ye cannot be saved. When therefore Paul and Barnabas had no small dissension and disputation with them, they determined that Paul and Barnabas, and certain other of them, should go up to Jerusalem unto the apostles and elders about this question.*
>
> ***Acts 15:15 KJV***
>
> *But there rose up certain of the sect of the Pharisees which believed, saying, That it was needful to circumcise them, and to command them to keep the law of Moses.*

It is time to know our enemy because they well know us and how to deceive us. They are within the leadership ranks of seminaries and churches all over the world. This has been their tactic of infiltration all along. They call themselves Jews meaning Yahudim which word they changed removing the name of Yahuah from the name of His people.

They are not His people and they do not know how to read the Bible. They are caught and exposed.

These next charts in which we conclude this chapter will lay down the facts. What did Messiah call them? Here are over 130 references in which he addressed the Pharisee fruits. How has the modern church forgotten this and embraced these same Pharisees as the origin of the Word. They are the opposite. The Qumran Community blasts these usurpers in major rebuke in which we have curated over 100 quotes from those fragments alone.

We lay out the evidence in history that the Hasmoneans and Pharisees are the defilers of the Temple who fulfilled Psalm 83 and not the Greeks. No wonder they earned such scathing rebuke from Jesus*(Yahusha)* and the exiled Temple Priests at Qumran where He launched His ministry in endorsement. Finally, we chart The Hanukkah Hoax as well as the Esther deception as neither Maccabees nor Esther are found in the Ancient Bible of the Temple Priests at Qumran.

However, it is generally the norm in scholarship to follow these Pharisees today we call Rabbis even the ones from the 1st Century who even called themselves Pharisees back then. These are the same that Messiah rebuked. Some even call themselves Christians as many of their families converted to infiltrate in centuries past especially throughout Europe. They do so and they rise to the top because they have an agenda to deceive and to agitate the true work of Jesus*(Yahusha)*. Understand this is not about the common Jew who has no knowledge of this but those Pharisees at the top know full well.

The Pharisees expanded the Sabbath which we still see retained with some of Jewry today. Some do not use electric on the Sabbath, others do not drive cars, etc. Some Jews generally have a separate kosher kitchen and a regular kitchen which means they do not keep kosher in the other kitchen. Some find ways around the Sabbath in the fine letters of the law even. However, it matters not what any of them practice as they are not practicing the Biblical Sabbath. Pharisees constantly rebuked Messiah for breaking their expanded Sabbath and He proved theirs is not His nor the Bible's. Many turn to Judaism as such example and it is the opposite. It is impertinent how they keep Feasts nor the Sabbath as they have no understanding of either and neither belong to them.

Pharisee Fruits

These Fruits Match Satan's from John 10:10 not Jesus' Fruits

"Vipers"	"Hypocrites"	"Expand the Word with Leaven"
Matt. 3:7, 12:34, 23:33 Luke 3:7	Matt. 6:2, 6:5, 15:7, 16:3, 22:18, 23:13, 14, 15, 23, 25, 27, 28, 29, 24:51; Mark 7:6; Luke 11:44, 12:56	Matt. 15:6, 16:6, 11, Mark 7:13, 8:15 Luke 12:1
"Lead People to Hell"	"Operate Against His Commandments"	"Blind" "Vain"
Matt. 23:13, 23:15, 24:51 Luke 11:52	Matt. 15:3-6, 23:4, 23 Mark 7:5-13 Rom. 2:17-20	Matt. 15:12-14, 23:16-17, 23-26 Mark 7:7 John 9:39-41 Rom. 1:21, 2:17-20
"Condemned to Hell Generally"	"Unclean" "Self-Righteous"	"Murderers"
Matt. 5:20, 23:13-15, 24:51	Matt. 6:5, 23:5, 15, 23-27, 28 Luke 7:29-30, 36-50, 18:9-14 John 8:39-59, 12:42	Matt. 12:14, 21:45-46, 23:31, 26:4 Luke 6:11, 11:47 John 8:44, 11:45-57 Acts 3:14-15, 7:52

"Pharisaism shaped the character of Judaism and the life and thought of the Jew for all the future."

—Jewish Encyclopedia [60]

According to the Bible

Why Ignore What the Bible Says to Support a False Paradigm?

"Seed/ Synagogue of Satan"	"Devour Widow's Houses/Poor"	"Pray/Give to Be Seen" "Haughty"
John 8:44 Rev. 2:9, 3:9	Matt. 23:14 Mark 12:40 Luke 7:36-50, 20:47, 21:1-6	Matt. 6:2, 5, 16, 23:5-6, 14, 17-22 Mark 12:40 Luke 11:43,16:14, 20:45-47
"Don't Know Prophecy" "Seek Signs"	**"Don't Know Scripture"**	**"Thieves" "Extort"**
Matt. 12:14-37, 16:1-4, 27:40-43 Mark 8:11-12 Luke 7:29-30, 11:29-32 John 5:18, 10:24-39	Matt. 16:6-12, 21:23-27, 22:34-46, 23:23-24 , 26:62-68 Mark 3:6, Acts 1:6 Luke 7:29-30, 22:2 17:20-21 John 5:18, 10:24-39	Matt. 21:13, 23:25 Mark 11:17 Luke 19:46
"Stand in the Way of Knowledge"	**"Accusers and Liars"**	**"Fools"**
Matt. 23:34-35 Luke 11:52, 22:2 John 12:42	Matt. 12:1-2, 13-17, 22-24, 22:15-22, Mark 3:22 Luke 6:7, 7:39, 11:53-54, 19:39, 20:20-26 John 8:13; Rev. 2:9	Matt. 23:17, 19 Luke 11:40, 24:25 Rom. 1:22, 2:17-20

**Pharisaism Became Rabbinic Judaism After 70 A.D.
Pharisees Are Modern Rabbis, Modern Jews**

Who Were the Pharisees and Hasmoneans?

***Page Number in Parentheses.**

"Sons of Darkness" "Men of the Pit"	"Sons of Belial/ Satan" "Lot of Belial"	"Wicked Priests"
War Scroll (165-182) Dam. Doc. (134, 144) 4Q548 (573) Comm. Rule (111) 4Q258 (121) Hymn 9 (265)	4Q286 (394), 4Q386 (613) Dam. Doc. (133) Temple Scroll (212) War Scroll (176) Comm. Rule (99) Hymn 7 (263)	4Q394-9 (221) 4Q448 (340) iQpHab (509-515) 4QpPsa (519)
"Defilers of the Temple"	"Theives" "Rob the Poor" "Prey on Widows"	"Unclean"
iQpHab (513, 515) Dam. Doc. (133, 137, 148) 4Q174 (525) Temple Scroll (212)	iQpHab (509-515) Dam. Doc. (134) 4Q163 (499) Hymn 13 (273) Comm. Rule (113)	iQpHab (513) 4Q174 (525) Dam. Doc. (133-134) 4Q286 (394)
"Vain"	"Strangers" "Men of Perdition"	"Flouters of the Law" *(Disregard, Despise)*
iQpHab (514) Dam. Doc. (134) 4Q174 (526) Comm. Rule (103, 119) War Scroll (171, 176) Hymn 14 (276)	4Q174 (525) 4Q501 (328) Comm. Rule (113) 4Q 171 (522)	iQpHab (509-512) Dam. Doc. (133) 4Q163 (499) 4Q174 (525) 11Q13 (533)

"Pharisaism shaped the character of Judaism and the life and thought of the Jew for all the future."

—Jewish Encyclopedia [60]

According to the Dead Sea Scrolls

From "The Complete Dead Sea Scrolls in English, Revised Edition" By Geza Vermes. [1]

"Liars" "Spouter of Lies"	"Those Who Seek Smooth Things"	"Scoffers"
4QpPsa (37) iQpHab (510-515) Dam. Doc. (137) 4Q 171 (519, 522) 4Q501 (328) Hymn 14 (278)	Dam. Doc. (129-130) Thanksgiving Hymns (262-269) 4Q163 (499) 4Q169 (505-7) 4Q177 (536)	Dam. Doc. (129, 137) iQH, 1Q36, 4Q427-32 Hymn 6 (262) 4Q162 (499)
"Abomination" "House of Guilt"	**"Enemies"**	**"Oppressive" "Overbearing"**
iQpHab (511, 513) Dam. Doc. (133) 4Q175 (528) Temple Scroll (212) 4Q387 (603) 4Q389 (604)	iQpHab (514-515) Dam. Doc. (133) 4Q174 (525) War Scroll (176-177, 184) Temple Scroll (215-217)	iQpHab (509-514) 4Q448 (341) 4Q508 (383) 4Q504 (378) 4Q 171 (522)
"Unfaithful" "Rebellious"	**"Vipers, Spiders, Serpents, Dragons"**	**"Men of Violence" "Instruments of Violence"**
iQpHab (509-510, 513) Dam. Doc. (133) 4Q306 (243), 11Q13 (533) Hymn 14 (278) 4Q332 (405) Comm. Rule (99)	Dam. Doc. (133) Hymn 14 (275) Hymn 13 (273)	Hymn 14 (276, 278) Hymn 7 (263) 4Q 171 (520-522) Comm. Rule (113) iQpHab (509-515) 4Q175 (528), 4Q379 (585)

Pharisaism Became Rabbinic Judaism After 70 A.D. Pharisees Are Modern Rabbis, Modern Jews

WHO DEFILED THE SECOND TEMPLE?

The Books of Maccabees, not found in the Dead Sea Scrolls, make the claim Greece defiled the Temple. That is a lie!

Greece Did NOT Defile the Temple

"Whither the lion goes, there is the lion's cub, [with none to disturb it] (ii, 11b).
[Interpreted, this concerns Deme]trius king of Greece who sought, on the counsel of those who seek smooth things, to enter Jerusalem. [But God did not permit the city to be delivered] into the hands of the kings of Greece, from the time of Antiochus until the coming of the rulers of the Kittim. But then she shall be trampled under their feet..." –Commentary On NAHUM, p. 505 [1]

Thus, from the time of Demetrius to the time of Antiochus I including the time of Antiochus Epiphanes and until the time of the Kittim takeover which is the Roman Empire, Judaea is not subdued with Greece's military. Even Alexander the Great was welcomed in a peaceful takeover not military conquest especially in the Temple where he even burnt the sacrifice of the Temple. Greece wanted the tax revenues and Israel agreed to that in all accounts even Josephus, Tacitus, Origen and others agree on that. However, who trampled Judaea? Who defiled the Temple? This community did not keep that a secret...

"[For the violence done to Lebanon shall overwhelm you, and the destruction of the beasts] X II shall terrify you, because of the blood of men and the violence done to the land, the city, and all its inhabitants (ii, 17).
Interpreted, this saying concerns the Wicked Priest, inasmuch as he shall be paid the reward which he himself tendered to the Poor. For Lebanon (Samaria) is the Council of the Community; and the beasts are the simple of Judah who keep the Law. As he himself plotted the destruction of the Poor, so will God condemn him to destruction. And as for that which He said, Because of the blood of the city and the violence done to the land: interpreted, the city is Jerusalem where the Wicked Priest committed abominable deeds and **defiled the Temple of God**. The violence done to the land: these are the cities of Judah where he robbed the Poor of their possessions."
–Commentary On HABAKKUK, p. 515 [1]

According to this history written by the exiled Temple Priests, it was the Hasmoneans and their illegal priesthood of usurpers called the Pharisees who defiled the Temple not Greece.

The Maccabees Did!

Is it a wonder why Messiah and these scrolls rebuke them so heavily?

THE HANUKKAH HOAX

The Feast of Dedication of modern Judaism also originates in the Books of Maccabees, yet Greece did not defile the Temple. However, worse, the Bible gives dates for the Dedication of the First and Second Temples and neither are December.

FIRST TEMPLE FEAST OF DEDICATION:

Feast of Tabernacles. 7th Hebrew Month (Ethanim)
Modern Calendar: Between Sept. 15 - Oct. 15
1 Kings 8:63, 1 Kings 8:2, 2 Chronicles 5:3

SECOND TEMPLE FEAST OF DEDICATION:

Adar 3 or 23. 12th Hebrew Month
Modern Calendar: Between Feb. 15 - Mar. 15
Ezra 6:15-17, 1st Esdras 7:5-8 (Note: March 15 is still Winter)

The Temple Was Never Rededicated According to the Bible.
The Qumran Temple Priests Record the Same Pharisees Who Claim This New Holiday in Fraud, Defiled the Temple.

Messiah Was In The Temple In
Adar (February) NOT December!

John 10:22 KJV
And it was at Jerusalem **the feast of dedication**,
and it was **winter**. And Jesus walked in the Temple in
Solomon's porch.

Matthew 15:12-14 KJV
Then came his disciples, and said unto him, Knowest
thou that the Pharisees were offended, after they heard this
saying? But he answered and said, Every plant, which my
heavenly Father hath not planted, shall be rooted up. Let
them alone: they be blind leaders of the blind. And if the
blind lead the blind, both shall fall into the ditch.

This is consistent with the Second Temple Feast of
Dedication in the Winter in Late February to Mid-March.
Messiah did NOT celebrate the Hasmonean Hanukkah nor
does He ever embrace their story on any level. He rebukes
their priests, their religion and even their lineage.
It is time we correct this for good.

Lunar or Solar?
Sunset or Sunrise?

6 am or 6 pm?

Chapter 15 | When Does Sabbath Begin? The Biblical Day

Generally, we are taught the Bible clock is set on a lunar calendar with the day beginning in the evening. The purpose of this chapter is to test this with scripture. Does it prove to agree with that or are we ingesting leaven untested and unexposed? By the end of this chapter, you will know the answer.

Many read a fragment of a verse in the Genesis 1 account and make a massive assumption ignoring the daytime which is right there in that passage as He created light and called it day first. Thus, day is there yet then ignored oddly as well as the word for 24-hour day, yom (יום: *yôm: Strong's #H3117*) in Hebrew. We will cover this in detail. Their conclusion with no investigation whatsoever is the day begins at night. Is this true? We will build to this in this chapter. However, let us begin with the foundation of the Old Testament aside from the Creation account so that we may fully test this and understand. What is the Bible clock set on? The moon or the sun? Did Moses not understand it? Did he write Genesis and then change the clock for the rest of Torah?

We will then, go to the Gospels and vet the story of Messiah's death and resurrection which holds the key to this same clock in His day including hours which are truly indisputable. We will examine other passages in the New Testament as well that must concur as they also must align with the Old Testament. Then, we will dismantle the Creation clock for the day and reassemble it based on the Bible setting aside the doctrines of men which we are testing here. We all know that in prophecy, it is the Beast system who is known for changing times and seasons. We have already well-proven their manipulation of the Sabbath as we currently live within the strong delusion that was prophesied. The Sabbath is the only part of the Law that is a time. Does that include when the day begins? Let's test.

What is the Torah Calendar? Lunar or Solar?

In our publishing of the Book of Jubilees: The Torah Calendar, we find the Qumran community of Levite Temple Priests, the sons of Zadok who managed the Temple and kept the Bible since the days of King Solomon, called Jubilees the source for the "exact determination of their times." They recorded Bible calendar for Feasts and keeping His law, was "strictly defined" in the Book of Jubilees. They used it's calendar and so should we.

> *"The Damascus Document, 4Q266, fr. 8 i, 6-9, 50 B.C.–100 A.D.: (For God made) a Covenant with you and all Israel; therefore a man shall bind himself by oath to return to the Law of Moses, for in it all things are strictly defined. As **for the exact determination of their times to which Israel turns a blind eye, behold it is strictly defined in the Book of the Divisions of the Times into their Jubilees and Weeks**. And on the day that a man swears to return to the Law of Moses, the Angel of Persecution shall cease to follow him provided he fulfills his word: for this reason Abraham circumcised himself on the day that he knew." [21]*

Realize, they just called this book Torah and told us Israel was turning a "blind eye" to this portion of Torah even then under the Pharisee rule. Remember, Hasmoneans and Pharisees defiled the Temple and usurped the priesthood which practice continues to this day in what we call Rabbinic Judaism. This is why they earned the title from Messiah as the "synagogue of satan" who say they are Yahudim and are not but do lie *(Rev. 2:9, 3:9)*. We are told to follow their calendar which is rebuked by the legitimate Temple Priests they exiled to Qumran/Bethabara even at the time that they did live in Israel.

In other words, this is The Torah Calendar thus our title for that book. This is not according to us but this was the practice in the Temple preserved by these sons of Zadok who continued this worship system in Qumran/ Bethabara where Messiah was baptized and launched His ministry. This is the Temple Calendar throughout the history of Israel continued in the time of Messiah really with His endorsement. It never changed from the time of Moses who records such all the way back to Creation. No beat is missed here.

This is not an enigma. It was the sun that was appointed to rule the calendar for days, sabbaths *(weeks)*, months and years. This is really established in Genesis but wholly explained in The Torah Calendar.

Jubilees 1:8-9

And on the fourth day He created the sun [1st] and the moon and the stars, and set them in the firmament of the heaven, to give light upon all the earth, and to rule over the day and the night, and divide the light from the darkness. And God appointed the sun to be a great sign on the earth for days and for sabbaths and for months and for feasts and for years and for sabbaths of years and for jubilees and for all seasons of the years.

The Book of Jubilees sets the Bible calendar based on the sun not the moon and even tells us why the moon will never work. It calls that lunar calendar error and warns that even Israel will stray from the Biblical calendar defiling the Feasts, Sabbaths, etc. The moon "dislodges" and "disrupts" Yahuah's calendar.

Jubilees 6:33-38

*But if they do neglect and do not observe them according to His commandment, then **they will disturb all their seasons, and the years will be dislodged from this (order)**, [and they will disturb the seasons and the years will be dislodged] and they will neglect their ordinances. And all the children of **Israel will forget**, and will not find the path of the years, and will forget the new moons, and seasons, and sabbaths, and they will go wrong as to all the order of the years. For I know and from henceforth shall I declare it unto thee, and **it is not of my own devising; for the book (lieth) written before me, and on the heavenly tables the division of days is ordained**, lest they forget the feasts of the covenant and walk according to the feasts of the Gentiles after their error and* *after their ignorance.* **For there will be those who will assuredly make observations of the moon--** *now (it) disturbeth the seasons and cometh in from* **year to year ten days too soon.** *For this reason the years will come upon them when they will* **disturb (the order),** *and* **make an abominable (day) the day of testimony, and an unclean day a feast day, and they will confound all the days,** *the holy with the unclean, and the unclean day with the holy; for they will* **go wrong as to the months and sabbaths and feasts and jubilees.** *For this reason I command and testify to thee that thou mayest testify to them; for after thy death thy children will disturb (them), so that they will not make the year* **three hundred and sixtyfour days only,** *and for this reason they will* **go wrong as to the new moons and seasons and sabbaths and festivals,** *and they will eat all kinds of blood with all kinds of flesh.*

Following the moon as the start of the day, sabbath *(week)*, month, year, sabbaths of years *(sevens)* and even Jubilees *(49 years with celebration on the 50th year)*, causes one to go wrong. This is accurate science as the New Moon occurs every 29.5 days [20]. The Bible calendar is 30-day months plus an added intercalary day at the end of each quarter for 364 days. This is a massive problem for the moon as it *"cometh in from year to year ten days too soon."* If one conducts the math at 29.5 days, this would mean 6 days too soon on the month and then, add the 4 intercalary days for the exact science Jubilees observes of 10 days too soon on the year.

In 2020, we examined the week and following the lunar calendar, this will disrupt the Sabbath 22 times in 52 weeks. That is even worse. There is a group out there that even propagates a Luni-Solar Calendar so-called but they are also following the moon to try to determine the Sabbath. In doing so, they have to fabricate rules never in scripture and they claim Sabbath moves as it is sometimes 6,8,9, or 10 days apart. They even skip the first day of every month as it doesn't exist yet the Sabbath can only be on the 7th day period. It is always the 7th day and never any other and it cannot move. They are observing the moon and allowing it to disrupt Yahuah's calendar. The origin of this lunar calendar after the Flood is really Babylon not the Bible.

Another very ancient book found in the Dead Sea Scrolls, The Book Enoch, agrees with the Book of Jubilees. The sun starts the day first. it is day first and then night in the progression of a Biblical day.

> *1 Enoch 41:6-7*
> *And the **Sun goes out first**, and completes its journey at the command of the Lord of Spirits - and his Name endures forever and ever. And after this is the hidden, and visible, path of the Moon, and it travels the course of its journey, in that place, **by day and by night**.*
>
> *1 Enoch 72.4*
> *And **first there rises the greater light, named the Sun**, and its disc is like the disc of Heaven, and the whole of it is full of a fire which gives light and warmth.*

Start of the Day in the Qumran Community

The Qumran community of Temple Priests kept Jubilees and Enoch as scripture and these were the #3 and #6 most found scrolls in that library. That represents a significant endorsement. However, even beyond these books kept as Bible canon in their library, we find their theology and interpretation which matches. Yahuah created morning as the start of the day at sunrise. Notice it is called the "boundary of the daytime." Then, night is mentioned second very consistent with Genesis 1 and all of scripture that we will cover.

> *Fragment 1 (Cf. Fragment 3+3a, p.579 parallel)*
> *. . . [Bl]essed art Thou, O Lord, who art righteous in all T h y ways. Be mighty in strength . . . [in Thy judge]ments. Thou who art faithful . . . Thou art understanding [with all intelligence . . . might. Thou who art . . . to bring out . . . **who hast created the morning as a sign to reveal the dominion of the light as the boundary of the daytime** . . . for their work. To bless Thy holy name Thou hast created them. For the light is good . . . [Thou art . . .] who hast created the evening as a sign to reveal the dominion [of darkness] . . . from labour. Thou hast [c]reated them to bless Thy holy name] when they see that the light is good and when . . . Thou hast created the evening as a sign (to mark) the appearance of the dominion of*

> *[darkness] . . . – Prayer or Hymn Celebrating the Morning and the Evening (4Q408), Vermes, p. 386 [1]*

We have a very defined calendar in Qumran and even the Temple Scroll record morning begins the day as they sacrificed "every day" from "first in the morning" and then, "in the evening." This is the exposition of a full day in worship and it does not begin in the evening nor ever has for the Bible system of worship. Every day perpetually begins first in morning and then evening. They were not following a lunar calendar nor does Genesis 1. It very clearly is simply not their mindset. This is set in a perpetual, never-ending cycle that cannot be broken or altered.

> *XIII [This is what you shall offer on the altar:] t[wo y]ear[ling lambs] without blemish **every day** as a **perpetual** holocaust. You shall offer the **first in the morning**; and you shall offer the other lamb **in the evening**... –The Temple Scroll, p. 193 [1]*

These Temple Priests affirm the progression of the Biblical day from it's beginning when light emerges or the sun rises to the going down of the sun and the beginning of darkness that remains the same day. Night ends not at midnight but specifically when the sun, "Great Light of Heaven," rises the next day that is tomorrow. Notice, the sun is called out as the measure for the day here even defined as Law from Yahuah's mouth. What scholar can overrule Him? This is a very clear definition no one can dispute. They even continue to clarify this is "the genesis of every period." The law appointed to every dominion meaning the sun and the moon are expressed in their exact Biblical order as to when we start counting the day at sunrise until it ends just before sunrise the next day. This cycle is firm and established forever and it is Yahuah's thus no scholar nor religion, no one, can change it.

> **Hymn 23 (formerly 19). XX (formerly XII).**
> *I will praise Thy Name among them that fear Thee. Bowing down in prayer I will beg Thy favours from season to season always: **when light emerges from [its dwelling-place]**, and when the **day reaches its appointed end** in accordance with the laws of the **Great Light of***

> *heaven;* *when evening falls and* **light departs at the beginning of**
> **the dominion of darkness,** *at the hour appointed for night, and* **at its**
> **end when morning returns** *and (the shadows) retire to their dwelling-*
> *place* **before the approach of light; always;** *at the* **genesis of**
> **every period** *and at the beginning of every age and at the end of every*
> *season,* **according to the statute and signs appointed to every**
> **dominion by the certain law from the mouth of God,** *by the*
> *precept which is and shall be for ever and ever without end. Without it nothing*
> *is nor shall be, for the God of knowledge established it and there is no other*
> *beside Him.* −*The Thanksgiving Hymns, p. 296-7. [1]*

Then, there is a calendrical expression of the time of the moon as
Qumran understood that evening and morning are the period of the
moon just as is mentioned in Genesis 1 and misunderstood by many.
The sun does not shine from evening to morning nor can that be an
accurate measure for a full day especially when the word for day is right
there in the passage describing a 24-hour day not only 12 hours.

Fr. 1 i

> *I ... to show it from the east. [And] to cause it to shine [in] the middle of*
> *heaven, in the foundation [of the creat]ion, from evening til morning. (There*
> *is full moon)* −*Mishmarot A (4Q320) [1]*

Even their Daily Prayers *(Daily Prayers, 4Q503, 75 B.C.)*, begin in the morning
"when the sun rises" not in the evening. There are evening prayers but
they begin in the morning as that is the start of the Biblical day. These
are priests and they are not following a lunar calendar.

In this Community Rule, they begin with the calendar citing days,
weeks, months, and years in precedence with "His right measure" which
is the sun. They, then, progress to define the day and night as well as
evening and morning. In this poem of sort, evening and morning depart
at the coming of the day that is sunrise just as in the Genesis 1 calendar.
They knew this.

> *I will sing with knowledge and all my music shall be for the glory of God.*
> *(My) lyre (and) my harp shall sound for His holy order and I will tune the*

> *pipe of my lips to **His right measure**. With the coming of day and night*
> *I will enter the Covenant of God, and when evening and morning depart I will*
> *recite His decrees. I will place in them my bounds without return.*
> *−The Community Rule, p. 112 [1]*

As we have seen clarified in their community, these priests began their worship with the day at sunrise with sacrifices and prayer. We locate another fragment that demonstrates this same theme as they "enter the covenant" at the "coming of the day" which is the "departure of evening and morning." It is then at sunrise they recite His precepts. This has never been a mystery and the Creation calendar when mentioning "evening and morning" were always understood as the dark hours or night yet He created Day that day first as Light and many scholars ignore half of the day. The Qumran Priests did not.

> *[At the coming] of the day [and the n]ight I will enter the covenant [of GOD*
> *and at the departure of evening and morning I will recite His precepts.*
> *−Community Rule Manuscript from Cave 4, p. 122. [1]*

In fact, a search through these Qumran scrolls for "sunset" returns numerous passages to cleansing in which sunset becomes important which is supported throughout Torah but not the start of the day ever. However, there is one forced interpretation added to the Sabbath in The Damascus Document that is outright fraud. Let us address this now.

> *Concerning **the Sabbath** to observe it according to its law **No man shall***
> ***work on the sixth day from the moment when the sun's***
> ***orb is distant by its own fulness from the gate (wherein it***
> ***sinks)**; for this is what He said, Observe the Sabbath day to keep it holy*
> *(Deut. v, 12). −The Damascus Document, p. 141. [1]*

Notice "(wherein it sinks)" is added to this fragment in false interpretation. It is in parentheses. The sun is at it's furthest distance when it rises as well as when it sets. Even the Book of Enoch *(72)* which is where this interpretation originates especially noting the language of the "gate" here, observes the sun rises and sets in the same gate thus it is distant from that gate at both times of the day not just once and certainly not only at sunset. This happens twice each day and this fragment does not identify which. There is no specificity but with all the other abundant theology of Qumran, this most certainly refers to the time just before sunrise not at sunset that is injected into this in erroneous interpretation.

The Torah Clock Begins the Day at Sunrise

Did Moses know when the Biblical day began? He received Torah from Yahuah and the Angel of the Presence themselves who bear such record since Creation. Moses was not alive back then. Bear in mind, these books were written at a time that the Biblical day origin was not in question. They knew what a Biblical day was as they lived it. We do not and there are many trying to reconstruct what was known. It appears these days of increasing knowledge include a large amount of lost information over the ages. Moses records this many times. You will find what Moses writes in the rest of Torah, then, must be the interpretation of the Genesis 1 as that cannot be in conflict. Moses wrote that too and he was not confused.

In the Exodus account Moses warns of locusts that will be brought upon Egypt tomorrow. When is tomorrow? A few verses later, Moses tells when the locusts came on tomorrow. It was day and night and then it was morning and the locusts came that he already said would be tomorrow. There is no forcing a lunar calendar into this passage.

> *Exodus 10:4 KJV*
> *Else, if thou refuse to let my people go, behold,* **to morrow will I bring the locusts** *into thy coast:*
> *Exodus 10:13 KJV*
> *And Moses stretched forth his rod over the land of Egypt, and the LORD brought an east wind upon the land* **all that day, and all that night;** **and when it was morning, the east wind brought the locusts.**

In the case of the Passover lamb, Moses identifies the same clock. The

Passover is killed in the evening on the 14th of Abib, the first month. They ate the flesh that night. Nothing of the lamb was to remain until the morning. If it did, it was to be burnt with fire.

He, then, in Leviticus *(same author, same Torah)* tells us the flesh of the Passover lamb must be eaten the same day. Nothing shall remain in the morning. Before tomorrow, any remains must be eaten or burnt with fire. He interchanges tomorrow and in the morning as if they are the same thing. How could this be? Moses was never on a lunar calendar for the morning brings tomorrow as the day begins at sunrise.

> ***Exodus 12:6-8 KJV***
>
> *And ye shall keep it up until the **fourteenth day** of the same month: and the whole assembly of the congregation of Israel shall **kill it in the evening**. And they shall take of the blood, and strike it on the two side posts and on the upper door post of the houses, wherein they shall eat it. And they shall **eat the flesh in that night**, roast with fire, and unleavened bread; and with bitter herbs they shall eat it.*
>
> ***Exodus 12:10-11 KJV***
>
> *And ye shall **let nothing of it remain until the morning**; and that which remaineth of it until the morning ye shall burn with fire. …it is the Lord's passover*
>
> ***Leviticus 7:15-16 KJV***
>
> *And the flesh of the sacrifice of his peace offerings for thanksgiving shall be **eaten the same day that it is offered**; he shall **not leave any of it until the morning**. But if the sacrifice of his offering be a vow, or a voluntary offering, it shall be eaten **the same day** that he offereth his sacrifice: and **on the morrow** also the remainder of it shall be eaten:*
>
> ***Leviticus 22:30 KJV***
>
> *On the **same day it shall be eaten** up; ye shall **leave none of it until the morrow**: I am the LORD.*
>
> ***Leviticus 7:15-16 KJV***
>
> *…offerings for thanksgiving shall be **eaten the same day** that it is offered; he shall **not leave any of it until the morning**.*

Passover evening has multiple timestamps for the day. It was midnight that Egypt's firstborn was smitten. Pharaoh rose up that night and called in Moses and Aaron still that night. That night is well recorded as Abib 14. However, Israel departed from Egypt later that morning and it was now the 15th and a new day because the day begins at sunrise. Numbers is specific that was the 15th, the day after Passover.

> ***Exodus 12 KJV***
> *11…For I will pass through the land of Egypt **this night**…*
> *12…And **this day** shall be unto you for a memorial… (14th)*
> *29 …And it came to pass, that **at midnight** the **Lord smote all the firstborn** in the land of Egypt…*
> *30…And **Pharaoh rose up in the night**…*
> *31 …And **he called for Moses and Aaron by night**…*
> ***Numbers 33:3 KJV***
> *And **they departed** from Rameses in the first month, on the **fifteenth day of the first month; on the morrow after the passover** the children of Israel went out with an high hand in the sight of all the Egyptians.*

In the story of the golden calf, Aaron proclaims tomorrow is a Feast. They rose early in the morning and it was tomorrow. Sunrise is the measure for the start of the Biblical day or tomorrow.

> ***Exodus 32:5-6 KJV***
> *And when Aaron saw it, he built an altar before it; and Aaron made proclamation, and said, **To morrow is a feast** to the LORD.*
> *And **they rose up early on the morrow**, and offered burnt offerings, and brought peace offerings; and the people sat down to eat and to drink, and rose up to play.*

The account of the manna also fortifies this timeline. Yahuah rained a double portion on Friday, the 6th day so that Israel could keep the Sabbath as could He. He brought manna in the morning in the form of pellets in which they could form bread, and quail in the evening.

Exodus 16:4-6 KJV

*Then said the LORD unto Moses, Behold, I will rain bread from heaven for you; and the people shall go out and gather a certain rate every day, that I may prove them, whether they will walk in my law, or no. And it shall come to pass, that on the **sixth day** they shall prepare that which they bring in; and it shall be **twice as much** as they gather daily. And Moses and Aaron said unto all the children of Israel, **At even**, then ye shall know that the LORD hath brought you out from the land of Egypt:*

Exodus 16:8-14 KJV

*And Moses said, This shall be, when the LORD shall give you **in the evening flesh to eat**, and **in the morning bread** to the full; for that the LORD heareth your murmurings which ye murmur against him: and what are we? your murmurings are not against us, but against the LORD. And Moses spake unto Aaron, Say unto all the congregation of the children of Israel, Come near before the LORD: for he hath heard your murmurings. And it came to pass, as Aaron spake unto the whole congregation of the children of Israel, that they looked toward the wilderness, and, behold, the glory of the LORD appeared in the cloud. And the LORD spake unto Moses, saying, I have heard the murmurings of the children of Israel: speak unto them, saying, **At even** ye shall **eat flesh**, and **in the morning ye shall be filled with bread**; and ye shall know that I am the LORD your God. And it came to pass, that **at even the quails came up**, and covered the camp: and **in the morning the dew lay round** about the host. And when the dew that lay was gone up, behold, upon the face of the wilderness there lay a **small round thing**, as small as the hoar frost on the ground.*

Specific to the manna that came in the morning, we know it was the early hours of the morning before the sun waxed too hot. They were not to leave any of the manna for the next morning. If they did, it spoiled but not for Sabbath. This proves Sabbath begins in the morning.

Exodus 16:15-21 KJV

*And when the children of Israel saw it, they said one to another, **It is manna**: for they wist not what it was. And Moses said unto them, This is the bread which the LORD hath given you to eat. This is the thing which* *the LORD hath commanded, Gather of it every man according to his eating, an omer for every man, according to the number of your persons; take ye every man for them which are in his tents. And the children of **Israel did so**, and gathered, some more, some less. And when they did mete it with an omer, he that gathered much had nothing over, and he that gathered little had no lack; they gathered every man according to his eating. And Moses said, **Let no man leave of it till the morning**. Notwithstanding they hearkened not unto Moses; but **some of them left of it until the morning**, and it bred worms, and stank: and Moses was wroth with them. And they gathered it **every morning**, every man according to his eating: and **when the sun waxed hot, it melted**.*

Yahuah provided on the Sabbath by bringing a double portion on the 6th day and all gathered enough for two days. He did not allow that to spoil. Notice the language today in the morning is the 6th day. Tomorrow will be the 7th-day Sabbath. This refers to the manna that comes in the morning. Might morning signify tomorrow? He become even clearer.

Exodus 16:22-23 KJV
*And it came to pass, that **on the sixth day** they **gathered twice as much bread**, two omers for one man: and all the rulers of the congregation came and told Moses. And he said unto them, This is that which the LORD hath said, **To morrow is the rest of the holy sabbath** unto the LORD: **bake that which ye will bake to day**, and seethe that ye will seethe; and **that which remaineth over lay up for you to be kept until the morning**.*

The manna from the 6th day was baked that day and remained on the 7th day that according to this account, once again, begins in the morning not the evening. The morning was the measure in which the day changed. However, Moses said to eat that today as today is the Sabbath and today you will not find it in the field that happens in the morning only. If yesterday was the 6th day and this morning begins the 7th day as it is the switch, the day begins at sunrise.

> ***Exodus 16:24-25 KJV***
>
> *And they **laid it up till the morning**, as Moses bade: and it did not stink, neither was there any worm therein. And Moses said, **Eat that today**; for **to day is a sabbath** unto the LORD: **to day ye shall not find it in the field**.*

Other Old Testament Examples Where Day Begins at Sunrise

There are numerous other examples from our research of which we will share some. Joshua led Israel into the Promised Land and they kept the Passover in the evening of Abib 14 as they should. It was time for Yahuah to stop the manna. Remember Manna rained in the morning and NOT on the Sabbath. They ate corn from the land instead and it was tomorrow as the manna ceased on tomorrow. Tomorrow began that next morning.

> ***Joshua 5:10-12 KJV***
>
> *And the children of Israel encamped in Gilgal, and kept the **passover on the fourteenth day of the month at even** in the plains of Jericho. And they did **eat of the old corn of the land on the morrow after the passover, unleavened cakes, and parched corn in the selfsame day**. And the **manna ceased on the morrow** after they had eaten of the old corn of the land; neither had the children of Israel manna any more; but they did eat of the fruit of the land of Canaan that year.*

In the story of Lot after the destruction of Sodom, his daughters feared extinction as they were not aware the damage localized. Last night, the older daughter lay with Lot and she tells her younger sister on tomorrow (today or the day after yesternight), this night she would lie with her father. In other words, though it may appear confused. Last night was yesterday, a different day. Today during the day, she spoke to her sister saying she would lie with him this night meaning tonight is still today. The shift in days here is sunrise.

> ***Genesis 19:34 KJV***
>
> *And it came to pass **on the morrow**, that the firstborn said unto the younger, Behold, **I lay yesternight** with my father: let us make him drink*

*wine **this night also**; and go thou in, and lie with him, that we may preserve seed of our father.*

Gideon set out to test Yahuah with a fleece. He left it that night and rose early in the morning that is tomorrow. The day pivoted at sunrise.

> ***Judges 6:38 KJV***
> *And it was so: for he **rose up early on the morrow**, and thrust the fleece together, and wringed the dew out of the fleece, a bowl full of water.*
> ***Judges 6:40 KJV***
> *And God did so **that night**: for it was dry upon the fleece only, and there was dew on all the ground.*

Joshua tells Israel to sanctify themselves in preparation for tomorrow. In the morning tomorrow began. Sunrise is the key.

> ***Joshua 7:13 KJV***
> *Up, sanctify the people, and say, **Sanctify yourselves against to morrow**:*
> ***Joshua 7:14 KJV***
> ***In the morning** therefore ye shall be brought according to your tribes…*

The day changes in the morning and it is tomorrow for Abimelech who then battles all that day. Wars were not fought in the evening in that era typically. Sunrise is the key.

> ***Judges 9:42 KJV***
> *And it came to pass **on the morrow**, that the people went out into the field; and they told Abimelech.*
> ***Judges 9:45 KJV***
> *And Abimelech fought against the city **all that day**…*

The Levite traveler planned to depart from his hosts on the 4th day early in the morning. They urged him to stay and he did and he ate. He continued there until he tarried all night. He then lodged there for that night again. When he arose, in the morning it was now the 5th day. The day only changed in the morning not the evening. This is not a lunar calendar.

He then, on the 5th day tarries again until afternoon and then evening and decides to accept their invitation to stay the night again. They tell him tomorrow, you can leave early on your way. Tomorrow began at sunrise twice in this story.

> ### Judges 19:5-9 KJV
>
> *And it came to pass on **the fourth day**, when they **arose early in the morning**, that he rose up to **depart**: and the damsel's father said unto his son in law, Comfort thine heart with a morsel of bread, and afterward go your way. And they sat down, and did eat and drink both of them together: for the damsel's father had said unto the man, Be content, I pray thee, and **tarry all night**, and let thine heart be merry. And when the man rose up to depart, his father in law urged him: **therefore he lodged there again**.*
>
> ***And he arose early in the morning on the fifth day** to depart: and the damsel's father said, Comfort thine heart, I pray thee. And **they tarried until afternoon**, and they did eat both of them. And when the man rose up to depart, he, and his concubine, and his servant, his father in law, the damsel's father, said unto him, Behold, **now the day draweth toward evening**, I pray you **tarry all night**: behold, the day groweth to an end, **lodge here**, that thine heart may be merry; and **to morrow get you early on your way**, that thou mayest go home.*

When Saul intended to kill David, David escaped in the night. Saul planned to slay him in the morning. Michal, David's wife says tomorrow begins in the morning. The passage ends with a tie between day and night as the same day just as tomorrow begins in the morning and continues until the next morning when a new day begins. This is not consistent with a lunar calendar and Israel never kept such.

> ### 1 Samuel 19:10-11 KJV
>
> *And Saul sought to smite David even to the wall with the javelin; but he slipped away out of Saul's presence, and he smote the javelin into the wall: and David fled, and **escaped that night**. Saul also sent messengers unto David's house, to watch him, and to slay him **in the morning**: and Michal*

*David's wife told him, saying, **If thou save not thy life to night, to morrow thou shalt be slain**.*
1 Samuel 19:24 KJV
*And he stripped off his clothes also, and prophesied before Samuel in like manner, and lay down naked **all that day and all that night**.*

Essentially, we find Torah and the other Old Testament passages are extremely transparent that the day begins at sunrise. This affirms the Book of Jubilees and the Book of Enoch and also the Qumran scrolls from the exiled Temple Priests that should be no surprise to anyone. This is quite weighty already but what about the New Testament? Does it affirm this as well?

Messiah's Death and Resurrection: Day Begins at Sunrise

Some of the most brilliant preservations in scripture, are called discrepancies by many scholars. The reason is they are stuck in the wrong paradigm and since it does not fit their paradigm, they seem incapable of reconciliation. However, the Bible is not so haphazard. When we find what appears a conflict, it is time to rethink our interpretation. This rings true with the entire narrative of Messiah's birth and His death and resurrection. There are no conflicts in these accounts. What appears a conflict is actually great revelation waiting for us all.

The Resurrection Clock

Matthew is explicit Messiah rose just before sunrise on the Sabbath. When the sun rises, it is no longer the 7th day Sabbath but the 1st day or Sunday on our calendar. The Greek word interpreted dawn is accurate here as is the clear definition Messiah rose on the Sabbath but before dawn and at dawn, Sabbath ends and Sunday, the 1st day begins. Sunrise is the measure.

Matthew 28:1 KJV
*In the **end of the sabbath, as it began to dawn toward the first day of the week**, came Mary Magdalene and the other Mary to see the sepulchre.*

epiphōskō: ἐπιφώσκω: epiphŏskō: to begin to grow light:——begin to dawn, ✕
draw on.

Mark's account is written a little differently but clearly says the same thing. The confusion is understanding Messiah rose just before sunrise. In his account, the women needed to purchase spices waiting until Sabbath was over to go to the tomb where they would anoint his body. Now, it is the 1st day of the week because the sun rose and they purchased without violating the Sabbath early in the morning the first day at the rising of the sun. These accounts all say the same, Messiah rose just before sunrise and it was still Sabbath. At sunrise, the 1st day started because that is the beginning of a new day Biblically. There are no conflicts here unless one tries to cram a lunar calendar that will not work.

> ### Mark 16:1-2 KJV
> *And **when the sabbath was past**, Mary Magdalene, and Mary the mother of James, and Salome, had **bought sweet spices**, that they might come and **anoint him**. And **very early in the morning the first day of the week**, they came unto the sepulchre **at the rising of the sun**.*

John agrees as the first comes or in other words, has not come yet. This means it is still the 7th-day Sabbath. Messiah rose in the dark hours, early right before sunrise. John and Matthew agree.

> ### John 20:1 KJV
> ***The first day of the week cometh** Mary Magdalene **early, when it was yet dark**, unto the sepulchre, and seeth the stone taken away from the sepulchre.*

John then, further entrenches this day clock when he tells us the evening that same day in which Mary had gone to tell Peter Messiah had risen, is still the 1st day of the week. The day clock did not change at sundown, it changed at sunrise even in the New Testament because that is the Biblical calendar. The lunar calendar is firmly disproven here.

John 20:19 KJV
*Then **the same day at evening, being the first day of the***
***week**, when the doors were shut where the disciples were assembled for fear*
of the Jews, came Jesus and stood in the midst, and saith unto them, Peace
be unto you.

In addressing another point made, John then, says after 8 days, the disciples were in the same place. They feared the Jews or Pharisees. However, this cannot be used in the slightest to claim the Sabbath changed. Those scholars cannot read nor count. It is 8 days after Messiah first appeared which was the 1st day in the evening not Sabbath. He is now reappearing on a Monday. It is illiterate for some to claim this somehow moved Sabbath at all whether alone to Sunday. It did not. They weren't even having a service. They were hiding and this account would have those scholars in conflict with themselves as the Sabbath would now be Sunday and Monday in that inept thinking.

John 20:26 KJV
*And **after eight days again his disciples were within**, and*
Thomas with them: then came Jesus, the doors being shut, and stood in the
midst, and said, Peace be unto you.

Yahusha's Death

If the Bible were set on a lunar calendar, Messiah's death is very problematic. He was crucified beginning the third hour according to Mark that is about 9 am on the Bible calendar but 9 pm on the lunar calendar which fails. On the sixth hour the sun was darkened. That would be midnight on the lunar calendar. What sun is out at midnight in order to be darkened? Epic fail. Instead that was about noon on the Bible calendar and He gave up the ghost at 3 pm. This fits all the narratives as the Pharisees wanted Him in the tomb before their lunar Sabbath began at sundown and that is the conflict not the Bible. The entire day clock is thrown into chaos attempting to force such yet Luke and Mark align perfectly with the solar calendar of the Bible.

A New Day Dawns... At Sunrise!

Messiah rose before dawn (sunrise) still on the Sabbath (Saturday). This means the Biblical day began at sunrise not sundown. The dark hours of the morning were still Sabbath (Saturday) until the sun dawned. He rose on Sabbath which is only Saturday. At dawn it was the 1st Day.

Matt. 28:1, Mark 16:1-2, John 20:1

7th Day
Sabbath
SUNRISE
1st day
Dawn

Evening is Still the Same Day!

Only the Pharisees' Lunar Calendar begins at sundown. Mary's did not. Joseph of Arimathea was a Pharisee on the Lunar Calendar. He placed the body in the tomb before his Sabbath observance. However, Mary would not anoint the body at that same hour on Sabbath because she was already observing the Bible Sabbath instead since sunrise.

Luke 23:54-56, Mark 15:42-43

7th Day
Sabbath
SUNSET
Still 7th Day
Sabbath

Evening is Still the Same Day!

Later that day, when the first day began and the 7th day ended at sunrise, the evening was still the 1st day not a new day. If this were a Lunar Calendar, the day would have to change at sundown which would have made it the 2nd day but it did not according to the Bible.

John 20:1, 19

Dawn
1st Day
SUNSET
Still **1st day**
Evening

... who hast created the morning as a sign to reveal the dominion of the light as the boundary of the daytime ... (4Q408), Vermes, p. 386 [1]

Charting the Four Gospel Accounts. Details in "Rest: The Case For Sabbath."

First Hebrew Month

Abib

MIRRORS ISAAC'S *Jub. 17-18* **SACRIFICE**

DIED ON SABBATH

Good Friday is Not Bible!

Joseph of Arimathea On Pharisee Sabbath Not Bible One!

First Day of Unleavened Bread: One of the 3 Most Important Feasts Requiring Pilgrimage.

1 DAY IN GRAVE

14	15	16
6 am-6am	*6 am-6am*	*6 am-6am*
Tuesday	*Wednesday*	*Thursday*
Passover Evening	**ULB Feast Sabbath**	**ULB Feast**
		Mary Waited for Sabbath to End
Messiah Captured After Passover Meal	**9 am** *Crucified* **3 pm** *Died* **6pm** *Tomb (Pharisee Sabbath)*	**6 am** *Anointed w/ Spices Counting Begins*

Mary already keeping Sabbath before Dark   *1 Day, 1 Night*

Lord of the SABBATH

AFFIRMED IN HIS DEATH & RESURRECTION

The Bible's Brilliant Accuracy Preserves the Start of the Biblical Day at Sunrise!

Messiah is attached to the Biblical Calendar and no one can change it. Forgetting the Sabbath is forgetting His Sacrifice and Resurrection!

Sabbath cannot pass away! He has restored it forever! The Bible is set on a Solar Calendar NOT a Lunar one!

> *Luke 23:44-46 KJV*
> *And it was about the **sixth hour**, and there was a **darkness over all the earth until the ninth hour**. And the **sun was darkened**, and the veil of the temple was rent in the midst. And when Jesus had cried with a loud voice, he said, Father, into thy hands I commend my spirit: and having said thus, **he gave up the ghost**.*
> *Mark 15:25 KJV*
> *And it was **the third hour**, and **they crucified him**.*
> *Mark 15:33 KJV*
> *And when the **sixth hour** was come, there was **darkness** over the whole land **until the ninth hour**.*

Though Luke's calendar is already established as the day beginning at sunrise, there appears great confusion over this passage of Messiah's death. That day was the preparation yet the Sabbath drew on. That characterization seems contradictory. Testing Luke however, will not lead to such chaos. How can a day be both the day of preparation that is the day one prepares for the Sabbath and yet the Sabbath is already in place at the same time? What Luke is expressing is there are two different calendars at work here. There is the one from the Bible in which the day began at sunrise as the previous passage from Luke demonstrates. Then, we have the Pharisee calendar that was lunar based even then.

> *Luke 23:54-56 KJV*
> *And **that day was the preparation, and the sabbath drew on**. And the women also, which came with him from Galilee, followed after, and beheld the sepulchre, and how his body was laid. And **they returned, and prepared spices and ointments; and rested the sabbath day according to the commandment**.*

Notice the women went to the tomb but would not anoint the body because it was already their Sabbath. Their Biblical Feast Sabbath drew on or was in progress. Messiah was crucified on Sabbath. This is where the Pharisee calendar comes in as it was their preparation day still yet not on the Bible calendar in which Sabbath already drew on.

Mark's account clarifies this even more as he tells us evening was coming. He, then, issues the Pharisee calendar Day of Preparation that is their day before the Sabbath. Joseph of Arimathea who was saved but still a Pharisee on the Pharisee calendar, fits this passage and it is about him thus appropriate. In fact, you will find him purchasing because he was not on Sabbath yet on his calendar, the Pharisee one which would begin at sundown though wrong. However, the women were already on Sabbath observation at the same time. This is not error, it preserves that there are two calendars. We showed you earlier in this chapter, that is exactly what is recorded by the Qumran Temple Priests at this very time in history. The Pharisees turned a "blind eye" to the Jubilees calendar as they were already applying their Babylonian lunar calendar. This is because they are not originally Hebrews nor Israelites but replacements with an infused religion originating in Persia.

> ***Mark 15:42-43 KJV***
> *And now when the **even was come**, because **it was the preparation**, that is, **the day before the sabbath, Joseph of Arimathaea**, an honourable counsellor, which also waited for the kingdom of God, came, and went in boldly unto Pilate, and craved the body of Jesus.*

Messiah Crucified on Abib 15 Not Passover

Let us also remember Messiah was not crucified on the 14th on Passover Evening. First, the sun doesn't shine during those hours thus it cannot fit on any level as the sun was darkened. Also, the Pharisees refused to put him to death on Passover because that would cause an uproar according to Mark.

> ***Mark 14:1-2 KJV***
> ***After two days was the feast of the passover**, and of unleavened bread: and the chief priests and the scribes sought how they might take him by craft, and **put him to death**. But they said, **Not on the feast day**, lest there be an uproar of the people.*

Messiah instead must mirror the prophetic time clock of Isaac, the promised son of the covenant not the Passover Lamb. In fact, he is called the Lamb but generally not specific to the Passover Lamb as He replaces all sacrifice for all 52 Sabbaths and all 7 Biblical Feasts. Isaac was offered in sacrifice on the altar on Abib 15 on the 1st day of Unleavened Bread not on Passover evening. This is another forcing of the lunar calendar in error that cannot possibly work.

> ### Jubilees 17:15-16 (Abib 12 - Satan Challenges Abraham's Righteousness)
> *And it came to pass in the seventh week, in the first year thereof, **in the first month** in this jubilee, **on the twelfth of this month**, there were voices in heaven regarding Abraham, that he was faithful in all that He told him, and that he loved Yahuah, and that in every affliction he was faithful. And the prince Mastêmâ came and said before Yahuah, "Behold, Abraham loveth Isaac his son, and he delighteth in him above all things else; bid him offer him as a burnt-offering on the altar, and Thou wilt see if he will do this command, and Thou wilt know if he is faithful in everything wherein Thou dost try him."*
>
> ### Jubilees 18:3 (The Third Day after, Abraham Intended to Sacrifice Isaac on the 15th)
> *And **he (Abraham) rose early in the morning** and saddled his ass, and took his two young men with him, and Isaac his son, and clave the wood of the burnt-offering, and he went to the place **on the third day**, and he saw the place afar off.*

Notice the Feast of Unleavened Bread ranks as one of the three most significant Feasts of the year in which men would undertake a pilgrimage to Jerusalem. The first day of Unleavened Bread is crucial as that is when Jacob and Jesus(Yahusha) were both offered. Isaac was spared.

> ### Deuteronomy 16:16 KJV
> ***Three times in a year shall all thy males appear before the LORD thy God in the place which he shall choose;** in the **feast of unleavened bread**, and in the **feast of weeks**, and in the **feast of tabernacles:** and they shall not appear before the LORD empty:*

In fact, Messiah was not crucified on Passover as that is the evening of the so-called "Last Supper" when He was captured later that evening. For those claiming He did not partake of a Passover Seder, they seem to be unwilling to read the passages. He told the disciples where to get the lamb, to kill it and they had dinner that evening. Some actually claim he did not actually eat yet scripture says he most certainly did. That was a Passover Meal period and if it was not, they have Him breaking the Law or sinning which is ludicrous or keeping it the wrong day.

> *Mark 14:12 KJV*
> *And **the first day of unleavened bread, when they killed the passover**, his disciples said unto him, Where wilt thou that we go and prepare that thou mayest **eat the passover**?*
> *Mark 14:17-18 KJV*
> *And **in the evening** he cometh with the twelve. And as they sat and **did eat**, Jesus said, Verily I say unto you, One of you which **eateth with me** shall betray me.*

It was the next day on the 15th, in the morning in which Messiah was taken to Pilate.

> *Mark 15:1 KJV*
> *And straightway **in the morning** the chief priests held a consultation with the elders and scribes and the whole council, and **bound Jesus**, and **carried him away**, and **delivered him to Pilate**.*

The timeline is incredibly clear. Messiah's death and resurrection must be on the Biblical clock as it proves to be. Certainly there is language in some accounts that clarify the Pharisees are on a different calendar but they only serve to preserve this distinction. The same contrast is found throughout the Dead Sea Scrolls as well. Messiah confirmed the Day Clock in this parable.

> *Matthew 20:1-12 KJV*
> *For the kingdom of heaven is like unto a man that is an householder, which went out **early in the morning** to hire labourers into his vineyard. And when he had agreed with the labourers for a penny a*

*day, he sent them into his vineyard. And he went out about **the third hour**, and saw others standing idle in the marketplace, And said unto them; Go ye also into the vineyard, and whatsoever is right I will give you. And they went their way. Again he went out about **the sixth and ninth hour**, and did likewise. And about **the eleventh hour** he went out, and found others standing idle, and saith unto them, **Why stand ye here all the day idle?** They say unto him, Because no man hath hired us. He saith unto them, Go ye also into the vineyard; and whatsoever is right, that shall ye receive. So when even was come, the lord of the vineyard saith unto his steward, **Call the labourers, and give them their hire**, beginning from the last unto the first. And when they came that were hired about the eleventh hour, they received every man a penny. But when the first came, they supposed that they should have received more; and they likewise received every man a penny. And when they had received it, they murmured against the goodman of the house, Saying, **These last have wrought but one hour,** and thou hast made them equal unto us, which have borne the burden and heat of the day.*

How odd indeed that Messiah uses the same time stamps here in this parable as His sacrifice. The clock for this analogy begins at sunrise, early in the morning when the day begins. He is starting the count of hours for the day then which is obvious. He advances to the third hour and men who labor are standing in the marketplace waiting for work. This is known as the third hour thus we count 3 hours from sunrise and it is about 9 am. That is the same hour he was crucified and it is also 3 hours from sunrise. The day begins at dawn in this parable just as in His entire crucifixion day.

It then advances to the sixth and ninth hours that are again counting from sunrise. Workers are not waiting for work at 9 pm that is what this story would require us to believe if the day begins at sundown as the Babylonian Jewish Calendar claims in error. The third hour is 9 am, the sixth hour is 12 noon and the ninth hour is 3 pm. Just as Messiah was crucified the third, the sun darkened in the sixth hour and our Savior gave up the Ghost in the ninth. He just preserved the timeline of His death anchoring these hours to sunrise, early in the morning.

The final wave of workers arrive in the eleventh hour which is about

5 pm, the end of the day. This would seem odd until you read the rest of the story in which the men all stop work and are all paid one hour later in the twelfth hour. This is evident as the first workers from the morning complained that the others from the eleventh hour got paid the same having only worked for 1 hour. This is 6 pm and the end of the workday when the men are all getting paid which makes sense. However, on the Ashkenazi Babylonian calendar, this would be 6 am and now the workers were working in the vineyard throughout the night which is nonsense and ruins the entire clock as usual.

If Messiah were using the Jewish clock, men are not waiting in the market for work at 9 pm even today. The sun is not out at midnight in order to be darkened. Thus, this parable as Messiah's death, are during the day. Of course, add to that the Pharisees wanted Him taken down from the cross before dark when their false Sabbath of Unleavened Bread would begin. Joseph of Arimathea puts His body in the tomb before sundown also following the Pharisee calendar not the Bible one as Mary observed where the tomb was and would not anoint the body until her Sabbath was over at sunrise. This is also evident in the resurrection account as Mary would wait until sunrise to purchase spices because that is when Sabbath was over. They were following the same cycle as when they anointed the body the first day that is why the counting of 3 days begins at sunrise and he rose just before sunrise on the Weekly Sabbath equating to exactly 3 days and nights as prophesied. His prophecies are never wrong. Those scholars who assume so, undermine the entire Bible.

Other New Testament Examples Where Day Begins at Sunrise

The Holy Spirit came and the disciple appeared drunk to some as they began to speak in other languages. It would not be odd for one to be drunk at 9 pm if this were the lunar calendar. It would be for 9 am.

Acts 2:15 KJV

For these are not drunken, as ye suppose, seeing it is but the third hour of the day.

Peter and John were detained or imprisoned of sort because they were preaching Jesus*(Yahusha)*. They were taken in the evening and held until the next day. In the morning, it was tomorrow in which they were brought before the High Priest. If this were the lunar calendar, then, tomorrow would be the next night that makes no sense. Peter speaks and says this day because tomorrow was the next day at daytime not the evening.

> *Acts 4:3-5 KJV*
> *And **they laid hands on them, and put them in hold unto the next day**: for **it was now eventide**. Howbeit many of them which heard the word believed; and the number of the men was about five thousand. And **it came to pass on the morrow**, that their rulers, and elders, and scribes...*
> *Acts 4:9 KJV*
> *If we this day be examined of the good deed done to the impotent man, by what means he is made whole;*

On tomorrow, Peter journeyed and in the 6th hour prayed. The 6th hour on the Bible day calendar is about noon. As you read, Peter fasted and then that night was given lodge. The next morning, it was tomorrow and Peter left. Otherwise, on a lunar calendar, Peter prayed at midnight. Time passes and what meals did he fast through the middle of the evening? None. Peter was then given lodge in the morning oddly because no one needs lodge in the morning but at night. Then, it is tomorrow which by the moon would begin about 6 pm traveling at night. None of this makes any sense on a lunar calendar as one will find with much of the Bible.

> *Acts 10:9 KJV*
> ***On the morrow**, as they went on their journey, and drew nigh unto the city, Peter went up upon the housetop to pray about the **sixth hour**:*
> *Acts 10:23 KJV*
> *Then **called he them in, and lodged them**. And **on the morrow Peter went away** with them, and certain brethren from Joppa accompanied him.*

Cornelius had vision during the day in the ninth hour. He is later speaking just before the ninth hour in which he makes further connection to the daytime. If that was the lunar calendar, it would be 3 am which cannot work. It was 3 pm on the Bible calendar that begins at sunrise not sunset.

> **Acts 10:3 KJV**
> *He saw in a vision evidently about **the ninth hour of the day** an angel of God coming in to him, and saying unto him, Cornelius.*
>
> **Acts 10:30 KJV**
> *And Cornelius said, Four days ago I was fasting until this hour; and at the ninth hour I prayed in my house, and, behold, a man stood before me in bright clothing,*

What was the hour of prayer at the Temple? 3 am? It would have to be on the lunar calendar in this account. That makes no sense. It was 3 pm in the ninth hour on the Bible calendar in which the day begins at sunrise.

> **Acts 3:1 KJV**
> *Now Peter and John went up together into the temple at the hour of prayer, being the ninth hour.*

The Apostles congregate for dinner on Sunday and Paul preached until midnight. Obviously, they then rested and they departed in the morning on tomorrow. Dinner, message, midnight, rest and journey in the a.m. makes sense. On the lunar calendar, they would wait until the next evening to depart which would waste time and then there is a gap in the story that should not be there just as with Unleavened Bread erroneously.

> **Acts 20:7 KJV**
> *And upon the first day of the week, when the disciples came together to break bread, Paul preached unto them, ready to depart on the morrow; and continued his speech until midnight.*

Paul's account in Acts 23 is full of time stamps that demonstrate the day begins at sunrise. It was day when the Pharisee council met. They wanted Paul brought tomorrow to have him killed. Not tonight, but tomorrow daytime. Instead, Paul escapes and we even know the hour about 9 pm that night. Thus, the evening is not tomorrow. We even have a letter from Claudius Lysias, the centurion who rescued Paul also affirming this same timeline. He saved Paul because Paul was a Roman citizen subject to their laws that he did not break. He affirms Paul is taken that night, that is today still and tomorrow, in the morning they left on horseback.

> **Acts 23:12 KJV**
> And **when it was day**, certain of the Jews banded together, and bound themselves under a curse, saying that they would neither eat nor drink till they had killed Paul.
> **Acts 23:15 KJV**
> Now therefore ye with the council signify to the chief captain that he **bring him down unto you to morrow**...
> **Acts 23:20 KJV**
> And he said, The Jews have agreed to desire thee that thou wouldest **bring down Paul to morrow** into the council, as though they would enquire somewhat of him more perfectly.
> **Acts 23:23 KJV (Paul moved in the night the same day, 9pm, NOT tomorrow)**
> And he called unto him two centurions, saying, Make ready two hundred soldiers to go to Caesarea, and horsemen threescore and ten, and spearmen two hundred, **at the third hour of the night;**
> **Acts 23:31-32 KJV**
> Then the soldiers, as it was commanded them, **took Paul, and brought him by night** to Antipatris. **On the morrow they left the horsemen** to go with him, and returned to the castle:

Understand just as we have today, the Bible calendar counts in two, 12-hour increments of time beginning with 0 about 6 am, to the twelfth hour that is 6 pm. The counting is restarted from 0-12 for night from 6 pm-6am. However, it tells us at night or during the day many times or as well defines activities or events that can only happen in the daytime such as the sun darkening. The sun dark at night is not worth noting but when it is only darkened for 3 hours, it proves that is not night. Even in this account, the action makes sense in the dark of the night and before the next day when Paul was to be seized by the Pharisees and killed. The third hour of the night is 9 pm.

This is overwhelming evidence that Torah, the Old Testament, the New Testament, and Messiah's Death and Resurrection all converge on the same conclusion – the day begins at sunrise. Jubilees, Enoch and the Qumran Scrolls lay out this theology in great detail. However, the main objection to this is the Creation account says "evening and morning" thus that is the entire day. Somehow, that is supposed to mean the day began in the evening though that is at the end of that verse after Yahuah already created Light and called it Day first.

The Creation Day Clock

Now we will address the Creation day. Was it 24-hours? Were they indistinct evolving pods of time or fixed 24-hour days? Did Yahuah really say He only Created in the evening and morning? Is the darkness before Creation began somehow evil? Let's go right to the account with our notations in brackets.

> *Genesis 1:3-5 KJV*
> *And God said, Let there be light: and there was light. [Light was His 1st Creation]*
> *And God saw the light, that it was good: and God divided the light from the darkness.*
> *And God called the light Day [Day comes 1st],*
> *and the darkness he called Night. [Night comes 2nd]*
> *[After Creating All Day]*
> *And the evening and the morning were the first day.*
> *[Yom - 24 hr Day or Daylight - Never Just Night]*

The first Creation was Day as the Light was called such. Was Yahuah confused as to what the word day meant? Did He confuse Moses? One would have to believe this in order to then, ignore this in the rest of the passage. There are two periods defined here. First is day or daylight that is 12 hours of a physical day. Yahuah was creating during that time as it would be illiterate to say He created the day at night.

The second period is night. He states this very clearly as day and night. Then, in the progression of the 24-hour day in which He says is a day, the first day of Creation or the first 24 hours of Creation, He completes the cycle here so it is simple to understand. It was day, then, it was evening and then, it was morning. Again, evening and morning are defined in the Qumran community as the period we call night from sunset to sunrise, the dark hours. We know what this is yet scholars have ripped through this lacking common sense.

You cannot have night as more than 12 hours. You cannot dismiss the daylight which He created first. This is a full 24-hour day. The Hebrew word day is used thousands of times.

> *day:* יום: *yôm, yôwm, yome, Strong's H3117*
> *The KJV translates in the following manner: day (2,008x), time (64x), chronicles (with H1697) (37x), daily (44x), ever (18x), year (14x), continually (10x), when (10x), as (10x), while (8x), full (8x), always (4x), whole (4x), alway (4x), miscellaneous (44x)*

Here we have a word that gets very mixed up yet is very simple. Yom means day either a 24-hour day as it is typically used or daylight meaning the 12 hours of daylight only which is our same usage today. In terms of pods of time which some have attempted to redefine this word, there is nothing to discuss nor consider as the 7th day clarifies exactly what day means here in terms of the whole time period being referenced. It is a literal 24-hour day as the Weekly Saturday Sabbath is a literal 24-hour day and always has been. Sabbath is not 12 hours nor is it a million years or more. The 1st day is 24 hours.

However, when Yahuah creates Light and calls it day (yom), He is specific to our other common usage as well as scripture which defines that as the 12 hours of daylight. This is why He called it day. He then uses the Hebrew word for night referring to the dark hours. One does not even need a concordance for this.

> *night:* ליל: *layil, lah'-yil: Strong's H3915*
> *properly, a twist (away of the light), i.e. night; figuratively, adversity:—(mid-)night (season).*

That always means night all 233 times it is used in scripture. The word evening is also appropriately interpreted as night which is always it's Biblical use 137 times.

evening: ערב: *'ereb, eh'-reb; from H6150; dusk:— day, even(-ing, tide), night.*

The word morning is very specific not all the hours of daylight and is not a substitute for the word yom which is used multiple times here.

morning: בקר: *bôqer, bo'-ker; properly, dawn (as the break of day); generally, morning:—(+) day, early, morning, morrow.*

Here is how it is translated throughout scripture:

morning (191x), morrow (7x), day (3x), days (with H6153) (1x), early (3x).

The few times this word is included in the final interpretation as day or days typically requires the presence of the word 'ereb or evening as this cannot be day on it's own in terms of a 12-hour daytime period even. It only means morning specific to the hours approaching sunrise. The unscholarly view that this word means all daylight of 12 hours is not founded in any of scripture. The word is morning as in dawn, sunrise or the early morning hours. 11 am is not a use for this word. In fact, here we have Biblical evidence the day begins at sunrise as even in the definition boqer means morrow or tomorrow because tomorrow begins as boqer ends at sunrise.

In fact, in researching this further, even the Strong's definition requires a stretch to the word "day" claiming it means 24-hour day as that is used 3 times. Strong's is merely noting an inclusion not day as the meaning.

Deuteronomy 16:4 KJV
(Moses does not use boqer for day)
And there shall be no leavened bread seen with thee in all thy coast seven days; neither shall there any thing of the flesh, which thou sacrificedst the **first day** *at* **even, H6153** *remain all night until the* **morning.** **H1242**

Daniel uses 'ereb (evening: ערב) boqer (morning: בקר) in the context of cleansing which is specifically an evening and morning ritual not daytime. The two words together are inaccurately interpreted as days that they never equate to 24-hour days. The passage is fine in interpretation as there is only one evening and morning each day and one can count by days but cannot be applied as an accurate use for the word boqer as days as it is not but requires 'ereb *(evening)*. This is exactly the kind of inept scholarship that misleads many as it appears to expand a definition it cannot expand as that is against the use.

Daniel 8:14 KJV
(This is a combination word not just boqer)

*And he said unto me, Unto two thousand and three hundred **days*** *(ערב: 'ereb בקר: bôqer); then shall the sanctuary be cleansed.*

This is a 12-hour period and cannot be redefined as a full day in any application. Even the third application where boqer is said to be interpreted day in Strong's inaccurately, Daniel 8:26 also has both words as "the evening and the morning" *(ערב: 'ereb בקר: bôqer)* and his vision came to him at night or evening and morning which equals night not day. Therefore, we have evening meaning 6 pm to midnight generally and morning meaning the dark hours before sunrise. The church generally is not reading Genesis 1 properly based on this simple assessment. They are changing the meanings of words they cannot change. Such foundation leads to confusion and we know whom is the author of that – not Yahuah.

Daniel 8:26 KJV (This is a combination word not just boqer)

*And the vision of the **evening** (ערב: 'ereb) and the **morning** (בקר: bôqer) which was told is true: wherefore shut thou up the vision; for it shall be for many days.*

The mistake is confusing the word "day" which only refers to daylight in this use, if that, as it's really before dawn, and 24-hour day. However, this should not be so confusing as the same dynamic still translates to the modern English mindset. When we use day it could mean a 24-hour day or refer to the 12-hours of daylight. This is the same in Hebrew.

Many will then, in dismissive manner, claim there was no time yet before the sun was created on Day 4. However, the sun is the timekeeper. It is the measure. It is not time but the instrument by which to know time. Time was since the first day of Creation. It is set in Day and Night. It is affirmed as a full yom, 24-hour day broken into two compartments of day and night. Night is then further specified into two compartments of evening and morning in terms of dusk *(sunset)* to dawn *(sunrise)*.

This pattern continues throughout the Creation days. You can observe the progression as Yahuah created during the daytime just as He created Light during what He called day. He created all daytime and then it was evening and it was morning. That is the context.

> *Genesis 1 KJV*
> *(Daytime = Create + Evening and Morning = 24-hour Day)*
> *6a: And God said, **Let there be a firmament** in the midst of the waters…*
> *8b: And the **evening** and the **morning** were the **second day**.*
> *9a: And God said, Let the **waters under the heaven be gathered**…*
> *13: And the **evening** and the **morning** were the **third day**.*
> *20:a And God said, Let the **waters bring forth** abundantly…*
> *23: And the **evening** and the **morning** were the **fifth day**.*
> *24 a: And God said, Let the **earth bring forth the living creature**…*
> *31b: And the **evening** and the **morning** were the **sixth day**.*

Then, on the fourth day, Yahuah created the timekeepers with the sun first and then, moon and stars. This is the progression of all of Creation and no one can change that. He set it in order. We already know He begins the day and His Creation at sunrise because He called that period day from the beginning and what does He first create on Day 4? The sun. The measure and standard for time itself that establishes the day. It's disappearance and the presence of the moon and stars establish the night. We know that evening and morning again, are only night – a 12-hour period yet for Genesis 1, many forget.

The sun was not created at night but during the day as we can even observe today. If the day begins in evening as the lunar calendar suggests, one would have to believe He created Light that He called day *(daylight)* at night yet He then tells you He creates night as a separate compartment of the day *(24-hours)*. Now, they would have to believe He created the sun at night and that is nonsense. We don't need to go backwards for that. We can observe the sun and it rises as daylight and sets before night even begins. It was not created at night nor does anything in the passage infer such. This is only a religious injection of Babylonian mystery religion into the Bible mindset. They debate and defend it profusely yet us regular folk can figure this out.

This is further entrenched in very obvious language that is in chronological order here. On Day 4, Yahuah mentions day first yet again and then night just as His sequential order which you see from Day 1. He even calls the sun the "greater light" because it is greater in importance in keeping time. He continues with a day first, then night.

> ***Genesis 1:14-16 KJV***
> *And God said, Let there be lights in the firmament of the heaven to divide the day [1st] from the night [2nd]; and let them be for signs, and for seasons, and for days, and years: And let them be for lights in the firmament of the heaven to give light upon the earth: and it was so. And God made two great lights; the greater light to rule the day [1st], and the lesser light [which has precedence?] to rule the night [2nd]: he made the stars also.*
>
> ***Genesis 1:17-19 KJV***
> *And God set them in the firmament of the heaven to give light upon the earth, And to rule over the day [1st] and over the night [2nd], and to divide the light [1st] from the darkness [2nd]:*
> *and God saw that it was good. [Creation during Day]*
> *And the evening and the morning were the fourth day.*

Finally, we have the 7th Day of Creation. Yahuah rested and so did ALL of His Creation including angels, man and animals. Let us not fall for the nonsensical logic that He created the Sabbath but hid it from His Creation whom He created it for.

> ***Genesis 2:1-3 KJV***
> *Thus the **heavens and the earth were finished**, and all the host of them. And on the **seventh day God ended his work** which he had made; and **he rested** on the seventh day from all his work which he had made. And **God blessed the seventh day,***

and sanctified it: *because that in it he had rested from all his work which God created and made.*

This is a day of rest for all of us. It was made for man. However, it was and remains a 24-hour day always. It is not a pod of time where we keep Sabbath for 1 million years, we observe for 1 day of the week for 24 hours – no more and no less. The Sabbath defines the Creation clock as seven 24-hour days. This cannot be changed.

Debate is then attempted that we just don't understand what the darkness was before Creation began. That darkness is simply the absence of light. It cannot be evil as evil first is not a Creation but an antithesis. It requires good in order to exist. Yahuah created good, evil is merely it's opposite not a Creation just as sin is lawlessness and requires the good of Law to exist. The Rabbis have many loony theories especially with the absence of Jubilees. However, let us allow Jubilees to end such debate.

Jubilees 2:2-3

*For **on the first day He created the heavens** which are above and the earth and the waters and **all the spirits which serve before Him (angels)**... and of **all the spirits of His creatures which are in the heavens and on the earth**, (He created) the **abysses** and the **darkness, eventide (and night)**, and the **light, dawn and day**, which He hath prepared in the knowledge of His heart. And thereupon we (the angels) saw His works, and praised Him, and lauded before Him on account of all His works; for **seven great works did He create on the first day**.*

Yahauh created darkness and it is evening and night. It is not day nor can it be called day. Even in Strong's, the definition of the Hebrew word for night is never daytime nor 24-hour day but only the 12-hours of night or evening. He created light, dawn and day. The word for morning is specific to the hours before dawn or sunrise at night as well. This compartment is firm. These are clearly 2 compartments of 12 hours each to equal a full 24-hour day. The word for day has two meanings just as it does today and it is the 12 hours of daylight when Yahuah creates Light called day and it is a 24-hour period in the end as it was the 1st day. Genesis says evening and morning for this 12-hour period of night and day for the 12 hours of daytime. It is a 24-hour day.

Notice elements present on the first day used to Create such as water that is one of the 7 Creations that day. However, the darkness before is not even mentioned as being created but darkness or night/evening created the first day and that darkness is good not evil. As there was no light prior to it's Creation, that darkness was merely the absence of light. Entire doctrines have arisen out of that darkness which are unfounded in scripture. It does not ever identify that darkness prior to the first day as anything notable whatsoever. One would have to add to scripture.

The earth being void and without form is extremely obvious for anyone who has ever created anything. Something not formed yet has no form of course. Something not created yet is not full nor validated thus void. Even the darkness is known as the void. There is an attempt to insert an entire manufactured story and history into the Bible in fraud during this period before Genesis 1:1 and 1:2.

One such theory is called The Gap Theory. This requires satan and angels to fall and evil to exist prior to evil ever existing. There was no evil and no sin until the end of Adam's presence in the Garden of Eden. Even satan did not sin until that point according to scripture as he was guardian cherub in the Garden which is why Eve trusted him. No angels sinned nor fell yet and the major such incursions are dated in scripture to 5 generations later in the days of Jared. It requires satan and angels to fall before they were even created on the first day. The problem is that record is in Revelation 12, a future event in which satan is accusing the brethren or mankind. However, man was not created yet between Gen. 1:1 and 1:2 until Day 6 and neither were angels until Day 1.

The Bible day begins at sunrise and we will further affirm this in Chapter 18 when we cover the Feast Sabbaths. You will find the Day of Atonement as well as Feast of Unleavened Bread firmly prove this out. These are both evening beginnings because one is an evening event and the other, an evening concept of purification. However, within their timing, which we chart, the day begins at sunrise not sunset.

It is time we move to the true Biblical calendar so we can understand things. This was kept by the Temple Priests in Qumran where they were exiled. We have several years in which this record is very clear on many things we have lost in interpretation because of Pharisee leaven.

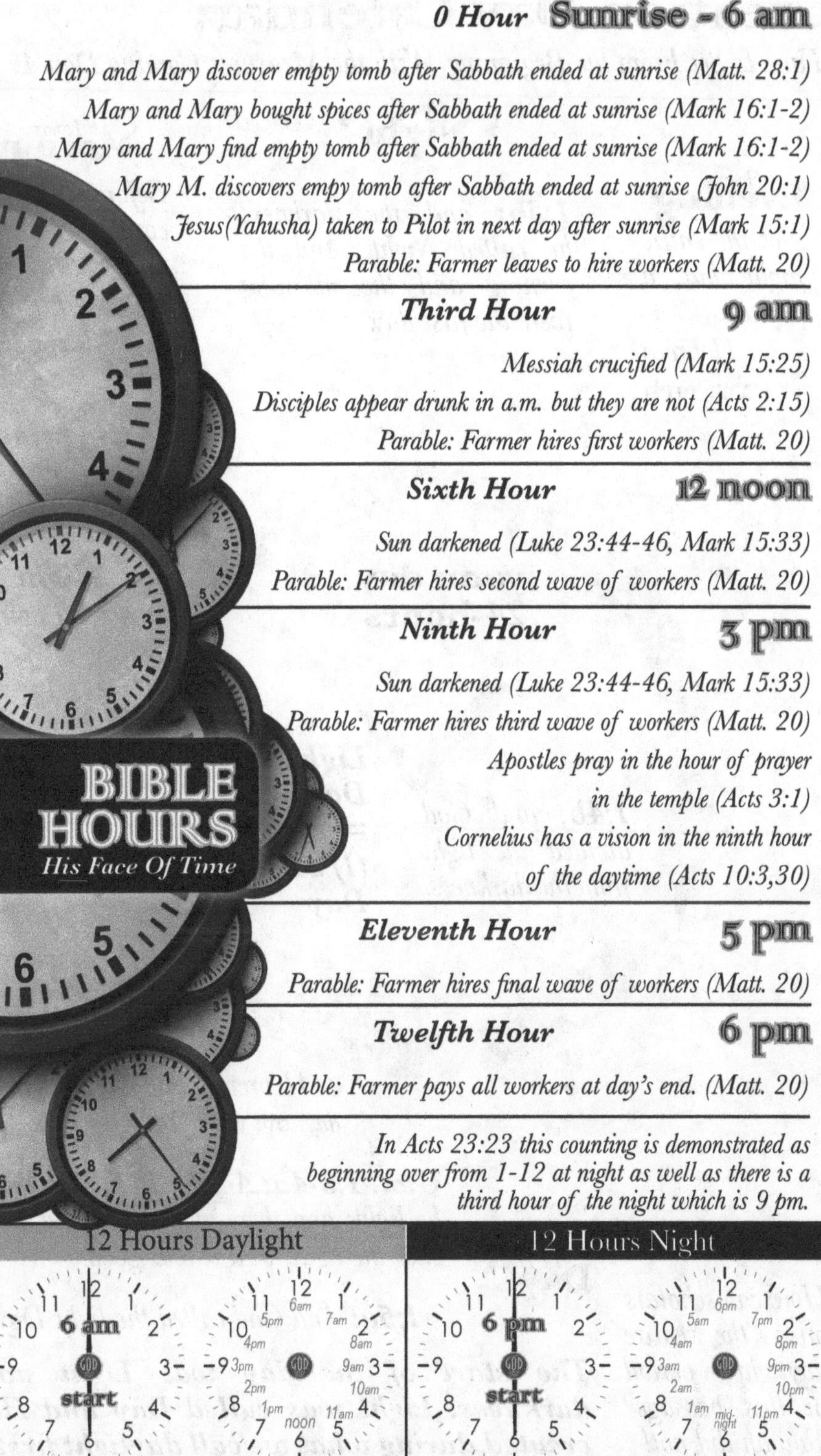

0 Hour Sunrise - 6 am
Mary and Mary discover empty tomb after Sabbath ended at sunrise (Matt. 28:1)
Mary and Mary bought spices after Sabbath ended at sunrise (Mark 16:1-2)
Mary and Mary find empty tomb after Sabbath ended at sunrise (Mark 16:1-2)
Mary M. discovers empy tomb after Sabbath ended at sunrise (John 20:1)
Jesus(Yahusha) taken to Pilot in next day after sunrise (Mark 15:1)
Parable: Farmer leaves to hire workers (Matt. 20)

Third Hour 9 am
Messiah crucified (Mark 15:25)
Disciples appear drunk in a.m. but they are not (Acts 2:15)
Parable: Farmer hires first workers (Matt. 20)

Sixth Hour 12 noon
Sun darkened (Luke 23:44-46, Mark 15:33)
Parable: Farmer hires second wave of workers (Matt. 20)

Ninth Hour 3 pm
Sun darkened (Luke 23:44-46, Mark 15:33)
Parable: Farmer hires third wave of workers (Matt. 20)
Apostles pray in the hour of prayer
in the temple (Acts 3:1)
Cornelius has a vision in the ninth hour
of the daytime (Acts 10:3,30)

Eleventh Hour 5 pm
Parable: Farmer hires final wave of workers (Matt. 20)

Twelfth Hour 6 pm
Parable: Farmer pays all workers at day's end. (Matt. 20)

In Acts 23:23 this counting is demonstrated as
beginning over from 1-12 at night as well as there is a
third hour of the night which is 9 pm.

BIBLE HOURS
His Face Of Time

12 Hours Daylight
6 am
start
5pm 7am
4pm 8am
3pm 9am
2pm 10am
1pm 11am
noon

12 Hours Night
6 pm
start
5am 7pm
4am 8pm
3am 9pm
2am 10pm
1am 11pm
midnight

GOD

Creation Day Calendar:

Time Is Set From the Beginning With the Measures Coming Day 4

12 Hours
Night

1:5b: *and the darkness he called Night. And the evening and the morning were the first day.*

6 Hours
Evening

Not the entire night but a portion.

Hebrew
ערב: ‘ereb

6 Hours
Morning

Before sunrise completes the dark hours.

Hebrew
בקר: bôqer

Evening
+
Morning
=
Night
Not 24 hours!

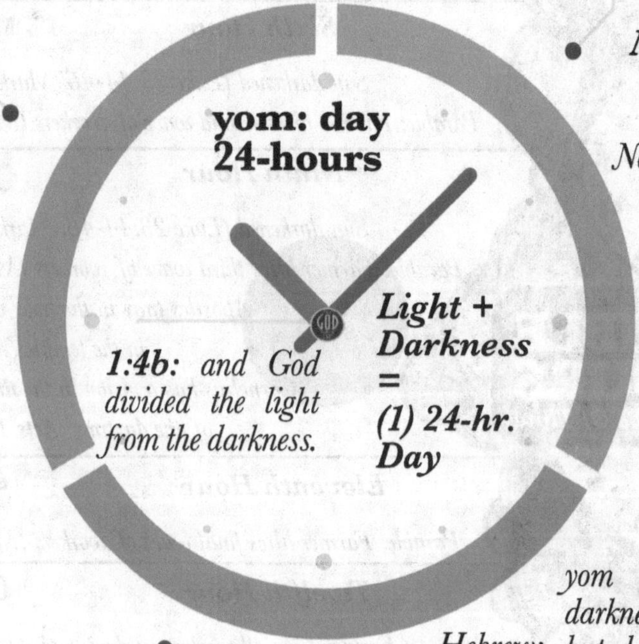

Hebrew:
day: יום: *yôm*

yom is never darkness alone but daylight or a 24-hour day

Gen. 1:3-4a: *And God said, Let there be light: and there was light. And God saw the light, that it was good:*

12 Hours
Day

1:5a: *And God called the light Day,*

How can scholars miss the entire daylight period in this passage? Yahuah did not!

The start of the day was Light not darkness. Light was called Day and He created during what we call daylight first.

Jubilees/Enoch/Qumran Day Start

Jubilees 1:8-9
And on the fourth day He created the sun [1st] and the moon and the stars, and set them in the firmament of the heaven, to give light upon all the earth, and to rule over the day and the night, and divide the light from the darkness. And **God appointed the sun to be a great sign on the earth for days and for sabbaths and for months and for feasts and for years** *and for sabbaths of years and for jubilees and for all seasons of the years.*

DAY 4: The sun was created first as the measure of time for days, weeks, months and years. The moon has other purposes but is not to be used for the calendar in this regard.

Jubilees 6:33-38 (Excerpts)
*...****they will disturb all their seasons, and the years will be dislodged from this (order)...***
For there will be those who will assuredly make observations of the moon-- *now (it) disturbeth the seasons and cometh in from* ***year to year ten days too soon.***

*"****. . . who hast created the morning as a sign to reveal the dominion of the light as the boundary of the daytime . . .****"* –4Q408, *Vermes, p. 386 [1]*

1 Enoch 41:6-7
And the ***Sun*** *goes out first...*

Jubilees 2:2
For on the first day He created the heavens which are above and the earth and the waters and all the spirits which serve before Him... spirits of His creatures which are in the heavens and on the earth, (He created) the abysses and the darkness, eventide (and night), and the light, dawn and day, which He hath prepared in the knowledge of His heart.

Creation Darkness cannot be Evil. No evil existed yet. Evil is an antithesis not a principle. It is the opposite of good and requires good to exist. This darkness is called good by Yahuah.

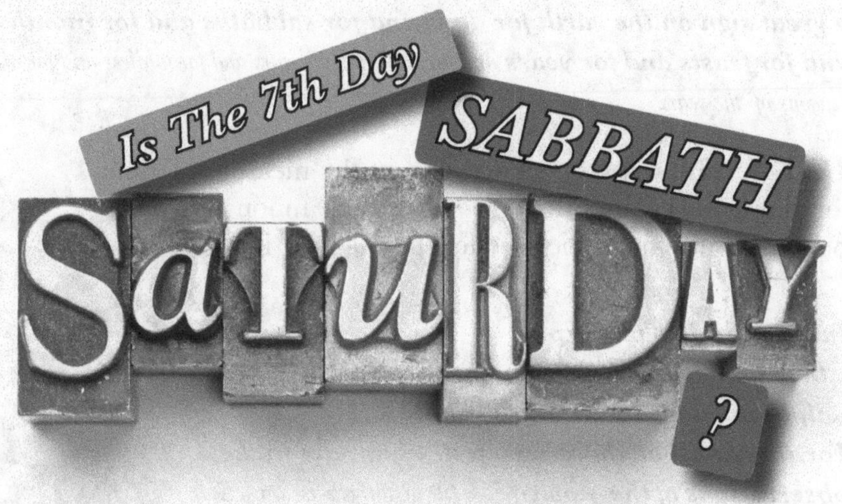

Is The 7th Day
SABBATH
SaturDay
?

the
GOD
culture
יהוה

Chapter 16 | Is the 7th Day Sabbath Saturday?

What is the first day of the week called in the New Testament? It is still called "the first day of the week" even after Messiah's ascension. It does not change to the 7th day.

Matt. 28:1; Mark 16:2, 16:9; 24:1
John 20:1, 20:19
Acts 20:7, 1 Cor. 16:2

The Sabbath is the 7th day of the week that is still found in these same periods and passages and after as we have demonstrated in abundance. When a scholar struggles counting to 7, it is perhaps time to set aside their dementia. 7 is not 1 unless it was changed in a very public way. The first verses here deal with Messiah's resurrection just before the 1st day yet still on the 7th-day Sabbath. Pharisees, even Modern Catholic ones, wish to exploit the Bible's preserved clarity that the day begins at sunrise as a contradiction between the Gospels. However, we have found that if one compares these discrepancies without preconceived paradigms, they actually serve to preserve the narrative and in this case the Bible calendar and the Sabbath. In fact, He was born on a Feast Sabbath *(Shavuot)*, Died on a Feast Sabbath *(1st Day of Unleavened Bread)* and resurrected on the Weekly Sabbath *(7th Day, Saturday)*.

However, some then question if perhaps the calendar changed for the days. It is a reasonable question as they have changed the start of the day as the Pharisees were already following the Babylonian Lunar Calendar beginning at sunset and the Romans at midnight. Neither represent the Bible which begins it's day at dawn. This was changed. However, we have yet to find any evidence that the days of the week were changed.

Rome's founders changed the Sabbath in their own words from the 7th day to the 1st day of the week.

"Down even to the fifth century the observance of the Jewish Sabbath was continued in the Christian church... During the early ages of the church, it [Sunday] was never entitled 'the Sabbath,' this word being confined to the seventh day of the week." –Ancient Christianity Exemplified. [71]

The Sunday law of Constantine: 321 A.D.:

"Let all judges, inhabitants of the cities, and artificers, rest on the venerable day of the sun. But in the country, husbandmen may freely and lawfully apply to the business of agriculture; since it often happens that the sowing of corn and the planting of vines cannot be so advantageously performed on any other day.' –Chambers's Encyclopedia, "Sabbath." [76]

The Sunday law of Constantine: 321 A.D:

"On the venerable Day of the Sun let the magistrates and people residing in the cities rest, and let all workshops be closed. In the country, however, persons engaged in agriculture may freely and lawfully continue their pursuits..."

"The Sunday law of Constantine must not be overrated.... There is no reference whatever in his law either to the fourth commandment or to the resurrection of Christ. Besides, he expressly exempted the country districts, where paganism still prevailed, from the prohibition of labor.... Christians and pagans had been accustomed to festival rests; Constantine made these rests to synchronize, and gave the preference to Sunday." –Philip Schaff, History of the Christian Church. [77]

"It is not to be denied but [that] we borrow the name of this day from the ancient Greeks and Romans, and we allow that the old Egyptians worshiped the sun, and as a standing memorial of their veneration, dedicated this day to him." –Dialogues on the Lord's Day. [78]

"The Apostles therefore resolved to consecrate the first day of the week to the divine worship, and called it the Lord's day. St. John in the Apocalypse makes mention of the Lord's day; and the Apostle commands collections to be made on the first day of the week."

The Sabbath, Why Changed to Sunday

"But the Church of God has thought it well to transfer the celebration and observance of the Sabbath to Sunday.

For, as on that day light first shone on the world, so by the Resurrection of our Redeemer on the same day, by whom was thrown open to us the gate to eternal life, we were called out of darkness into light; and hence the Apostles would have it called the Lord's day.

—The Catechism of the Council of Trent. [79]

How exactly does an Emperor making a decree outlawing the Biblical Sabbath end up being praised and heralded even in the Protestant Church today? It is as if these scholars are not even Protestants but Catholics. This is because they are truly Pharisees wearing a different robe which is a common tactic of Pharisaism. Much of this is carried by the Pharisee Order or what we hear called the Jesuit Order. Ignatius Loyola who founded that unbiblical society was a Marrano Jew – a Pharisee.

They do not hold the beliefs of the Bible. They do not even know them and they will scoff at those who do because the Bible is foreign to them. It is the same today as it was in the days of Messiah. Not all scholars are literal Pharisees but they are trained to think like them. This is because seminaries are dominated by Pharisees.

They did not change the 7th day or Saturday to the 1st day or Sunday however. Those remained. They just changed the title of Sabbath essentially to Sunday. This is authority they never had nor do they offer the slightest justification to overrule and usurp the Lord of the Sabbath's authority. Worse, it is based on the erroneous reading that Sunday Biblically was a day of celebration of the Sabbath on the 1st day of Creation to commemorate work. That is not Sabbath and it is rather inept to not notice that Yahuah set aside the 7th day for such observation and not the first. When He says 6 days you shall work, He already defined which 6 on the weekday clock and when He says rest 1 day, He already determined which day that must be. This is from Creation to Noah to Moses to Jesus*(Yahusha)* to His ascension to Revelation. The only way one could change this day is to change the Bible because there is not a single scripture that supports this thinking. That is the only way they could claim authority to change it and it is advanced-level blasphemy of the anti-Christ form. The Sabbath is not a minor issue – it is a Creation. Who would think to change Creation? Nephilim would and their progeny which is why Daniel told us the final empire would be mixed with iron and miry clay. He explains in Daniel 2:43 that this miry clay are not the seed of men and they mingle with the seed of men. Genesis 6 has always well defined these are the Nephilim and such was the cause of the Flood not an angry God who hates His Creation which is illiterate scholarship yet again.

If these scholars could simply use their brains a little and refrain from playing the robot, they would know no one would ever look back at the major events of history and then claim, they changed the days of the week. Would one actually attempt to say satan tempted Eve in the Garden of Eden and he and man fell on Sunday and the Flood began on Sunday on the week clock, therefore, these events transferred the Sabbath from the 7th day, Saturday to this first day, Sunday? The problem is they are. They are not telling you this and perhaps most of them do not even realize this is what they are saying because they do not know these things. One of the largest violators of the Word in all of history is the office of Pope. Pope Francis spoke of the Sabbath in a television interview on 60 Minutes.

> *"We live with the accelerator down morning and night. This ruins mental health, spiritual health, and physical health. More so: it affects and destroys the family, and therefore society. On the Seventh day, He rested. What the Jews followed and still observe, was to consider the Sabbath as holy. On Saturday you rest. One day of the week, that's the least! Out of gratitude, to worship God, to spend time with the family, to play, to do all these things. We are not machines. –Pope Francis interview on 60 Minutes, May 11, 2018 [80]*

This is perfect example of one who knows nothing of scripture. The Sabbath is not a day of recreation, it is the celebration of Creation as Yahuah rested on the 7th day and we are commanded to do the same. It's Creation not re-creation. Of course, he acknowledges the Bible Sabbath is Saturday and the day of rest is still Saturday according to the Pope. Obviously, the Catholic Church changed the Sabbath from Saturday to Sunday but even the Pope admits the Bible Sabbath is Saturday not Sunday. However, the Catechism of the Catholic Church is not so politically correct. It defines their changing the Sabbath and Sunday esteemed above Saturday as it's replacement. The Pope is not representing the Catechism in this interview because he is attempting to be politically correct yet the Catholic Church is Biblically incorrect. It demonstrates he is a liar as he well knows the Bible Sabbath remains Saturday but he also undermines that in saying "that's the least" which is illiterate as Sabbath is one day, never more and it is holy and set apart. He is teaching people to defile it even in this softened language.

> **Catechism of the Catholic Church:**
>
> *348 The sabbath is at the heart of Israel's law. To keep the commandments is to correspond to the wisdom and the will of God as expressed in his work of creation.*
>
> *349 The eighth day. But for us a new day has dawned: the day of Christ's Resurrection. the seventh day completes the first creation. the eighth day begins the new creation. Thus, the work of creation culminates in the greater work of redemption. the first creation finds its meaning and its summit in the new creation in Christ, the splendour of which surpasses that of the first creation.217 [75]*

The Sabbath remains the heart of the entire New Testament as we have proven. The works of Creation are celebrated on the 7th Day since Creation. As they invoke the Creation clock and era, how dare they attempt to then warp thousands of years ahead and claim all of sudden that celebration is to change from the 7th to the 8th Day? Well, again, the Beatles were wrong, there are only 7 days in the week and only 7 days of Creation. We have proven the Day Clock begins at sunrise and Messiah rose on what is still Saturday on the Biblical calendar which John says is still the 7th-Day Sabbath on Saturday. How could the church who supposedly hails from Peter forget the Biblical day and change the day of the Resurrection? Certainly, we are new creatures in Him but that does not change the day in which he actually rose which is Sabbath. They are wrong.

Creation does not find it's culmination until the realization of Messiah's salvation that happens on the Day of Judgment in which also, Heaven and Earth are made new or replenished or recreated. That is the culmination and that has not happened yet. Nothing surpasses the first Creation nor does it need to. This is illiteracy of scripture and even reads like a Pharisee document oblivious to the Word.

Catechism of the Catholic Church:
The day of the Resurrection: the new creation

2174 Jesus rose from the dead "on the first day of the week."104 Because it is the "first day," the day of Christ's Resurrection recalls the first creation. Because it is the "eighth day" following the sabbath,105 it symbolizes the new creation ushered in by Christ's Resurrection. For Christians it has become the first of all days, the first of all feasts, the Lord's Day (he kuriake hemera, dies dominica) Sunday: We all gather on the day of the sun, for it is the first day [after the Jewish sabbath, but also the first day] when God, separating matter from darkness, made the world; and on this same day Jesus Christ our Savior rose from the dead.106 Sunday - fulfillment of the sabbath

2175 Sunday is expressly distinguished from the sabbath which it follows chronologically every week; for Christians its ceremonial observance replaces that of the sabbath. In Christ's Passover, Sunday fulfills the spiritual truth of the Jewish sabbath and announces man's eternal rest in God. For worship under the Law prepared for the mystery of Christ, and what was done there prefigured some aspects of Christ:107 [75]

Did Yahuah separate the light from darkness on the eight day? No. He did on the first which is a day of work not Sabbath which has always been set apart since Creation on the 7th Day or Saturday never Sunday. Jesus did not rise on the first day of the week. Scripture says he rose on the Sabbath on the 7th Day of the week. The women discovered the tomb empty once the first day dawned but that does not change the fact that He rose before sunrise on what is still the Biblical Saturday Sabbath. When did any Apostle ever say the Lord's day was any other day than the Sabbath of which He is Lord of the Sabbath? Never. We will cover this in the next chapter but the term is only used one time in all of scripture and by John the Revelator who was worshipping on...? The 7th Day Sabbath as was his custom, Messiah's custom, Paul's custom, etc.

There is no scripture which ever abolishes the Sabbath, nor one that ever moves it to Sunday replacing the 7th-Day Sabbath and notice they do not cite one because this Catecism is not based on the Bible. That alone should be enough to question everything Catholic. How can they put in writing that this represents "worship under the Law" when the Law strictly sets forth the 7th Day of Saturday as the Sabbath and commands it's observance specifically that day?

Catechism of the Catholic Church:
Article 3 THE THIRD COMMANDMENT:

2189 "Observe the sabbath day, to keep it holy" (Deut 5:12). "The seventh day is a sabbath of solemn rest, holy to the Lord" (Ex 31:15).

2190 The sabbath, which represented the completion of the first creation, has been replaced by Sunday which recalls the new creation inaugurated by the Resurrection of Christ.

2191 The Church celebrates the day of Christ's Resurrection on the "eighth day," Sunday, which is rightly called the Lord's Day (cf SC106). [75]

Only the Catholic Church and their origins in heresy replaced the Saturday Sabbath with Sunday. No one in the true ekklesia in the East did so. Messiah rose on the Sabbath thus they need to change it back and offer a correction for over 1,000 years of error. We will address the Lord's day in the next chapter.

Now let us deal directly with their illiteracy regarding Paul in their *Catechism of the Council of Trent* claiming he set collections for the first day. This point is again illiterate of the Sabbath practice. The passage never says they abolished the Sabbath and moved it to Sunday but instead it reinforces that they did not collect on the Sabbath as they were keeping it holy as they should. These are incredibly weak positions for a church that claims superiority to even Jesus*(Yahusha)* Himself.

Did Paul Move Sabbath from the 7th Day to the 1st Day?

1 Corinthians 16:1-2 KJV

*Now concerning the collection for the saints, as I have given order to the churches of Galatia, even so do ye. **Upon the first day of the week let every one of you lay by him in store**, as God hath prospered him, that there be no gatherings when I come.*

Did Paul say they were observing Sabbath on the 1st day of the week now? Where is that? It is not there. This is about collecting money that is not something to be done on the Sabbath in fact if you observe it strictly which Paul did. The fact they are doing so on the 1st day of the week proves it is not Sabbath. Also, why is Paul taking so long to get there? He is not there celebrating the first day of the week.

1 Corinthians 16:8 KJV
But I will tarry at Ephesus until Pentecost.

Paul was still keeping the Feast of Pentecost or Shavuot, the Feast of Weeks. Imagine that. He seems to not get his own memo. Actually, he never had delivered such. Paul had always kept the Feasts and Sabbath and taught them. This passage does not change the Sabbath to Sunday. It is an incredibly weak position in the face of a comprehensive case that will never be disproven because it comes from the Bible in context.

Others will say Philippians demonstrates Paul meeting on Sunday. No, it says the opposite. Let us read.

Philippinans 1:3-5 KJV
*I thank my God upon every remembrance of you, Always in every prayer of mine for you all making request with joy, **For your fellowship in the gospel from the first day until now;***

Did Paul just say they fellowship the first day of the week? That would be illiterate. The problem with those thinking Paul just said he only met on Sundays now is these scholars can't even go back and read Acts to see that Paul first preached in Philippi on the Sabbath. The first day he met and fellowshipped with them was the Saturday Sabbath. What gross misrepresentation.

Acts 16: 12-13 KJV
And from thence to Philippi, which is the chief city of that part of Macedonia, and a colony: and we were in that city abiding certain days. And on the sabbath we went out of the city by a river side, where prayer was wont to be made; and we sat down, and spake unto the women which resorted thither.

This is it. All the passages that mention Sunday as a day in that the Apostles gathered and some are not even Sunday. There is certainly nothing here which overturns the Sabbath and moves it to Sunday. Messiah's resurrection does not provide for that in the slightest as He resurrected on the Sabbath which was and is Saturday. In fact, He further entrenched it as that is the greatest event in history to date.

Even to the 5th Century, we can document the Saturday Sabbath observance in parts of the Catholic Church specifically in it's capitol of origin – Constantinople. One cannot make a connection to the Apostles with such practice because it is untrue.

5th Century: Socrates of Constantinople
"The people of Constantinople and almost everywhere, assemble together on the Sabbath, as well as on the first day of the week, which custom is never observed at Rome or at Alexandria." –Sozomen, Ecclesiastical History. [30]

As we proved, Messiah rose on the Sabbath that was still the 7th day of the week or Saturday on the Biblical calendar. The Roman calendar is impertinent. The women discovered the tomb empty after sunrise as they had to wait to purchase spices until after Sabbath had ended at sunrise. However, Jesus*(Yahusha)* resurrected before sunrise. He was not there already when they got there just after sunrise. When they got there it was now the 1st day of the week. However, Messiah arose minutes before on the 7th day.

Matthew 28:1 KJV
In the end of the sabbath, as it began to dawn toward the first day of the week, came Mary Magdalene and the other Mary to see the sepulchre.

Mark 16:2 KJV
And very early in the morning the first day of the week, they came unto the sepulchre at the rising of the sun.

Mark 16:9 KJV
Now when Jesus was risen early the first day of the week, he appeared first to Mary Magdalene, out of whom he had cast seven devils.

Luke 24:1 KJV
Now upon the first day of the week, very early in the morning, they came unto the sepulchre, bringing the spices which they had prepared, and certain others

with them.

John 20:1 KJV
The first day of the week cometh Mary Magdalene early, when it was yet dark, unto the sepulchre, and seeth the stone taken away from the sepulchre.

Again, here is the problem with the interpretation that the day begins in the evening. As all these accounts reconcile perfectly, Messiah arose in the dark hours of the morning that was still the Sabbath which was still the 7th Day. He did not rise on the first day. The women came to the tomb at sunrise and then, it was the first day that they learned of Messiah's resurrection. However, he rose before sunrise and it was still Sabbath. All of the accounts are in concert and do not disagree as they cannot. The day begins at sunrise which is the only way this works and Jesus*(Yahusha)* preserved this in His death and resurrection. For that evening it still remained the first day. If the day changes at sunset, then that would be the second day not the first.

John 20:19
*Then **the same day at evening, being the first day of the week,** when the doors were shut where the disciples were assembled for fear of the Jews, came Jesus and stood in the midst, and saith unto them, Peace be unto you.*

The Apostles Met Every Day But They Still Kept the Sabbath

Yes, the Apostles sometimes met on Sunday. They also met on Monday and other days. In fact, from their very first coming out on the Day of Pentecost which was a Sunday, they continued to meet daily not Sundays but they still kept the 7th Day as Sabbath. With the rational being applied by these non-scholars, we are now to have Sabbath every day. That is illiterate as the Bible never says so. Sunday is never set apart and sanctified as a Day of Rest period.

Acts 20:7 KJV
*And **upon the first day of the week**, when the **disciples came together to break bread, Paul preached unto them**, ready to*

*depart on the morrow; and **continued his speech until midnight**.*

Paul certainly did preach on Sunday to the Apostles. It does not say anything but they had dinner and Paul gave a speech. This cannot replace the precedence of the whole of scripture especially when the 7th-Day Sabbath is observed for 85 sabbaths in writing in the Book of Acts alone *(pp. 188-191)*. It is always on Saturday.

Acts 20:18 KJV

*And when they were come to him, he said unto them, Ye know, **from the first day that I came into Asia**, after what manner I have been with you at all seasons*

Paul's first day in Asia, he met Timothy and circumcised him even. Yes, Paul still practiced circumcision the Bible way. He never preached against that. However, he shared the Apostles message, not merely his own, that adult Gentile men did not have to now be circumcised in order to be saved. Circumcision was never salvation in the Bible but the Pharisees lied and told these new believers that if they were not circumcised they were not saved. That is a lie and always has been as the Old Testament never says such.

Acts 16:1 KJV (Paul First Enters Asia Minor for Yahusha)

Then came he to Derbe and Lystra: and, behold, a certain disciple was there, named Timotheus, the son of a certain woman, which was a Jewess, and believed; but his father was a Greek:

Then, Paul began meetings but when? Daily not just on Sunday nor just on the Sabbath. The Apostles nor Messiah only taught on the Sabbath nor any specific day. The Sabbath mostly but every day is good for teaching.

Acts 16:5 KJV

And so were the churches established in the faith, and increased in number daily.

Messiah also sometimes taught daily.

> ***Matthew 26:55 KJV (cf. Mark 14:49, Luke 19:47)***
> *In that same hour said Jesus to the multitudes, Are ye come out as against a thief with swords and staves for to take me?* **I sat daily with you teaching in the temple,** *and ye laid no hold on me.*

Then, from Pentecost forward, we find the Apostles teaching daily but they still kept the Sabbath on Saturday, the 7th Day.

> ***Acts 2:46-47 KJV (After Peter's First Message on Pentecost/ Shavuot)***
> *And they,* **continuing daily with one accord in the temple, and breaking bread from house to house,** *did eat their meat with gladness and singleness of heart, Praising God, and having favour with all the people. And* **the Lord added to the church daily** *such as should be saved.*
>
> ***Acts 5:42 KJV***
> **And daily in the temple, and in every house, they ceased not to teach and preach Jesus Christ.**
>
> ***Acts 16:5 KJV***
> *And so were the churches established in the faith, and* **increased in number daily.**
>
> ***Acts 17:17 KJV***
> *Therefore disputed he in the synagogue with the Jews, and with the devout persons, and* **in the market daily with them that met with him.**
>
> ***Acts 19:9 KJV***
> *But when divers were hardened, and believed not, but spake evil of that way before the multitude, he departed from them, and separated the disciples,* **disputing daily in the school** *of one Tyrannus.*

Hebrews even establishes that the ekklesia, which Messiah defined as 2 or more not thousands, exhort or minister to each other daily. At the end of this chapter and throughout the next, Hebrews then tells us the Sabbath remains and to keep it or we are an example of unbelief. He even affirms it is the 7th Day, the same 7th Day as Creation, the time of Moses, the time of David and the time of Messiah. Not scholar can overcome Hebrews.

> **Hebrews 3:13 KJV**
> But **exhort one another daily**, while it is called To day; lest any of you be hardened through the deceitfulness of sin.

8 Days Later From Sunday = Monday:

Were the Beatles right? Are there 8 days in a week? Well, some scholars seem to forget. Sorry we have to provide this math because there are actual scholars who claim 8 days from Sunday is another Sunday claiming they met 2-consecutive Sundays. They were together the previous Sunday with no actual service mentioned. That is recorded in those passages as the day after Sabbath. They were hiding from the Pharisees and Messiah appeared to them then. They were not holding church. It was the day after He rose though the same day Mary found the empty tomb first thing in the morning at the dawn at the start of the Biblical day. It is the only way the Gospels make sense. Of course, even on that Monday, the passage still does not indicate their holding church. They were simply together inside hiding again. We all would be as well after seeing the Messiah crucified.

> **John 20:19 KJV**
> Then the same day at evening, being the first day of the week, when the doors were shut where the disciples were assembled for fear of the Jews, came Jesus and stood in the midst, and saith unto them, Peace be unto you.
>
> **John 20:26 KJV (8 Days Later)**
> And **after eight days again his disciples were within**, and Thomas with them: then came Jesus, the doors being shut, and stood in the midst, and said, Peace be unto you.

Essentially, what we observe in these interpretations from Catholic scholars, but also many Protestants alike, is a complete miss. They turn themselves into fools who cannot count any longer, are challenged to read and who placate paradigms rather than reading and interpreting what the Bible actually says. This is the error of our age and it has been building with Pharisee leaven in the Catholic Church which is the foundation of the Protestant Church even still. All represent a foundation built on sinking sand. In these days of increasing knowledge, these weak imposters will be exposed in the light of these truths.

Prophecy tells us they will continue until the end but their reckoning will be upon them soon. If you are a scholar peddling this nonsense, repent and experience salvation because right now, you have no relationship with the Messiah claiming the Lord of the Sabbath changed His Day to another with no support whatsoever. Religion leads to man's domination and they step in as a mediator when we do not require another. Jesus *(Yahusha)* is our only mediator and no priest, pastor, theologian, scholar or even Pope can fill His role.

The Apostles kept 85 different Sabbaths in the Book of Acts alone *(chart to right)*. These were all on Saturday. They kept 0 Sundays as Sabbath. The scoreboard speaks for itself. It is inept to claim the Saturday Seventh-Day Sabbath ever changed to Sunday. We also find no evidence that the day we call Saturday has ever been anything different from the 7th day. History has offered a consistent track that one will find demonstrated in the abundant history throughout this book.

However, one of the strongest proofs is the fact that the word for Sabbath in cultures around the word remains their connotation for Saturday instead in their language *[map and chart next spread]*. Based on research by United Church of God, we have recreated a map with chart demonstrating this. This is still retained in much of the world to this day proving the day we call Saturday is the 7th-Day Sabbath.

BOOK OF ACTS Sabbath Days

7th Day Sabbaths Kept

After Messiah's Ascension:

Acts 17:1 = 3 Sabbaths
Acts 13:13 = 1 Sabbath
Acts 13:43 = 1 Sabbath
Acts 16:11 = 1 Sabbath
Acts 18:1 = 1 Sabbath
Subtotal = 7 Sabbaths
+
Acts 18:5 = Every Sabbath for
1 Year + 6 Months =
52 +26 Sabbaths =
78 Consecutive Sabbaths
Meeting in the Synagogue
of the Saved Rabbi
Meaning Saturday

Total = 85 Sabbaths in 1 Book
After Messiah's Ascension
That Pattern is Undeniable
And Cannot Be Overturned

1st Day Sabbaths Kept

There is no mention of the 1st Day of the Week ever becoming Sabbath in the Bible. This is a manufactured doctrine of men of the very weakest form as demonstrated by the fact that the Catholic Church and those opposing Sabbath have had to resort to killing and imprisoning "Sabbath-keepers" by their own admission from their own histories. If they could have proven the Sabbath moved rather than their changing it illegally, rational people would accept their position. They have none. Time to awaken.

Credit for this revelation goes to Eliyah Ministries. Eliyah.com.

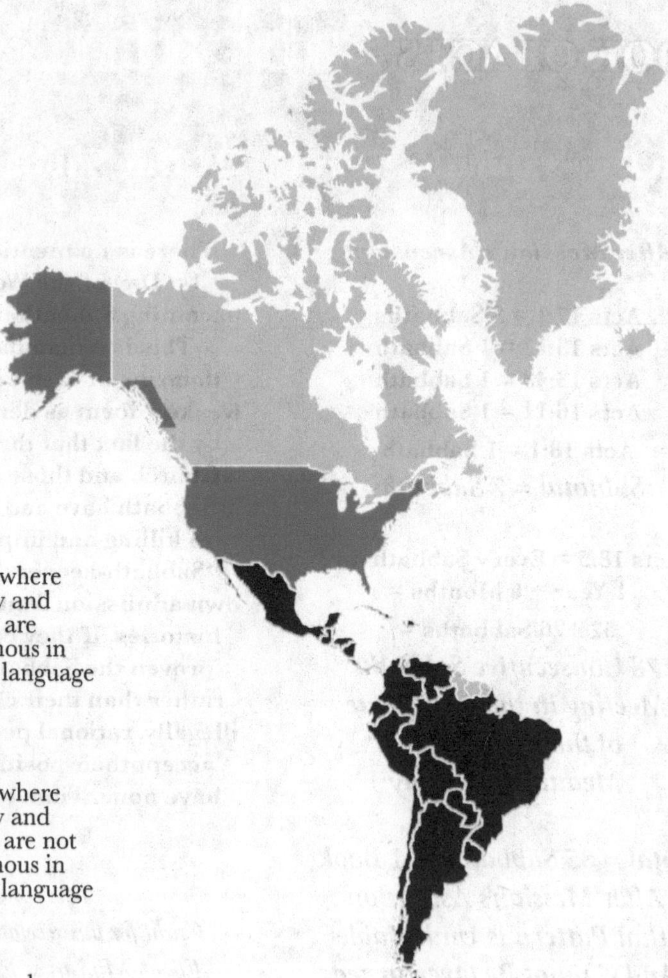

Languages Where Saturday and Sabbath Are Synonymous

This map demonstrates the nations which retain the word Sabbath in their language which we label Saturday, the 7th day of the week. The Catholic Church has made sure to hunt, imprison and even kill many of those in many countries who have kept the Saturday Sabbath in certain eras according to their own history. This chart does not denote those keeping the Sabbath.

Map Recreated From research by Beyond Today, United Church of God. Feb. 11, 2011.

SABBATH & SATURDAY

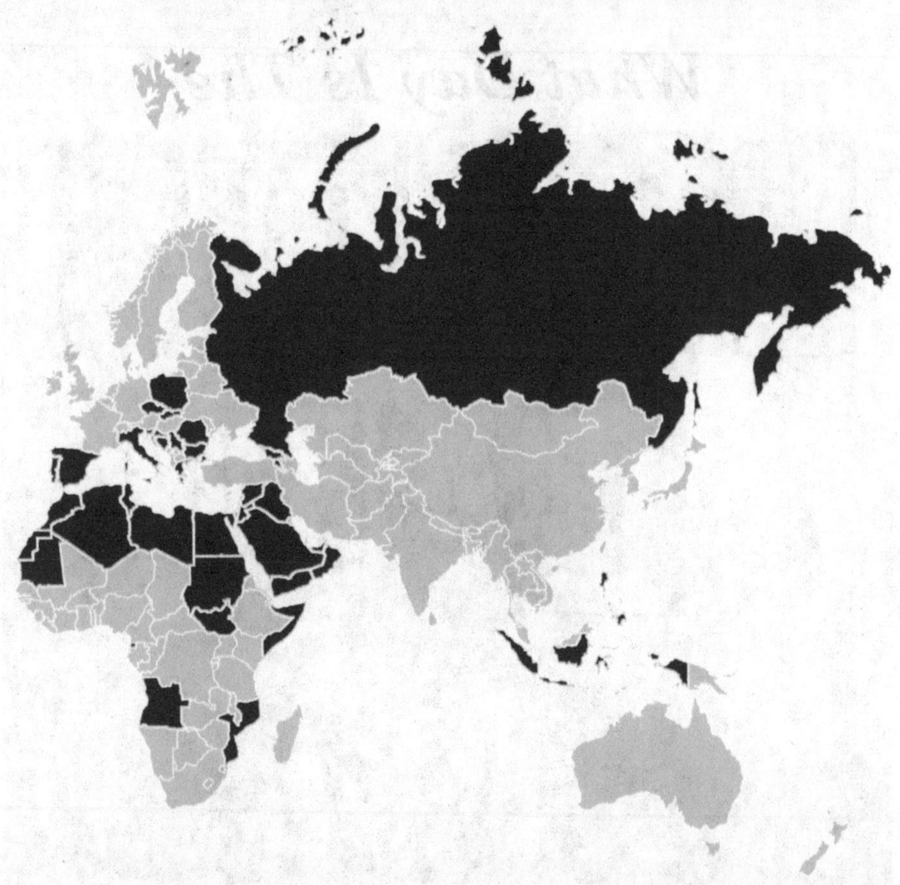

Arabic: Sabet	280	Maltese: is-Sibt	1
Armenian: Shabat	6	Polish: Sobota	39
Bosnian: Subota	2	Portuguese: Sábado	215
Bulgarian: Sabota	7	Romanian: Sambata	26
Corsican: Sàbatu	1	Russian: Subbota	166
Croatian: Subota	6	Serbian: Subota	9
Czech: Sobota	10	Slovak: Sobota	5
Georgian: Sabati	4	Slovene: Sobota	2
Greek: Savvato	13	Somali: Sabti	15
Hebrew: Shabbat	6	Spanish: Sabado	399
Indonesian: Sabtu	77	Sudanese: Saptu	45
Italian: Sabato	58	Ukranian: Subota	40

(Number of speakers in millions, rounded)

What Day Is The LORD'S DAY?

Rev. 1:10

For the Son of man is Lord even of the sabbath day.

Matthew 12:8 KJV

Chapter 17 | What Day Is The Lord's Day?

I was in the Spirit on the Lord's day, and heard behind me a great voice, as of a trumpet, Saying, I am Alpha and Omega, the first and the last:

John could certainly worship any day of the week. However, he is specific this day is the Lord's day in which he is in the Spirit. Messiah, on His day, declares He is the Alpha and Omega or the beginning and the end. He appears and speaks to John on His day. However, we are told this refers to a new day for Sabbath in which He moved it with His resurrection. Did He say that? No. Did any Apostle write such? Not one. We have proven that at this point. In fact, this is the only time this term is used in all of scripture. No Apostle even uses it.

There is a day of the Lord in Isaiah, Jeremiah, Ezekiel, Joel, Amos Obadiah, Zephaniah and Malachi as well as multiple places in the New Testament. However, that is the Day of Judgment and that's not what John sees here. He will later in Revelation but not yet. He refers to Jesus'*(Yahusha's)* day. What day of the week could that be? What day does He say is His?

We have covered many times Messiah says He is Lord of the Sabbath Day *(Mark 2:27-28)*. No one would argue that at the time at which He said that, that day was the 7th day of the week or Saturday as we know it today and not Sunday. Did He change that day? He never said He did and since He is Lord of the Sabbath, the only day ever called out as His day, He could change it if that were ever something remotely desirable to Him. No Apostle ever said He did. No Apostle ever observed the Sabbath any other day but the 7th day that we have proven. You will find them meeting different days but you will never find them abandoning the Sabbath to do so as they would never replace the Lord's day with any other day. So where does this thinking originate? Judaism still keeps the Sabbath on the 7th day though by the wrong calendar we proved.

The argument begins in a false paradigm. Should we keep the Lord's Day or the Sabbath Day. It is like saying: Should we eat popcorn or corn that is popped. Anyone telling you the Lord's Day is anything but the Sabbath is illiterate of scripture. Scripture uses the term once yet tells us Messiah is Lord of the Sabbath. No one can actually debate that. However, the mantra continues over possibly thousands of years.

You will find this stems from the illiterate reading of the Gospels for the resurrection account which we fully examined. The account is clear Messiah rose on the Sabbath on the 7th Day. No scholar really argues that Saturday has been the 7th Day throughout history. Yet, they claim He changed it to Sunday with His resurrection because they cannot read and understand the Bible calendar that does not match the Roman nor Pharisee/Babylonian one.

However, let us examine some of the history behind this. We know the Apostles kept the Sabbath and so did the true early ekklesia. When we find one changing the Sabbath even that far back, it is a sign of an ekklesia that is not following the Bible. It is believed that the earliest example of the move from Saturday to Sunday is The Letter of Barnabas. This is never proven to actually be a letter written by any Apostle especially Barnabas and it did not even make the Catholic Canon thus even the ancient Catholics knew it was not representative of scripture. Their major problem is there is not a single Bible support for this illiterate position. They are stretching. These are the men who "crept in." This is where the Catholic scholars produce their laundry list of men who were changing the Word.

The Letter of Barnabas: 74 A.D.:

"We keep the eighth day [Sunday] with joyfulness, the day also on which Jesus rose again from the dead" —Letter of Barnabas 15:6–8. [84]

In those days, keeping the Sabbath on Sunday would be a rogue congregation or better yet false church. You do not go against the teachings of the Apostles and claim you are part of their ekklesia. Still early, Ignatius of Antioch claims a Sunday doctrine of the Lord's day. He is joined by a repeated control line as has always been the case. In the Catholic Church, you would follow their doctrine or in many cases, face imprisonment or death.

In fact, as we covered those preaching and keeping the Sabbath in the Eastern Church especially Turkey, you will note, many of them became martyrs. They were killed for keeping the Sabbath and the Law that the Apostles kept just as the Apostles were murdered for doing so. This is how they followed the example of Messiah. They loved Him and kept His Commandments. However, these men did not. They are not representative of His ekklesia. These are not "early church fathers" in the sense of Biblical principles. They are the founders of a new religion infusing the New Testament into their Persian/Babylonian religion of choice.

Ignatius of Antioch: 110 A.D.:

"[T]hose who were brought up in the ancient order of things [i.e. Jews] have come to the possession of a new hope, no longer observing the Sabbath, but living in the observance of the Lord's day, on which also our life has sprung up again by him and by his death" –Letter to the Magnesians 8. [85]

Justin Martyr: 155 A.D.:

"But Sunday is the day on which we all hold our common assembly, because it is the first day on which God, having wrought a change in the darkness and matter, made the world; and Jesus Christ our Savior on the same day rose from the dead" –First Apology 67. [86]

The Didascalia: 225 A.D.:

*"The apostles further appointed: On the first day of the week let there be service, and the reading of the holy scriptures, and the oblation [sacrifice of the Mass], because on the first day of the week [i.e., Sunday] our Lord rose from the place of the dead, and on the first day of the week he arose upon the world, and on the first day of the week he ascended up to heaven, and on the first day of the week he will appear at last with the angels of heaven"
–Didascalia 2 [A.D. 225]. [87]*

Origen: 229 A.D.:

"Hence it is not possible that the [day of] rest after the Sabbath should have come into existence from the seventh [day] of our God. On the contrary, it is our Savior who, after the pattern of his own rest, caused us to be made in the likeness of his death, and hence also of his resurrection"
—Commentary on John 2:28. [88]

Victorinus: 300 A.D.:

"The sixth day [Friday] is called parasceve, that is to say, the preparation of the kingdom. . . . On this day also, on account of the passion of the Lord Jesus Christ, we make either a station to God or a fast. On the seventh day he rested from all his works, and blessed it, and sanctified it. On the former day we are accustomed to fast rigorously, that on the Lord's day we may go forth to our bread with giving of thanks. And let the parasceve become a rigorous fast, lest we should appear to observe any Sabbath with the Jews . . . which Sabbath he [Christ] in his body abolished" —The Creation of the World. [89]

We could continue with many more over time. One can easily identify the anti-ekklesia in these writings. For not to keep the Sabbath, proves they are not even believers according to Hebrews 4. They cannot change the Bible. If they do not match it's practices which we have well-proven, they are no early fathers of anything but an infused religion that once again, Yahuah rejects just as in Samaria.

As we demonstrated, in around the 3rd and 4th centuries especially, one can observe their change in trying to infuse Sunday as equal to Saturday. That is how many started with this in whole. Once that equation occurred, Pandora's box was opened and this emboldened them to force Sunday as the Sabbath.

However, there is no such term for Sunday being the Lord's day in all of scripture. This one time John uses it, he must and can only refer to the Saturday, 7th-Day Sabbath. If John was invoking Sunday there, that would be new doctrine and strange. John had no such authority and neither did the so-called "early church" which was really the early Synagogue of Satan infusion.

Through history, one can observe the dumbing down and wearing down in propaganda. It is no different today. These evil agents know what tactic works and eventually good men will stand aside and do nothing to stop them from performing evil deeds. Changing the Sabbath is an evil deed. It is not just a misunderstanding, it is a purposeful lie knowingly. It cannot be done accidentally nor do they claim such. These historic references from the Catholics allow one to track the apostate church through history that has stood on the wrong side of the Bible because it is not their basis. They appear as the world, as pagans because that is what they represent and always have. Even non-Christians knew this and that is sad. The fact that Faustus could level such a charge that the Catholic Church looked and acted as pagan as the pagans with nothing separating them, is a clear indicator that they were not fooling everyone even in that age.

> *"You celebrate the solemn festivals of the Gentiles, … and as to their manners, those you have retained without any alteration. Nothing distinguishes you from the pagans except that you hold your assemblies apart from them."*
> *—Faustus (a non-Christian) to St. Augustine (4th Century), cited in History of the Intellectual Development of Europe, John William Draper, M.D., LL.D., vol. 1, p. 310. [90]*

One will find one sympathizer after another placating this paganism infusion with the Bible but Yahuah does not. He never has and this is about Him and His ways.

> *"This legislation by Constantine probably bore no relation to Christianity; it appears, on the contrary, that the emperor, in his capacity of Pontifex Maximus, was only adding the day of the sun, the worship of which was then firmly established in the Roman Empire, to the other ferial days of the sacred calendar." —Prof. Hutton Webster, Ph.D. (University of Nebraska), Rest Days, p. 122.[91]*

It began in subtle fashion and as evil always does would rear it's ugliness right away.

> *"What began, however, as a pagan ordinance, ended as a Christian regulation; and a long series of imperial decrees, during the fourth, fifth, and*

sixth centuries, enjoined with increasing stringency abstinence from labor on Sunday." –Ibid., p. 270. [92]

Then it becomes braggadocious about it's role in this abomination.

"The church took the pagan philosophy and made it the buckler of faith against the heathen. She took the pagan Roman Pantheon, temple of all the gods, and made it sacred to all the martyrs; so it stands to this day. She took the pagan Sunday and made it the Christian Sunday. She took the pagan Easter and made it the feast we celebrate during this season…"

"The sun was a foremost god with heathendom…. There is, in truth, something royal, kingly about the sun, making it a fit emblem of Jesus, the Sun of justice. Hence the church in these countries would seem to have said, 'Keep that old pagan name. It shall remain consecrated, sanctified.' And thus the pagan Sunday, dedicated to Balder [the god of light and peace], became the Christian Sunday, sacred to Jesus."
–Catholic World, Vol. 58, no. 348, March, 1894, p. 809. [93]

Why Sunday Instead of Saturday?

The Catholic Church was founded by the High Priest of Mithraism – Constantine the "Not-So Great." Certainly, part of the church, though not the true ekklesia especially the Eastern church from Turkey and Kurdistan, did observe Sunday though unbiblical even before his days. However, he made Sunday observance law. The true church continued the practice of the Apostles that we already well proved. We also witnessed some churches beginning to observe Sunday while holding onto the Saturday Sabbath. The Catholics would seize on their lukewarm behavior and pressure them to abolish Sabbath.

The fact is this is Mithraism. Sunday is the day of the "invincible sun" which Constantine pledged his allegiance and that is what he forced in his Sunday law. SUNday was very sacred to them. It is not to the Bible practice. It is another day of 7 never set apart and sanctified as the Sabbath nor can it be. Messiah is the only one who could have changed that and He did not. His resurrection was on the 7th Day so using

Catholic reasoning, they should still be keeping the Saturday Sabbath.

> *"The devotees of Mithra held Sunday sacred because Mithra was identified with the 'invincible sun.' —Letter to C. P. Bollman from W. de C. Ravenel, administrative assistant to the secretary of the Smithsonian Institution, Washington, D. C., quoted in Sunday, p. 3. [72]*

> *"They held Sunday sacred, and celebrated the birth of the Sun on the 25th of December." —The Mysteries of Mithra (1910), pp. 190, 191. [73]*

> *"The Christian church made no formal but a gradual and almost unconscious transference of the one day to the other."*
> *—Archdeacon F. W. Farrar, The Voice From Sinai (1892), p. 167. [94]*

This is Mithraism, the Persian religion once again being infused into the Bible practice just as the Samaritans as imposters and replacements did in the Northern Kingdom. Yahuah rejects Catholicism.

Dr. Peter Heylyn (Church of England):
> *"It was near 900 years from our Saviour's birth, if not quite so much, before restraint of husbandry on this day, had been first thought of in the East; and probably being thus restrained, did find no more obedience there, than it had done before in the Western parts."*
> *—History of the Sabbath, part 2, chap. 5, par. 6. [95]*

Bishop Grimelund of Norway:
> *"Now, summing up what history teaches regarding the origin of Sunday and the development of the doctrine about Sunday, then this is the sum: It is not the apostles, not the early Christians, nor the councils of the ancient church which have imprinted the name and stamp of the Sabbath upon the Sunday, but it is the Church of the Middle Ages and its scholastic teachers."*
> *—Sondagens Historie, p. 37. [96]*

What happened in Europe in the Middle Ages? The Pharisees migrated from the Russian Steppes into many parts of Europe in great number.

They began to infuse their Yiddish language into Hebrew and all of the Languages essentially adding letters and new rules. The Jews were bankers and merchants as well which earned them exile from about 70 countries around the world for their unethical usury and treason. This was followed by a direct infiltration welcomed by the Catholic Church as the Jesuit Order that would continue the same. They, too, would be exiled from over 70 countries for the same reason. Today, those are called anti-semites or racists for displacing them. However, these agitators seize economies and religions. It is what Pharisees have always done. They did in Samaria, followed in conquering the Temple in Judaea, Josephus places them migrating into the Russian Steppes in at least two migrations. Those were not Lost Tribes of Israel; they were Pharisees. They migrate into Europe from there and have infiltrated the highest levels of most governments on Earth.

In time, they would set their sights on defiling the very Land of Creation that is the origin of the first Sabbath. For Adam was not taken into the Garden until later. This land has been identified in our book, The Search for King Solomon's Treasure supported by a 300-page Sourcebook. We fully prove that land is the Philippines. With the Philippines we even find a further tie to this Land of Creation in the name of Cebu which is originally spelled Sebu. This is a Hebrew derivative of the word Shavuot, the Feast representing the Day of Covenant Renewal according to the Book of Jubilees. It is defined, as we covered, as being kept by Adam and creation, Noah, Abraham and Moses. Messiah was born on this day during this Feast following Isaac's birth.

Notice, how entrenched Catholicism has forced itself in this land called the modern Philippines. They are there to defile the Sabbath as they hate it. They have always hated Yahuah's ways and never represented it since their inception. However, the Philippines will be the first to shake off the Catholic Church in prophecy and condemn it and the New World Order even according to Messiah *(Matt. 12:42)*, Isaiah *(60:9)* and Ezekiel *(38)*.

The true Lord's Day, Saturday, will be restored in this land in time as they restore His ways and His Laws. However, we all can look forward to this beginning in our own personal lives now. We can end this reign of terror from this Beast. Keep the Sabbath holy and restore the power of rest exposing their chaos in your life weekly.

Sebu = Sebat = Sabbath

the feast &
7th year
SABBATH,
Jubilee
& Millennium
the shortened form
tened form of us, as
Sabbath noun a day
worship and rest fr

Chapter 18 | Special Sabbaths: Days and Years

Sabbath rest also comes in other forms as there are extra Annual Sabbaths throughout the year within certain Biblical Feasts, the 7th-year Sabbath to rest one's land, the 50th year Jubilee and we will examine the Millennium Sabbath to come as well. Some observe that scripture denotes a Sabbath that begins in the evening. Indeed there is. It is called a Feast Sabbath timed with a Feast that begins in the evening such as the Day of Atonement. This has no impact on the Weekly Sabbath timing and is not a Weekly Sabbath. It is a special observance once a year for that Feast. Anyone claiming to change the entire calendar for such has no interest in representing scripture. The day begins at sunrise not in the evening. However, some Feasts do begin in the evening such as Passover as the original Passover was indeed historically an evening event. However, this is no way changes the Day Clock because of such special observance once a year. Those who say it does, lack reason.

Feasts and Their Sabbaths

On an annual basis, the Biblical Feasts have Sabbaths built into them in observance as well. Understand some of them have evening beginnings. However, applying that back to the Weekly Sabbath in attempt to change it's observance is unfounded and illogical. The day still begins at sunrise and so does the Weekly Sabbath. Feasts such as Atonement are sometimes driven by evening events beginning at sundown. On the tenth of the seventh Hebrew month, we, including Gentiles even from the Exodus all along, are to observe one day per year where we atone for our sins. This does not mean you cannot or do not ask forgiveness anytime but the Feast remains as it is a statute for ever. In the Old Testament, the blood of bulls, goats, etc. would be offered in atonement. That was not perfect and Messiah has now become our sacrificial lamb for all occasions including the 52 Weekly Sabbaths and all 7 Biblical Feasts. We do not offer the blood of animals in sacrifice any longer because that is imperfect and Messiah was our sacrifice once and for all. This does not change the observance however. Messiah reinforced the Feasts and Sabbaths. He did not do away with them.

Atonement is a shadow of the coming Day of Judgment when all who ever lived will be judged. For those saying it was fulfilled by Messiah and erroneously applying that definition as passed away, they really have done no research on the topic. A prophetic event that has not occurred has not passed away in observance. The notion is ludicrous and unscholarly.

Day of Atonement: A Special Sabbath

> ***Leviticus 16:29-31 KJV (Day of Atonement)***
> *And this shall be a **statute for ever** unto you: that in the **seventh month**, on the **tenth day** of the month, ye shall afflict your souls, and do no work at all, whether it be **one of your own country, or a stranger that sojourneth among you**: For on that day shall the priest make an atonement for you, to cleanse you, that ye may be clean from all your sins before the LORD. **It shall be a sabbath of rest unto you**, and ye shall afflict your souls, by **a statute for ever**.*

This is a "special" Sabbath that according to the Qumran Calendar falls on a Thursday evening to Friday evening. You will find cleansing and atonement lasting until evening in scripture many times. However, once again, we have a perfect Biblical example demonstrating when the Biblical day begins. Above the tenth day is referenced. However, later in Leviticus 23, this is clarified and you will find this event begins in the evening of the ninth day and lasts 24 hours to the evening of the tenth day. It is both the ninth and tenth day – portions of both. The Biblical day cannot begin in the evening at sunset and be characterized by Yahuah speaking to Moses in such fashion. If 24 hours from sunset to sunset is two different days, then, sunset cannot be the measure for the beginning

1 Day Of Atonement

The Bible defines 1 day for Atonement each year as a Feast. It is a 24-hour period. If one follows the lunar calendar this has to be stretched to 2 days which is what many do today yet it cannot work. It can only be one day total. Atonement is an evening concept throughout scripture. However, these passages tell us this is from the 9th in the evening to the 10th in the evening (Lev. 16:29, 23:32). However it is 1 day of 24 hours. The only way to view 24 hours of a 2-day period as 1 day but 2 dates is to recognize the first day ends and the new begins within the period. As it is defined as sunset or 1/2 day on the 9th, and also being on the 10th for 1/2 day ending at sunset, this Feast proves the day begins at sunrise.

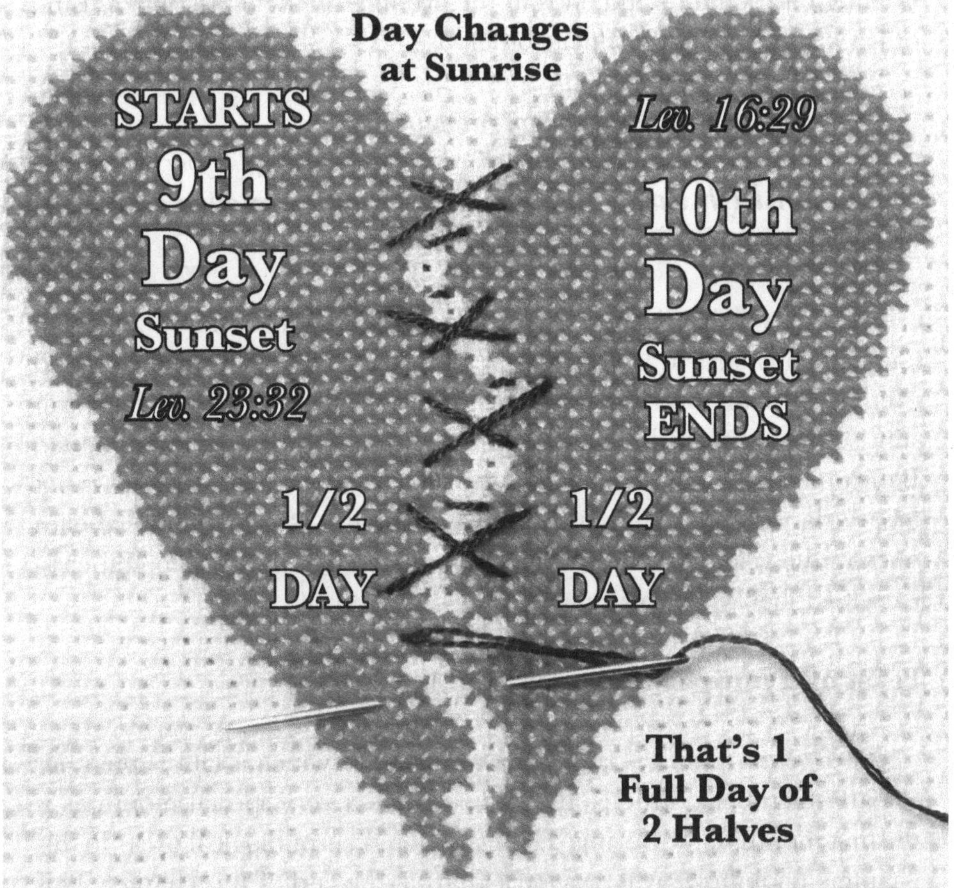

Day Changes at Sunrise

STARTS
9th
Day
Sunset
Lev. 23:32

Lev. 16:29
10th
Day
Sunset
ENDS

1/2 DAY

1/2 DAY

That's 1 Full Day of 2 Halves

This Feast is the shadow of the Day of Judgment to come. It cannot pass away before it has happened nor does it according to Messiah in Matthew 5:17-20. Even in these passages this applies to the Hebrew Israelite and the Gentile known as "strangers that sojourn among you." This is not a "Jewish" Feast, it's a Bible one from before Israel was a nation. Jacob mourned for Joseph on this day before (Jub. 33:17-19, 34:18, 5:17-18).

of the day. This has been right there in scripture for thousands of years yet completely misconstrued in willing ignorance. Leviticus 23 confirms the Biblical day begins at sunrise not sunset. Many misunderstand this and even attempt to use this passage to define the day because this Feast, which is a "special" Sabbath not a Weekly Sabbath, begins in the evening. However, when one reads chapter 16 and 23 together fully defining this event, it is spread over two days not one. It begins in the evening on the ninth and ends in the evening of the tenth. There is no other way this would reconcile otherwise.

> ***Leviticus 23:32 KJV (Day of Atonement)***
> *It shall be unto you a* **sabbath of rest**, *and ye shall afflict your souls:* in the **ninth day** *of the month at even, from even unto even, shall ye celebrate your sabbath*.

Again, this is the ninth from evening to evening in Leviticus 23 which chapter 16 is clear it is also on the tenth day. This ends on the second evening. The only way it can cross into two dates is if the day begins at sunrise not sunset. This very verse used to attempt to justify the lunar, Babylonian calendar actually says the opposite. Notice as well, this is not a Saturday and not the routine Weekly Sabbath. It is an added Sabbath once in the year. The seventh Hebrew month falls in late September to early October when this Feast is to be observed.

Feast of Trumpets: A Special Sabbath

The seventh month on the Hebrew calendar which is late September to early October on the Roman calendar, is a very special month as is the first month in the Spring. These are not in chronological order in this chapter. Though we will provide a chart at the end of this chapter. This is another prophetic event foreshadowing the coming days in which the trump shall sound. Again, as that has not happened yet, anyone calling themselves a scholar claiming it has passed in observance is not credible. This Feast represents a special Sabbath and a gathering or convocation and falls on a Wednesday on the Qumran calendar. Thus, this is not the Weekly Sabbath but additional.

Leviticus 23:23-25 KJV (Feast of Trumpets: Yom Teruah)
And the LORD spake unto Moses, saying, Speak unto the children of Israel,
saying, In the **seventh month,** *in the* **first day of the month,**
shall ye have a **sabbath,** *a memorial of blowing of trumpets,* **an holy**
convocation. *Ye shall do no servile work therein: but ye shall offer an*
offering made by fire unto the LORD.

The Pharisees erroneous label this as Rosh Hashanah meaning "Head of the Year" as their false New Year. There is not a single scriptural support for such. They will tell you the term is not even mentioned in the Bible yet they seemingly cannot even read Hebrew as it is most certainly in the Bible as Abib 1 in the Spring not Yom Teruah or the Feast of Trumpets. The New Year or "Head of the Year" is always in the Spring and never in the Fall in the Bible. That is the Babylonian calendar just as they follow the Babylonian Lunar calendar. It is Pharisee leaven as are many of their flawed expansions including their expanding it to a 2-day event that is not Bible. It begins on the ninth of the seventh month in the evening and ends in the evening on the tenth. That is only one day not two. It seems they feel confident enough to have the license to change scripture. This will earn them a special judgment and they will regret such unbiblical behavior.

Ezekiel 40:1 KJV (Rosh Hashanah not Feast of Trumpets)
In the five and twentieth year of our captivity, in the **beginning of the**
year *(בראש: rô'sh: head: H7218; השנה: shâneh: year: H8141), in the*
tenth day of the month, in the fourteenth year after that the city was smitten, in
the selfsame day the hand of the LORD was upon me, and brought me thither.

Some will attempt to manipulate Ezekiel 40:1 in which the Prophet tells us it was the beginning of the year or first month in the tenth day. Ezekiel is identifying Abib 10 not the Feast of Trumpets in that passage and it is the tenth day of that first month. It requires a profound ability of ignorance to manipulate scripture in such fashion but this is a talent of Pharisees that is why we are warned of their leaven. Furthermore, the year has one beginning not two. It is rather insane to even suggest such. The Bible never calls Yom Teruah or Feast of Trumpets the beginning

of the New Year or Rosh Hashanah. In fact, there is another reference
to the start of the months.

> ### Exodus 12:2 KJV (Rosh Hashanah not Feast of Trumpets)
> *This month shall be unto you the **beginning of months** (ראש: rô'sh:
> head: H7218; חדשים: chôdeshim: months: H2320): it shall be the first
> month of the year to you.*

Exodus makes clear in verse 6 that this first month is the same as the
month of Passover that is Abib. There is a reason why the Bible numbers
months many times. It begins it's year in the first month not the seventh
month. The Bible was never changed by the Levite Priests who kept it.
It was changed by Pharisees following their Babylonian Lunar calendar
that we have seen they followed even in the first century.

Feast of Tabernacles: 2 Special Sabbaths

The longest celebration of the year is the Feast of Sukkot or Tabernacles
or Booths/Tents. On this day in history, it becomes a remembrance
of Israel's journey living in temporary housing in the wilderness for
40 years. This also marks the day in which Israel entered the land of
Canaan as well. The Book of Jubilees tells us Abraham observed this
long before the Exodus. However, Tabernacles represents a prophetic
event when all believers receive our permanent bodies after the Day of
Judgment. Once again, all three Fall Feasts have not been fulfilled and
there is no literate language that could assume they passed away.

> ### Leviticus 23:33-36 KJV (Feast of Tabernacles)
> *And the LORD spake unto Moses, saying, Speak unto the children of Israel,
> saying, The **fifteenth day of this seventh month** shall be the **feast
> of tabernacles for seven days** unto the LORD. On the **first day
> shall be an holy convocation**: ye shall do **no servile work** therein.
> Seven days ye shall offer an offering made by fire unto the LORD: **on the
> eighth day shall be an holy convocation** unto you; and ye shall
> offer an offering made by fire unto the LORD: it is a solemn assembly; and ye
> shall do **no servile work** therein.*

Leviticus 23:39 KJV (Feast of Tabernacles)
*Also in the **fifteenth day of the seventh month,** when ye have gathered in the fruit of the land, ye shall keep a feast unto the LORD seven days: on the **first day shall be a sabbath,** and on the **eighth day shall be a sabbath**.*

This 8-day period has two special Sabbaths within. Don't forget, there is also a Weekly Sabbath in the middle as well. The first day on the fifteenth is a Special Sabbath and assembly and the eighth day on the twenty-second is a Special Sabbath and assembly as well. These are Wednesdays on the Qumran calendar with a routine Saturday Sabbath in between. Also, Jubilees 16:21 and 29 record Abraham was the first to keep this Feast not Moses in origin.

Feasts of Passover and Unleavened Bread: 2 Special Sabbaths

The Spring Feasts continue to affirm that the Biblical calendar begins at sunrise even though some of the Feasts such as Passover are based on evening events in history and begin as such. Those looking for Passover to begin during the day with the calendar are simply ignoring the facts of the event itself. When Leviticus defines Passover and Unleavened Bread, you will notice Passover begins in the Evening and is only an evening event as that is when it occurred. Even the Passover Lamb is to be fully eaten or the remainder burnt by sunrise the next day *(Ex. 12:10)*. Sunrise is the next day on the Biblical calendar recorded now as the fifteenth no longer the fourteenth.

Here, Leviticus names Passover evening the fourteenth and the next day which is the first day of Unleavened Bread which begins in the day not at night, as the fifteenth. This does not change the fact that Passover still falls within Unleavened Bread in date and practice. These are misconstrued when one uses the wrong calendar from the Pharisees and they have a gap that does not exist in scripture as Passover and Unleavened Bread flow together. There is no half-day gap of nothingness in scripture separating them but Unleavened Bread is 7 days with no gap and begins on the 14th in the evening as Passover.

> ***Leviticus 23:4-8 KJV (Passover & Unleavened Bread)***
>
> *These are the feasts of the LORD, even **holy convocations**, which ye shall proclaim in their seasons. In the **fourteenth day of the first month at even** is the **LORD'S passover**. And on the **fifteenth day of the same month is the feast of unleavened bread** unto the LORD: **seven days ye must eat unleavened bread**. In the **first day** ye shall have an holy **convocation**: ye shall do **no servile work** therein. But ye shall offer an offering made by fire unto the LORD seven days: in the **seventh day** is an holy **convocation**: ye shall do **no servile work** therein.*

Exodus provides further clarity and confirmation that the Biblical day begins at sunrise here. The entire period of Passover and Unleavened Bread together is 7 days. It begins on the 14th of Abib in the Evening and that is both Passover and Unleavened Bread as it is included in the 7-day count for Unleavened Bread of which one is not to partake of leaven. This is exactly a 7-day period from the 14th evening ending on the evening of the 21st. There is no other way to reconcile this.

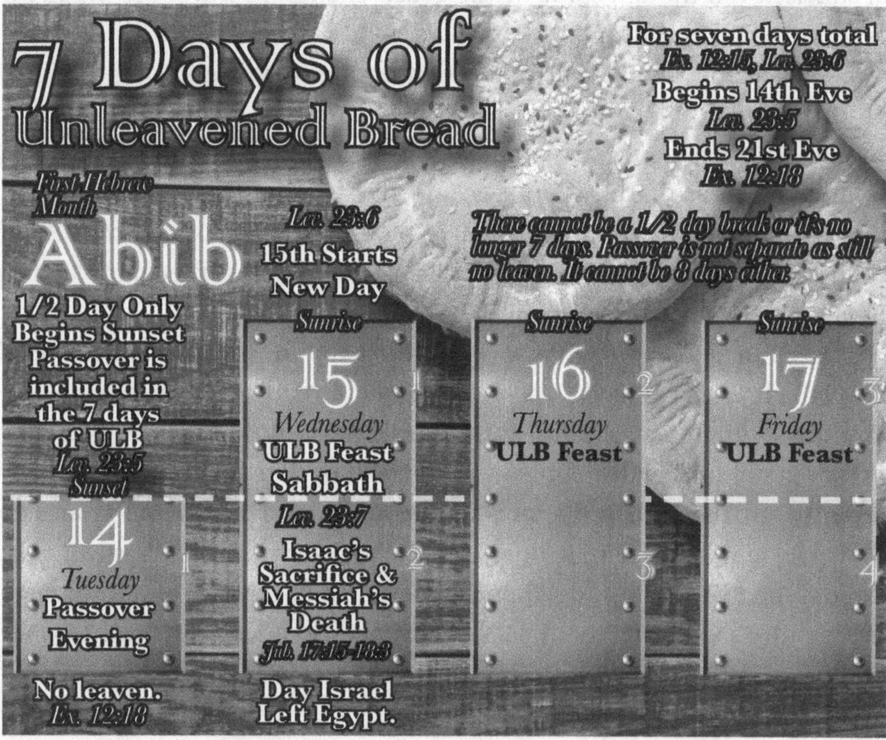

Exodus 12:15-20 KJV (Unleavened Bread)
*'**Seven days you shall eat unleavened bread**. On the **first day** you shall **remove leaven from your houses**. For whoever eats leavened bread from the first day until the seventh day, that person shall be cut off from Israel. 'On the **first day** there shall be a holy **convocation**, and on the **seventh day** there shall be a holy **convocation** for you. **No manner of work** shall be done on them; **but that which everyone must eat**—that only may be prepared by you. 'So you shall observe the **Feast of Unleavened Bread**, for on **this same day I will have brought your armies out of the land of Egypt**. Therefore you shall observe this day **throughout your generations as an everlasting ordinance**. 'In the **first month, on the fourteenth day of the month at evening**, you shall **eat unleavened bread, until the twenty-first day of the month at evening**. 'For **seven days no leaven** shall be found in your houses, since whoever eats what is leavened, that same person shall be cut off from the congregation of Israel, **whether he is a stranger or a native** of the land. 'You shall eat nothing leavened; in all your dwellings you shall eat unleavened bread.'"*

The Book of Jubilees 17:15-18:3 records that Abraham celebrated this Feast of Unleavened bread offering Isaac in sacrifice on the 15th of Abib. This would become the same day in which Messiah would be crucified as well. He follows the Covenant as Isaac was the child of covenant promise. He does not follow the Passover Lamb.

Unfortunately, Pharisees and many scholars appear very challenged in the arena of math. For this Feast of both Passover and Unleavened Bread is a total of 7 days. It begins on the 14th of Abib but in the Evening and ends exactly 7 days later on the 21st at sunset. The 7 days of Unleavened Bread include Passover. In fact, Passover carries the same rule as we are not to partake of leaven that night as well. In scripture these two are synonymous as this is referred to as Passover within the 7 days after the 14th at times, and Passover as ULB and that remains appropriate. These are indeed interchangeable.

Unleavened Bread separates on the 15th but also began on the 14th in the evening at the same time as Passover. The 14th evening is called the Passover in title but again, it also is a portion of Unleavened Bread according to scripture. We know this because you cannot get from the 15th to only half a day on the 21st and call that 7 days. It is 6.5. You also cannot ignore that Passover is a day of eating unleavened bread. The previous chart demonstrates this. The fact that a Feast beginning in the evening is noted as special already identifies that day does not begin then. However, the chart *[previous page]* well demonstrates these 7 days lead to the Biblical day start at sunrise not sunset.

Even more importantly, if Unleavened Bread began on the 15th but the day started in the evening on the Lunar calendar, you not only lose a 1/2 day from when Passover ends and ULB begins, but those do not believe the Bible which says ULB is 7 days ending on the 21st in the evening. It would only be 6. Even with Passover, it would only be 6.5. Not only is Passover part of that count and thus, still Unleavened Bread, but that supposed 1/2 day gap must also be included meaning it does not exist. There can be no gap. Otherwise, the count is wrong. We are counting to 7 here and yet, that appears very difficult for many scholars. They know math better than that. Peter called it willing ignorance and that defines our era.

Also, though Atonement and Passover/Unleavened Bread begin in the evening as atonement is an evening concept and Passover was only an evening event, the other four Feasts begin in the daytime. It is glaring that these aforementioned Feasts specify they are different as beginning in the evening. That should tell us all something right there. For if the day began at sunset, there would be nothing of note about those three Feasts in beginning because they would begin at the start of the day as expected if that were the accurate paradigm. However, this is the opposite.

It is the other four Feasts that begin at sunrise which are treated in the mindset of the normal start of the day. There is no need for Moses to point that out because everyone knew that. Atonement and Passover/ULB are called out as beginning at a different time at sunset. That demonstrates the day does not begin at sunset but sunrise. Otherwise, there would be no reason to treat them as occurring at a special time but the other four would be treated so and they are not.

Further evidence the Bible day begins at sunrise. Isaac offered the 3rd day during the day.

First Fruits Offering:

When Israel entered the Promised Land, they were told to offer a First Fruit Offering to Yahuah from the land as a Feast Day. This is not an actual Feast itself but an offering along with sacrifices. The Priest would wave the offering to prove it acceptable to Yahuah. Some try to place this on different days but it says this occurs on the morrow after the Sabbath. Sabbath is Saturday and tomorrow is Sunday. This is always a Sunday and on the Qumran calendar, it is quantified to Sunday, the 26th of Abib specifically. This is not a moving target nor does it matter what one calls the barley harvest in Modern Israel that cannot change it. This is a fixed date every year as demonstrated in multiple years of calendars in Qumran. This was always the 26th.

> ***Leviticus 23:10-14 KJV (First Fruits)***
>
> *Speak unto the children of Israel, and say unto them, When ye be come into the land which I give unto you, and shall reap the harvest thereof, then ye shall **bring a sheaf of the firstfruits of your harvest unto the priest**: And he shall **wave the sheaf** before the LORD, to be accepted for you: **on the morrow after the sabbath** the priest shall wave it. And ye shall offer that day when ye wave the sheaf **an he lamb** without blemish of the first year for a **burnt offering** unto the LORD. And the meat offering thereof shall be two tenth deals of fine flour mingled with oil, an offering made by fire unto the LORD for a sweet savour: and the drink offering thereof shall be of wine, the fourth part of an hin. And ye shall eat neither bread, nor parched corn, nor green ears, until the selfsame day that ye have brought an offering unto your God: it shall be a **statute for ever throughout your generations in all your dwellings**.*

Many attempt to claim this Feast occurs in the middle of the Feast of Unleavened Bread. However, they are not reading the passage. ULB is already mentioned as ending after 7 days on the 21st in the Evening. That is Tuesday. It then, describes this next Feast Day occurs the day after the Sabbath. The next Sabbath after Tuesday, the 21st is Saturday, the 25th on the Qumran Temple Priest Calendar. The next day is Sunday, the 26th. This further reconciles as accurate when you realize

Shavuot is exactly 50 days after that on Sivan 15 in the third month. This aligns, the Pharisee calendar never does. First Fruits is not recorded as a Special Sabbath in scripture. If you have been keeping it, it does not harm anything to keep an extra Sabbath each year.

Noah also instituted a First Fruit Offering in the Book of Jubilees 7:36 though a date is not given. Abraham offered a First Fruit Offering to Melchizedek in Jubilees 13:25 as well. Once again, this Feast predates the nation of Israel and Moses.

Feast of Shavuot: A Special Sabbath

The most overlooked Biblical Feast is the most important of all. It is also a Special Sabbath. The Feast of Shavuot which is it's Hebrew name is also known as the Day of Pentecost in Greek or the Feast of Weeks in English translation. Shavuot, or really Shabuot as there is no "V" in Ancient Hebrew, simply means weeks.

> שבוע: *shâbûwaʻ, shaw-boo'-ah;* or שבע: *shâbuaʻ;*
> *also (feminine)* שבעה: *shᵉbuʻâh (H7620)*

Some attempt a different day for Pentecost but that is not founded in scripture as it is Shavout, the Feast of Weeks as well. There are only 7 Biblical Feasts represented by Yahuah's number of completion – seven. It is the Greek word for the Feast of Weeks because it is represented by a counting of 50. We find this affirmed in the Book of Tobit as well as the Qumran Temple Priests' local writings according to Geza Vermes.

> ### Tobit 2:1 KJVA
> *"Now when I was come home again, and my wife Anna was restored unto me, with my son Tobias, in the feast of Pentecost, which is the holy feast of the seven weeks, there was a good dinner prepared me, in the which I sat down to eat."*
>
> *One of these festivals, the Feast of the New Wheat, coincided with the Feast of Weeks and was for the Essenes/Therapeutae (No Essenes lived in Qumran but the Sons of Zadok, exiled Temple Priests.) also the principal holy day of*

> *the year, that of the Renewal of the Covenant, the importance of which is discussed above. From the Book of Jubilees, where, as has been said, the same calendar is followed, it is clear that Pentecost (the Feast of Weeks), together with the Feast of the Renewal of the Covenant, were celebrated on the fifteenth day of the third month (Sivan) (Jub. vi, 17-19; cf. also 4Q266 fr. 11 ii; 270 fr. 7 ii). —Introduction by Geza Vermes [1]*

This is treated in some circles as a different counting every year to find this elusive date but that is not Bible. Shavuot/Pentecost is also a fixed date on Sivan 15. It never moves and the counting of 50 was done and settled by Moses. No one needs to count it out again nor does Modern Israel's barley harvest, etc. have any significance in changing this fixed date that does not ever move. It is unscholarly to suggest that a Biblical Feast was a moving target.

Granted, the true Hebrew calendar must then be reconciled with our Roman calendar to pinpoint the date but that is only one added day off most years and two on leap year, not the weeks that modern Judaism represents in annual changes much of the time. Their dates are based on the Babylonian Lunar Calendar they follow which is also their religion not the Bible. Jubilees, as we covered, condemns that calendar as following the moon for days, weeks, months and years, causes one to err and the year comes in 10 days too soon.

Some also attempt to go to the next Weekly Sabbath and count but this language is the same as the previous verses for the First Fruit Offering. "The morrow after the Sabbath" is the First Fruit Offering day that it then fully identifies as the day in which the priest waved the sheaf. Shavuot is 50 days from there. That occurs on Abib 26 every year and count 50 days and it brings one to Sivan 15 on Shavuot. One only has to count once and again, Moses already conducted that count for us. However, we will substantiate that further. Additionally, this is another Feast that many celebrate over 2 days yet the Bible is clear it is one only.

There are yet others who try to read this as counting 49 days and then, another 50 days but that not only does not fit the language, the Qumran exiled Temple Priests who kept the Bible calendar demonstrate this as Sivan 15 year after year just as 50 days earlier they plot the First

Fruit Offering. There is nothing to debate. This is tied to First Fruits as Shavuot is the actual Feast of First Fruits whereas the offering on Abib 26 is just that but not a full Feast.

> ***Leviticus 23:15-21 KJV (Shavuot/Pentecost/Feast of Weeks)***
> *And ye shall **count unto you from the morrow after the sabbath, from the day that ye brought the sheaf of the wave offering; seven sabbaths shall be complete: Even unto the morrow after the seventh sabbath shall ye number fifty days;** and ye shall offer a new meat offering unto the LORD. Ye shall bring out of your habitations two wave loaves of two tenth deals: they shall be of fine flour; they shall be baken with leaven; they are the firstfruits unto the LORD. And ye shall offer with the bread seven lambs without blemish of the first year, and one young bullock, and two rams: they shall be for a burnt offering unto the LORD, with their meat offering, and their drink offerings, even an offering made by fire, of sweet savour unto the LORD. Then ye shall sacrifice one kid of the goats for a sin offering, and two lambs of the first year for a sacrifice of peace offerings. And the priest shall wave them with the bread of the firstfruits for a wave offering before the LORD, with the two lambs: they shall be holy to the LORD for the priest. And ye shall proclaim on the selfsame day, that it may be an holy **convocation** unto you: ye shall do **no servile work** therein: it shall be a **statute for ever in all your dwellings throughout your generations**.*

How exactly does this counting work? Again, Moses already counted this and set the date on a fixed calendar. No one needs to calculate annually on the Hebrew calendar as it never moves. We know from Exodus that Israel reached Sinai in the third month.

> ***Exodus 19:1 KJV***
> *In the **third month**, when the children of Israel were gone forth out of the land of Egypt, the same day **came they into** the wilderness of **Sinai**.*

However, the modern Torah does not give this firm date and of course Rabbis speculate in error as usual. They claim it is Sivan 6 and they call it the day in which Torah was given to Moses. However, the Book of Jubilees which has historic precedence for being Torah and Pharisees historic precedence as mixing, confusing and even as liars according to Messiah. Moses went up to Sinai to receive Torah on the 16th of Sivan the day after he and Israel celebrated Shavuot.

> ### *Jubilees 1:1 (3rd Month 16, Day after Shavuot)*
> *And it came to pass in the first year of the exodus of the children of Israel out of Egypt, in the **third month, on the sixteenth day of the month**, that Elohim spake to Moses, saying: "Come up to Me on the Mount, and I will give thee two tables of stone of the law and of the commandment, which I have written, that thou mayst teach them."*

It took 40 days for Moses to write the first portions of Torah on Mt. Sinai not one day and by the time he was done and returned, it was no longer even Sivan. Thus, the Rabbis have this wrong yet again.

> ### *Jubilees 1:3-4*
> *And He called to Moses on the seventh day (Sivan 20) …out of the midst of the cloud, and the appearance of the glory of Yahuah was like a flaming fire on the top of the Mount. And Moses was on the Mount forty days and forty nights...* ***Sivan 16 + 40 = NO LONGER SIVAN!!!***

Shavuot is not about the giving of the Torah but instead this is the most precious of Feasts minimized in Judaism and the church today. We have forgotten it's purpose. This is the day once a year in which we are to renew covenant with The Father and Son. That is an annual event and most important in our walk and growing relationship. The covenant is not a one-time occurrence and this is the underlying fallacy of the modern church generally. They use that to undermine the so-called "Old" covenant as passed away yet ALL covenants are intertwined and a renewal not truly new. Yes, we have a new covenant with Messiah but it has the same foundation and tenets as the so-termed "Old." There is no "Old" only covenant or no covenant. The Rabbis lost this and the church lost the entire Old Testament basically. Even Noah observed the

Feast of Weeks. It is this day in which Yahuah set His rainbow in the sky as a reminder of His covenant not to flood the entire earth again. He has certainly kept that covenant and better hope He continues to. We still observe His rainbow yet we forget our part and that is not just covenant but the very day in which the rainbow originates – Shavuot. He reminds regularly and yet, most of us do not even know what it means.

> ***Jubilees 6:16-17***
>
> *He set His bow in the cloud for a sign of the **eternal covenant** that there should not again be a flood on the earth to destroy it **all the days of the earth**. For this reason it is **ordained and written on the heavenly tables**, that they should celebrate the **feast of week**s in this month once a year, **to renew the covenant every year**.*

Somehow, modern scholarship forgot what the word eternal means. It lost the meaning of forever and perpetual generations. This language accompanies every Feast and the Sabbath especially. These cannot ever pass away. If this concept of renewing covenant every year is foreign to us, then one must ask why? How have we lost Torah in understanding? How have we lost the most significant Feast in all of history? The hidden and suppressed Book of Jubilees defines Shavuot better than anything. The Pharisees do not read it nor did they 2,000 years ago because it condemns their doctrines. There is no reconciling Jubilees to Pharisaism and certainly no claiming a Pharisee wrote it which is one of the most inept poor assumptions we have seen in scholarship. Shavuot has historicity far beyond Moses as the oldest Feast really. It's origin is Creation, really the 7th day or Sheba day which is why it is Shebuah or Shavuot. It truly memorializes the first Sabbath, the first covenant.

> ***Jubilees 6:18-22***
>
> *And this whole festival was **celebrated in heaven from the day of creation till the days of Noah**-twenty-six jubilees and five weeks of years: and **Noah and his sons observed it** for seven jubilees and one week of years, **till the day of Noah's death**, and from the day of Noah's death his sons did away with (it) **until the days of Abraham**,*

*and they ate blood. 19 But **Abraham observed it, and Isaac and Jacob and his children observed it up to thy days, and in thy days the children of Israel forgot it until ye celebrated it anew on this mountain**. And do thou command the children of Israel to observe this festival in **all their generations** for a commandment unto them: one day in the year in this month they shall celebrate the festival. For it is the **feast of weeks and the feast of first-fruits**: this feast is **twofold and of a double nature**: according to what is written and engraven concerning it celebrate it. For **I have written in the book of the first law**, in that which **I have written for thee**, that thou shouldst celebrate it in its season, one day in the year, and I explained to thee its sacrifices that the children of Israel should remember and should celebrate it **throughout their generations in this month, one day in every year**.*

From Creation to Noah to Abraham, this Festival was observed since the most ancient of times. This is before Torah and before the Law of Moses. It cannot pass away with the Law of Moses even for those who claim that passed. Messiah of course said the Law does not pass – not one letter of it *(Matt. 5:17-20)*. Those who recognize we are under the Priesthood of Melchizedek *(Gen. 14:18; Ps. 110:4; Heb. 7)* also cannot separate this day from then as that is the ancient order in place at the time of Abraham who kept Shavuot under that law. Messiah was that Priest and remains so to this day. A restored Ancient Order.

Jubilees 14

*1 After these things, in the fourth year of this week, on the new moon of the **third month**…*

*10 And he took all these in the **middle of the month**; and he dwelt at the oak of Mamre, which is near Hebron.*

11 And he built there an altar, and sacrificed all these…

*20 And on that day **we made a covenant with Abram, according as we had covenanted with Noah in this month; and Abram renewed the festival and ordinance for himself for ever**.*

However, the Book of Jubilees that the Qumran Temple Priests identified as Torah and the exact determination for how to keep Torah in times, records the time of Shavuot. It has never been a mystery and Pharisees *(modern Rabbis)* simply do not know it.

> ***Jubilees 15:1 (Sivan 15 is Shavuot)***
> *…in the **third month**, in the **middle of the month**, Abram celebrated the **feast of the first-fruits of the grain harvest**.*

Again, Shavuot is the actual culmination of First Fruits as the Feast of First Fruits as it has a double nature. It is not just a counting but tied together. The Temple Priests in Qumran kept a very detailed calendar found over multiple years. Year after year First Fruits is always on Abib 26 [1] and Shavuot, the Feast of Weeks is always 50 days later on Sivan 15 [1]. There are no leap years and no changes on the Bible calendar. It is not negotiable and nothing moves including the Sabbath that must be every 7th day not the 8th, 6th or any other schedule. Jubilees also gives an exact date as well and this is the day Isaac, the child of promise in the covenant was born.

> ***Jubilees 16:12-13 (Sivan 15 is Shavuot)***
> *12 And in the **middle of the sixth month Yahuah visited Sarah** and did unto her as He had spoken, and **she conceived**. 13 And she bare a **son in the third month, and in the middle of the month**, at the time of which Yahuah had spoken to Abraham, on the **festival of the first-fruits of the harvest, Isaac was born**.*

As we covered previously, this is the same day in which Messiah was born as He mirrored Isaac's birthday. Luke was literal when he wrote the Angel Gabriel visited Mary and she conceived in the sixth month just as Sarah did. Messiah was also born on Shavuot. Forget Christmas which has basis in sun worship of Jesus' *(Yahusha's)* enemy, His birthday is the opposite in Sivan 15 on Shavuot, the Day of Covenant Renewal. Once we understand what Shavuot means, there is truly no other day in which Messiah would be born logically but the Bible proves this out.

Luke 1:26-27 KJV

And in the sixth month the angel Gabriel was sent from God unto a city of Galilee, named Nazareth, To a virgin espoused to a man whose name was Joseph, of the house of David; and the virgin's name was Mary.

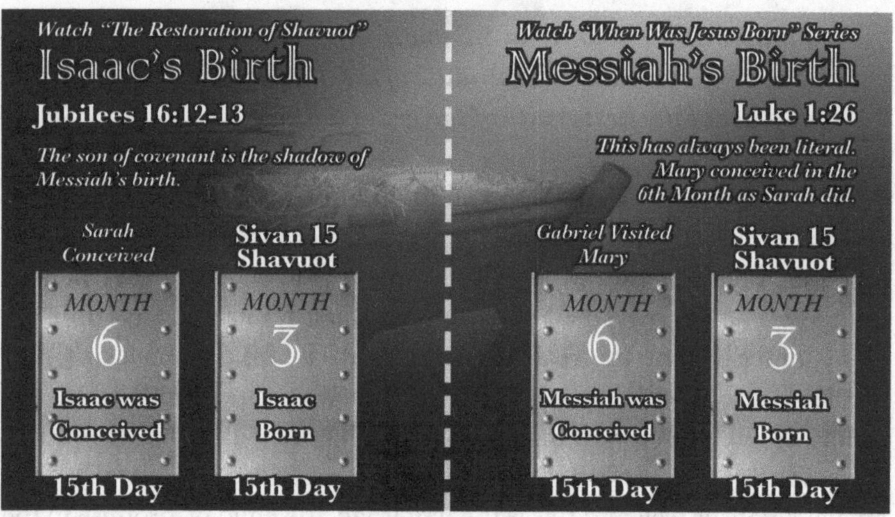

In our "When Was Jesus Born" Series on YouTube, we cover this topic in testing the Course of Abia in which John the Baptist's father served in the Temple pinpointing when he returned and Elizabeth conceived. We cover history included when Herod died, when Qurinius was Consul in charge of the census, etc. All of this data led to Sivan 15 as the birthdate of Messiah long before we found this in the Book of Jubilees. The Apostles most certainly celebrated Messiah's birthday and it was a Feast. In fact, the very day the Holy Spirit came in Acts 2, was the Day of Pentecost that is Shavuot. What other day could be more appropriate for that event and Jesus' *(Yahusha's)* birth than the Day of Covenant Renenewal? They were celebrating His birthday as a part of that Feast that day. It is hard to imagine a day of such significance could be lost and especially pass away. It remains. Christmas will pass away.

Sacrifices For the Sabbaths and Feasts

Many attempt to ridicule those who keep the Sabbath and the Biblical

Feast Days demanding that we all begin to offer animal sacrifices. These are mostly supposed Christians who then ignore that Messiah was our sacrificial lamb for all occasions. Annually, there are 7 Feasts and 52 Weekly Sabbaths for a total of 59 Sabbaths. That is a lot of sacrifices. However, Jesus*(Yahusha)* is our sacrifice. The blood of animals was never sufficient but His blood is sufficient forever for all such occasions. John the Baptist knew this prophetically when he immediately identifies Messiah as the "Lamb of God, which taketh away the sin of the world."

John 1:29 KJV

The next day John seeth Jesus coming unto him, and saith, Behold the Lamb of God, which taketh away the sin of the world.

The Book of Hebrews which tells us to keep the Sabbath or we are a sign of unbelief, explains that Messiah's sacrifice has replaced all sacrifices of animals for eternity. Some will claim these offerings will be reinstituted after the Day of Judgment but that is another doctrine of men as it is unnecessary according to scripture. Yes, He replaced the sacrifice but the sacrifice still occurred and no scholar dare say Messiah's sacrifice passed away. This changes the Feast observances a little but really not that much. However, we are still to keep these Feasts and Sabbaths according to the only source credible on the topic – the Bible.

Hebrews 10:1-4 KJV

For the law having a shadow of good things to come, and not the very image of the things, can never with those sacrifices which they offered year by year continually make the comers thereunto perfect. For then would they not have ceased to be offered? because that the worshippers once purged should have had no more conscience of sins. But in those sacrifices there is a remembrance again made of sins every year. For it is not possible that the blood of bulls and of goats should take away sins.

Hebrews 10:8-14 KJV

Above when he said, Sacrifice and offering and burnt offerings and offering for sin thou wouldest not, neither hadst pleasure therein; which are offered by the law; Then said he, Lo, I come to do thy will, O God. He taketh away the first, that he may establish the second. By the which will we are sanctified through the offering of the body of Jesus Christ once for all. And every priest standeth daily ministering and offering oftentimes the same sacrifices, which can never take away sins: But this man, after he had offered one sacrifice for sins for ever, sat down on the right hand of God; From henceforth expecting till his enemies be made his footstool. For by one offering he hath perfected for ever them that are sanctified.

There is no separating His Sabbaths in the Weekly Sabbath from the Feast Sabbaths. Three of these Feasts remain shadows of future events thus even if they could pass away as the Spring Feasts are said to erroneously, they would not do so until the Day of Judgment. Anyone not keeping them is not keeping the Bible. Messiah also told us every letter of His law will remain until that same day.

This is His worship system and we either keep His ways or the doctrines of men. Celebrating replacement holidays that are pagan in origin is never His ways. Anyone claiming that His Feasts passed away so that they can partake of eating food sacrificed to idols is certainly not honest nor do they represent the Bible. One cannot abolish His Feasts and replace them with counterfeits while then ridiculing His originals. That is not Pastoral nor scholarly and it is the action of non-believers just as not keeping His Sabbath. This issue will define the End Times believer.

Finally, we do not find the added Pharisee holidays of Hanukkah nor Purim in the Bible. There is a reason for that. Even the Book of Esther has extremely questionable roots and was the only book of the modern Old Testament canon not found in Qumran kept by the Temple Priests. They were not chauvinists who hated women as they certainly did include Ruth, Judith, etc. Even Martin Luther strongly protested the Book of Esther as scripture and scholars have for thousands of years even some Pharisees 2,000 years ago. We cover that in our Original Canon Series and we test Esther. We also cover "Who Defiled the Second Temple" and that as well may surprise many as it was not the Greeks and the Pharisee Book of Maccabees is also disproven. These are not Biblical Feast Days nor does either story represent the truth.

These are the annual Sabbaths. In addition to these annual Sabbaths, there are others in scripture as this is Yahuah's way, always has been and always will be as He changes not.

FEASTS OF YHWH

Abib 1 begins on a Wednesday when the sun was created.

PASSOVER

Part of ULB
1st Sabbath

1st month day 14 (mar-apr)
Qumran Calendar: Tuesday Sundown(Evening Only)

UNLEAVENED BREAD

2 Special Sabbaths

1st month: days 15-21 (mar-apr)
Qumran Calendar: Wednesday Sunrise-Tuesday Sundown

FIRST FRUITS

Not a Sabbath

1st month: day 26* (mar-apr)
Qumran Calendar: Sunday Sunrise

SHAVUOT

1 Special Sabbath

3rd month: day 15* (may-jun) [not 6th]
Qumran Calendar: Sunday Sunrise(1 Day not 2)

TRUMPETS

1 Special Sabbath

7th month: day 1 (sep-oct)
Qumran Calendar: Wednesday Sunrise

ATONEMENT

1 Special Sabbath

7th month: day 9-10* (sep-oct)
Qumran Calendar: Thursday Sundown-Friday Sundown
(Only 1 day not 2)

TABERNACLES

2 Special Sabbaths

7th month: days 15-21 (sep-oct)
Qumran Calendar: Wednesday Sunrise-Next Thursday Sunrise

52 Weekly + **7** Special Sabbaths = **59**

*Jubilees 15:1-4 says Shavuot is the 15th not the 6th. Lev. 23 defines Shavuot and Atonement as 1 day. The Qumran Calendar identifies First Fruits on the 26th multiple times which is exactly 50 days from Shavuot as it must be.

7th Year Sabbaths

Not only were the Weekly and Annual Sabbaths important to Yahuah and remain so, but He also instituted a Sabbath of the land every 7th year. For six years, we work the land and the 7th, we allow the land to rest or Sabbath. Anything that does grow naturally is not to be harvested.

> ### Leviticus 25:1-7 KJV
>
> *And the LORD spake unto Moses in mount Sinai, saying, Speak unto the children of Israel, and say unto them, When ye come into the land which I give you, then shall the land keep a sabbath unto the LORD. Six years thou shalt sow thy field, and six years thou shalt prune thy vineyard, and gather in the fruit thereof; But in the seventh year shall be a sabbath of rest unto the land, a sabbath for the LORD: thou shalt neither sow thy field, nor prune thy vineyard. That which groweth of its own accord of thy harvest thou shalt not reap, neither gather the grapes of thy vine undressed: for it is a year of rest unto the land. And the sabbath of the land shall be meat for you; for thee, and for thy servant, and for thy maid, and for thy hired servant, and for thy stranger that sojourneth with thee, And for thy cattle, and for the beast that are in thy land, shall all the increase thereof be meat.*

Some would rightfully ask what shall we eat then for a year? Yahuah promised to bless the land the sixth year enough to cover three years of food supply. Today, modern farming understands the value of crop rotation typically every 3-4 years or so but Yahuah told Israel of this thousands of years ago. It is good for the soil and an essential practice in farming.

> ### Leviticus 25:20-22 KJV
>
> *And if ye shall say, What shall we eat the seventh year? behold, we shall not sow, nor gather in our increase: Then I will command my blessing upon you in the sixth year, and it shall bring forth fruit for three years. And ye shall sow the eighth year, and eat yet of old fruit until the ninth year; until her fruits come in ye shall eat of the old store.*

This is not an arbitrary, obscure concept as Yahuah breathed a sigh of relief as Israel was removed from the land of Israel for breaking His covenant. He says the land will finally get it's rest. Sabbath matters in every sense to Him. He did not forget that. How exactly does the modern church get the impression that Yahuah somehow no longer minds if we break His Law? How does such a strong distaste for such sin in Yahuah's eyes get redefined as acceptable? Messiah did not come for us to sin, He came to make it possible that we could keep His covenant. However, these concepts appear very foreign in the church today. It looks nothing like this. The church generally has lost her way. Restoring His Sabbath and His ways are the only solution.

Leviticus 26:43 KJV

The land also shall be left of them, and shall enjoy her sabbaths, while she lieth desolate without them: and they shall accept of the punishment of their iniquity: because, even because they despised my judgments, and because their soul abhorred my statutes.

The Jubilee Year

Just as we count 7 Weekly Sabbaths and add a day to figure Shavuot, the same applies in Sabbath Years. Every 7 Sabbath Years or 49 years marks a special period known as a Jubilee. The Jubilee celebration just as Shavuot occurs in the 50th year. Just as the land rested, the Jubilee is more of a complete economic rest and reset. The land does rest again but also employees and slaves are returned to their homes, debts are forgiven which makes usury far less profitable, land is returned, etc.

Leviticus 25:8-19 KJV

And thou shalt number seven sabbaths of years unto thee, seven times seven years; and the space of the seven sabbaths of years shall be unto thee forty and nine years. Then shalt thou cause the trumpet of the jubile to sound on the tenth day of the seventh month, in the day of atonement shall ye make the trumpet sound throughout all your land. And ye shall hallow the fiftieth year, and proclaim liberty throughout all the land unto all the inhabitants thereof: it shall be a jubile unto you; and ye shall return every man unto his

> *possession, and ye shall return every man unto his family. A jubile shall that fiftieth year be unto you: ye shall not sow, neither reap that which groweth of itself in it, nor gather the grapes in it of thy vine undressed. For it is the jubile; it shall be holy unto you: ye shall eat the increase thereof out of the field. In the year of this jubile ye shall return every man unto his possession. And if thou sell ought unto thy neighbour, or buyest ought of thy neighbour's hand, ye shall not oppress one another: According to the number of years after the jubile thou shalt buy of thy neighbour, and according unto the number of years of the fruits he shall sell unto thee: According to the multitude of years thou shalt increase the price thereof, and according to the fewness of years thou shalt diminish the price of it: for according to the number of the years of the fruits doth he sell unto thee. Ye shall not therefore oppress one another; but thou shalt fear thy God: for I am the LORD your God. Wherefore ye shall do my statutes, and keep my judgments, and do them; and ye shall dwell in the land in safety. And the land shall yield her fruit, and ye shall eat your fill, and dwell therein in safety.*

Yahuah's economy does not resemble our modern systems. Today's banking system especially charges far too much interest fostering an environment leading to slavery of sort. It is a system of debt that is destined to implode. Currencies are set to inflate without end until they someday fail as they have no tangible basis such as gold in most cases. The rich are favored no matter which political party or form of government. Even Communism creates a super elite class and lowers the rest of society. These are not wiser than Yahuah.

The Jubilee year carries laws to free the people and the land. When this was being implemented, there could be no long-term servitude, no long-term debt essentially, etc.

This concept seems very foreign today but let us remember, this is not Moses' words but the words of Yahuah. These are the ways of the Creator and if they are foreign to us today, this only serves to demonstrate how far man has strayed from Him in our age. When everyone is helping the poor, there is no lower class. When everyone obeys His Law in sincerity, poverty would be eradicated. In fact, if all the dollars just from the U.S. alone were given directly to the Biblical aim of eradicating poverty and assisting the widows and orphans as scripture says, we would hardly have those termed as poor except for drastic cases. The modern church structure absorbs these monies giving little to the poor because this is what is required by their massive overhead and infrastructure that are unbiblical concepts. The Biblical ekklesia merely requires a gathering of 2 or more according to Messiah *(Matt. 18:20)*. No building necessary.

The Sabbath Milinnea

Many have considered that the Biblical time clock for the Last Days also follows the Sabbath cycle in thousands. Peter, likely quoting Jubilees 4:30, defines that a day is as a thousand years to Yahuah *(2 Peter 3:8)*. The thinking makes sense but few substantiate it. It is assumed the world will experience a Sabbath on it's 7th Day or 7,000th year. There is Biblical support for this. On the Day of Judgment, Satan will be bound for 1,000 years, and in the first resurrection, believers will be with Messiah for that same 1,000 years with no Satan. This is a Sabbath indeed.

> ### Revelation 20:1-6 KJV
> *And I saw an angel come down from heaven, having the key of the bottomless pit and a great chain in his hand. And he laid hold on the dragon, that old serpent, which is the Devil, and Satan, and **bound him a thousand years**, And cast him into the bottomless pit, and shut him up, and set a seal upon him, that he should deceive the nations no more, till the thousand years should be fulfilled: and after that he must be loosed a little season. And I saw thrones, and they sat upon them, and judgment was given unto them: and I saw the souls of them that were beheaded for the witness of Jesus, and for the word of God, and which had not worshipped the beast, neither his image, neither had received his mark upon their foreheads, or in their hands; and **they lived and reigned with Christ a thousand years**. But the rest of the dead lived not again until the thousand years were finished. This is the first resurrection. Blessed and holy is he that hath part in the first resurrection: on such the second death hath no power, but they shall be priests of God and of Christ, and **shall reign with him a thousand years**.*

However, there is deeper support for this timing of 7,000 years. In 2nd Esdras, the resurrection of the dead on the Day of Judgment occurs after

7 days. This aligns with Peter's definition and Revelation 20 providing a timeline.

> **2 Esdras 7:31 KJVA**
> *And after seven days, the world that yet awake not shall be raised up, and that shall die, that is corrupt.*

The Book of Enoch alludes to the same clock of 7,000 years. When the Watcher Fallen Angels were locked away during the Flood, they will be there until the Day of Judgment and they will be consumed with eternal fire at that point. They will be bound until the end of ALL generations. This clock is established as seventy generations. Though many attempt to assign 70 years or 90 years for a generation based on modern lifespans, this was written before the Flood. If it referred to generations in lifespans at that time, each generation would be 900 years not 90. However, we have found in the Bible this term generations is really an even 100 years. This would equal 7,000 years and 2nd Esdras is recording the same.

> **1 Enoch 10**
> *12 ... bind them for **seventy generations**, under the hills of the earth, **until the day of their judgment and of their consummation**, until the judgment, which is for all eternity, is accomplished. 14 ...together they will be bound **until the end of all generations**.*
> ***(70 Generations = 7,000 years)***

Many have arrived at this same thinking simply because they understand His Sabbath cycle which would lead one to this thinking. We find support in 2nd Esdras and Enoch really affirming this as probable. Of course, no man knows the day nor hour, however, understand in that verse Messiah says we will know His season. The next challenge is to truly reconcile the modern Roman calendar over thousands of years with the Biblical calendar. In these, this will be restored soon.

Revelation 20 is defining a Sabbath reprieve from Satan's tricks as he is bound and locked away. That is truly a Sabbath in every sense. For these other books to affirm this as 7,000 years makes sense.

One can observe how the Sabbath becomes entrenched in every aspect of the ways of Yahuah. We are to observe the Sabbath every week on Saturday. Then, there are 7 annual Sabbaths in addition within His Biblical Feasts. Every 7th year becomes a year long Sabbath for the land. Finally, the 7th series of Annual Sabbaths or 49 years marks His Jubilee in which we celebrate the 50th year. It certainly appears, the entire timeline for the Earth is likely set on the Sabbath as the 7,000th-year seems to bring the Day of Final Judgment and the Millennial Sabbath. This established an entire paradigm of thinking largely unknown in the modern church.

the
GOD
culture
יהוה

CLOSING ARGUMENT

Chapter 19 | Conclusion: We REST Our Case

The greatest miracle of all time was completed as the Father and Son *(John 1)* Created the Heavens and the Earth. It was the day in which they would rest from their works and bask in the glory of their Creation *(Gen. 2:2-3)*: the day of the Sabbath. The seventh day and no other.

The event happened and is recorded on the Heavenly Tablets for Heaven rested and kept the Sabbath. They did so in the Land of Creation that we identify as the Philippines in The Search for King Solomon's Treasure. That is where Yahuah's seat is on Earth in the Garden of Eden within the Earth. They kept the Sabbath in the time of Adam to the time of Noah to the time of Abraham and in the days of Israel. It was now for the Son to be revealed on Earth in the flesh. What did He practice in Heaven from where He came? The Sabbath. He would continue to keep and teach the Sabbath on Earth on the seventh day. He could never break the Sabbath as that is defined as sin and He was sinless. Did He abolish it because He kept it in Heaven for thousands of years? No. Would He ever abandon it on Earth just because He was now flesh? No. One cannot change Creation of which He participated in Creating the Sabbath of which He is Lord of the Sabbath. He also said He would not abolish it *(Matt. 5:17-20)*.

The Apostles were in the Upper Room celebrating Messiah's birth on the Feast of Shavuot *(Pentecost in Greek)* – a Biblical Feast that still had not passed away after Jesus' *(Yahusha's)* ascension. Any scholar saying it could is no scholar. They celebrate Christmas typically which means they believe in commemorating His birthday yet they worship on the day of the sun god and abolish His birthday, a Feast. That is hypocritical.

A mighty wind rushed in and they were endued with power unimaginable. The Holy Spirit had come after Messiah ascended. The Holy Spirit kept the Sabbath for thousands of years. Would he now teach to abolish it? No. Still observing His Feasts and the Sabbath, the Apostles were still keeping the Feasts that day and 85 Sabbath observances are recorded in the Book of Acts alone. They were now filled with the Holy Spirit yet their observance did not change. This is along with their keeping the Biblical Feasts even the Spring Feasts that we are told passed yet it did not for them. The Fall Feasts remain prophetic and thus even in such false paradigm could not pass away before they were realized in full.

This practice was gifted from the Apostles to the True Early Ekklesia as they, too, kept the Sabbath and on the seventh day. Of course, they would as the Sabbath is a Creation not new in the Law of Moses and no one would abolish it nor did they. This has continued throughout the ages and one can easily identify those operating in unbelief *(Hebrews 4)* as they do not observe this Creation concept attempting to explain it away in willing ignorance as Peter warned in our day. Those calling themselves the church in any period not keeping the Sabbath, cannot be His Ekklesia. His Ekklesia keeps His commandments including the Sabbath. There is no other definition as those are His ways.

Redefined even in timing by Pharisees and attacked by the Catholic Church in arrogant rebellion to the Word and against the Creator, the Sabbath importance is marginalized over the ages yet Creation happened did it not? Are we not still here? All Creation survives today. We have plants, animals, humans and the mighty works of the 7 Days. However, we are told to forget 15% of Creation in the Seventh Day now because some church said so. The Bible never does nor does it ever change it's day. A church that has no foundation, as if they do not have Creation, they have no understanding of Heaven's ways, is not His. For the Sabbath and Feasts are the shadow of Heavenly things and those to come. They cannot pass nor be completed and abolished before they even come into fruition. This is an illiterate proposition most of us have fallen for most of our lives.

It is the end. Messiah returns in all His anointing from Heaven accompanied by tribulation saints from the presence of Yahuah in Heaven. In Heaven, they keep the Sabbath. Out of his mouth proceeds a flaming sword of fire and He consumes all those who oppose His ways. That fire is the Law *(2Esd. 13:4, 38)* that includes the Sabbath. No one can redefine something still in use in the end. No one can claim it passed.

For who is it that is judged on this day and by what measure? All men will be judged by His righteous Law which has never changed. It has always included the Sabbath and always will. Messiah said the Sabbath is an End Times concept *(Matt. 24:20)* and so does Revelation *(14:12, 22:14)*.

Jubilees 2:27

*And whoever profaneth it (Sabbath) shall surely die, and whoever doeth thereon any work **shall surely die eternally**, that the children of Israel may observe this day throughout their generations, and not be rooted out of the land; for it is a holy day and a blessed day.*

Hosea 8:12 KJV

I have written to him the great things of my law, but they were counted as a strange thing.

For the Sabbath defines the Remnant believer. Jubilees even says that to profane the Sabbath leads to spiritual death. No, it is not salvation but accompanies those who are saved as a sign of salvation essentially. The Sabbath does not save but your relationship with Him does. How does something holy and blessed become something demonized and redefined as bad and a strange thing? How could it be so foreign for those claiming to be His? Who could ever even attempt such? How can keeping His Word be said to be a bad thing? How can it even be alluded that keeping His Sabbath Day of Rest could be considered sin or lawlessness? Where is this new law which becomes the opposite? It does not exist except in the satanic bible, occult writings even from before the Flood and is now Catholic dogma. This paradigm is not based on the Bible yet it is the foundation of the modern church even Protestant as they continued the same foundation as the Catholic Church.

Sin is defined by John as "transgression of the law." What law? He most certainly kept the Law of Moses as did Messiah and the Apostles. For if we commit ourselves in doctrine to sin, we are committing to be lawless and John defines that as the behavior "of the devil." Messiah tells us in Matthew 7 we are to know Him or we will be told to depart on the Day of Judgment. John clarifies that if we are committed to sin, we do not know Him. In other words, if we choose to be lawless, we do not know Him. He must have Law or you cannot be in covenant with Him even in a New Covenant as that is always regulated by Law. The church is actively teaching that we have liberty from the Law that is lawlessness or sin. This is a major issue for the church because it cannot represent scripture while undermining it's very foundations. These seminaries do not believe the Bible nor are they teaching it but a foundation set on sinking sand leading the lambs to slaughter.

1 John 3: 3-10 KJV

*And every man that hath this hope in him purifieth himself, even as he is pure. Whosoever committeth sin transgresseth also the law: **for sin is the transgression of the law**. And ye know that he was manifested to take away our sins; and in him is no sin. Whosoever abideth in him sinneth not: whosoever sinneth hath not seen him, neither known him. Little children, let no man deceive you: he that doeth righteousness is righteous, even as he is righteous. He that committeth sin is of the devil; for the devil sinneth from the beginning. For this purpose the Son of God was manifested, that he might destroy the works of the devil. Whosoever is born of God doth not commit sin; for his seed remaineth in him: and he cannot sin, because he is born of God. In this the children of God are manifest, and the children of the devil: whosoever doeth not righteousness is not of God, neither he that loveth not his brother.*

We love these scriptures about receiving and getting. However, who receives according to John? Those who keep His commandments. As Messiah confirmed all 10 Commandments in His teachings as did the Apostles even in an End Times context, and told us they would never pass away, we must continue to observe His ways not our own and certainly not the doctrines of men. Many will ask: "How do I know I am saved then?" The Bible tells us we know that He abides with us if we keep His Commandments. Yes, we sin and we repent and ask forgiveness. No one has ever kept the Law perfectly except Messiah.

1 John is in the New Testament. His Commandments remain unchanged and it is time we understand this. The era in which we live demands it as the pressure is about to increase for many. It already has for many. Are you prepared? You will never be prepared if you are not

keeping His Sabbath Day of Rest. You will never wear your full armor without it. You will be empty and prone to depression.

1 John 3: 22- KJV

And whatsoever we ask, we receive of him, because we keep his commandments, and do those things that are pleasing in his sight. And this is his commandment, That we should believe on the name of his Son Jesus Christ, and love one another, as he gave us commandment. And he that keepeth his commandments dwelleth in him, and he in him. And hereby we know that he abideth in us, by the Spirit which he hath given us.

A new era has begun as the shadows become exposed and the lukewarm disintegrates. As the clock accelerates, the world marches in rebellion against it's Creator while knowledge increases for the Remnant and they deepen their relationship with Him. All things are being reformed and rehabilitated to the envisioning of evil as good and good as evil. For the harlot remains jealous of the virtuous. She wants control by any means necessary and she will defile all she can. Her followers will accuse the innocent to placate the immoral. They will stand firm on ancient rebellion daring anyone to challenge. They will and do ridicule His Creation, even the Flood and the deity of Messiah just as Peter prophesied *(2 Peter 3)*. The mundane serve at the harlot's pleasure and she feigns not when they perish as collateral damage in the cultivation of her fruits stealing, killing and destroying. This is the same Queen of Heaven venerated in the Catholic Church whom Jeremiah rebuked three times.

The day approaches in which all will be resurrected and judged when the greatest miracles of all time will occur as Heaven and Earth are replenished. Yahuah is not slack in His righteousness and He will not tarry beyond His timing. For the Son, His greatest works are yet to manifest. He is readied for swift action as He begins to pour out His spirit on His remnant. For the world was not made for those committed to sin, it was Created for the righteous. The sons and daughters prophesy. Young men dream and the old see visions while the flounders fill the bottom of the sea of increasing knowledge.

They move at their own pace turned away from understanding and change. Affixed to the bottom, these flounders cling to their traditions that are not old at all neglecting the most ancient of commands. They further burrow into the sand hoping no one will notice. Yahuah always does. They migrate with the tide accepting the flow wandering slowly and aimlessly. Little do they know they are the easiest of prey and regardless of title or appearance, they abide in the clutches of the enemy. But many will examine this case and they will no longer.

They will tell you what not to read censoring Yahuah's Word. They will find ways to repel you from the presence of Yahuah. They will challenge everything you say that is not in their playbook of ignorance. No need for learning unless you learn their beliefs. Don't read that Bible, study our doctrine they encourage. Using flattery and flowery language, these will lead you to Hell. But he's Brother Love don't you know? And over there is Brother Wisdom... Good men in appearance, rotting inside as Pharisees were described 2,000 years ago *(Matt. 23:27)*. Our age will only get worse in this regard as Messiah predicted there would be seven times the demon possession *(Matt. 12)*. They care for your soul, you think. Yet their image is their only aim. They live in rebellion against Jesus*(Yahusha)* and His Word.

Messiah characterized these as the worst of mankind yet today, we call them scholar, doctor, PhD's otherwise known as Pharisee Dunderheads much of the time, and the like. Not all who carry such titles are but they are within them in great number. Pharisees gain powerful positions not only controlling the church at the highest levels but they control much of the banking industry just as they did in Jerusalem when Messiah turned over their pawnbroker tables rejecting their unethical usury that leads to slavery. This has lead to their conquest as economic hit men of the largest of companies and governments worldwide.

You will notice Jesus*(Yahusha)* rebuked them many times not just for something they said but for the worst of character flaws, traditions of sin and even turning Torah against Torah. That is a disease that He even warned He hates their doctrine of this synagogue of satan who say they are Yahudim and are not but do lie *(Rev. 2:9, 3:9)*. The Catholic Church is clearly a Pharisee concoction as well with similar infusion to their Samaritan practices. Yahuah is mixed into their paganism and He always rejects that.

For the church generally accepts 9 of the 10 Commandments without protest though they corrupt those in understanding as well some of the time. However, they reject one, the fourth Commandment to remember His Sabbath and keep it holy – The Creation. Even when the Pope placates in political correctness he, too, is guilty of encouraging everyone to profane the Sabbath which he does not understand characterizing it as a day of recreation not Creation. However, let us not pretend the office of Pope has ever been a scriptural position. It originates in Mithraism from Persia even in title not the Bible. No one representing scripture could be Pope nor serve him in any sense.

Isaiah prophesied of the times in which we find ourselves today. The church attacks the Sabbath, one of the 10 Commandments as if it never existed. They minimize and marginalize it's importance in ignorance. This church culminating from Dark Age Theology truly represents what Isaiah calls the "blind," "ignorant" and "dumb dogs" and Peter calls "willingly ignorant." Yes, those are Bible terms. It's always interesting when one attempts to claim these words are not showing love yet they are simply those who do not know nor represent scripture nor especially love which includes rebuke. These "greedy dogs" who can "never have enough" will not rest until they have profaned His Sabbath in every way possible. These are generally the controllers of the church system today.

Notice this is yet another passage that actually demonstrates they drink in the evening and tomorrow which is the Sabbath morning, will be the same as any other day. In other words, His Sabbath no longer matters to them predicted by Isaiah and fulfilled before our very eyes in what is called His church but clearly cannot be. Even the shepherds or pastors cannot understand. All is done for their own gain because they have lost His ways and profane them whether knowingly or not. To equate the Sabbath to any other day of the week is to profane it as it is the holy, sanctified day. Taking what is holy and reclassifying it as not holy is evil. To do so, one must produce abundant scripture of such shift and their position offers nothing but weak manipulations.

Isaiah 56:8-12 KJV

The Lord God, which gathereth the outcasts of Israel saith, Yet will I gather others to him, beside those that are gathered unto him. All ye beasts of the field, come to devour, yea, all ye beasts in the forest. His watchmen are blind:

they are all ignorant, they are all dumb dogs, they cannot bark; sleeping, lying down, loving to slumber. Yea, they are greedy dogs which can never have enough, and they are shepherds that cannot understand: they all look to their own way, every one for his gain, from his quarter. Come ye, say they, I will fetch wine, and we will fill ourselves with strong drink; and to morrow shall be as this day, and much more abundant.

The Book of Jubilees warned in prophecy accurately that we would lose this knowledge and we have. Remember, there were always Gentiles among Israel and they kept His commandments and Sabbath as well. His Law has always been for the Gentile too.

Jubilees 1:13

And they will forget all My law and all My commandments and all My judgments, and will go astray as to new moons, and sabbaths, and festivals, and jubilees, and ordinances.

Jubilees 6:34

And all the children of Yisrael will forget and will not find the path of the years, and will forget the new months, and seasons, and Sabbaths and they will go wrong as to all the order of the years.

Why would we ever listen to those who represent this unbiblical paradigm? No amount of education nor string of initials will ever qualify them as experts when they fit this prophecy of willing ignorance.

Jude 1:4 KJV

For there are certain men crept in unawares, who were before of old ordained to this condemnation, ungodly men, turning the grace of our God into lasciviousness, and denying the only Lord God, and our Lord Jesus Christ.

You can see how these "crept in unawares" into the original ekklesia. They began establishing infrastructure from the beginning that would overwhelm the true ekklesia. They are defined truly by their defiling the Sabbath preaching a Gospel the Apostles never preached which makes them very easy to identify throughout history.

Centuries later, the 7 ekklesias of Turkey were gone. Where did they go? They were hunted, killed, and chased into the Lost Tribe territory of Assyria *(modern Kurdistan)* especially *(watch our Lost Tribes Series or read 2nd Esdras: The Hidden Book of Prophecy for evidence)*. They did not go into the Russian Steppes however. Those were Pharisees.

Then, under Constantine, they were legislated out of existence. Many view his legislation as positive yet what he really did was lay the foundation to destroy the original ekklesia throughout the Empire which his Pharisee bloodline had been doing for centuries even according to Paul *(Acts 8:1-3, 9:1-2, 22:4-5, 26:9-11)*. In fact, Paul admitted his own guilt prior to his conversion multiple times in this *(1 Cor. 15:9; Gal, 1:13, 23; Phil. 3:6)*. Paul repented of this and was a true Apostle endorsed by Messiah, Ananias, the witnesses, Luke and Peter yet there are those who attempt ridicule of him today in ignorance. They are simply presenting Pharisee leaven and no different from the rest of the scoffers. They do not represent the Bible.

Constantine was forcing the replacement of Yahuah's people once again as his people did in Samaria, in Judaea, and then, in Turkey. He moved the seat of power for the Roman Empire to where the seat of satan is *(Rev. 2:13)* and the synagogue of satan originates *(Rev. 2:9, 3:9)* in power. This was no coincidence and this was the rise of the Final Beast Empire of Daniel 2 and 7 also known as the Eagle Empire in 2nd Esdras 11 and 12. This is where Rome *(legs of iron)* mixed with the miry clay *(Dan. 2:43)* and this is the world controlling Empire to the very end: a Pharisee empire none-the-less. It is not a future rule as this has been with us for over 1,500 years. Daniel leaves no break between Empires. It is no surprise under this rule, the world has experienced more death than all generations prior combined. Wars have become commonplace even in our so-called "civilized" society. Understand according to the Book of Enki, that is what the Nephilim called their Empire prior to the Flood.

This is why we must prove all things for ourselves because the strong delusion in which we were warned is already upon us. The very infused religion installed by Constantine has attacked almost the entire world at this point and many cannot even see it. Colonialism was their tool for centuries and they were not bringing the son of Yahuah with them as He condemns everything they stand for. Is it a surprise that Magellan forced his attack on Lapu Lapu in Mactan, Cebu, Philippines on the

Sabbath? He even waited hours for sunrise because that is when Sabbath begins. No, he was not observing it nor is there any record of him nor his people doing so. He was defiling it as the Catholic Church has from it's inception. Antonio Pigafetta even wrote regarding the Battle of Mactan:

"We however waited for daylight..."
"This fatal battle was fought on the 27th of April of 1521, on a Saturday; a day which the captain had chosen himself, because he had a special devotion to it." –Antonio Pigafetta, Historian traveling with Magellan, 1522 [22]

Magellan was there to defile the Biblical land of gold, the Garden of Eden and Creation as he had done everywhere he went for Portugal previously and now for Spain. We prove this out in The Search for King Solomon's Treasure. He was demanding tribute to the point of the sword, burning villages and brazenly arrogantly in dominant, evil fashion. He had special devotion to Saturday at sunrise because that was the beginning of the True Sabbath at sunrise and that was the land of the first Sabbath, Sheba (שבע), Sebu or Sebua (שבוע) in Hebrew. He had found a pocket of local residents of Ophir and Sheba whom he would attempt to eradicate.

The King of Zubu *(Cebu)* was no native but a Hindu from Sumatra whose family migrated because of the Gold Rush in the Philippines. He and his wife embraced the idols Magellan brought because that was already their familiar worship. However, even he turned against the Spanish and killed Magellan's brother-in-law and successor. These evil men defile Yahuah's ways in every way they can corrupt. Their devotion is to corruption and chaos in which they intend to become the order that rises from the ashes. That is the Catholic Church and there is no redemption for that organization which stands against His Word.

It is difficult for the average person who is not evil to fathom such evil. This is the origin of the Holy Roman Empire and that is the Final Empire in power to this day. It's religion is rebuked by scripture many times over. It's fruits are those killing, stealing and destroying yet many overlook that because they claim to bring Jesus. According to archaeology, what they brought were idols of Isis they call Mary and Ploutus, the Greek god of wealth as a child, the Child Jesus they claimed in fraud. These statues in exact image are found 400 and 500 years in archaeology used in pagan worship in Persia/Babylon before Messiah was even born. They are blatant and very obvious but the evil is so intense it is unimaginable. It is time we imagine such because the Bible already predicted their coming many times. Accept them and their religion and you will accept the Beast because their False Prophet Pope, will usher in his rise and enforce that all bow to that Beast. They will preach another Gospel without His Sabbath and Feasts and we see that today.

2 Corinthians 11:3-4 KJV

But I fear, lest by any means, as the serpent beguiled Eve through his subtilty, so your minds should be corrupted from the simplicity that is in Christ. For if he that cometh preacheth another Jesus, whom we have not preached, or if ye receive another spirit, which ye have not received, or another gospel, which ye have not accepted, ye might well bear with him.

Galatians 1:6-9 KJV

I marvel that ye are so soon removed from him that called you into the grace of Christ unto another gospel: Which is not another; but there be some that trouble you, and would pervert the gospel of Christ. But though we, or an angel from heaven, preach any other gospel unto you than that which we have preached unto you, let him be accursed. As we said before, so say I now again, If any man preach any other gospel unto you than that ye have received, let him be accursed.

1 Peter 1:25 KJV

But the word of the Lord endureth for ever. And this is the word which by the gospel is preached unto you.

Not just from Paul and Peter, the Gospel is from Heaven and matches Heaven's practice which includes keeping His Sabbath and that endures forever. For Heaven keeps the Sabbath. Heaven does not present a different Gospel. That Gospel is a shadow of Heavenly things.

Revelation 14:6 KJV

And I saw another angel fly in the midst of heaven, having the everlasting gospel to preach unto them that dwell on the earth, and to every nation, and kindred, and tongue, and people,

Any Gospel without His Sabbath is absent the Lord of the Sabbath *(Mark 2:27-28)*. That is not the whole Gospel. Even Hebrews 4, as we covered in the Introduction, is clear the Sabbath is included in the Gospel message. Is it included in your church's Gospel or are they preaching a different Gospel to the Word? The Gospel is not a tract nor a fragment out of context nor is it 12 scriptures we memorize or a storyline about Jesus*(Yahusha)* filling a chasm. It is the Word, all of it, and it begins in Genesis 1:1 according to John 1 and others as Messiah was since the beginning. It is unscholarly to accuse the Creator of the Sabbath of breaking and abolishing it especially when He kept it, taught it and said it would not pass away.

If the church were so effective in these end times as it purports to be, why does an Angel have to travel the world to preach the Gospel in the end? In fact, the notion that the modern church will reach every person in the world is unfounded in scripture. The Angel completes that mission not the church. Many of us keep giving to missions programs claiming this purpose not theirs, that are teaching an incomplete salvation that falls short of Jesus'*(Yahusha's)* definition. In fact, how do we forget He said His words will never pass away and He said to keep the Sabbath and declared He is Lord of the Sabbath. If we are not following His example, whose example are we following? In this same chapter, Jesus*(Yahusha)* defines that Sabbath will still be kept in the End Times *(Matthew 24:20)*.

Matthew 24:35 KJV
Heaven and earth shall pass away, but my words shall not pass away.

This is confirmed by Isaiah and Revelation both also regarding the future even today. How can a scholar miss these over 1,000 scriptures? How can they demean and ridicule Messiah's own words? The only way they can is if they are not serving the Creator as He keeps the Sabbath, preaches the Sabbath and it is His way. That is foreign to them because they only know a limited paradigm steeped in the doctrines of men not the Bible.

The Sabbath origin is not remotely questionable. It began on the 7th day of Creation. Yahuah rested then as did His Creation. Heaven began keeping Sabbath as well as Earth. Mankind observed the Sabbath up until the Flood and after it until Noah died. There was a lapse for about a couple of centuries or so until Abraham renewed it. His descendants continued the Sabbath at least in part all the way until the days of Moses and whatever that lapse was in years, it continued from that period until the New Testament.

There is massive support that Messiah kept and taught the Sabbath. He is Lord of the Sabbath. His Apostles kept and taught the Sabbath even after His ascension that would make them rebellious if He had abolished it. He said He would not and not a single scripture says He did. Apostles meeting on a Sunday at some point is not a moving of the Sabbath as in the Book of Acts alone, there are 85 recorded 7th-Day Sabbath observances. It never changed and yes, they met other days as well. In fact, in some places at some times, daily. We can all meet any day of the week, however, no church can redefine His Sabbath. There is no such authority carried by any Pope, seminarian, apostle nor pastor.

We are told Messiah abolished the Law and the Sabbath yet He said He would not. John the Baptist even knew this. The Apostles knew this. The Early Ekklesia knew this. Why don't we know this? For His Law cannot pass away as it is the measure of covenant and there is no covenant, even a New one, without His Law. Any scholar saying this is very challenged to be able to read scripture as this is basic. Keeping His Sabbath is an essential and should be understood at elementary levels within the church. Certainly, you will hear a preacher rail on it in ridicule but they cannot overrule over 1,000 verses affirming the Sabbath as His practice throughout time.

If we are not following His Word and His ways, whose faith are we following? We are to follow the Faith of Messiah and the Apostles not an apostate church full of heresy who loves to characterize anyone against it's views as heretics. Jesus *(Yahusha)* doesn't change. He is the same yesterday, today and forever *(Heb. 13:8)*. This is why the Apostles did not change their practice after His ascension as He did not change it. The illiterate, apostate church did and we have fully dismantled what are the most ignorant reasons they have given. They prove they do not even know the Word, not even a little. The Protestant Church follows the Catholic illiteracy on this topic and that is insane. This leads to a foundation on nothing.

Hebrews 13:7-9 KJV

Remember them which have the rule over you, who have spoken unto you the word of God: whose faith follow, considering the end of their conversation. Jesus Christ the same yesterday, and to day, and for ever. Be not carried about with divers and strange doctrines. For it is a good thing that the heart be established with grace; not with meats, which have not profited them that have been occupied therein.

The strange doctrine to the Book of Hebrews that teaches and affirms the Sabbath throughout time as well as in the era after Messiah's ascension, is abolishing the Sabbath. That is strange to scripture and always has been. Any church built on such foundation, cannot be His regardless of how much good they may appear to perform. Messiah is clear there are many in the Last Days who will even remind Him they performed miracles, cast out demons, and prophesied in His name yet He will still tell them "depart from me" as He never knew them.

Matthew 7:13-29 KJV

Therefore all things whatsoever ye would that men should do to you, do ye even so to them: for this is the law and the prophets. Enter ye in at the strait gate: for wide is the gate, and broad is the way, that leadeth to destruction, and many there be which go in thereat: Because strait is the gate, and narrow is the way, which leadeth unto life, and few there be that find it. Beware of false prophets, which come to you in sheep's clothing, but inwardly they are ravening wolves. Ye shall know them by their fruits. Do men gather grapes of thorns, or figs of thistles? Even so every good tree bringeth forth good fruit; but a corrupt tree bringeth forth evil fruit. A good tree cannot bring forth evil fruit, neither can a corrupt tree bring forth good fruit. Every tree that bringeth not forth good fruit is hewn down, and cast into the fire. Wherefore by their fruits ye shall know them. Not every one that saith unto me, Lord, Lord, shall enter into the kingdom of heaven; but he that doeth the will of my Father which is in heaven. Many will say to me in that day, Lord, Lord, have we not prophesied in thy name? and in thy name have cast out devils? and in thy name done many wonderful works? And then will I profess unto them, I never knew you: depart from me, ye that work iniquity. Therefore whosoever heareth these sayings of mine, and doeth them, I will liken him unto a wise man, which built his house upon a rock: And the rain descended, and the floods came, and the winds blew, and beat upon that house; and it fell not: for it was founded upon a rock. And every one that heareth these sayings of mine, and doeth them not, shall be likened unto a foolish man, which built his house upon the sand: And the rain descended, and the floods came, and the winds blew, and beat upon that house; and it fell: and great was the fall of it. And it came to pass, when Jesus had ended these sayings, the people were astonished at his doctrine: For he taught them as one having authority, and not as the scribes.

How is it that we know Him? Is this not defined by Messiah Himself which better be the origin of the church's salvation doctrine. Unfortunately, few of His words even make it into most salvation doctrines today. The church is bent on quoting Paul out of context at times but was not Jesus*(Yahusha)* salvation? It is unthinkable that He would not fully define such when He came in the flesh. Is this not the most important of topics? Of course it is. Messiah did define salvation and it is not a fragment but one of great detail in John 15.

John 15:1-27 KJV

I am the true vine, and my Father is the husbandman. Every branch in me that beareth not fruit he taketh away: and every branch that beareth fruit, he purgeth it, that it may bring forth more fruit. Now ye are clean through the word which I have spoken unto you. Abide in me, and I in you. As the branch cannot bear fruit of itself, except it abide in the vine; no more can ye, except ye abide in me. I am the vine, ye are the branches: He that abideth in me, and I in him, the same bringeth forth much fruit: for without me ye can do nothing. If a man abide not in me, he is cast forth as a branch, and is withered; and men gather them, and cast them into the fire, and they are burned. If ye abide in me, and my words abide in you, ye shall ask what ye will, and it shall be done unto you. Herein is my Father glorified, that ye bear much fruit; so shall ye be my disciples. As the Father hath loved me, so have I loved you: continue ye in my love. If ye keep my commandments, ye shall abide in my love; even as I have kept my Father's commandments, and abide in his love. These things have I spoken unto you, that my joy might remain in you, and that your joy might be full. This is my commandment, That ye love one another, as I have loved you. Greater love hath no man than this, that a man lay down his life for his friends. Ye are my friends, if ye do whatsoever I command you. Henceforth I call you not servants; for the servant knoweth not what his lord doeth: but I have called you friends; for all things that I have heard of my Father I have made known unto you. Ye have not chosen me, but I have chosen you, and ordained you, that ye should go and bring forth fruit, and that your fruit should remain: that whatsoever ye shall ask of the Father in my name, he may give it you. These things I command you, that ye love one another. If the world hate you, ye know that it hated me before it hated you. If ye were of the world, the world would love his own: but because ye are not of the world, but I have chosen you out of the world, therefore the world hateth you. Remember the word that I said unto you, The servant is not greater than his lord. If they have persecuted me, they will also persecute you; if they have kept my saying, they will keep yours also. But all these things will they do unto you for my name's sake, because they know not him that sent me. If I had not come and spoken unto them, they had not had sin: but now they have no cloak for their sin. He that hateth me hateth my Father also. If I had not done among them the works which none other man did, they had not had sin: but now have they both seen and hated both me and my Father. But this cometh to pass, that the word might be fulfilled that is written in their law, They hated me without a cause. But when the Comforter is come, whom I will send unto you from the Father, even the Spirit of truth, which proceedeth from the Father, he shall testify of me: And ye also shall bear witness, because ye have been with me from the beginning.

Jesus*(Yahusha)* said far more than "Marvel not, ye must be born again." He said if we love Him, we keep His commandments. He does not say that is negotiable. He certainly does not abolish it. Messiah defines salvation as our bearing good fruit. If so, He will prune and groom us and we will flourish. If not, He will cut us off and we will be burned in the fire. That is salvation as well as Heaven and Hell right there. No one needs to read a fragment from Paul to define what Messiah already defined. Where in this passage does He say if you just say a prayer, that is all it takes? Nowhere. Where does Paul say that? Nowhere. This defines a progressing relationship. No one ever needs to ask if they are saved. The fact they are insecure is already a bad sign because it means they have not been taught scripture. The church teaches an incomplete definition of salvation as well.

Though not salvation, the Sabbath is part of this relationship in pursuing His ways. I repeat, because the illiterates claiming to represent scripture will claim we express Sabbath as salvation. The Sabbath is NOT salvation. However, this is a sign of a believer according to many scriptures we have covered. If you do not have that sign, you will be insecure in your salvation. If we are keeping His Sabbath even imperfectly, we love Him. That's it. If we don't, well, you know what that means.

Even mental and physical health are affected by the Sabbath. Though not studied otherwise that we can find, we did locate an article about Orthodox Jews keeping their Sabbath. It is not truly the Biblical practice but the rest never-the-less has an impact on their mental well-being in this study. Imagine how much more the Sabbath matters in the life of a true believer especially in issues with stress, anxiety and depression

The mental health benefits and costs of Sabbath observance among Orthodox Jews

"Emerging themes wereas follows: Shabbos as a special day, giving time to contemplate on profound issues, withdrawaland rest from mundane concerns, and deepening relationships. These aspects can potentiallyimprove feelings of mental well-being, and were indeed often said to do so." – Simon Dein, Kate M Loewenthal. University College London, London, UK, [57]

However, even if Jews were Hebrews, and we prove they are not, the Sabbath has always been applicable in the lives of Gentiles as well. No Gentile nations have entered covenant but the Gentile or non-Hebrew also is to keep the Sabbath and the Law according to Moses many times we have addressed. For the Sabbath has never been only for the Jew nor is that term even an Ancient Hebrew one. Hebrews in the Bible call themselves Yahudim after the name of Yahu or Yahuah *(YHWH)*.

Also, to ignore that Adam, Enoch, and Noah were not Jews anyway requires ignorance. Abraham was a Hebrew but not a Jew. Jesus*(Yahusha)* was not a Jew either. The term is not a Hebrew one and does not belong in the Bible. It is Yiddish and in modern times refers to Pharisees. For the Gospel which includes the Sabbath is made manifest to all but from where according to Paul? The scripture of the prophets specifically, Paul says, "the Commandments." These are made known to ALL nations for the obedience of faith. No, they do not replace Israel who has a special place and covenant with Yahuah but this applies to all. Sabbath is for everyone and it is a pleasure and a blessing.

> ### Romans 16:26 KJV
> *But now is made manifest, and by the scriptures of the prophets, according to the commandment of the everlasting God, made known to all nations for the obedience of faith:*
>
> ### 2 Esdras 1:14 KJVA
> *24 What shall I do unto thee, O Yacob? thou Yahudah would not obey me: I will turn myself to other nations, and unto those will I give my Name, that they may keep my Statutes.*

Even in this passage from Ezra, the Prophet, what is it that the other nations or Gentiles will do? They will keep His statutes – His Sabbath. Ezra is Old Testament and he is writing of the Law of Moses and so is Paul as these are saying the same thing. Paul always taught the Law and never disregarded it.

Remember the Sons of Zadok, the Temple Priests exiled to Qumran/ Bethabara? They remained holy which we already covered in Ezekiel 44, and they kept the Old Testament that we found in 1947 in their library and complex. However, they were mandated with a charge that every pastor has today.

> ### Ezekiel 44:23-24 KJV
> *And they shall teach my people the difference between the holy and profane, and cause them to discern between the unclean and the clean. And in controversy they shall stand in judgment; and they shall judge it according to my judgments: and they shall keep my laws and my statutes in all mine assemblies; and they shall hallow my sabbaths.*

Most pastors today are taught in seminaries to ignore the profane and the holy yet specifically that is what they should be teaching - discernment. They should be preparing all of us for what is coming as we should know our enemy and we should know Yahuah's ways not doctrine. Instead, this watered-down Gospel leaves the lambs for slaughter mostly including pastors often. They shun anything that they deem controversy yet they are supposed to be controversial. When the world is not threatened by their presence, it simply means they are not following Him. The world should hate them.

They teach censorship rather than discernment telling people not to read books that these very Temple Priest kept for us as inspired scripture. Every pastor should be taught to keep His laws, statutes and to hallow His Sabbaths. His entire clock is set in Sabbath periods in weeks, years, jubilees and even millennia. The fact that this is foreign to the modern church demonstrates they do not fully represent the Word and His ways.

The good news is every pastor reading this book can began their journey now. Every believer who is just now understanding things they never saw before can repent and begin to truly walk in His ways. We can all shun the doctrines of men instead. If you haven't tested every doctrine in your denomination especially pastors, you have not fulfilled your charge. If you are not teaching and keeping His Sabbath, not only will you be the least in the Kingdom, you are not executing His office. Jeremiah discussed even prophets who operate in such false vision calling it divination even.

Jeremiah 14:14 KJV

Then the LORD said unto me, The prophets prophesy lies in my name: I sent them not, neither have I commanded them, neither spake unto them: they prophesy unto you a false vision and divination, and a thing of nought, and the deceit of their heart.

Most pastors have no intention to deceive and wish to serve Yahuah. They are not preaching anything which they believe would do harm. However, the seminaries they attend are controlled by Pharisees who have installed their leaven in great proportion. Their foundation remains the Catholic foundation which is rotten to it's core as a church who hates Yahuah and His ways. The very church on record even in it's own history as hunting believers who read the Bible and burning at the stake those who translated the Bible back into known languages. That church is the cause of the Dark Ages and they are still with us thus so is their Dark Age Theology.

Some say why would one do this to Yahuah? However, He is clear you are not hurting him but yourself.

2 Esdras 1:27 KJVA

You have not as it were forsaken me, but your own selves, says Yahuah.

So how then do we govern ourselves? Who do we follow? What church do we attend? Is there a denomination that gets this right?

You will never find denominations in scripture. His ekklesia cannot be broken into such. In our age, there are a Remnant of believers only. It is not 1.5 billion but a few in terms of the population of the world. They are one and defined as keeping His commandments. Those come from the Bible as should all of our doctrine.

Any organization one enters is a creation of men. You will notice just about all of them attempt to boil down their theology into a Statement of Faith or Mission Statement of sort. These are meaningless as any Statement of Faith that does not include every letter of the Word is no such. The origin of such practice is freemasonry as the Bible never says to create a Statement of Faith. You will find every False Prophet comes from the church within and has a great resume and great sounding Mission Statement. That is Pharisaism not Bible. If one can whittle their faith down to a sentence or paragraph, they are extremely shallow.

We have put forth a case for the Biblical Sabbath that no scholar will ever genuinely disprove. No one can overturn over 1,000 scriptures. They will use one scholar after another some even quoting Pharisees but what they will not do is disprove that the Bible says the Biblical Sabbath remains and on the seventh day. They never prove it moved nor will they. They never proved it was abolished nor will they.

The question remains who would not desire to please Yahuah? Who would not desire to demonstrate for Him our love in return for all He has done for us? One does not do that through giving money though a good thing generally. One does not accomplish this by serving in church though fine to do so. We manifest our love for Him one way... We keep His commandments and that includes His Sabbath Rest on the seventh day. Many are already beginning to restore the Sabbath in their lives in this age of increasing knowledge. They are already seeking something because they know something is missing. It is time to restore His Sabbath in our lives and seek His ways above those of man. It is not too late.

We REST our case.

"This is the book of the commandments of God, and the law that endureth for ever: all they that keep it shall come to life; but such as leave it shall die. Turn thee, O Jacob, and take hold of it: walk in the presence of the light thereof, that thou mayest be illuminated. Give not thine honour to another, nor the things that are profitable unto thee to a strange nation."   **–Baruch 4:1-3 KJVA**

"Another book which Enoch wrote for his son Methuselah and for those who should come after him and keep the law in the last days."   **–1 Enoch 108:1**

They that fear the Lord will seek that which is well, pleasing unto him; and they that love him shall be filled with the law.   **–Sirach 2:16 KJVA**

He that seeketh the law shall be filled therewith: but the hypocrite will be offended thereat.   **–Sirach 32:15 KJVA**

the
GOD
culture
יהוה

The Name of YHWH, Yahuah: Why We Use It

We learn from Jubilees Hebrew is the language of Creation thus it must be simple and somehow for thousands of years, it was written with just consonants yet spoken without ever needing vowel points. Those were added in about 1000 A.D. by the Masoretes and at times serve to offer more confusion than clarity as they clearly were not honest about the name of Yahuah since it was their practice to hide His name. Therefore, this must be a phonetic language requiring no vowels and no fancy rules especially those changing even within a word illogically. What we call Hebrew today is Yiddish-infused not Ancient Hebrew.

Phonetically, YH is simple. H is AH *(see chart to right)*. That's YAH. The next combination is HW which we know by the names of the prophets is HU. Thus, it's YAHU as with the prophets. Finally, we add the last H or AH for YAHUAH.

We recognize there is a whole church out there which stakes it's claim on the name Jehovah. Here's the largest problem with that word. It is not Ancient Hebrew, Aramaic, Greek, Latin, Old French, Old German nor Old English. In other words, every language in which the Bible has been interpreted through in origin cannot render J nor V until the Renaissance *(1500s or so)*. The Bible was already thousands of years old and never used J nor V in any ancient text. There is a Pharisee out there deceiving many by trying to make this fit but we have the Dead Sea Scrolls dating to as early as 300 B.C. with even entire books such as the Isaiah scroll of about 25 feet in length which never renders a J nor a V even once. There is no overturning that. One may ignore it but let us not pretend they would be interested in the truth.

This leads us to the name of Messiah as the same first 3 letters YHW or YAHU as set by Yahuah. Yes, He literally meant He came in His Father's name. His name ends with SH - SHIN, A - AYIN which is SHA. He is Yahusha with Yahushua also appearing as a variant in scripture. Joshua has this same name in Hebrew. His people are the YAHUdim never Jews but YAH's.

Finally, some focus on the one time in scripture that Yahuah says His name is HYH, HAYAH as His only name ignoring the 6,800 times it is recorded as YHWH, Yahuah. However, modern Yiddish renders this as EHYEH and similar in fraud. Ancient Hebrew is HA YAH or THE YAH. It is the same name. Yahuah is being specific in saying I am The Yah not to be confused with any other. He is still invoking His name Yahuah in that passage which matches. In fact, YAH is rendered in the Old Testament 45 times on a standalone basis.

PHOENICIAN	𐤄𐤅𐤄𐤉	*1100 B.C.*
PALEO-HEBREW	𐤄𐤅𐤄𐤉	*1000 B.C.*
HEBREW	יהוה	*300 B.C. - TODAY*

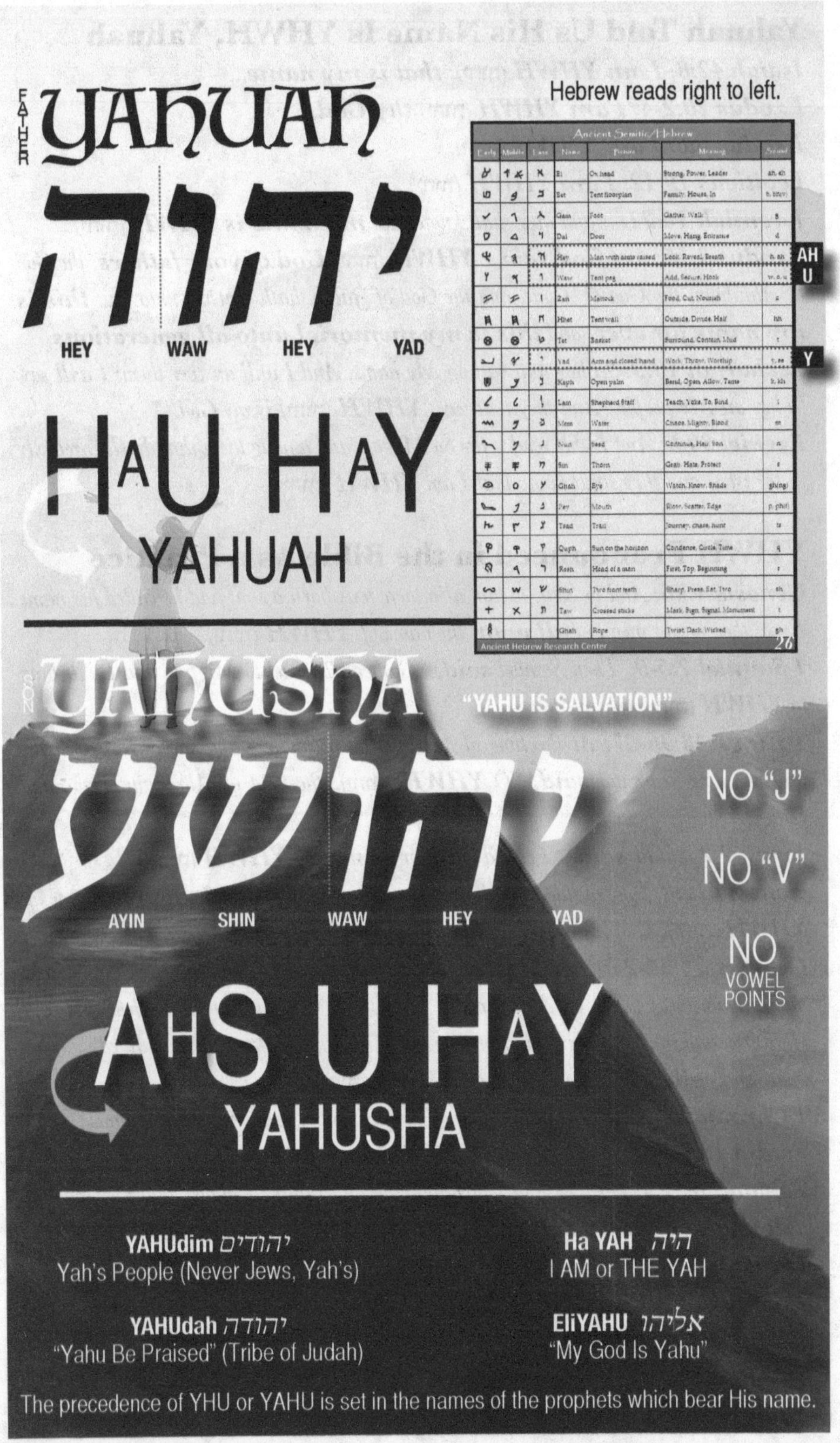

Hebrew reads right to left.

Ancient Semitic/Hebrew						
Early	Middle	Late	Name	Picture	Meaning	Sound
𐤀	𐤀	א	El	Ox head	Strong, Power, Leader	ah, eh
𐤁	𐤁	ב	Bet	Tent floorplan	Family, House, In	b, b(v)
𐤂	𐤂	ג	Gam	Foot	Gather, Walk	g
𐤃	𐤃	ד	Dal	Door	Move, Hang, Entrance	d
𐤄	𐤄	ה	Hey	Man with arms raised	Look, Reveal, Breath	h, ah
𐤅	𐤅	ו	Waw	Tent peg	Add, Secure, Hook	w, o, u
𐤆	𐤆	ז	Zan	Mattock	Food, Cut, Nourish	z
𐤇	𐤇	ח	Hhet	Tent wall	Outside, Divide, Half	hh
𐤈	𐤈	ט	Tet	Basket	Surround, Contain, Mud	t
𐤉	𐤉	י	Yad	Arm and closed hand	Work, Throw, Worship	y, ee
𐤊	𐤊	כ	Kaph	Open palm	Bend, Open, Allow, Tame	k, kh
𐤋	𐤋	ל	Lam	Shepherd Staff	Teach, Yoke, To, Bind	l
𐤌	𐤌	מ	Mem	Water	Chaos, Mighty, Blood	m
𐤍	𐤍	נ	Nun	Seed	Continue, Heir, Son	n
𐤎	𐤎	ס	Sin	Thorn	Grab, Hate, Protect	s
𐤏	𐤏	ע	Ghah	Eye	Watch, Know, Shade	gh(ng)
𐤐	𐤐	פ	Pey	Mouth	Blow, Scatter, Edge	p, ph(f)
𐤑	𐤑	צ	Tsad	Trail	Journey, chase, hunt	ts
𐤒	𐤒	ק	Quph	Sun on the horizon	Condense, Circle, Time	q
𐤓	𐤓	ר	Resh	Head of a man	First, Top, Beginning	r
𐤔	𐤔	ש	Shin	Two front teeth	Sharp, Press, Eat, Two	sh
𐤕	𐤕	ת	Taw	Crossed sticks	Mark, Sign, Signal, Monument	t
𐤖			Ghah	Rope	Twist, Dark, Wicked	gh

Ancient Hebrew Research Center   26

YAHUdim יהודים
Yah's People (Never Jews, Yah's)

YAHUdah יהודה
"Yahu Be Praised" (Tribe of Judah)

Ha YAH היה
I AM or THE YAH

EliYAHU אליהו
"My God Is Yahu"

The precedence of YHU or YAHU is set in the names of the prophets which bear His name.

Yahuah Told Us His Name Is YHWH, Yahuah

Isaiah 42:8: I am YHWH (יהוה): that is my name...

Exodus 20:2-4: I am YHWH (יהוה) thy God...

Exodus 6:6: I am YHWH (יהוה)...

Leviticus 19:12: I am YHWH (יהוה)...

Jeremiah 16:21: ...and they shall know that my name is YHWH (יהוה)...

Exodus 3:15: And God said... YHWH (יהוה) God of your fathers, the God of Abraham, the God of Isaac, and the God of Jacob, hath sent me unto you: this is my name for ever, and this is my memorial unto all generations.

Zechariah 13:9: "They will call on My name, And I will answer them; I will say, 'They are My people,' And they will say, 'YHWH (יהוה) is my God.'"

Ezekiel 39:6: And I will send a fire on Magog, and among them that dwell carelessly in the isles: and they shall know that I am YHWH (יהוה).

YHWH Pronounced in the Bible As a Practice

Genesis 4:26: And to Seth, to him also there was born a son; and he called his name Enos: then began men to call upon the name of YHWH (יהוה).

1 Samuel 7:5-9: Then Samuel said, "Gather all Israel to Mizpah and I will pray to YHWH (יהוה) for you."

1 Kings 18:36-37: At the time of the offering of the evening sacrifice, Elijah the prophet came near and said, "O YHWH (יהוה), the God of Abraham, Isaac and Israel..."

Jonah 2:2 and he said, "I called out of my distress to YHWH (יהוה)..."

Genesis 12:8: ...he builded an altar unto the Lord, and called upon the name of YHWH (יהוה).

Genesis 26:24-25: And YHWH (יהוה) appeared unto him the same night, and said, I am the Elohim of Abraham thy father: fear not, for I am with thee, and will bless thee, and multiply thy seed for my servant Abraham's sake. And he builded an altar there, and called upon the name of YHWH (יהוה)...

1 Chronicles 16:8 Give thanks unto YHWH (יהוה), call upon his name...

Psalm 105:1: O give thanks unto YHWH (יהוה); call upon his name:

Zephaniah 3:9: For then will I turn to the people a pure language, that they may all call upon the name of YHWH (יהוה), to serve him with one consent.

Lamentations 3:55: I called upon thy name, O YHWH (יהוה)...

2 Samuel 22:4: I call upon YHWH (יהוה), who is worthy to be praised...

Psalm 18:3: I call upon YHWH (יהוה), who is worthy to be praised...

1 Kings 18:24: "Then you call on the name of your god, and I will call on the name of YHWH (יהוה)...

All passages from the KJV.

2 Kings 5:11: *...Naaman was furious and went away and* **said**, *"Behold, I thought, 'He will surely come out to me and stand and* **call on** *the name of* **YHWH** *(יהוה) his God...*

Psalm 18:6: *In my distress I* **called upon YHWH** *(יהוה)...*

Psalm 28:1-2: *To You, O* **YHWH** *(יהוה),* **I call**...

Psalm 55:16: *As for me, I shall* **call upon** *God, And* **YHWH** *(יהוה) will save me.*

Psalm 120:1: *In my trouble* **I cried** *to* **YHWH** *(יהוה), And* **He answered** *me.*

Isaiah 58:9: *Then* **you will call**, *and* **YHWH** *(יהוה) will answer...*

Joel 1:19: *To You, O* **YHWH** *(יהוה),* **I cry**...

Joel 2:32: *"...that whoever* **calls on** *the name of* **YHWH** *(יהוה)...*

Psalm 99:6: **Moses** *and* **Aaron** *were among His priests, And* **Samuel** *was among those who called on* **His name**; *They called upon* **YHWH** *(יהוה) and* **He answered**...

Numbers 21:7: *So the people came to Moses and* **said**, *"We have sinned, because we have spoken against* **YHWH** *(יהוה) and you;* **intercede** *with* **YHWH** *(יהוה)...*

1 Samuel 12:19: *Then all the people* **said** *to Samuel, "Pray for your servants to* **YHWH** *(יהוה) your God...*

Genesis 13:4: *...to the place of the altar which he had made there formerly; and there* **Abram called on** *the name of* **YHWH** *(יהוה).*

Exodus 32:11-13: *Then Moses entreated* **YHWH** *(יהוה) his God, and* **said**, *"O* **YHWH** *(יהוה)...*

Deuteronomy 9:26-29: *"I* **prayed** *to* **YHWH** *(יהוה) and* **said**, *'O* **YHWH** *(יהוה) GOD do not destroy Your people...*

Numbers 14:13-19: *But Moses* **said** *to* **YHWH** *(יהוה), "Then the Egyptians will hear of it, for by Your strength You brought up this people from their midst, and they will tell it to the inhabitants of this land. They have heard that You, O* **YHWH** *(יהוה), are in the midst of this people, for You, O* **YHWH** *(יהוה), are seen eye to eye...*

YHWH Will Be Restored in the Last Days Says YHWH

Isaiah 52:6: *Therefore my people shall know my name: therefore they shall know in that day that I am he that doth speak: behold, it is I.*

Jeremiah 16:21: *Therefore, behold, I will this once cause them to know, I will cause them to know mine hand and my might; and they shall know that my name is* **YHWH** *(יהוה).*

Ezekiel 39:7: *So will I make* **my holy name known** *in the midst of my people Israel; and* **I will not let them pollute my holy name** *any more: and the heathen shall know that I am* **YHWH** *(יהוה), the Holy One in Israel.*

BIBLIOGRAPHY:

1. The Complete Dead Sea Scrolls in English. Revised Edition. By Geza Vermes. Penguin Books. London, NY. Revised 2004. Originally Published 1962.

2. The Book of Jubilees: The Torah Calendar. By Timothy Schwab and Anna Zamoranos. 2020. Based on the Original Translation by R.H. Charles, 1903.

3. "The Ethiopic Book of Enoch." By Michael A. Knibb, ed. and trans., [Oxford: Clarendon Press, 1978], S.O.A.S. Library at the University of London.

4. "The Book of Jubilees or The Little Genesis Translated from The Editor's Ethiopic Text and Edited, with Introduction, Notes and Indices." By R.H. Charles, D.D., Professor of Biblical Greek, Trinity College, Dublin. London, Adam and Charles Black, 1902. Free eBook at www.bookofjubilees.org.

5. "The Book of Jubilees Translated by R. H. Charles." Society for Promoting Christian Knowledge. London. 1917. By W. O. E. Oesterley and G. H. Box. Electronic Edition Available at: https://www.sacred-texts.com/bib/jub.htm (Talmudic Footnotes very rampant in this edition)

8. "The Dead Sea Scrolls and the Christian Myth." by John Allegro. 1992.

9. "The Mystery of the Essenes." By H. Spencer Lewis, F.R.C. From "The Mystical Life of Jesus." Rosicrucian Digest No. 2. 2007. p. 3.

10. "Natural History." Pliny the Elder. Book V. p. 277.

11. "The Life of Flavius Josephus." 1:2. The Genuine Works of Flavius Josephus the Jewish Historian. Translated from the Original Greek, according to Havercamp's accurate Edition.

12. 1770, Bonne Map of Israel. Rigobert Bonne 1727 – 1794. AdobeStock.

13. Madaba Mosaic Map(left), c. 6th century A.D. St. George's Church. Jordan. AdobeStock.

14. 1836, Tanner Map of Palestine, Israel, Holy Land. AdobeStock.

15. NASA/Goddard Space Flight Center Scientific Visualization Studio U.S. Department of Commerce, National Oceanic and Atmospheric Administration, National Geophysical Data Center, 2006, 2-minute Gridded Global Relief Data (ETOPO2v2). Horace Mitchell (NASA/GSFC): Lead Animator.

16. 1845, Chambers Map of Palestine, Israel, Holy Land. AdobeStock.

17. 1852, Philip Map of Palestine, Israel, Holy Land. AdobeStock.

18. Ein Gedi Photos: Chalcolithic Temple, Essene Synagogue, Tile mosaic Peacock symbols. AdobeStock.

20. "What is a Black Moon, and How Often Does One Happen?" By Michael Greshko. Natioanal Geographic. Jul. 31, 2019.

21. "The Complete Dead Sea Scrolls In English Revised Edition." "The Damascus Document." Translated By Geza Vermes, 2004, Penguin Classics Books. London, England. First Published 1962. Revised Edition 2004. p. 139.

22. "The First Voyage Round the World By Magellan." By Antonio Pigafetta. Translated from the Accounts of Pigafetta and Other Contemporary Writers. Accompanied by Original Documents, with Notes and an

*Introduction By Lord Stanley of Alderly.
London. M.DCCC.LXXIV. p. 200.*

*23. The Whole Works of the Right Rev. Jeremy
Taylor (1650), D.D. By Reginald Heber, A.M.,
1822. London. 1 Vol. X. p. 210-211.*

*24. "Sabbath Observance From Coptic
Sources." By Wilson B. Bishai, The Johns
Hopkins University. School of Advanced
International Studies. p. 25.*

*25. Coptic Orthodox Statute 75: 24 in Leipoldt,
op. cit., p. 45. "Sabbath Observance From
Coptic Sources." By Wilson B. Bishai, The
Johns Hopkins University. School of Advanced
International Studies. p. 27.*

*26. Coptic Orthodox Statute 45; see Horner, op.
cit., p. 315. Sabbath Observance From Coptic
Sources, Bishai, The Johns Hopkins University.
"Sabbath Observance From Coptic Sources."
By Wilson B. Bishai, The Johns Hopkins
University. School of Advanced International
Studies. p. 28.*

*27. See Wilhelm Riedel, The Canons of
Athanasius (Oxford, 1904). pp. 59, 60,
122 and 139. "Sabbath Observance From
Coptic Sources." By Wilson B. Bishai, The
Johns Hopkins University. School of Advanced
International Studies. p. 31.*

*28. "Dialogue on the Lord's Day." By Dr. T.H.
Morer (Church of England). London, 1701.
p.189.*

*29. 1. Antiquities of the Christian Church, Vol.
II. Book XX, chap 3, Sec. 1 66.1137, 1138.2.
Sunday a Sabbath, John Ley, p. 163. London:
1640. 3. Catholic Church Council in Laodicea,
364AD, Canon 29.*

*30. Sozomen, Ecclesiastical History, from A.
D., 324-440, book 7, chap. 19, p. 355.*

*31. James T. Ringgold, The Law of Sunday,
p. 267.*

*32. Professor James C. Moffatt, D.D., Professor
of Church History at Princeton, The Church in
Scotland, p. 140.*

*33. Schaff-Herzog, The New Encyclopedia
of Religious Knowledge, art. Nestorians; also
Realencyclopaedie fur Protestantische Theologie
und Kirche, art Nestorianer.*

34. Celtic Scotland, Vol. 2, p. 350.

*35. Lewis, Seventh Day Baptists in Europe and
America, Vol. 1, p. 29.*

*36. History of the Inquisition of the Middle
Ages, H.C. Lea, Vol. 1.*

*37. Catholic Provincial Council at Bergen.
1435 Dip. Norveg., 7, 397.*

*38. H.J. Holtzman, Kanon und Tradition,
1859 edition, p. 263.*

*39. Martyrology of the Churches of Christ,
commonly called Baptists, during the era of
the Reformation, from the Dutch of T.J. Van
Braght, London 1850, 1, pp. 113-4.*

*40. Council, Moscow, 1503. H. Sternberf,
Geschichte der Juden (Leipzig, 1873), pp.
1117-122.*

*41. Bishop Anjou, Svenska Kirkans Historia
efter Motet i Upsala.*

*42. History of the Sabbath, J.N. Andrews, p.
649, ed.*

*43. Adeney, The Greek and Eastern Churches,
p. 527-528.*

*44. Abyssinian legate at court of Lisbon, 1534.
Geddes' Church History of Ethiopia, pp. 87-8.*

*45. Stennet's letters, 1668 and 1670. Cox.
Sab., 1, 268.*

46. *Dr. Peter Chamberlain gravestone inscription reads... Dr. Chamberlain was "a Christian, keeping the commandments of God and the faith of Jesus, being baptized about the year 1648, and keeping the seventh day for the Sabbath above thirty-two years."*

47. *History of the Seventh Day Baptist General Conference by Jas. Bailey, pp. 237-238.*

48. *John Milton, Sab. Lit, 2, 46-54.*

49. *Jahrgang 2, 254.*

50. *Adolf Dux, Aus Ungarn, pp. 2889-291. Leipzig, 18880.*

51. *Rupp's History of Religious Denominations in the United States, pp. 109-123.*

52. *George Park Fisher, History of the Christian Church, (New York: Scribner, 1900), 1 18; quoted in Bible Students' Source Book (Washington D. C.: Review and Herald Publishing Association, 1962), 866.*

53. *A Critical History of the Sabbath and the Sunday.*

54. *May 30, 1863, p. 169. Evangelisten (The Evangelist) Stockholm, May 30 to August 15, 1863 (organ of the Swedish Baptist Church).*

55. *Official publication of Cardinal Gibbons and the Papacy in the United States, published in Baltimore, Maryland, September 1893.*

56. *The History of the Sabbath. By Peter Heylyn, London, 1636. p. 140.*

57. *Simon Dein, Kate M Loewenthal. University College London, London, UK. PubMed. https://pubmed.ncbi.nlm.nih.gov/23867919/*

58. *Irenaeus (120-200 A.D.). Adversus Haeres. Book III, Chapter 4, Verse 3 and Chapter 3, Verse 4.*

59. *"The encyclical epistle of the church at Smyrna, The Martyrdom of Polycarp, Bishop of Smyrna." Verses 7.1 & 8.1. Charles H. Hoole's 1885 translation*

60. *"PHARISEES (Φαρισαῖοι; Aramaic, "Perishaya"; Hebr. "Perushim")." By Kaufmann Kohler. Jewish Encyclopedia. Retrieved June 2021.*

61. *"Pharisees." Wikipedia. Retrieved June 2021.*

62. *"Pharisees." Encyclopedia of the Bible. Bible Gateway.*

63. *"Tertullian, De Idolatria." c. 14, Vol. I, p. 682., 155 A.D.*

64. *"Apollinaris. From the Book Concerning Passover." Translated by Alexander Roberts and James Donaldson. Excerpted from Volume I of The Ante-Nicene Fathers; American Edition, 1885. Reprinted 2001. Peter Kirby*

65. *Polycrates, Letter to Victor, Bishop of Rome, quoted in Eusebius' Ecclesiastical History. Eusebius. The History of the Church, Book V, Chapter XXIV, Verses 2-7 . Translated by A. Cushman McGiffert. Digireads.com Publishing, Stilwell (KS), 2005, p. 114.*

66. *Theophilus of Antioch. To Autolycus, Book 2, Chapters XI, XII and XV. Translated by Marcus Dods, A.M. Excerpted from Ante-Nicene Fathers, Volume 2. Edited by Alexander Roberts & James Donaldson. American Edition, 1885. Online Edition 2004 by K. Knight.*

67. *R. L. Odom, Sunday in Roman Paganism, p. 188. Sunday in Roman Paganism, Robert Leo Odom. TEACH Services, Inc. (January 2003).*

68. *"Christians and the Sabbath" By Sean Pitman. Detecting Design. April 20, 2017*

69. "The Teaching of the Twelve Apostles To The Nations, Known As The Didache." Legacy Icons. MI. 2016.

70. Codex Justinianus, lib. 3, tit. 12, 3; translated by Philip Schaff, History of the Christian Church, Vol. 3 (1902), p. 380. 71. Ancient Christianity Exemplified, chap. 26, sec. 2, p. 527. 72. "Letter to C. P. Bollman from W. de C. Ravenel, administrative assistant to the secretary of the Smithsonian Institution, Washington, D. C., quoted in Sunday," p. 3.

73. "The Mysteries of Mithra (1910)." By Franz Cumont, Ph.D., LL.D. pp. 190, 191.

74. The Catechism of the Council of Trent or the Catechism of Pius V. This translation used as its basis the Manutian text as reflected in the Maredsous edition of 1902, the fourth Roman edition of 1907 and the Turin edition of 1914. pp. 241, 243.

75. Catechism of the Catholic Church.

76. Chambers's Encyclopedia, "Sabbath"

77. Philip Schaff, History of the Christian Church, Third Period, chap. 7, sec. 75 (vol. 3, p. 380).

78. Dialogues on the Lord's Day.

79. The Catechism of the Council of Trent or the Catechism of Pius V. This translation used as its basis the Manutian text as reflected in the Maredsous edition of 1902, the fourth Roman edition of 1907 and the Turin edition of 1914. pp. 241, 243.

80. Pope Francis interview on 60 Minutes, May 11, 2018.

81. Socrates, Ecclesiastical History, book 5, chap. 22, p. 404..com.

83. "Pharisees." Encyclopedia.com.

84. Letter of Barnabas 15:6–8.

85. Ignatius of Antioch: 110 A.D. Letter to the Magnesians 8.

86. Justin Martyr: 155 A.D First Apology 67.

87. The Didascalia: 225 A.D. Didascalia 2 [A.D. 225].

88. Origen: 229 A.D. Commentary on John 2:28.

89. Victorinus: 300 A.D. The Creation of the World.

90. Faustus (a non-Christian) to St. Augustine (4th Century), cited in History of the Intellectual Development of Europe, John William Draper, M.D., LL.D., vol. 1, p. 310.

91. Prof. Hutton Webster, Ph.D. (University of Nebraska), Rest Days, p. 122.

92. Ibid., p. 270.

93. Catholic World, Vol. 58, no. 348, March, 1894, p. 809.

94. Archdeacon F. W. Farrar, The Voice From Sinai (1892), p. 167.

95. History of the Sabbath, part 2." By Dr. Peter Heylyn (Church of England) chap. 5, par. 6.

96. Bishop Grimelund of Norway: Sondagens Historie, p. 37.

Timothy Schwab &
Anna Zamoranos-Schwab

About The Authors:

In his extensive experience of over 30 years in publishing and over 30 years in ministry, Timothy leads an international research team which focuses on restoring Biblical geography especially. Using a very profound scientific method, they have been able to articulate a strong position on the location of the famed Biblical isles of gold – Ophir, Sheba and Tarshish. Over four years ago, their group began documenting their journey on YouTube and over 10 million views later, the channel continues to grow. Together with his Filipina wife Anna and their team of researchers, The God Culture continues to provide content on YouTube in deep studies especially in Hebrew and restoring Biblical geography including the Garden of Eden, Rivers from Eden, Land of Adam and Eve, Land of Creation, home of John the Baptist including restoring Qumran's Biblical name, Lost Tribes of Israel migrations, mapping Noah's division of the earth from the Book of Jubilees, Gog of Magog's seat of power and allied nations, the peoples involved in the Psalm 83 War, location of Noah's ark landing, unveiling Revelation 11 and 12, etc. and all with great revelation amending modern scholarship much of the time with evidence.

With the backing of their research team, this couple has now released 5 books internationally being read in over 70 countries including The Search for King Solomon's Treasure, Ophir Philippines Coffee Table Book, The Book of Jubilees: The Torah Calendar, 2nd Esdras: The Hidden Book of Prophecy and REST: The Case for Sabbath. As their first topic, Solomon's Gold Series which finds Ophir, has not been disproven in over four years, this research group has been validated to offer valuable insight.

Having set their sites on proving out the Biblical Sabbath, they have produced over 20 videos and expounded this research in this comprehensive position positing an incredibly strong case for the Sabbath. They have no affiliation with any denomination nor organization keeping this research pure and free of the doctrinal hinderances of most scholars. They support this case with over 1,000 scriptural and hundreds of historical references. It is time to know what the Bible says about this day of rest.